Deceptions and Myths of the Bible

Deceptions and Myths
of the Bible

by
Lloyd Graham

BELL PUBLISHING COMPANY   NEW YORK

Library of Congress Cataloging in Publication Data

Graham, Lloyd.
Deceptions and myths of the Bible.

Reprint of the ed. published by University Books,
Secaucus, N. J.
Includes index.
1. Bible—Criticism, interpretation, etc.
2. Christianity—Controversial literature. I. Title.
[BS533.G68 1979]   220.6   79-103
ISBN 0-517-27834-0

Table of Contents

The Bible is the Book of the Church . . . The Jewish Church stands behind the Old Testament. The Christian Church stands behind the New Testament.

The Bible in the Making,
J. Patterson Smyth, B. D. Litt. D., D.C.L.

And behind the Church stands the priesthood.
L.G.

Preface

Is the "Holy Bible" holy? Is it "the word of God"? And can it be disproved?

There is nothing "holy" about the Bible, nor is it "the word of God." It was not written by God-inspired saints, but by power-seeking priests. Who but priests consider sin the paramount issue? Who but priests write volumes of religious rites and rituals? No one, but for these priestly scribes sin and rituals were imperatives: their purpose was to found on them an awe-inspiring religion. By this intellectual tyranny they sought to gain control, and they achieved it. By 400 B.C. they were the masters of ancient Israel. For so great a project they needed a theme, a framework, and this they found in the Creation lore of more knowledgeable races. This they commandeered and perverted—the natural to the supernatural, and truth to error. The Bible is, we assert, but priest-perverted cosmology.

The process began with the very first chapter—the world's creation. This *first* was not the original first; it is priestly cosmology substituted centuries later and for a priestly purpose. The original *first* was written by the same hand as the second. To scholars its author is known as the Jhwhist, a by no means pious mythologist. He was the Hebrew Homer, and as with the Greek, his God was never meant to be worshiped. His characters, including God, are personifications, and through them he tells us plainly the true nature of Causation: fratricidal Cain, drunken Noah, dishonest Jacob and murderous Joshua and Moses. His account of Creation was, no doubt, of like nature—mythic but true. This would not serve the priestly purpose and so it was removed, and the supernaturalistic and fiatic version known as the Priestly put in its place. Here the personifications became the realities and their meaning lost.

The prerequisite of a priesthood is a divine Avenger with man as a sinner and hence dependent on priests for salvation. To this end the process was continued: first, the semimythic Elohist, rewriting and holifying the Jhwhist's characters, and finally the Priest declaring a personal God created the world in six days and by saying Let it be. This God-concept of the priestly mind is the cornerstone of the Bible, and if it be false, everything based upon it is also false.

Literally, the priestly account of Creation is but kindergarten cosmology, yet we have accepted it for two thousand years. This is because Western man is incapable of abstract thought. All the metaphysical and cosmological knowledge Western man has, came to him from the East. The ancient Orientals were capable of such thought but not Western man, and this includes the Jews. In his metaphysical incompetency Western man puts the stamp of his own ego on everything, including the Creator. Now blinded by his own error, he cannot see that it is only that part of the race incapable of abstract thought that believes in his anthropomorphic creation. That part of him called Christian could not even create a God or religion for itself; it had to borrow these from the Middle Eastern Jews. And what did they know about other worlds and galaxies? They did not even know this world is round. How then could their cosmology be right?

In spite of their pretended intimacy with the Creator, the Jews never had great knowledge of things cosmic and metaphysical; they were but plagiarists culling mythic artifacts they did not understand. In their day the wisdom-knowledge was lost and so they were but epigonists—"the unworthy descendants of the mighty Homer," their own included. This brings us to another point that must be understood—a prereligious age of enlightenment, and the loss of its knowledge.

Time was when man knew vastly more about Causation and

Creation than he does today—the Mythopoeic Age. We call its enlightened ones Initiates and their knowledge, The Ancient Wisdom. With reason uncorrupted by false theologies they were able to study Reality and thus arrive at Truth. But due to a change in the cyclic law that knowledge was lost; priests took the place of the Initiates and religion of metaphysics. This was wisdom's Gotterdammerung and likewise of spiritual man. We had entered a period of materialism and hence spiritual blindness—the Kali-yuga of the Hindus. Here we became "the children of darkness" and "children of darkness" we still are concerning Causation and Creation.

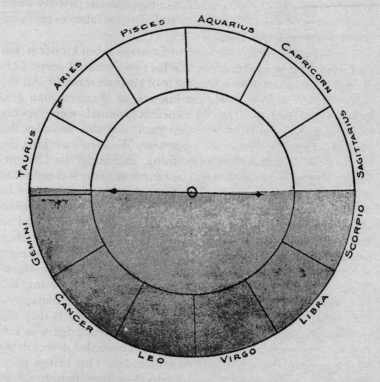

Acceptance of this depends upon our knowledge of the law of cycles, and particularly that cycle known as "The Precession of the Equinoxes"—a matter of some twenty-five thousand years. This is divided into two equal and opposite halves. See diagram. So opposite and different are they we might call the one the Zodiacal Day, the other the Zodiacal Night. The latter began about six thousand years ago when the zodiacal hand entered Taurus, and the nether hand, the real indicator, entered Scorpio. The lower half is the materialistic part and we are in it; at the very nadir in fact—Virgo-Leo. Oddly enough, it was when we reached this material nadir that we discovered the true nature of matter—atomic energy. This could happen only in an age dedicated to matter. But lacking the wisdom-knowledge we cannot see that material progress implies its spiritual opposite—you cannot serve two masters. This is the fact proud, materialistic Western man must learn, particularly in things religious. In these he believes what he believes only because he is ignorant of the *cosmic* "facts of life." As the Bible is a product of this same dark age, its authors were also ignorant of them.

From this we see that the Bible's theology and cosmology are not necessarily true, but only what "the children of darkness" believed was true. We should also see that the religions based on its so-called truth are not eternal verities, but only period pieces. They are of and for the Arian and Piscean cycles, and as these are now past their products must go with them. We are entering a new age, the so-called Aquarian, though even this is wrong, and for it we need a new cosmology, a new philosophy, and above all else a new dimension of consciousness—cosmic consciousness to wisely handle cosmic energy. This comes only with knowledge of those *cosmic* "facts of life," and this we cannot get from false theology and cosmology. We must therefore recognize the fraudulent nature and false security these offer and learn again the true nature of Causation and our place in Creation. Of these things the aforesaid Initiates had great knowledge and they left us that knowledge in prereligious records—myth and scripture, zodiac and pyramid. These are the archives of the Ancient Wisdom but modern man cannot read them. It was this knowledge the priesthood copied and then destroyed. But only physically; it is not lost and now the cyclic law has decreed its return; it is coming back to destroy its destroyers.

The Bible is not "the word of God," but stolen from pagan sources. Its Eden, Adam and Eve were taken from the Babylonian account; its Flood or Deluge is but an epitome of some four hundred flood accounts; its Ark and Ararat have their equivalents in a score of Deluge myths; even the names of Noah's sons are copies, so also Isaac's sacrifice, Solomon's judgment, and Samson's pillar act; its Moses is fashioned after the Syrian Mises; its laws after Hammurabi's code. Its Messiah is derived from the Egyptian Mahdi, Savior, certain verses are verbatim copies of Egyptian scriptures. Between Jesus and the Egyptian Horus, Gerald Massey found 137 similarities, and those between Christ and Krishna run into the hundreds. How then can the Bible be a revelation to the Jews?

The masses never read these other sources and the churchmen who do keep silent about them. Today these sources are few because Bible inspired fanatics destroyed them. The ancient Jews, however, had access to a multitude of them quite unknown to us. In 125 A.D. St. Irenaeus said, "There was a multitude of gospels" in his day. Those that came down to us are but the ones the priesthood needed for its purpose, the rest it destroyed. To realize these things the reader must know there was a vast conspiracy afoot when this book was written.

Part of this lies in its structure. It is written in two languages; esoteric and exoteric—the hidden truth and its deceptive garment, the literal word. The latter is all we know today and so the simple mind still thinks of the world's beginning in terms of Adam and Eve, Cain and Abel, sin, the Fall, and hence salvation. The esoteric completely refutes these literalisms. Secretly it tells us Adam and Eve were not the first human beings; that Cain and Abel were not Adam's sons; that Solomon was not David's son; that the Jews were never in bondage in Egypt, nor is Exodus their escape therefrom; that the moral laws are not the laws of the tablets, nor were they handed down at Sinai; that the Jews never conquered Canaan, nor were they promised Palestine; that the modern Palestine is not the "Promised Land," or even the "Holy Land." Who does not know these things is wholly ignorant of the Bible's true meaning. He is also ignorant of the fact that he has been deceived.

We little realize the price we've paid for this deception: two thousand years of worship instead of welfare, one thousand and six hundred of darkness, disease and war, the Crusades, Inquisition, massacre, prejudice and bigotry. Even today the religions founded on it are dividing the race and fomenting war. Because of its diversionary influence we are thousands of years behind the planetary schedule; our consciousness is wholly inadequate to our place in Evolution. It is not qualified for the coming Aquarian Age, in fact, it cannot solve the problems of this one. It's time this scriptural tyranny was broken that we may devote our time to man instead of God, to civilizing ourselves instead of saving our souls that were never lost.

Its foes have labored long to destroy this tyranny yet its source is still a best-seller and its victims distribute fifty million copies every year. Such foes have failed and for two good reasons: First, because they lacked the knowledge necessary, now fortunately available, and second, because they employed the wrong method. Lacking the necessary knowledge, they resorted to ridicule and exposé; they pointed out its obscenities, absurdities and atrocities and all to no avail. This priestly hoax cannot be destroyed by ridicule, modern science or our kind of "higher learning." The only weapon that can destroy it is greater knowledge than that of its authors, and the only time is when the race acquires sufficient enlightenment to see for itself that it is false. It must acquire such knowledge of natural Causation and Creation as will render scriptural supernaturalism unnecessary; it must become so aware of the evolutionary genesis of moral qualities that it can no longer accept the scriptural account of their source. This is our method and the reason for the lengthy approach to the scriptures. Unfortunately this is necessary, for without such knowledge the reader cannot see these subjects in the scriptures. That Causation is still a mystery implies an ignorance that is appalling. It is also unnecessary for we have, thanks to science, a vast amount of unrelated data. The reason the mystery still exists is because we lack the philosophic ability to collate them. The following pages will at least illustrate the collative process.

The mystery and the tyranny exist only because there is still so much that cannot be explained without their hypothesis—a supernatural Creator and source of moral good. As Richard Carrington said in *A Million Years of Man:* ". . . scientists who have so often attempted to eliminate a creative God from the universe in the interest of truth, are now finding that they can ultimately explain nothing at all unless they are prepared to put him back." This is the dilemma that must be disposed of. Could we find a natural, reason-satisfying cause that does explain, instead of the reason-offending cause religion offers, we could then say with Monsieur LaPlace, "We have no need of that hypothesis." This would mean the end of superstition and the beginning of enlightenment.

We have been told that the tall tales of the Bible are "revealed truth." What we need now is to have that "revealed truth" revealed, for as yet it never has been. What follows are but scraps of the required knowledge.

Premise: A Genetic Cosmo-Conception

Say first, of God above or man below,
What can we reason but from what we know?[1]

ALEXANDER POPE

A world is a vast and complex thing, its life and economy far too teleological to be accidental. Its cause can be none other than an intelligence of some kind, and since all nature bears witness to such an element, the intelligent cosmologist will begin with intelligence. What this intelligence is constitutes the cosmic mystery.

Concerning this, there need be no mystery. This intelligence has been staring us in the face since the dawn of life; it is all around us everywhere but because of false theologies we cannot see it. It is here in this world, not heaven above, and science is well aware of it. The mystery still persists because the scientist has never seen its cosmic significance.

The key to Causation is in the effect. This, for us, is the known world, and as the Zohar says: "If you would know the unknown, observe carefully the known." So let us observe the known and by a process of extrapolation apply what we know about the known to the unknown. By this process we will arrive at a Cause in keeping with the effect—the opposite of the priestly method. This should result in two prerequisites of the future: correct orientation of the mind with Reality, and a *new dimension of consciousness.*

[1] *An Essay on Man*, Epistle 1, line 17.

Causation

The seeds of things, the primal germs we teach,
Whence all creation around us came to be.

Lucretius

In observing the known, we might "consider the lilies, how they grow" but wheat is better. There may be in a field of wheat as many stocks as there are stars (visible) in the heavens, but there is no collective creator and governor over them. The creator and governor of wheat is within each wheat stock, and because of this we may sweep them all away save one, and that one will grow, mature and reproduce itself. Now if this be so of plants, it is so of planets also, for in spite of etymology, they are one and the same genetically. Suns and worlds are celestophytes—cosmic plants and space is the soil in which they grow. As poets are wiser than priests, poetry is sometimes truer than scripture:

Then in the infinite meadows of heaven,
Blossomed the lovely stars,
The forget-me-nots of the angels.

Longfellow, in *Evangeline*

Now we know that all terrestrial plants spring from a seed, and that this seed contains both the cause and ideation of all subsequent growth and expression. Now if this be so of terrestrial plants, it is so also of celestial plants. *Worlds come from world seeds.* This is the "master key"—gonos, not theos. It is from *cosmos* and *gonos* we derive the word *cosmogony*, creation. Only in the seed do we find combined the two essentials, creative intelligence and energy. These are nature's symbionts and together they constitute Causation, a principle, not personality. Space is their field of expression and in this, world seeds are indigenous, and just as with terrestrial seeds their germination sets in motion the dynamics of creation. And just as biologic seeds draw their substance from the terrestrial fields, so do cosmic seeds draw theirs from the celestial fields. "Chaos is the seed-ground of the cosmos." This is pagan wisdom destroyed by Hebrew theology.

Like all other seeds these cosmic seeds have within them a creative intelligence, the cause of all creative activity; like all other seeds they create the forms in which this principle manifests; and like all other seeds they have the power of self-generation, motivation and sustention; in other words, the active agent in Creation is within the created. We would like to call it the Life Principle to distinguish it from life, its evolutionary construct, of which more later.

In all terrestrial seeds there are what science calls genes, the carriers of the creative ideation and hereditary characteristics. This it calls *genetic*. So we assume there are planetary genes, "monads," the carriers of planetary ideation and characteristics of a world to be. As the original ideation is inherent in the seed, its development but follows as in any seed or embryo; in other words, genetic intelligence is creative but not discriminatory. It has no choice, but creates only after the innate plan or idea. Thus there is no "free will" or fiatic choice in Creation, nor is it a reasoned process. Ask not then the Creator for his reasons: Why did you make the world and me? Why did you make pain and suffering, disease and death? Reasons imply reason, Creation does not. Neither does it imply moral qualities. The creation of matter is purely dynamic, a matter of violent and terrible forces. It is also purely quantitative. Thus no moral qualities are necessary to the creation of a world. They are, however, necessary to the civilizing of one, and here is where moral qualities appear, in biogenesis, not cosmogenesis. To put it another way, in Creation, sometimes called Involution, quantity is made but no quality (moral or rational); in Evolution quality is made but no quantity. Herein lies the error of scriptural theology.

In all terrestrial seeds this Creative Principle is nonmoral and non-self-conscious, and its first creations are savage, merciless and warlike; such then is its nature *per se*. This it is that has the creative "know-how" but not the love and mercy to realize the consequence of its creating—five billion years of conflict, pain and death. Nothing endowed with pity, love or mercy could create a thing so horrible as a primeval world, or permit catastrophes in it billions of years thereafter. Thus in arguing for nonmoral and non-self-conscious Causation we are absolving not accusing.

Another word for seed is egg, and the Oriental cosmologists spoke of "the mundane egg" or world seed. In either case Creation implies growth. World creation is therefore not just a *modus operandi* but a *modus vivendi* as well. The Hindus likened world growth to that of a tree with its roots in the Absolute and its branches hanging downward.

As for worlds in the aggregate: Here in this world biologic aggregates are not resolutions of a common bioplasm, but distinct and separate constructs of distinct and separate genes. So is it with worlds. Each is a distinct and separate entity, a god in its own right, conditioned only by its relationship with other entities. From this it follows that cosmic aggregates, solar systems and galaxies, are not resolutions of a common substance, gas or nebula, but congeries of separate entities, each going through its own life cycle and fulfilling its own life purpose. Is it not so of us and all things known to us? It is, for the law is one and the method is universal.

Considering then this universality of the law and consistency of method, may we not draw the conclusion that the creative factor in cosmic forms is identical in nature with that of biologic forms, namely, the prolific but nonmoral Genetic Principle, amazingly creative but unconscious of what it creates? With this, Creation is no longer a mystery incomprehensible to man, but only a part of Reality not yet comprehended by man. If man would comprehend it, he has only to reduce it to the comprehensible, namely, planetary genetics—seed, growth and organism. This is Creation reduced to intelligible nature; this is Causation without supernaturalism. It is also the ancient and prereligious doctrine of analogy and correspondence, "As above, so below, and as below, so above." This is another master key but nowhere has it been applied to Creation itself, yet so applied, it becomes that natural key so necessary to sound knowledge of ourselves, the world, the universe. It means, as we said, the end of superstition and the beginning of enlightenment. The aforesaid archives all confirm it and later we will present them in proof thereof.

Creation is a process, not an act. It is cosmic "big business" and like its human similitude its purpose is to supply a lack, in this case qualitation. If this be not so, what is Creation for? What is Evolution for? So vast and painful a process cannot be just for the pleasure of something that needs nothing. And we might well add, What is man for? Is he just a lost soul living by grace, or is he a partner in the business? This cosmo-conception gives to man a majestic *raison d'être*, not just that of saving his soul but of creating soul—qualitation. Sometimes we say God is a spirit, but never do we say he is a soul, and rightly so, for soul is man's creation. Man is the moral and spiritual qualifier, and this qualifying of the purely quantitative is the purpose of Creation. This the scriptural authors did not know, and so they perverted the mind of man and the purpose of God. Their personal and fiatic Creator is but their alibi for ignorance of Causation and the creative process. The world exists and knowing not how or why, they said a God created it. If our more natural theory is correct, it completely refutes this priestly concept, and everything based upon this concept.

To the religionist it will seem horrendous, opposed to the "revealed truth" of the scriptures. To this we reply, it is their *concealed* truth finally revealed. What does "the seed of Abraham" mean? Abraham, formerly Abram, is but the Hindu Creator Brahma, formerly Brama, with the *a* as prefix instead of suffix. Therefore Abraham's seed is the Creator's seed. And what is Genesis but *gene* with another suffix? Testament itself is derived from *testes*, and the Bible is but the testi-mony of a cosmic teste's work—Creation. Such is the Old Testament and such is the New. Originally the latter's Creator was called monogene—one gene, wrongly and maliciously translated as "only begotten son," so even here we see the monstrous hoax in the making. The Bible is, we repeat, but priest-perverted cosmology, its God, but the creativity in nature.

With its Causation concept, nothing can be explained; with ours everything can be, including the second mystery—life from so-called "dead matter."

In world creation, called in metaphysics Involution, the creative intelligence became involved in that substance that became matter; it ensouled and intelligized it creatively. Together they constitute that aforesaid Life Principle. Because of this, matter is not "dead"; it is instinct with creativity. But matter is the polar opposite of space in which this genetic intelligence lay inactive and asleep; so in matter it is again inactive and asleep. To become active it must free itself from matter, and here the process is radiation, the opposite of congelation. Once free, an aspect of that intelligence that creates cosmic forms, creates biologic forms to complete its purpose, namely, the development of qualities. These forms through experience with the quantitative (environment) develop an intelligence of their own, moral, rational, and so forth. Here we have another name for intelligence: we call it consciousness—funded experience. As this is something added, we call it epigenetic consciousness to distinguish it from the genetic. This is the work of Evolution, the sequel to Involution, and here science calls the biologic intelligence genetic, but it has never carried the idea to its logical conclusion, namely, that the biologic and the cosmologic must be of like nature. Yet there are not two Creators, one for the cosmic the other for the biologic. To this cosmic genetic we may attribute all the creative wisdom we have attributed to religion's God, with this difference: it is neither moral nor self-conscious. This alone explains the earthquake and volcano, the hurricane and flood. These are not conscious "acts of God," but only planetary functionalism. They are energy acting without consciousness; biologic forms are energy controlled by consciousness. There are, in fact, just two principles in the entire universe, consciousness and energy, and they are inextricably bound together throughout the entire creative process. Without energy, consciousness can do nothing, and energy without consciousness will do nothing constructive. It is of these two then that we must learn.

From all this we see that the mystery of life is man-made, not God-made. When an ignorant priesthood introduced the supernatural into a perfectly natural universe, it threw confusion into the human mind. The result was a myriad warring religions and philosophies all trying like the blind men with the elephant, to explain the whole by something felt (emotional) instead of seen (mental). Only in our theory can these warring elements be harmonized, and the paradox posed by religion—divine source and savage nature—be resolved.

Energy (Source)

Silence! coeval with eternity,
Thou wert ere Nature's self began to be:
'Twas one vast Nothing all, and all
Slept fast in thee.[1]

ALEXANDER POPE

For the creation of a thing so vast as a world, Creative Intelligence must have a vast amount of matter. The second question then is: Where did this matter come from? Though scoffed at but a few years ago, it is now known that matter is but "congealed energy." This implies a congealing process and a prephysical source of matter, something like that of the nonphysical electron. Dr. I. Langmuir called this source the *quantel*, a significant term and we shall use it. A more familiar name, however, is etheric energy. But is this the ultimate source of matter? May it not be but one of the many vibratory rates of energy? It is.

We are all familiar with the many vibratory rates of the electromagnetic spectrum, but this spectrum itself is but a section of the total cosmic spectrum; it is, in fact, the lowest part of it. In all ancient cosmologies, that of Genesis included, there are seven stages in the creative process, each with its own vibratory rate and each rate producing a different element—the planetary precedent of the seven divisions in the atomic table.

Now creation implies action, and energy is the active agent. This being so, precreation implies energy not in action, that is, motionless and attenuate beyond our ken. This is the nature of nonmanifesting space, the ultimate source. In metaphysics it is called the Absolute, "inactive and asleep," and in scripture "the

[1] "On Silence," in *Imitations of English Poets.*

deep," "without form and void." Space is the field of cosmic manifestation, suns, planets, moons, and these are the aforesaid "congealed energy." The time and means of this congelation and condensation constitute the creative process of worlds, a matter not of solar days but of cosmic days. Primordial energy cannot become dense matter in time as we reckon it, hence the intermediate stages. In passing through these it becomes more and more substantial, and so we might call it primordial substance, evenutally the quantel and finally the chemical. This being the process, we might say that this earth is a precipitate of primordial substance and a congelation of cosmic energy. But energy of itself is neither constructive nor purposive. For it to become such it must have a guiding, directing intelligence, and as that intelligence here on earth is genetic, so is it in heaven, space—". . . as below, so above."

One vast Nothing materially, all things potentially. This is the true beginning and therefore the beginning of truth. And such it was for all the ancient races, save one, for it is the Chaos of the Greeks, the Nox or night of the Romans, the Nir or nothing of the Egyptians, the Po of the Polynesians, the Parabrahm of the Hindus, and the Tao of the Chinese. Of the latter, the wise and enlightened Lao-tze said: "There is something chaotic yet complete which existed before heaven and earth. Oh how still it is and formless, standing alone without changing, reaching everywhere without suffering harm. Its name I know not. To designate it I call it Tao." So with the Polynesians: "In the beginning," said they, "there was no life, no light, no sound. A brooding night called Po enveloped all, over which Tanaoa (darkness) and Muti-Hei (silence) reigned supreme." And from the Assyro-Babylonians: "Chaotic darkness brooding over a waste of waters (space). Naught existed save primordial ocean Mommu Tiawath or Tiamat."

But again this would not do for a religion, so the Hebrew priests personified, deified and endowed this silent waste with vocative wisdom, moral perfection and even self-consciousness—the greatest mistake mankind has ever made for it confused all human thought, divided the race into a thousand sects and sowed the seeds of unending warfare. To escape its tragic consequence we must reverse this process; we must begin with nothing qualitative, thus giving meaning to Evolution, namely, qualitation; we must realize that the glory of Creation lies in its consummation, not its inception. As this consummation is perfected humanity, this gives meaning to man as well. In due time he becomes a divine being, and so, divinity is made by man, not man by divinity. This the scriptural authors did not know and so they put divinity at the wrong end of Being. And what good does that do man? Though God were divine to infinity it would not change savage-nature-molded humanity. For divinity to become factual on earth it must first become functional in man. This is the goal of Evolution and the purpose of man, both concealed from us by priestly falsehoods. If we would understand Creation, Evolution and ourselves, we must put these aside and learn an entirely new system of thought. And by this I do not mean that of science. Its theories of Creation and Evolution are also false.

Prephysical creation is a metaphysical subject and neither the scientist nor the religionist can deal effectively with it. The religionist begins with a "living God" and the scientist with "dead matter," whereas matter is the end of world creation not the beginning. No, only the metaphysician can reach out and grasp the totality of things, and it is still a mystery only because there has not been a genuine metaphysician in the world for six thousand years. If there had been, he would have seen the fallacies of both science and religion and exposed them.

Planetary Elements

With science, as stated, everything begins with matter, no intelligence, no ideation, no prephysical process. In all ancient cosmologies there were seven stages in the creative process, each producing a different element and rate of vibration. Were the nature and purpose of these known to us, life would not be the mystery that it is. Time was when they were known, but our scientists brand all reference to them as "mere metaphysics," yet without them they cannot explain such things as sentiency, emotion, mind or even life, neither can they solve the riddle of the universe. Thus they lay themselves open to the taunt of religion, equally ignorant of them: "The evolutionary expositor . . . cannot pretend to have no lacuna in his history." Martineau. With the addition of the missing elements the lacunae in both science and religion could be filled and the "mysteries" now "known only to God" explained. That the scientist does not recognize these elements is no proof that they do not exist; they are but the *eka* elements of a system beyond his ken. When someday he wearies of the physical and needs them to explain the superphysical, he will admit them; then, as always, they will become another "great scientific discovery"—like the Van Allen belt, known always to the metaphysician.

In the interest of future explanation of scriptural mysteries we will name these elements as they were known of old. As the three highest were beyond the ken of anyone, they were called spirit in lieu of knowledge. They did not remain spirit, however; as the ancients said, Spirit became matter. This being so, they are no longer spirit. What then are we worshiping? On the three planes below they were called mental, astral, and etheric matter or elements. These we will call Planetary Elements to distinguish them from the chemical elements. In the congealing process these six became No. 7, dense matter. Here we can learn again from analogy and correspondence.

When hydrogen becomes helium, it is no longer hydrogen, save potentially. And when helium becomes lithium it is no longer helium, save potentially. So is it with the planetary elements. When No. 2 comes into being, No. 1 ceases to be, save potentially. So with Nos. 2 and 3, and all three (the Trinity) ceases to be when No. 4 appears; and this applies to all six when No. 7 is formed. Thus does the Creator burn his bridges behind him. He (it) is now in matter below, not heaven above. Of this too the scriptural priests were ignorant and so they left their Creator behind to fear and worship. The Greeks, knowing better, called this succession of powers *henotheism*. The word means one god as does *monotheism*, but with this difference—one god at a time. Here in our world, No. 7, that god is the aforesaid creativity in nature, hence violence not providence. Only this as we said explains the earthquake and the hurricane. Besides this god, there are as many gods as there are bodies in the cosmos. Monotheism is therefore priestly ignorance of nature's complexity.

Apart from genetic ideation, these elements in Involution are unqualified, thus a sort of planetary *tabula rasa* (blank tablet), on which evolutionary life is to write its entire experience. Their purpose is that of registration and what they register is the aforesaid qualitation—mental, moral and rational. Everything man has thought or done is registered here and can be drawn upon. This is the "akashic record" of the Hindus and "the recording angel" of the Jews. This qualifying of the purely quantitative, we repeat, is man's task and purpose, and this being so, he should cease attributing moral qualities to the Creator and begin contributing them. To paraphrase a president: Ask not what God will do for you but what you can do for God.

Qualities

According to the scriptures all good qualities come from God and all evil ones from the devil or Satan. They little knew these two are one. The wiser pagans knew it and reduced it to an epigram: *Demon est Deus inversus*—the devil is God inverted—the original Dr. Jekyll and Mr. Hyde. In other words, when spirit became matter it became evil, or the source of evil. This is from the Romans, the Greek equivalent was *Diabolos*, and when written thus, dia-bolos it means thrown down, from the spirit plane to dense matter. They also knew that human desire, the cause of our evil, was in the planetary elements. The word comes from *desidero* and again divided, de-sidero, it too becomes revealing. *De* means of or from and *sidero* is the root of our word sidereal, of or pertaining to the stars. And star comes from *aster* and aster from astral, that is, astral matter. Thus human desire and the stars are of the same substance. And who created that? And if it be evil who is to blame? This is scriptural evil; this is the source of those sins of "the flesh and the devil." It is this the scriptures admonish us to overcome. And he who overcomes it is called a Master, "I have overcome the world." Now Master is but the word aster, star, with an M as prefix. Overcoming this is scriptural "salvation," and it is accomplished in Evolution, not religion.

Here we see again the results of false theologies. By attributing all morality and virtue to the Creator of soulless, senseless matter, they hid from us the true nature of Causation and the purpose of our own being. And so ignorant have we become under them we are now, in business, destroying what morality and virtue our forebears did develop. Instead of increasing the better qualities we are daily augmenting the worse—cruelty, greed, selfishness and dishonesty. If these be registered, what kind of legacy are we leaving? If we reap as we sow, what will the racial karma be? We must now learn that the creative process has a will and a purpose and when we subvert it we pay with our lives, our peace and our freedom. Such we are paying today and because we are ignorant of the plan and opposing its impulse.

Now just as all qualities man will ever need are developed in Evolution, past, present and future, so are the powers he will need. Through eons of conflict with a savage environment, the astral element was so qualified as to become our psyche, the source of psychic power. Though now in abeyance that reason may be developed, it can still be aroused. The way is through the emotions, and the means is prayer, fervent, not formal. And this is the prayer-answering power, not religion's God. As man's four elements are affinitized with the planet's four, the aura, effects are sometimes possible which to the ignorant seem omniscient response. This the authors of the scriptures did not know and so to them every psychic phenomenon, dream, vision, was a communication from their God, Jehovah.

Laws

We have been taught to believe in "the laws of God," and "the laws of nature," when actually there are no such things, save those man makes. There are only things and their modes of action. But what determines modes of action? The nature of things, and the nature of things is the sum of their qualities or characteristics. An atom unites with another atom, but it isn't a law that makes it unite; it is because of its energy content. Because of this it acts (expresses itself) thus and so, and as in a world, a universe, we have many things, we have a vast interplay of self-expressions. These interacting one with another give rise to relationships. Among things constant these expressions and relationships are also constant, and man, perceiving this constancy, puts it into words and calls it a law. Thus man is the lawmaker, not God. God makes things, and laws are but man's interpretation of their functions.

As these functions so long antedate conceptual man and manifest in all things, he assumes they preexisted these things, that God in his wisdom conceived them to govern his creations. But laws are neither causative nor creative nor do they preexist things. They come into being with being and being is the result of ideation, not laws. As for those still vaster mysteries Time and Space the same holds true of them. The Creative Principle does not make time and space and put worlds into them; it makes worlds and time and space, concrete, result from them—the abstract always was. Worlds are autonomous Beings and their characteristics determine their laws and relationships; and their laws and relationships constitute celestial government, also placement. Thus the "divine lawgiver" here is but man's substitute for knowledge of celestial dynamics. What he has called God's geometrizing is but the equilibration of cosmic forces. As for the infinitude of these forces, in other words, numbers, it is but the result of genetic fecundity.

Biologic Forms

Another great mystery is the kingdom forms, plant, animal, man. Where did they come from? Out of "congealed energy," "dead matter"? That living forms should spring from "dead matter" is mystery enough, but that they should arrange themselves in a mutually dependent sequence shocks even our limited reason. We say these have a precedent and a preparation, both ideatively and substantially, and until this is recognized a scientific account of them is like that of a biographer trying to explain the achievements of a great man without reference to his parentage or childhood experience. Evolutionary phenomena cannot be explained without involutionary antecedents. What is more, nothing exists in Evolution that was not in Involution potentially.

The kingdom forms were part of the aforesaid planetary ideation, and if the energies came forth why not the ideas? The very word Evolution means a coming out, but a coming out of what? Why, what went in—planetary ideation. In Involution the form ideas were worked up in the aforesaid elements as archetypes, and like the energies appear in Evolution in inverse order, and also time. Thus man is not an evolved animal nor yet a special creation but only a special ideation among many. This is the key to the kingdom forms but what, you ask, has it to do with understanding the Bible? For want of such knowledge an entire section of this book has been misunderstood for two thousand years and today we're making fools of ourselves over it.

Cosmic Forms

In spite of our so-called enlightenment millions still believe God controls the weather, when actually it is the sun. Even climate is due solely to the relationship of the sun and earth. In like manner, millions believe God created the world, when again it was a sun, but not our sun nor as science presents it. A sun is a transmuter of cosmic energy into chemical matter— that aforesaid congealed energy. Up to this point the creative process is an invisible one and so quite unknown and unrecognized today; from here on there is another, a visible and obvious one, as little known and recognized as its antecedent, namely sun, planet, moon, asteroid, etc. These various cosmic bodies, wholly dissociate in our minds, are not different species in a divine economy, but only different stages in the one purposive process—the making of a life-bearing planet. This is the goal of all cosmic bodies, and every one of them is either this, a priori or subsequent to. In this a sun constitutes the higher subdivision

THE ABSOLUTE — INACTIVE ENERGY

CREATIVE ENERGY

NONCREATIVE ENERGY

Mental Matter

Astral Matter

Etheric Matter

Electrons
Atoms
Molecules

Dense Matter

Sun Period

Earth Period

Electrons
Atoms
Nebula
Planetary dust
Asteroids
Moon
Old planet

Invisible sun

Gaseous sun
Visible sun
Old sun

Young planet
End of Involution

BEGINNING OF EVOLUTION

END OF EVOLUTION

EVOLUTION

LIFE HISTORY OF A COSMIC BODY

of the seventh plane, and its work is that of transforming the primal gas into the many, and finally their mineral compounds—the homogeneous into the heterogeneous as in the beginning. In this way the sun is laying down within itself the physical basis of a future planet. The process is that of fusion and by means of it the elements in the atomic table are created. These contain the life-force and the life-bearing period of a planet is one with the time it takes for them to radiate themselves away. When released they become the planetary aura, the energy substantive of biologic forms, and as their vibration rises, so does life. By the end of Evolution they stand in inverse order identical with those in Involution. And as the three highest there were spirit, so we must assume the three highest in Evolution will be likewise. Here man will be a spirit being with all the knowledge, wisdom and power that evolution affords. Thus does he, himself, create what he imagined his Creator to be—Omega not Alpha, and the scriptural error is as vast as the invo-evolutionary process.

A sun is a cosmic crucible in which that cross called matter is made, in other words, a transmuter of cosmic energy—a fact known thousands of years ago and also reduced to a myth: "Prometheus was the first to transmute atoms fit for human clay." Horace. And Prometheus, who stole fire from heaven and brought it down to earth, is but solar fire personified. Here that fire is imprisoned in matter. This is "Prometheus Bound." When released by radiation it is "Prometheus Unbound." Today we are releasing it without that cosmic consciousness necessary to use cosmic energy wisely.

But this is not all the sun is doing; it is also laying down within itself a future moon. A moon is the slag pile left by the solar furnace in the creation of the mineral kingdom—lava, pumice, not mud from the Pacific ocean. Nor are its pockmarks and tors the result of bombardment by meteors. This was an "inside job"—bubbles and flares caught in the congealing process, much like sun spots and prominences. When, throughout Evolution, the mineral covering is radiated away and life has left it, naught remains but the slag pile with some mineral relics. Such is our moon today, a corpse in space. That we today are seeking the key to life in this cosmic corpse shows how far our science still is from the heart of the cosmic mystery. Had our scientists knowledge of the creative process they would know what the moon is made of without spending the nation's wealth and maybe lives. Had they knowledge of the planetary sequence they would know, without space travel, what planets have life and what have not. It's a matter of understanding, not money and machines. As Lao-tze said, "Without going out of my door I can know the universe."

They would also know how solar systems are formed. When an old sun dies it becomes a young planet, but not immediately. For millions of years, perhaps, it wanders in space to cool its internal heat. Here it becomes a cosmic bomb, radioactive and deadly. This is Apollyon, "Chief of the wandering spirits," simply Apollo, sun, now dead and deadly. This in the plural are the "wanderers" the ancients had in mind, not the present planets. In due time this wanderer is picked up by the magnetic, not gravitational, force of another sun and thus are solar systems formed. The process is sequential and in this sequence is the key to life on other planets, also its condition. This the ancients also knew and named them accordingly: Mars, where it begins, martial and warlike, and where it ends, Venus, love. Love is the fulfilling of the law of Evolution. From this we can see just where we and our world are in this process—neither one nor the other but half way between. The process is inward, hence opposite to all past theories. Our place on the evolutionary ladder is also midway, 3½ planes, counting the physical.

As for Apollyon, "Chief of the wandering spirits," he was called "The Prince of Darkness, doomed to wander for ages and ages in the blackness of darkness." These are words from what is now a "dead language," a sort of cosmo-lingua modern man cannot read. Could he read it, he would know how false his theories are, both scientific and religious. It was a sun that created this world and not the God of Genesis. And instead of a Garden it was a Gehenna, all of which an ancient priesthood concealed or didn't know. Only in such knowledge as offered here can its frauds and fallacies be recognized.

Summary

A sun is a planet in the process of becoming. Such is the lord of our solar system today—a future earth, a forlorn moon. Our earth is now a planet, but it was not always so; it was once a sun. It was not, therefore, cast off from the sun; it is older by trillions of years than the sun: indeed suns are the youngest visible bodies in the universe. Our moon was once a life-bearing planet; it was not, therefore, cast off from the earth or sun; it is older by far than either of these; in fact, moons are the oldest globular bodies in the universe. Our moon is the last remaining member of a solar system when our earth was a sun. Jupiter, with its swarm of moons, was such a system once, a solar family when Jupiter was a sun and its moons were planets. And someday all our planets will be moons about a planet that is now our sun. In fact, Mercury is already moonlike. And if no life exists on Venus, it is not because its atmosphere is inimical but because its evolution is over and life has left it.

All this the Ancients knew and left to the world in what we call The Ancient Wisdom. This was known to the priestly founders of both Judaism and Christianity, and out of it they fashioned their scriptures and religions. That accomplished they destroyed every trace of their source material. That is why it is unknown to us. In what follows the reader will find these statements fully justified.

The Scriptures: The Concealed Truth Revealed

*The time will come when our
posterity will wonder at our ignorance
of things so plain.*

Seneca

Genesis or Creation

The Priestly Account

Divine Fiat

Heaven and earth, centre and circumference were made in the same instance of time and clouds full of water and man was created by the Trinity on the 26th of October, 4004 B.C., at 9 o'clock in the morning.

DR. JOHN LIGHTFOOT, 1654.

This was priestly knowledge of Creation in the seventeenth century A.D. What then of the seventh century B.C.? It should be understood that there was at that time no knowledge of man's natural development—anthropology, or of the creative process—cosmogony. To its priestly scribes this world was the center of the universe and man the sole concern of its Creator. That there were other worlds and galaxies was quite beyond their comprehension.

So let us realize that priests are not revealers of truth but only keepers of traditions, and that the purpose of both the scribes and their later translators was not to reveal the truth but to lay the basis of a theistic religion, based on the supernatural and the terrifying. This accounts for the presence here of the awesome word God. The original Hebrew did not use this singular word, or its equivalent, but the plural Elohim, many gods or aspects. Had this been followed, the mental darkness of monotheism might have been dispelled. It should also be noted that the word *genesis* does not mean "something out of nothing." It is a derivative of the word *gene*, the life germ, thus implying generation, growth. This is the key to the Mystery and if we would solve it we must make a clear distinction between the God of religion and the Creator of worlds. The one is a human ideal, the other a cosmic principle. These things understood, the interpretation offered here will not seem so preposterous.

We will not bore the reader with a verse-by-verse analysis but as with the Bible it seems a good way to begin. And so to Genesis 1:

1. In the beginning God created the heaven and the earth.

This very first verse disqualifies the Bible as authority, for it implies the aforesaid lack of knowledge. The author did not know how the world was created, and so he said a God created it. This is ignorance's way of explaining what it does not understand. The author's resort to it here is reminiscent of something a literary critic once said: "Whenever an author introduces a Chinaman in his story, I know that he is then writing about something he knows nothing about—'the inscrutable Chinee.' " So with the author here: he too is writing about something he knew nothing about, namely, Causation and Creation, "revelation" to the contrary.

2. And the earth was without form, and void; and darkness was upon the face of the deep. And the Spirit of God moved upon the face of the waters.

"The Spirit of God" is a false term due to the idea of a personal Deity. The Creator, on the contrary, is not a spirit, nor has it a spirit; it is spirit in the sense of substance, a morally unqualified principle, whose modus operandi is that of violence. Here it moved very gently upon the waters. No mention is made of the violence involved in the creation of a world which includes the sun period, nor the trillions of years of time. No word of a "war in heaven," as of John the Revelator, nothing about a beast, a devil, a Satan-opposer—just peaceful creation by word of mouth. This is woeful ignorance of cosmogony.

In all other ancient cosmologies we find the Creator battling with some cosmic monster, out of whose body the world was formed: Sosiosh with Tiamat, Odin with Ymir, the Rig-Veda gods with Parusha, etc. This we say is pagan ignorance and Genesis the Hebrews' superior wisdom. This, for instance: "Where the Babylonian poet saw only the action of deified forces of nature the Hebrew writer saw the working of God. And that insight was Inspiration." [1] And right there natural creation became supernatural, and that "inspiration," superstition. The result was twenty-five hundred years of benighted worship instead of welfare. This is the error and the evil this book fastened upon Western man and only now are we beginning to suspect it.

By the time this account was written the Hebrews had lost all knowledge of Causation and Creation and Genesis 1 is the result. In writings much older than this we find their Yahweh battling with Leviathan, the dragon, the serpent, Isaiah, 27:1. Psalm 74 reads thus: "Thou breakest the heads of Leviathan in pieces, and gavest him to be meat to the people inhabiting the wilderness." And in the Apocryphal Book of Enoch we read: "In that day shall be distributed for food two monsters; a feminine monster, whose name is Leviathan, dwelling in the depths of the sea, above the springs of waters; and a male monster whose name is Behemoth. . . ." In Job 41:10, God and Leviathan are as one: "None is so fierce that dare stir him (Leviathan) up: who then is able to stand before me?"

Why then is this aspect absent in the Priestly account? Besides the fact that the priests needed the divine, the perfect, the supernatural for their religion, its absence is due to the translators' ignorance of the words they were translating, words such as bārā tehōm, tōhū, bōhū, and others. These do convey a hint of warfare and violence. The original Hebrew reads thus: "In the beginning Elohim (many gods) bārā (not created, but cut out) the heavens and the earth. And the earth was tōhū and bōhū, and darkness was on the surface of the tehōm."

Tehōm is the primordial ocean, space or Absolute. Tōhū and bōhū, mistranslated "without form and void," connotes the monstrous and the violent. As Professor Jeremias, the German orien-

---

[1] J. Paterson Smyth, B.D., Litt.D., D.C.L. (Archbishop of St. Andrew, Montreal), The Bible in the Making, p. 61.

talist, says: "There can be no doubt that *tōhū* is connected with Ti(h)amat and *bōhū* with Behemoth. *Bōhū* is the equivalent of the Babylonian Apsu, the male mate of Tiamat." Thus *bōhū* and *Behemoth* are the Hebrew equivalents of Tiamat, Ymir, Purusha, and so on, all therianistic symbols of the violent elements with which the Creator had to contend. Elsewhere they are called *turbulentos*.

According to its apologists, the Bible is a Hebrew refinement of all pagan theologies and cosmologies, a process that completely obscured all knowledge of Causation and Creation. As Bellamy says: "But we must not forget that the report in Genesis has only come down to us in its sublimated—and therefore from the mythologists' standpoint, very unoriginal, not to say corrupted—form. Nevertheless, if we listen carefully to the Hebrew wording of the first verses in Genesis, we still find traces of the original meaning which no priestly editor has been able to extirpate." [2]

3. And God said, Let there be light: and there was light.

Here begins that fatal personification that has deceived the human race. A personal and vocal God said, "Let there be light." God said nothing of the kind; the allegorist said He said it, which makes all the difference between superstition and knowledge. Man puts words into the mouth of his creations then later believes these creations spoke.

4. And God saw the light, that it was good: and God divided the light from the darkness.

Here again, God *saw* the light, and thought it good, but how did this priestly scribe know that He did? Did God tell him so trillions of years after the act? No, the world exists and the author just assumed its various stages were right and proper. That this light is not sunlight is obvious, since the sun, the stars, were not created till the fourth day. On the contrary, this *light*

[2] From *Moons, Myths and Man.*

is that first primordial "light shining in darkness," and it was
not produced by some deity saying Let it be. The one creative
energy separated into two, positive and negative, and their in-
teraction produced something luminous compared to the darkness of the Absolute. According to the New Testament this
"light shining in darkness" was Christ, but actually it was
Lucifer, the Son of the Morning, of creation; in the power sense,
none other than the Creator himself. It is the Hebrew concealment of this fact that has hidden from us the true nature of
Causation; the result has been twenty-five centuries of spiritual
ignorance. This ignorance must now be dispelled. The time has
come for an "agonizing reappraisal" of the entire scriptures, and
Genesis is the place to start. Therefore we too say, Let there be
light, but this time the light of understanding.

5. And God called the light Day, and the darkness he called Night.
And the evening and the morning were the first day.

Please note the capitals here. As the earth has not yet been
formed nor the sun created, they are not our day and night; they
are what the Hindus call the Day and Night of Brahma, the
Creator—immeasurable periods in the creative process. In this
account the Days are from the evening to the morning; that is,
from the darkness of the Absolute (nonbeing) to the light of
Being. As these Days are billions if not trillions of years, we see
here how much is covered and covered up, by these four words,
"Let there be light," and also how little they explain.

6. And God said, Let there be a firmament in the midst of the
waters, and let it divide the waters from the waters.
7. And God made the firmament, and divided the waters which
were under the firmament from the waters which were above the
firmament; and it was so.
8. And God called the firmament Heaven. And the evening and the
morning were the second day.

The word *firmament* in Hebrew is *rakia* and means only a wide
expanse, namely, space. In this is the nascent planetary entity,

a vast globular field of cosmic energy—the "ring-pass-not" of ancient cosmology. The division of the waters (energy) above and below is but the division of the planetary elements from the Absolute, Being from nonbeing.

9. And God said, Let the waters under the heavens be gathered together unto one place, and let the dry land appear: and it was so.

By assuming that this "dry land" is our present physical earth we have missed the whole meaning of this chapter, namely, that it deals only with the prephysical world. The division here is not that between land and water but between the *spiritual* and the *material*, the Trinity and the Quaternary. This took place on the cusp of the third and fourth involutionary planes. The priestly error lies in leaving the *spiritual* behind to be worshiped and adored, whereas the *material* four are the concretion of the *spiritual* three. The Creator burns his bridges behind him, but this would never do for a religion and so the priest concealed it.

10. And God called the dry land Earth; and the gathering together of the waters called he Seas: and God saw that it was good.

The "earth" here is the earth-entity, at the fourth plane and still invisible. So with the "seas." Throughout both the Old and the New Testament the three planes between the *spiritual* and the *physical* are called "seas," "waters," etc. Between this fourth plane and physical earth is the sun period, a matter of trillions of years. This the priest was either ignorant of or did not want known. The authors of the New Testament knew it, but presented it in a manner too occult for modern man to grasp. Later we will explain it.

11. And God said, Let the earth bring forth grass, the herb yielding seed, and the fruit tree yielding fruit after his kind, whose seed is in itself, upon the earth: and it was so.

This priestly scribe saw clearly that everything in the world comes from a seed within itself, but he could not, or would not, see that this is so of the world also. Had he said that it is a cosmic plant "whose seed is in itself," what a difference it would have made. The supernatural would not have blinded us to the natural; "divinity" would not have diverted us from Reality.

12. And the earth brought forth grass, and herb yielding seed after his kind, and the tree yielding fruit, whose seed was in itself. . . .

Grass, trees, fruit, and all this before the sun was created or ever it had rained on the earth, according to Genesis 2:5. This is real occultism and not one of our ecclesiastics knows what it means. With our theory, however, its meaning is obvious. On this third day and plane, grass, trees and fruit are purely ideative, defined in our outline as planetary ideation. On the metaphysical planes below, this becomes archetypal. There can be no other meaning to Genesis 2:4–5. ". . . the Lord God made the earth and the heavens, and every plant of the field *before it was in the earth*, and every herb of the field *before it grew.*" The Jews got this bit of occult truth from the Hindus. According to their cosmology all evolutionary forms were first created in mental, astral and etheric matter in Involution, these serving later as models for the physical. This does not mean that every form that has appeared in Evolution was there in archetype, thus proving each a permanent entity as some would like to believe; on the contrary, the specie and kingdom prototypes were there and their first evolutionary counterparts were endowed from the beginning with the capacity for incalculable proliferation, hence the myriads today. Be this as it may, to understand the myths such as this we must cease to think of the earth as of now and think in terms of a cosmic entity, invisible but evolving and creating for trillions of years before it became a visible, concrete object. This is the aforesaid key to the biologic kingdoms. There the reader may have had his doubts, not knowing he had read it all before in his holy scriptures.

13. And the evening and the morning were the third day.

This third day and plane is the end of the ideative period and you will remember it was here Uranus, the last god in the Greek

trinity, was dispatched. This is correct since he represented the
end of ideation. Creation went on, however, under Cronos. This
is Greek henotheism—one god at a time. No such change is
recognized by the priest, however; to him the same God remains
throughout, external and omnipotent. Now since there is only
one Creator, this method is defensible, but it hides from us the
all important fact that the creation of worlds is a natural process,
cyclical in nature and incalculable in time.

14. And God said, Let there be lights in the firmament of the heaven
to divide the day from the night; and let them be for signs, and for
seasons, and for days and years:

15. And let them be for lights in the firmament of the heaven to give
light upon the earth: and it was so.

16. And God made two great lights; the greater light to rule the day,
and the lesser light to rule the night: he made the stars also.

17. And God set them in the firmament of the heaven to give light
upon the earth,

18. And to rule over the day and over the night, and to divide the
light from the darkness: and God saw that it was good.

19. And the evening and the morning were the fourth day.

And now that the earth is ready for business, it needs lights,
and presto! they're made. Kindergarten cosmology, also geocen-
tric—the sun, the moon, the stars were made just to give light
to the earth. Again we wonder what these semiancients knew
about galaxies a billion light years away. Yet here and there in
their borrowed cosmology we find traces of the original occult
meaning in spite of the priests' destruction thereof. This is such
a case and it is truer than modern science. For decades science
told us the earth was thrown off from the sun; now it is back
with Dr. Lightfoot and the priest—instantaneous creation, not
only of the world but the universe. The priest must have nodded
here for all unintentionally he tells us the earth was made first,
and this is correct. The earth is older far than the sun; as we
said, suns are the youngest visible bodies in the universe. At the
time in the earth's history referred to here, our sun was not yet
visible and the moon was a nascent planet. The contemporary

suns of that time had existed for billions of years and are now planets also.

20. And God said, Let the waters bring forth abundantly the moving creatures that hath life, and fowl that may fly above the earth in the open firmament of heaven.

The "waters" here are still prephysical substances. In Evolution these become the seven planes, and these are the seven heavens of the Cabala and some religions.

21. And God created great whales, and every living creature that moveth, which the waters brought forth abundantly, after their kind, and every winged fowl after his kind: and God saw that it was good.

Well, seeing's believing. Apparently this God wasn't sure until he did see. As for whales: if these creatures evolved from land animals, science would say this reveals a woeful lack of knowledge of Evolution, but this is not Evolution: it is Involution and the whales are archetypal whales. The Bible does not stop to explain; it merely states occult truths in cryptic fashion and leaves us to understand when and if we can. The tragedy is that it has never been understood in the Piscean Age.

22. And God blessed them, saying, Be fruitful, and multiply, and fill the waters in the seas, and let fowl multiply in the earth.
23. And the evening and the morning were the fifth day (of Involution).

Were every creature in Evolution a permanent monad, there would have been no need of multiplying at the start.

24. And God said, Let the earth bring forth the living creature after his kind, cattle, and creeping thing, and beast of the earth after his kind: and it was so.
25. And God made the beast of the earth after his kind, and cattle after their kind, and every thing that creepeth upon the earth after his kind (including disease germs): and God saw that it was good. ("Before it was in the earth and before it grew" [Gen. 2:5].)

26. And God said, Let us make man (should be Man) in our image, after our likeness: and let them have dominion over the fish of the sea, and over the fowl of the air, and over the cattle, and over all the earth, and over every creeping thing that creepeth upon the earth.

Here a singular Creator suddenly becomes plural, *us*, the Elohim. The word comes from *Alheim* and means a council, a council of the gods, the creative aspects of the one power. It was here at this same point in the Greek myth that the Titans began creating Man. The Elohim were inferentially twelve in number, since there are twelve Titans and twelve powers of the zodiac. [3] Were this physical man, the Bible would be wrong not once but twice. First, man did not have dominion over everything in the beginning; he achieved this only as he evolved. Second, man was not here, save potentially, at the beginning of biologic life. In the evolutionary process, the kingdom-forms came forth in a sequence the reverse of that in Involution; that is, the plant was first in Evolution, therefore last in Involution; man was last in Evolution, therefore first in Involution. "And the first shall be last and the last shall be first." Man is the consummator of the Creator's plan and therefore first in ideation. The priestly scribe did not know these things and so has man created last in Involution. The meaning here, however, is dual; this generic Man is the creative power when it got down on the lower planes. The dominion given to him is over the planetary entity. This is now Adam, and save for the priestly prerequisite, the God of the Bible could be dispensed with from here on. Biologically Adam

[3] It might be of interest to some to know that the numerical value of the word Alheim is 3.1415, the relation of a diameter to the circumference of a circle, here the zodiac. The zodiac is the story of Creation written in the stars and much of the Bible is based on it. But like the Bible it too has been changed and corrupted. Children are not the proper symbol for Gemini; Capricorn though very old was not originally a goat. And somewhere, sometime, "the children of darkness" transposed Virgo and Libra. Furthermore, it is not the large hand of this cosmic clock that locates our place and condition but a lesser hand, if added, pointing in the opposite direction. This is the true significator. Thus we are not entering the Aquarian Age but the Leonean Age. And Leo is the sun and the age will be as violent as the sun, more ideological than military, however. What then of the "peace and tranquillity" we've been promised? It is twelve thousand years from us. Aquarius does not bring us peace and tranquillity; we must bring peace and tranquillity to Aquarius.

THE ZODIAC

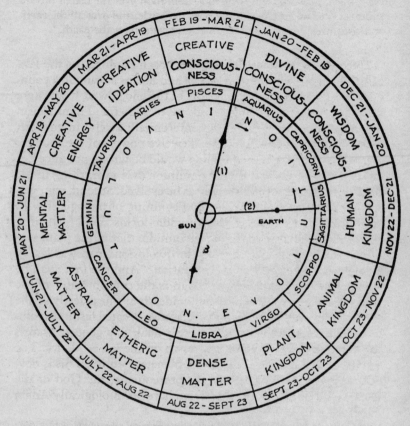

THE COSMIC CLOCK
(1) PRECESSIONAL HAND   (2) EVOLUTIONARY HAND
(3) THE CONDITION INDEX

is the creative genetic principle in matter, and I wonder how many realize that the biologic genetic is the only creatively active function of God in Evolution; all other activities in nature are but energy in action—wind, rain, earthquake, volcano, and so forth—not "Acts of God" but planetary functionalism, as we said.

In our cosmology, we did not make man and God identical, and we did not out of respect for man, the subsequent moral epigene. We did not want to make this moral being responsible for the murderous violence of a nonmoral Creator.

27. So God created man in his own image, in the image of God created he him; male and female created he them. (And that is the tragedy of man and the source of his violence.)

Has it ever occurred to you that this "image of God," your body, is a moral, spiritual and social know-nothing? Of your morals and manners it has no knowledge and so at the most inopportune moment it may want to relieve itself. On the very day you need your strength and wits the most, it will get sick or keep you awake the night before. Yet this know-nothing is the one part of us God made without man's help. Why then attribute morality and omniscience to its Creator?

Man is made in the image of God only substantially. If morphologically, we must conclude this God has a stomach and alimentary system like man, also sex organs. One might wonder what He does with them since in Judaism and Christianity He has no female consort. Well, He creates worlds with them. This is "the seed of Abraham" and the teste of the Testament. Thus this world was not created by God's *vox*, but by his *sex*.

Here as yet his creations are not physical man and woman but their involutionary archetypes after the ideation thereof. On the sixth plane, this involutionary image was in etheric matter, which gave rise to the false metaphysical doctrine that evolutionary man was first an etheric being. He was so only in Involution. In Evolution the organism acquires the etheric. It also acquires the astral and is today building an astral replica of the physical body. This will be our vehicle on the higher planes. It may be even now the vehicle of Venusians if such exist.

The words "male" and "female" in Hebrew were *sacr* and *n'cabvah*, one with *phallus* and *yoni*, the genetic principle. Throughout the Bible, the male represents creative ideation, which was first; the female represents substance, matter, created later. If this be not the meaning here, then this first chapter flatly contradicts the second, which says that man was created first and woman thereafter.

28. And God blessed them, and God said unto them, Be fruitful, and multiply, and replenish the earth, and subdue it: and have dominion over the fish of the sea, and over the fowl of the air, and over every living thing that moveth upon the earth.

Well, it's nice that God has someone now to talk to; hitherto He's been talking to himself. The word "replenish" here implies restoration of something previously taken away. That something was the fifth-plane creations in astral matter, which must now be recreated in sixth-plane etheric matter. Thus the Bible is not speaking of human beings or evolutionary life, but of involutionary archetypes, yet upon these literal words the Catholic Church urges its people to multiply regardless of means. God did not say these words; a Jewish priest said them—and he wasn't even talking about humanity. Yet his literal minded successor uses them to make irresponsible parenthood a virtue, and irrational proliferation a sacred duty. In spite of the population explosion parents must have six, eight, a dozen, not for society's sake, but for Catholicism's sake. The right to propagate at will is, I suppose, the fifth freedom, but like all other freedoms when exercised by ignorance it is inimical to social welfare. We have restraints against all others but not against the fifth; instead, it is politically encouraged, for security, and religiously sanctified, for the Church.

To the intelligent, however, an ignorant and prolific female mass-producing humanity is one of the most shocking things in human life. Every child is a potential for good or evil with which all human society must deal, yet here is a socially irresponsible creature turning out multiple problems in blissful ignorance of everything save the biologic function. Such procreation reduces man to the level of the beast. Instead of a sacred duty, it is one of the greatest of crimes; instead of a "blessed event," a monstrous impertinence. If the race would solve its crime and social problems, it must begin with these irresponsible problem-breeders. They must be made to realize there is no divine authority for ignorant propagation; it is but nature's prolific fecundity, over which man should also "have dominion." The Church's attitude towards this well illustrates the consequence of our ignorance of Causation and the facts of Reality, for, there is no soul involved in conception; there isn't even life, only the Life Principle. And this we destroy every day.

29. And God said, Behold, I have given you every herb bearing seed, which is upon the face of all the earth, and every tree, in the which is the fruit of a tree yielding seed; to you it shall be for meat.

30. And to every beast of the earth, and to every fowl of the air, and to every thing that creepeth upon the earth, wherein there is life, I have given every green herb for meat: and it was so.

And it was so because trillions of years thereafter man made it so. But he did not make it according to this command. God gave the plant kingdom to both man and animal for meat, but he did not give the animal kingdom to man for meat, yet God's "chosen people" ate meat and also sacrificed animals to their God, no mention of which is made here. Were this rite as important as it subsequently became, one would think it would be authorized here. If this sacrifice was not also mythological, it was probably a clever means of filling the priests' own larder. Bring us your lambs and your heifers but don't ask what we do with them.

31. And God saw everything that he had made, and behold it was very good. And the evening and the morning were the sixth day.

This sixth day is the last in which God looked upon his work and called it good. This, no doubt, was because the work of the seventh is the creation of matter, the source of evil.

We include here the first three verses of the second chapter because they belong to the priestly account. Such was the Editor's idea of sequence.

1. Thus the heavens and the earth were finished, and all the host of them.

Archetypally only, else later parts of the Bible are sheer nonsense, the Ark for instance, explained later.

2. And on the seven day God ended his work which he had made; and he rested on the seventh day from all his work which he had made.

The motion in an atom, great as it is, is but "slow motion" compared to that of the preatomic planes. Eventually, this high rate was *arrested* in dense matter, number 7. This does not mean, however, that the Creator did nothing on this day; he but "ended his work" on this day, and the end of his work was the creation of the whole physical world. The morning of this day is the early sun period, and all between this and the beginning of Evolution, condensation, radiation or devolution, was done on this day. Here, as in the polar opposite, the Absolute, the Life Principle was "inactive and asleep." Devolution is strictly an energy function; elsewhere the Bible tells us this began at the three-and-one-half point. (See diagram p. 44.)

The word for week in Hebrew is *seven;* this, however, is a cosmic week of seven planetary days. This seven-day creation is by no means original with the Hebrews; every ancient cosmology was based on it—the mystic seven. In Greek mythology the gods created the world in a week of seven days, and in the Hindu Purânas, Brahma does likewise. The names of these seven days are found in Hindu manuscripts as early as 5000 B.C.

Nor was it the Hebrews who first made the seventh day a sacred day. Before this Priestly account was written (fourth century), Hesiod (eighth century) said, "The seventh is the sacred day." And later Plato wrote thus: "The gods, pitying the laborious nature of men ordained for them as a rest from all their labors, the succession of religious festivals." The first of these was every seventh day, while the seventh day of every month was dedicated to Apollo, the sun, hence our Sunday. Not even the word *Sabbath* comes from the Hebrews. It derived from the Babylonian *Sabattu*, day of rest, observed by them long before the Hebrews. "The problem as to why the Hebrews chose the Babylonian *Sabattu* as a name for these days of rest is a mystery. The idea of a regular seventh day of rest arose in

Babylon—of that, there can be no doubt." Professor Langdon. There is no mystery about it; the Hebrews got all their metaphysical ideas from older races. There is practically nothing in the Bible that cannot be found in other literatures. Convinced of its originality and revelatory nature we just don't look elsewhere.

3. And God blessed the seventh day, and sanctified it: because in it he had rested from all his work which God created and made.

God did not call this day's work merely good; he did still better. He blessed and sanctified it, not because in it He had a good rest, but because in this seventh day and plane He achieved the goal and consummation of all his effort, namely, the material earth. Those despisers of matter should make a note of this. Trillions of years of involutionary labor are not for nothing; a physical world was the objective. Neither are millions of years of evolutionary labor, hence the significance of our physical body, the human correlate of the physical earth.

Now we have interpreted this chapter in terms of our own theory, but not in terms of it alone; these are the terms of every ancient cosmology of which we have knowledge. They tell only the story of the world's creation down to dense matter, and include Man only as the symbol of the Creative Principle. The Priestly account conforms to the pattern. There is in it no mention of Adam, only "man," a generic term. No doubt there was originally a Jhwhist chapter covering the same ground, but it is now lost. This is a great misfortune because it might have given us a viewpoint quite different. We said *lost*, but no, it was destroyed. To those who defend the Bible we should say, Produce this lost and destroyed original that the priestly substitute, and its perversion, may be made known.

Today we know the world was not created as per this Priestly account; why then do we respect it? Why do we accept it as part of "the word of God," and let it tyrannize over us? It is not God's account of Creation; it is priestly ignorance thereof, and we accept it only because we too are ignorant of the subject. The creation of a world is a metaphysical process, and we here repeat, Western man is incapable of true metaphysical thought, and so he blindly accepts this false account of it.

Suns are the creators of worlds, not gods. This the Ancients knew and it became the basis of their sun-worship. Today we think of this as pagan ignorance of "the one true God," but alas, the ignorance is ours, not theirs. The story is told of a Christian bishop who said to a Parsee:

"So you are one of those peculiar fellows who worship the sun."

"Yes," said the Parsee, "and so would you if you had ever seen it."

No, the bishop had never seen the sun mentally and so he worshiped a mythical Creator instead of the real one. And I'm sure he thought his form of worship vastly superior to the peculiar fellow's.

And now if this first chapter is false, what of the rest of the book? It is of like nature, a priestly hoax intended to deceive us. And nowhere has it succeeded more than in the first four chapters of Genesis.

Eden, the Garden of Eden, Paradise, etc.

Now to understand these chapters we must know where and what their Eden was, how it differs from the Garden of Eden, what Paradise was and what took place therein.

We generally think of Eden and the Garden of Eden as one, but the Bible says the Garden was planted "eastward in Eden." Eden then is something bigger than the Garden: it is, in fact, the planetary entity in its prephysical state, i.e., prior to matter, the mythic source of evil. Eastward, that is, forward in this, was planted a Garden. Now in cosmogony what other Garden is there save a life-bearing planet, in this case, the earth? The Garden of Eden is the earth itself, planted eastward, that is, forward in the creative process. The Hebrew word *Eden* comes from an old Babylonian name for Mesopotamia, *Gan-Eden*, the garden of the Middle East. The word *Meso-potamia* also means *middle land*, so also the Norse Midgard, home of the gods. Throughout mythology, which includes scripture, the "middle

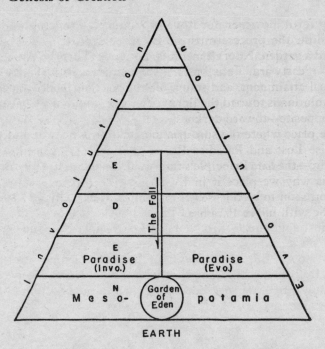

The "East" in Involution becomes the "West" in Evolution; thus "the happy lands" are always in the "West."

land" is that middle ground between Involution and Evolution, namely, the earth. How absurd then to think the Garden of Eden was somewhere in *our* Mesopotamia. How absurd also to call a primeval world a garden. This is some more priestly concealment of the truth. Now, billions of years later, it is something of a garden but Adam is still "raising Cain" in it, and not because he ate an apple, but because of the nature of Being.

Fair Eden is one with all the happy lands always in the west— the Hesperides, Elysian Fields, Fortunate Isles, Isles of the Blest, and brave Valhalla, whose passing is *Gotterdammerung*, the twilight of the gods. Prior to this all was well with them; there was no matter, the source of evil, and their food was nectar and ambrosia, symbols of the etheric, astral and mental elements. This was the Paradise mythological man lost. We need not mourn for it, however, for it was not only well lost but meant to be lost, the process must go on. So eastward in this was planted a garden. Now all members of secret orders know what "east," "eastward," etc., mean—forward, toward the light, spiritual attainment, and so on. This is all right in Evolution, for Evolution is toward the light, but in Involution it means the very opposite—toward darkness, matter, evil. Thus the West to us, the place where the sun *went down* to dense matter. This is Paradise Lost and Paradise Regained is but its evolutionary opposite—the Life Principle's freedom from bondage in matter. This is why we place it in Evolution also, and why another Creator, soon to be released from matter, said, "This day thou shalt be with me in Paradise."

The Jhwhistic Account

Genesis: Second Chapter

4. These are the generations of the heavens
and of the earth when they were created, in the
day that the Lord God made the earth and the
heavens.

Obviously this is not a reference to the
Priestly account of Creation, since the Jhwhist wrote hundreds
of years before the priests. It is either a conjunctional sentence
written by the Editor or the Jhwhist's reference to his own
account. Here, God becomes the Lord God, a term not used by
the priest in the first chapter.

5. And every plant of the field *before it was in the earth*, and every
herb of the field *before it grew*: for the Lord God had not caused it to
rain upon the earth, and there was not a man to till the ground.

This is the true meaning of the first account of Creation—archetypal and prephysical. The Jhwhist no doubt presented it as
such in his account but the priests obscured it in theirs. Would
the Jhwhist have written "There was not a man to till the

ground" if he had written the first account? Hardly, since in that one, man was already created. As he knew nothing about the present first chapter, he was writing in accordance with his own sequence. In this there was no physical man as yet, nor even a physical earth. Reference to this begins only in verse 8, therefore verses 6 and 7 are either out of place or refer only to prephysical Man.

6. But there went up a mist from the earth, and watered the whole face of the ground.

7. And the Lord God formed man of the dust of the ground, and breathed into his nostrils the breath of life; and man became a living soul. (Should be Man, not man.)

Physical man was not made before the physical earth, verse 8. "Nostrils" here is purely figurative, and so is "breath." The "living soul" is not the human psyche, but merely life. This is the translator's fault. The Hebrew word here was *nephish*, and under the Mosaic code, where restitution was demanded for a killed or stolen ox or sheep, the law was "nephish for nephish," a life for a life, not a soul for a soul. No good Christian would admit a sheep or ox has a soul.

This account of man created from the dust is also copied from the Babylonian epic, the Gilgamesh. In still another Babylonian myth, a woman, Aruru, creates him in like manner.

> *Aruru washed her hands;*
> *Clay she pinched off and spat upon it;*
> *Eaboni, a hero she created,*
> *An exalted offspring with the might of Ninib.*

Certainly not a mortal man, and neither was his Hebrew counterpart.

8. And the Lord God (law God) planted a garden eastward in Eden; and there he put the man whom he had formed.

Oh, no, the Lord God did not put the *man* into a garden; he put him into a hell in space, a violent, primeval world over which he has been trying ever since to gain dominion. If this Garden is not the earth but only that part called Mesopotamia, consider the absurdity of it. Can you imagine God planting a garden save as nature does it? And if this God is the Creator of the entire cosmos, we wonder how the rest of it got along while He was messing around in Mesopotamia. Here we see the logic of our theory: that each planet is its own creator and needs no attention from the creators of the others.

And here we come to another mystery no theologian can explain:

9. And out of the ground (earth) made the Lord God to grow every tree that is pleasant to the sight, and good for food; the tree of life also in the midst of the garden, and the tree of knowledge of good and evil.

Since there is no physical "tree of life" nor yet of "good and evil," this must be symbolic. Why then can't we see that the whole story, nay the whole book, is symbolic. The "tree of life" is life itself, more specifically, the Life Principle, growing in the midst, i.e., within the planetary entity. Calling it a tree is by no means peculiar to the Hebrews; every ancient race had its "tree of life." With the Greeks it was Gogard, with Ladon the serpent; with the Norse it was Yggdrasil, the ash, at the foot of which was Nidhogg, their serpent. According to Hesiod, Zeus created three races of men, the last out of ash trees. The Hindus pictured Creation as a tree, Ashvatta, with its roots in the Absolute and its branches (seven planes) hanging downward. From this word, Ashvatta, we see where the others got their *ash* tree, considered sacred. Among the Tibetans, the "tree of life" was Zampun, and among the Persians, Homa. The Druids honored the oak tree as a symbol of "the mundane tree of life." Even the Chinese had their "tree of knowledge," Sung-Ming-Shu. As moral good and evil are purely human and wholly epigenetic, this cannot be the good and evil of the second tree. On the contrary, it is that immemorial good and evil of myth and scripture—spirit and matter. It was of the latter that Man, spiritual substantially only, was warned not to partake, and yet how purely figurative that warning is, since material existence and all it implies was the goal and purpose of Creation. How then could it be sin and disobedience? Involution was, that Evolution might be. The "tree of life" and the "tree of knowledge" are the scriptural equivalents of our genetic and epigenetic.

Herein lies the source of many of our present false ideas about ourselves. This Man of the capital *M* was the subject of all the ancient cosmologists. It was of him they were thinking when they used such terms as immortality, reincarnation, etc. When man of the little *m* lost all knowledge of Man of the capital *M*, he applied such terms to himself, and so little *m* became immortal, reincarnated, and so on.

10. And a river went out of Eden to water the garden; and from thence it was parted, and became into four heads.

This is "the river of life," the creative energy, one with the waters of Aquarius. First, it flowed out of the Trinity to become the four *waters* of the Quaternary. This was Eden, from which it flowed into the Garden, earth, from whence it divided again into four parts, the four material elements of the planetary aura, that is, counting the physical. These, as we said, are the energy substantives of the four kingdoms. And this is their meaning here as their names imply.

11. The name of the first is Pison; that is it which compasseth the whole land of Havilah, where there is gold.

Seems a bit early to be talking about gold in the economic sense. Here it is but a symbol of the mineral kingdom. Pison means a multitude—atoms or mineral monads.

12. And the gold of that place is good; there is bdellium and the onyx stone (*Bedolach* and *shoham stone*).

We called the earth a cosmic *lithos*, or stone. Esoterically, this and the shoham stone are one.

13. And the name of the second river is Gihon: the same is it that compasseth the whole land of Ethiopia.

Gihon means "to break forth"—the life-force breaking forth from the earth, the etheric and plant kingdom. That this river flowed out of Mesopotamia (Asia) into Ethiopia (Africa) is not a mistake of ancient ignorance of geography, but a hint to modern ignorance about symbolic literature. This is not the African Ethiopia but the Greek Aethiopia, a mythic land of darkness and mystery. The word Ethiopia here is but a blind for the etheric or second plane.

14. And the name of the third river is Hiddekel: that is it which goeth towards the east of Assyria. And the fourth river is Euphrates.

Hiddikel means *rapid motion*, the animal kingdom with its freedom and mobility. Euphrates means *fruitful*, and represents the fruit or purpose of the others, the human kingdom. Later on in the Bible the land of Assyria is also used symbolically. The Bible is quite right in making but four rivers, for that is all there are today.

In the Brahmanical account, four primeval rivers pour out from the golden Mount Meru (earth), the city of Brahma. So likewise the Sineru of the Buddhists had its four sacred rivers which proceeded from Tawrutisa, the abode of Sikia, the god of Life. The Tien-Chan, or celestial mountains of the Chinese and Tartars, was watered by four perennial fountains of Tychin, or immortality. Asgard, the Eden of the Scandinavians, was watered by four rivers of milk. And so we see there is nothing original here. If Jews and Christians would but read others' mythology as well as their own, they would realize that this is cosmological symbolism, not geography and history. Even Josephus's words imply some recognition of its symbolic nature: "Now the garden was watered by one river, which ran round about the whole earth, and was parted into four parts." A literal river would not run "round about the whole earth" and through the oceans.

15. And the Lord God took the man, and put him into the garden of Eden to dress it and to keep it.

There is no mention of Adam yet, only "the man," symbolic of the life force. Only by realizing this can we understand the following verses.

16. And the Lord God commanded the man, saying, Of every tree of the garden thou mayest freely eat:
17. But of the tree of knowledge of good and evil, thou shalt not eat of it: for in the day that thou eatest thereof thou shalt surely die (spiritually).

Knowledge of good and evil comes from racial experience with Reality, matter in all its forms. This "tree of knowledge" is therefore life's experience with matter. To taste of this meant spiritual death in the involutionary sense—the great crime of mythology, perverted by priests. And yet how absurd is this command in any moral or literal sense, because tasting this fruit was the whole purpose of Creation. It is therefore a command against the Creator's own will.

18. And the Lord God said, It is not good that the man should be alone; I will make him an help meet for him.

Ladies, you're only an afterthought, a mere help meet for Mr. Big, still later, a "spare rib." This is what the literal word makes you; you must now learn what the occult word makes you. But first, this verse is out of place, or else the Lord God is unpardonably poor in literary sequence. It should follow verse 20.

19. And out of the ground the Lord God formed every beast of the field, and every fowl of the air; and brought them unto Adam to see what he would call them: and whatsoever Adam called every living creature, that was the name thereof.

More bad literary form, the hero introduced so abruptly, no buildup at all. Were this the Jhwhist's untouched original it would not have been done so undramatically.

20. And Adam gave names to all cattle, and to the fowl of the air, and to every beast of the field; but for Adam there was not found an help meet for him. (Here, read verse 18.)

As a human being, Adam naming the countless creatures including the fishes, the insects, and even the bacteria is naive, to say the least. Symbolically, it is but that identity of things as the Life Principle made them. And this is what Adam is. In the most esoteric sense, Adam is the genetic consciousness, but once in matter we speak of it as matter—"Spirit became matter." The word Adam is simply Hebrew for "red clay," and as such, is the earth. Here Adam and atom are one and the same. Adamah, the source of the word, means "that from which vegetation springs"; and what is that but atomic matter? Rabbi Jehuda said that when Adam stretched out his body he covered the whole earth. And why not, since he is the earth.

The name Adam is not Hebrew in origin. Adam Adami is found in Chaldean scriptures much older than those of the Hebrews; it was also known to the Babylonians. Among their clay tablets George Smith found an account of Creation identical with that of the Bible, and in this the first man is Adamu. And in a Hindu book two thousand years older than the Bible, *The Prophecies*, by Ramutsariar, the Hebrew story is given almost word for word, and there the first man is Adama and the first woman Heva. It is obvious then that Adam is not a personal name, but a generic term for the Life Principle. Indeed the Kabbalah confirms this. Its Adam, that is, Adam Kadmon, is the "only begotten," or first emanation from the source. Whose "sin" then was "Adam's sin"? and who responsible? What Adam did was wholly impersonal, nonmoral and nonhuman, and yet it is upon this "sin" our whole salvation madness rests. "What fools we mortals be!" In our Preface we said that Western man was not capable of metaphysical thought or perception; this, we think, should prove it.

21. And the Lord God caused a deep sleep to fall upon Adam, and he slept: and he took one of his ribs, and closed up the flesh instead thereof.

This "deep sleep" is that period of complete inactivity the Life Principle suffered when completely involved in matter— four planes and trillions of years removed from humanity. Thus

Adam's "sleep" is identical with God's "rest." It's nothing new in mythology. According to the Egyptians, their God caused a cloud to pass over the first men, "and while they slept he gave them wives." And the Tahitans tell us that their God, Taaroa, "put men to sleep for long ages," during which he pulled a bone, Ivi (Eve), from one of them and it became a woman.

The Creator pulled a bone, but our translators pulled a boner, for we have here, perhaps, the most tragicomic mistake a translator ever made.

22. And the rib which the Lord God had taken from man, made he a woman, and brought her unto the man.

A translator should understand the subject as well as the words he is translating. This is a good example of what happens when he does not. The subject here is the cosmic Man, but believing it was our first human parent, the translator made woman a "spare rib" and her creation a clinical operation.

23. And Adam said, This is now bone of my bones, and flesh of my flesh: she shall be called Woman, because she was taken out of Man.

In all biologic life man is taken out of woman. How is it then that the first woman was taken out of man? Because the Bible is not speaking of biologic or evolutionary man but of involutionary Man, the Life Principle. This was first and it subsequently generated matter, personified by woman. But how did the "rib" get into it? The word from which rib was translated is *tzala* and means side as well as rib. With this, and the subject, understood, the meaning becomes clear. The rib is one side of the, as yet, androgynous Life Principle. As this is both male and female, or positive and negative, taking a side of it away is separating the two, here only the negative and positive for not even a male and female amoeba existed for billions of years thereafter. We have said repeatedly that knowledge of the creative process is the key to the riddle of life, and we could add, the Bible. Had our translators possessed the slightest knowledge of this process, this story alone would have shown them the

Bible is not dealing with biologic man. They should have read other races' mythology as well as their own. The Chaldeans portrayed the Trinity as a triangle closed on two sides, the right and the base; the left side was open from which stepped Sephira, the female aspect. The Hindus picture the Creator with one side male and the other female. Respectful Christians pronounce this shocking and blasphemous, little suspecting their effeminate Christ implies the same thing. Implies but never states.

Here again we see the error of the Judeo-Christian concept. Whatever exists in Evolution existed also in Involution, potentially. Now the female exists in Evolution, therefore it too existed in Involution. Yet nowhere in the scriptures do we find a female consort of the Creator. God is a bachelor, yet He had a son. Too long these metaphysically ignorant priests have ribbed and robbed us of the truth.

The Bible was written by men, and men were masters then; so also in the days of the translators—the heyday of social chivalry and sociological inequality. Such are the errors of ignorance, and having made one like the rib, how can we trust our translators elsewhere? How can we occultly translate their translations? Our effort is only to make theirs cosmologically informative. And how greatly even this bit of knowledge changes things. Woman is not, after all, a "spare rib"; she is half of life itself, the negative half, but even this must be understood, for it does not mean inferior. In dynamics, the negative equals the positive and is just as important. What good is a positive proton without its negative electron? So with Mr. Big. "What signifies the life of man, if it wasn't for the ladies-o?" Burns.

24. Therefore shall a man leave his father and his mother, and shall cleave unto his wife: and they shall be one flesh.

This is imposing on chemical affinity the moral standard of humanity. Carried to the human plane it is using cosmology to point a moral.

25. And they were both naked, the man and his wife, and were not ashamed.

And why should they be? What have naked atoms to be ashamed of? Collectively, they are the "naked earth," and this too runs throughout all Creation myths. In those of Babylonia and Sumeria the female Creators Ishtar and Innana descend from the spirit plane to the material, seven steps and seven gates. As they pass through each, some garment or jewel is taken from them so that on arriving at the seventh plane (matter) they too are naked. This is the mythic way of telling us the Creative Principle loses its spirit nature when it becomes matter. The Romans said "Demon est Deus inversus." Others had a different name for it; they called it the Serpent.

Concerning this scriptural myth, we know that man was not created in this fashion. Why then do we accept and respect it? The answer is, because we are ignorant of the entire subject of beginnings, of world as well as man. Our Premise showed how knowledge eliminates religion's God concerning weather, climate and even worlds. So is it here. The Creator of biologic forms is the Creative Principle whose dwelling place is the parental genes. Of worlds it is planetary genes. This is the Creator of both cosmic and biologic forms and there is no other beyond it.

If now we see this part of the Bible is false, what of the rest of it? It is either priestly ignorance or priestly hoax intended to deceive us. If the latter, nowhere has it succeeded more than in the next chapter. Let us get behind the hoax that we too may partake of "the tree of knowledge."

3

The Serpent

In religion what damned error but some sober brow
will bless it, and approve it with a text.

SHAKESPEARE.

As a molder of religious thought, the third
chapter of Genesis has been, perhaps, the greatest influence of
any in the Old Testament. From it we get the idea of "original
sin," "the fall of man," the belief that we are "lost" and therefore
in need of "salvation." Because of this, we need to know something about the alleged cause of it all.

In this chapter a new character is introduced—Satan, the
priestly alibi of all religions. Here, however, this mighty fellow
is only a talking snake. Later, we will meet a talking ass—
Balaam's. In this case the author, knowing our weakness, tells
us in five different places that this is a fable. Then why not the
snake story also? Most people today accept it as such, yet even
these do not see in it the all-important point, namely, that it has
nothing whatever to do with us. This is a Creation myth, and
whatever happens in it happens to the Creator, not man.

Throughout the ancient world the serpent was the symbol of
the Creative Principle, and an excellent symbol it is, for the male
germ of both man and animal is a microscopic serpent, "armed
forward with a piercer and propelled by the violent lashing of
a formidable length of tail." Julian Huxley. This is the Creative

Principle in biologic forms. In this myth it has not reached that stage yet; it is still within the earth. Here it is "that old serpent, which is the Devil, and Satan" of Revelation. And so the serpent, Satan, the devil and the Creator are all one. According to the *Kabbalah* the true name of Satan is Yahveh reversed,[1] the *Deus inversus* of the Romans. This is the all-explaining truth a cunning priesthood hid from us.

In ancient Egypt, the symbol of the Creator was a snake, Kneph, encircling a water vase; the snake was breathing on the waters (space), and its breath, impregnating the water, produced matter and life. In the Mayan Naacl cosmology we find a seven-headed serpent called Naga, guarding its eggs beneath the ground—the germinal Life Principle, "the worm that never dies." In the Orient we find this identical symbol, a seven-headed serpent there called Nârâyana, the seven heads representing the seven planes and elements. The Hebrew idea of God moving on the waters came from this story of Nârâyana, called by the Hindus "The Mover on the waters." The name of these waters was Amriti, from which the Hebrews took the name of Jonah's father. In the Buddhist version the serpent was called Naga, a name identical with that of the Mayans in America. This itself is a hint of the once universal knowledge. According to the myth, as Buddha (genetic consciousness) sat under the Bodhi tree, that is, "tree of life," he attained enlightenment, "tree of knowledge," and Naga, perceiving that a Savior had been born, arose from Amriti and surrounding him with seven coils, auras, covered and protected him with its seven heads. And for seven days and seven nights (evolution) he sat thus protected by the royal snake. The legend ends thus: "These fearful serpents by the influence of Buddha's law (enlightenment) became the blessers of mankind." These seven serpents are identical with "the seven angels," "the seven spirits before the throne," etc., all symbols of the seven energies. When, in Evolution, these are qualified by epigenetic consciousness, they become "blessers of mankind."

As the creative process is both downward and upward, the

---

[1] Not in letters but in numbers, see p. 154.

Greeks had a symbol of both. This is the Caduceus of Hermes, the messenger (active agent) of the gods. The serpent on the left hand is Involution; that on the right is Evolution. As the creative force returns to its source, the Hindus gave it another twist, a serpent swallowing its tail. And the zodiac, beginning with Aquarius [2] and returning to Aquarius, embodies the same idea.

Thus the whole creative process is symbolized by the serpent, or Satan, rather than Divinity creating by divine fiat, as the priest would have us believe. Satan, or a satanic power, whichever you like, is the Creator of this world; this alone explains its satanic nature and without which it cannot be explained. The devil is but this involutionary power in evolutionary forms, the planetary Satan biologized. Thus in religion, the devil is but the priestly alibi for the Creator's diabolism.

Such was the teaching of a rival sect in the Dark Ages, but the Church put an end to that. It did not succeed, however, in extinguishing the idea. There is, even today, in Mosul, a people whom the Christians would call devil worshipers. These are the Kizelbash—the word means "red head." If you ask them why they worship an evil god rather than a good one, they will explain it thus: There were in the beginning two gods, a good one and a bad one. They went to war over the newly created world and the bad god won. He is now the devil and the Lord of this world—the Hebrews said "prince." The good god is now so far away it is useless to pray to him—and some theologians tell us God withdrew after the age of miracles. So why not pray to the god close at hand, the devil? The great mistake these people make is believing there ever was a good god in the moral sense. This is the mistake the Hebrews made and so endowed their murderous Jehovah with divinity. And how many of us know this word comes from the same root as the word devil? It is derived from the Sanskrit *deva*, and from it we get devil,

[2] There are two Zodiacs: (1) The Zodiac of Signs, beginning with Aries. This is the Zodiac of astrology. (2) The Zodiac of Constellations, a symbol of the Creative Process. This begins with Aquarius, pouring out the primordial waters and returning to Aquarius at the end of Evolution. This is the Zodiac of occult cosmology, the concealed theme of the Bible.

and the Greek demon. The devas were nature spirits, thus creative only.

The Bible calls Satan "the Prince of this world"; it should be King, for King he is until man takes over. As Evolution proceeds, man raises up this fallen King and, at its close, sets him free. His labors now ended, he returns to his former kingdom and "The Sorrows of Satan" are over. His "sorrows" today are due to the fact that man, by clinging to matter, denies him his rightful throne. All this has been hidden from us by religion; in Christianity it is Christ who is going to lift us up, the devil can go to hell. We must now learn that we rise only as we raise the devil. This may sound like what we are doing, but we mean a cosmic process not an idiom.

As the creative force rises and its energies are used benignly, the serpent becomes also the symbol of wisdom: "Be ye wise as serpents," said Christ. It was in the knowledge of this the ancient Midianites called themselves "sons of the snake." The Egyptian hierophant said, "I am a serpent, I am a snake," and the Druid, "I am a serpent," meaning "I am a student and exemplar of the wisdom-knowledge."

Come Back to Erin.

Someone much deeper in this wisdom-knowledge than the Catholic Church suspects has left us a legend based on this. It tells us St. Patrick drove the snakes out of Ireland, and he surely did. It was he who brought Christianity to Ireland, and by so doing drove out the Druid serpents and their wisdom-knowledge. St. Patrick was thorough to say the least, for wisdom-knowledge has never returned; on the contrary, Catholicism reigns supreme. This is the curse of Ireland, but sunk in the depths of their Christian ignorance its people cannot see it. It is tragic indeed that a people so potentially fine should be literally damned by their religion. If, as has been said, they are not mature emotionally and politically, the reason is obvious: two thousand years of religious error plus seven hundred of racial hatred. If the Irish would overcome this, they must *bring back to Erin* the ancient wisdom. With this, they would realize that the thing that's bedivilin' them now is not the Satan of religion but the religion of Satan, Catholicism. See p. 438.

Its teachers need this wisdom-knowledge that they may understand the book they preach from. According to that book Satan is one of the "Sons of God," "Lucifer, bright star of the morning," and as Virgil tells us, "Lucifer antevolent" leads on ahead. He is the actor, the doer, the *primum mobile*. It was he who, "in the beginning," aroused the genetic consciousness asleep in the Absolute, and eons later aroused it from sleep in the earth. All this the Jhwhist saw clearly and stated it plainly for those who can read occult literature. He described its nature as bloodthirsty Jehovah, murderous Joshua and dishonest Jacob, all Causation symbols. Perhaps he thought it not in the interest of the common people to openly attribute such qualities to its rightful source, and so used personification. He also made a distinction between consciousness, God, and energy, Satan, the one to warn, the other to disobey. He knew quite well the spiritually wise would see through the subterfuge, but what he did not know was that there would come a time when there are no spiritually wise, an age of materialism in which mankind could not distinguish truth from error or mythology from history. But now, having acquired some knowledge of Causation and Creation, let us see what the Jhwhist is trying to tell us.

4

Genesis: Third Chapter

1. Now the serpent was more subtil than any beast of the field which the Lord God had made. And he said unto the woman, Yea, hath God said, Ye shall not eat of every tree of the garden?

We assume that the word *subtil* here means morally evil, cunning, crafty, etc., but is not the word for this *subtle?* Our dictionary defines the latter word as evil, cunning, deceptive, but it defines subtil as "that which is fine drawn, ethereal, rarefied," and subtilize, to make less gross or coarse; in other words, to refine. Subtil is from the Latin *subtilus—sub,* beneath, and *tela,* web; and from *tela* we get *texo,* to weave, and *textile,* fabric. This is the real meaning of Satan's "subtil" nature. In Evolution he refines the coarse, material earth and weaves it into etheric, astral and mental matter; he also makes forms less gross than earth. Today these words are used interchangeably, but we should have a distinction here. Subtil should convey no evil qualities; the word for that is subtle.

There is plenty of the latter in the Bible. It tells this story, for instance, as though it were the first and only version, yet the legend existed long before the Hebrews. At Gawra, Assyria, a prehistoric seal was found bearing the figure of a man, a woman, a tree and a serpent, and this city had ceased to exist by 2000 B.C. In Greece, as stated, the serpent was Ladon, and in Scandinavia Nidhogg. In the Pelasgian myth of Creation, the goddess Eurynome created a wind by dancing over the waters of Chaos. The more she danced, the greater and stronger grew the wind, until it became the serpent Ophion, who, coiling himself about her, coupled with her. Thus impregnated she took the form of a dove and laid the cosmic egg. From this all things developed. And, according to Robert Graves, later becoming angry at Ophion, "she bruised his head, kicked out his teeth and banished him to the dark caves below the earth." And from this we get the story of Eve bruising the head of the serpent. As stated elsewhere the Jews of Bible times had at their disposal a vast store of creation myths wholly unknown to us.

2. And the woman said unto the serpent, We may eat of the fruit of the trees of the garden:
3. But of the fruit of the tree which is in the midst of the garden, God hath said, Ye shall not eat of it, neither shall ye touch it, lest ye die.

We have interpreted all things in terms of ourselves so long it is difficult for us to realize these are not human beings. They are personifications of planetary principles. The garden is the earth itself; the midst of the garden is the middle point between its involutionary creation and its evolutionary expression. It is at this point that Evolution starts, and "the tree of knowledge" is evolutionary experience. While the Life Principle was on the involutionary side it was spiritual in the sense of substance. When in Evolution it emerged as biologic life, it became subject to all "the ills that flesh is heir to," and "Death and Hell followed after" it, as per Revelation. In this Eden story it is still in Involution, and so this death is not physical but metaphysical. This is the death about which God allegorically warned Adam. He must not become material lest he die spiritually, as essence. But allegorically, Satan knew that Adam must die this death that he might become biological and *morally* spiritual. He therefore urged the more susceptible half of Being, matter, to eat, that is, act. And do you see the scientific aspect here? Actually we are reading nuclear physics—fission and radiation. The susceptible part, however, is not the scientifically negative electron, but the "unstable" proton, which by disintegrating sets the life-force free. This is matter and woman is its symbol.

At this point we have a complete about-face, an evolutionary power taking over the work of the involutionary Creator. It is not new in mythology, however, for in the Babylonian account of the same thing the lesser god Zu takes from "the father of the gods" the *umsimi*, or creative power, so in Greek henotheism. This is the difference, in personification, between the first two chapters of Genesis and the third. In the first two, God is the only actor; now we have another, Satan, as the acting force with God the restraining influence—Life asleep in matter, with "Don't disturb" on the door. This is the Great God Inertia whose motto is *Laissez faire*, let be, let be, and whose command is "Thou shalt not." He is thus a sort of mythological *Dieu fainéant*, or do-nothing God. It is this that Satan, the evolutionary impulse, must from here on urge and push and struggle with throughout all Evolution. Today, its followers, the pious and the reactionary, have gone a bit too far, and so seeing no other way, Satan has called on his good friend Mars for help. In this war-filled century these two symbionts are but trying to destroy the spiritual inertia of Piscean man. But not even these can do it unless they first destroy the spiritual error he has lived by.

4. And the serpent said unto the woman, Ye shall not surely die (that is, literally):

5. For God doth know that in the day ye eat thereof, then your eyes shall be opened, and ye shall be as gods, knowing good and evil.

Now which was right, God or Satan? Satan, apparently, since they ate and did not die, but only received the curse of sentient life. Here we see what the good and evil of the Bible really is—creative only, for the gods do not know moral good and evil.

6. And when the woman saw that the tree was good for food, and that it was pleasant to the eyes, and a tree to be desired to make one wise, she took of the fruit thereof, and did eat, and gave also unto her husband with her; and he did eat.

This is not the "fall"; that was involutionary. This is the evolutionary impulse urging energy to free itself from matter, hence a *rise*. This is wholly energic and its symbol, woman, being the more susceptible, partook of the fruit and passed it on to the reluctant Adam, genetic consciousness asleep in matter. And this is the awful "sin" from which we have been trying to save our souls for two thousand years. Again, "What fools we mortals be!" It's time we too had our eyes opened. The "original sin" was the sin of creation—what could be more original? However, the word is wrong; it should be crime. But as sin is the biggest thing priests can think about, they called it sin, and made it human to incriminate man and absolve the Creator. Yet if this world, with all its pain and suffering, is the work of a self-conscious Being, then Creation is a crime and its Creator a criminal. From this there is only one escape—unconscious Causation.

While our eyes were still closed we interpreted this "sin" as sex and so made for ourselves a "guilt complex." Perhaps now we can shift that guilt where it belongs. Perhaps we can even get rid of the complex, for the truth will set us free.

7. And the eyes of them both were opened, and they knew that they were naked; and they sewed fig leaves together, and made themselves aprons.

"The woman clothed with the sun," namely, the sun, now finds herself "naked earth," and Ishtar and Inanna were also naked at this point. Adam and Eve are the two principles with which we began, consciousness and energy; on the seventh plane they united and became "naked earth." As soon as the Life force freed itself from this, it clothed itself in organic matter—the literal grass, herbs, trees, etc., of the first chapter.

8. And they heard the voice of the Lord God walking in the garden in the cool of the day: and Adam and his wife hid themselves from the presence of the Lord God amongst the trees of the garden.

"The cool of the day" is the cooling-off period between Involution and Evolution. It is at this point that the genetic principle is hidden most completely in matter.

9. And the Lord God called unto Adam, and said unto him, Where art thou?

Yes, even the Lord God might have difficulty seeing life in a stone, or even a virus.

10. And he said, I heard thy voice in the garden, and I was afraid, because I was naked; and I hid myself.

"And Br'er Rabbit said, 'Whatever you do, don't throw me in the briar patch.' " This is allegory, and so is Genesis.

11. And he said, Who told thee that thou wast naked? Hast thou eaten of the tree, whereof I commanded thee that thou shouldest not eat?

What naiveté! As if God didn't know he would eat of it. The fruit of this tree is biologic existence, and this God labored six long eons that this might be. Why then should partaking of it be disobedience? This was not an act but part of the creative process, yet upon it our whole salvation nonsense is based. Had we possessed the slightest knowledge of the process we would not have been deceived. The story implies the first man had a sense of modesty and a conscience like ourselves. We should have known that such qualities are evolutionary constructs and imply millions of years. Therefore we have only ourselves to blame for the time we've wasted saving our souls from the "sin" of Adam.

Those who would save our souls don't know what the soul is; they don't even know the difference between soul and spirit, nor yet between spirit and spirituality. Apparently they think soul is spirit and that spirit is spiritual. Not so. Spirit is but the creative energy developed on the third plane in Involution—dynamic, not moral. It thus manifests in man as vitality only, physical and mental. Soul is the sum total of epigenetic qualities added to the genetic's construct, hence soul and body. Our task is to create soul, not just save it. Spirituality is the higher of these qualities dominating the lower, and this is the only salvation we need. From this we see that spirit and spirituality are at opposite ends of the creative process.

12. And the man said, The woman (matter) whom thou gavest to be with me (consciousness), she gave me of the tree, and I did eat.

Cherchez la femme! Not very gallant of the divine man Adam, but pardonable in an atom.

13. And the Lord God said unto the woman, What is this that thou hast done? And the woman said, The serpent beguiled me, and I did eat.

But *la femme* was not better, and so she put the blame on Satan—and the priest passed it on to man. And there it serves a double purpose: a help meet for the priest and an alibi for God. This serpent is God on the lower plane, and yet we read:

14. And the Lord God said unto the serpent, Because thou hast done this, thou art cursed above all cattle, and above every beast of the field; upon thy belly shalt thou go, and dust shalt thou eat all the days of thy life.

"Upon thy belly shalt thou go." Oh, no. Upon everybody's belly—"armed forward with a piercer and propelled by the violent lashing of a formidable length of tail." In the cosmological sense, "belly" represents the under and lowest part of the planetary entity, the seventh or material plane. The serpentine part of it is the genetic principle, in other words, the Creator; and if confirmation is needed for our contention that the genetic never becomes anything else, here it is. Its curse is that it must remain apart, forever denied the food of man, the epigenetic qualities, and even the Heaven that man creates. Exodus also confirms it.

All this is allegory, yet in our gullible literalness we have put its stigma upon even the serpent of the fields. It is not, of course, the cause of our dislike for this creature, but it lends support. The real cause is its ugly, venomous nature, but even this was put upon it by its Creator, but biologically, not mythologically. If otherwise, why do we not see its literal falsity? This lowly creature does not eat dust any more than we do, and it does not crawl on its belly because of our first parents. It crawled and wiggled thus for millions of years before an ancient allegorist perceived its symbolic usefulness.

But if the serpent is the genetic or Creative force, who is this cursing God? He is but an allegorical convenience, wholly redundant and unnecessary except to religion. There is nothing in all the universe save consciousness and energy, and these two deities are but their personifications. Collectively, they are one, the cursing God of the higher planes and the accursed Satan of the lower—and neither of them possesses moral qualities. Why then should moral man debase himself before them? There is nothing higher morally and spiritually than well developed man. As Eliphas Levi said: "The Angels aspire to become men; for the perfect Man, the Man-God, is above even angels." Above even gods also, for the gods died that they might become men.

15. And I will put enmity between thee and the woman, and between thy seed and her seed; it shall bruise thy head, and thou shalt bruise his heel (as in the case of Eurynome).

This enmity is purely symbolic and planetary, the woman and the serpent representing matter and the life-force. Such symbolism runs throughout all mythologies but having no understanding of them, we have inverted its hidden meaning and missed its subtil truth. To us woman is the ennobling and uplifting force and the serpent our moral opponent. The scriptures are telling us the opposite. Biologically, it is genetic consciousness that is trying to rise and matter is holding it down—and woman represents matter. And this applies all too aptly to epigenetic consciousness as well. Woman is the enemy of its progress. She opposes every new idea creative man proposes; she fears and resents change lest she lose security; she hates the truth and loves illusion; she does not want to know the truth about Reality; she prefers the escapism of religion. The reason is implied in the next verse, propagation and security.

16. Unto the woman he said, I will greatly multiply thy sorrow and thy conception; in sorrow shalt thou bring forth children; and thy desire shall be to thy husband, and he shall rule over thee.

And because of these words it has taken woman three thousand years to escape them. If she would be free and help man to be free she must learn to think; she must become enlightened. Thus intelligized and rationalized she would not believe mythology to be "the word of God," or oppose the truth when she heard it.

She has in this verse an excellent case could she but see it. Were her maternal lot the result of this curse, she should rise up in protest; she should charge the Creator with cruelty and injustice, for the command not to eat of the tree was not given to the woman; it was given to man before woman was created, as per the Jhwhist. Furthermore, Eve, poor girl, had no mother to tell her about the birds and the bees. And, of course, her father was too busy. But since we know this was not biologic woman, we withdraw the charge and also the sympathy. But not the original responsibility, for woman's biologic lot *is* the Creator's decree, and it is both cruel and unjust. How any woman who has borne the pangs of childbirth can believe in a God of love and mercy is difficult to see. Such a God would not have made her all-important part painful; such a God would not have made disease germs to kill her children; such a God would not have devised the jungle, or decreed that life must live on life. Only something devoid of all the finer qualities can be responsible. We have a name for it; we call it Nature. This understood, we see that these decrees are not punishment for "sin" but simply the nature of Nature. And blind and cruel as that nature is, it is not the result of an act half way in the process, but the inherent nature of the Life Principle itself. This is the Creator, therefore we should see clearly the distinction between God and Creator. The Creator created man and ruthless Nature, then man in his turn created God, a human ideal necessary to spiritually aspiring man, a goal he, himself, will someday become. So let us see clearly the difference between this man-made ideality and the ruthless Reality.

17. And unto Adam he said, Because thou hast harkened unto the voice of thy wife (matter), and hast eaten of the tree, of which I commanded thee, saying, Thou shalt not eat of it: cursed is the ground for thy sake; in sorrow shalt thou eat of it all the days of thy life.

Well, is not sorrow also inherent in life? Death is, and it causes sorrow. So does love. Our preachers have always told us this world is a vale of tears, but their only explanation of it is the literal word of a myth, and not original either. It was copied from the older Babylonian account. George Smith, speaking of this, writes thus: "Our fragment refers to the creation of mankind, called Adam as in the Bible; he is made perfect . . . but afterwards he joins with the dragon of the deep, the animal Tiamat the spirit of Chaos, and offends against the god who curses him and calls down on his head all the evils and troubles of humanity." In the Greek it was due to disobedience in opening Pandora's box. Of the Babylonian account we have only one comment: Tiamat was not "the spirit of Chaos," but the violent material substance in Involution out of which Sosiosh made the world. As such she is one with the troublemaking Eve.

By misinterpreting this scriptural myth we have missed the key to the very nature of Nature and our own estate. Because of it we believe all Nature cursed because of one man's "sin." So if men go to war, kill and enslave their fellow men, it is because of their subsequent fallen estate. Yet certain ant species invade other ant colonies, capture their workers and enslave them, and ants were here millions of years before man. Therefore man got his villainy from nature, not vice versa.

Were it otherwise Adam must have had amazing genes, that his sin be transmitted through millions of evolving generations. The absurdity of this lies in the fact that neither moral nor amoral qualities enter the genes; such qualities are strictly epigenetic. Only in our theory is this problem solved: Adam's genes were not human genes; they were our "planetary genes." Through them came all that is, including villainous Nature. It was this that came down, or rather up, to us, not Edenic "sin."

Another name for this "sin" is disobedience, but since we're dealing with Creation, not man, there must be some more cosmological meaning here that we have missed. We think there is.

Throughout Involution and part of Evolution the creative genetic directed all life. Now anything that refused this direction would be disobeying God's command. And something did. When man developed epigenetic intelligence he began to think for himself, and act accordingly. This is that "free will" we're told God gave man. But as he did not give primitive man the mind and morals to control it, he made mistakes and paid the price. Thus the disobedience was that of the epigenetic to the genetic's will. And that disobedience is still with us. Today the priest, subbing for God, tells man the genetic should be used only for procreation, and the epigenetic is still disobeying. The consequence is symbolized in the next verse of dual meaning.

18. Thorns and thistles shall it bring forth to thee; and thou shalt eat the herb of the field.

Thorns and thistles are not punishment for sin, but consequence of physical existence. They have also another meaning: they represent the infinite number of ways the Creator has of torturing man. This is the only way it has of sensitizing and civilizing its savage creation. In speaking of this Plato likened the growth of the soul in man to that of the pearl in the oyster, the cause of both being irritation. We learn only by experience and painful experience at that. The scholastic name for this is resipiscent—"made wise by experience." And it applies to the

Creator as well as man. All Involution was devoted to it; those prephysical archetypes were but trial and error "mock-ups" for the real thing, evolutionary forms. And this may be going on in worlds without end. To some this may be shocking, so contrary to all Bible teaching, but no, the Bible asserts it. It tells us plainly that the Creator learned by experience, but you will never find it unless you know it. The Greeks also knew it. They said Prometheus created man, and the name implies this: Pro, before, and metheus, learn. But before what? Before he brought solar fire down from heaven to make a world, and man from its dust just like Jehovah.

19. In the sweat of thy face shalt thou eat bread, till thou return unto the ground; for out of it wast thou taken: for dust thou art, and unto dust shalt thou return.

And how else would physical man live save by working? This God does not feed anyone, save as nature feeds him. If you think otherwise, sit down and wait for His ravens; devote your life to something great and this God will let you starve. This verse has no moral meaning whatever; the toil and sweat, the pain and sorrow are natural conditions, not punishment for sin. It's industrous nature whose law is work or starve. The ants, the bees and the beavers are slaves because of it. It was this that Man was warned against. While in Eden he did not have to work for food; he lived on ambrosia, the food of the gods. This is "the bread that cometh down from heaven," exclusively for gods, but the gods died as such, and became evolutionary beings requiring physical sustenance. They also became subject to physical death, which leads us to the next point.

Save at funerals, our preachers never take this verse for their text. They dare not, because it denies immortality. They could, however, if they understood it. This Adam is not a human being; he is the earth, and the earth is mundane dust, and to primordial dust it shall return. More definitely, he is genetic consciousness, and it is condemned to that dust called matter. This never enters the epigenetic's "heaven." The Bible tells us this too but again, you have to know it to see it.

20. And Adam called his wife's name Eve; because she was the mother of all living.

"Of all living." This includes plants and animals as well as humans. This ends her role as a woman. On the contrary, she is Mother Nature. As a symbol of matter, she is the Earth Mother—mother, mater, matter. Then there is *mere*, the sea. If then she sinned whose sin was it? The word Eve is but the latter part of the word Yahveh (heve), the Creative Principle. As with all the rest we have nothing new here. In the Hindu *Book of Prophecies* the first woman is called Heva, and the Babylonian name is similar. To the Tahitians it is Ivi. Thus, like Adam, Eve is not a personal name but a planetary symbol.

21. Unto Adam also and to his wife did the Lord God make coats of skins, and clothed them.

Together Adam and Eve are the naked earth, which must be covered with vegetation and an aura. And here we will quote from a book many thousands of years older than the Bible, the *Book of Dzyan*, stanza I. "Cease thy complaints. Thy seven skins are yet on thee. Thou art not ready." This is the earth entity complaining about its involutionary garments, aura. "After great throes she cast off her old three (mental, astral, and etheric) and put on her seven skins (evolutionary) and stood in her first one (physical matter)." These are Adam's and Eve's "coats of skin," seven theoretically, but at that time physical only. Later we will come to a misunderstanding of them as absurd as that of the rib.

22. And the Lord God said, Behold, the man is become as one of us, to know good and evil: and now, lest he put forth his hand, and take also of the tree of life, and eat, and live for ever:
23. Therefore the Lord God sent him forth from the Garden of Eden, to till the ground from whence he was taken.

"As one of us." Modern Jews and Christians should ponder well this reference to other gods. Here we repeat, by learning of them, the mental darkness of monotheism might be dispelled.

The earth now dressed in its evolutionary garments has become as it was in Involution. But it does not know moral good and evil. The good and evil of scriptural mythology is that between spirit and matter. This the Life Principle now has learned; it has eaten of "the tree of knowledge," matter, the source of knowledge. The meaning of the fear that Adam would also lay hold of "the tree of life and live forever" is the very opposite of our common belief. The "tree of life" is the Life Principle asleep in matter, and the fear is that its Adam would remain there and refuse to go out and eat of "the tree of Knowledge," biologic experience. This Life Principle is the genetic, neither moral nor self-conscious, and had Adam eaten of this (remained like it) epigenetic man would never have been. It was because of this, not sin, the Lord God drove Adam from the Garden. The plan was that Adam should go out, and once out the Law God saw to it that he did not return. There is a lesson here for all of us, but particularly for our religionists, our fundamentalists and reactionaries, those timid souls who cling to their God and refuse to go out. Their God has given them the privilege of eating of "the tree of knowledge," but not having eaten enough of it they are afraid. They should follow Abraham's example: he went out "not knowing whither he went."

24. So he drove out the man; and he placed at the east of the garden of Eden Cherubims, and a flaming sword which turned every way, to keep the way of the tree of life.

The cherubim are the forces that determine life's exit and entrance from plane to plane, identical with the seven angels who open the seven seals in Revelation. The scriptures make them divine beings; that the other races considered them but natural forces is obvious from the source of the word *cherub*, which is *kirub*, and means an ox, symbol of energy and power. On the third plane, as we made it, this was Taurus, the bull, but ox will do on the seventh. Here, we said, the creative force was slowed down, arrested. Be this as it may, ox and bull are a far cry from the saintly heads between two wings with which

Christian artists adorned their Madonnas and Conceptions; indeed, it well illustrates our Christian ignorance of Causation and Creation.

Now perhaps we can see that this account "revealed" only to the Jews is but one of innumerable Creation myths and follows the usual formula. Its characters are identical with those of the Greek. The Lord God is Jupiter, Satan is Prometheus, Adam is Epimetheus, and Eve is Pandora. That the woman caused all the trouble is also part of the formula. In Egypt, Noom, the heavenly artist, creates a beautiful girl and sends her to Batoo, the first man, after which all peace for Batoo is ended. According to the Chinese *Book of Chi-King*, "All things were at first subject to man, but a woman threw us into slavery, by an ambitious desire for things. Our misery came not from heaven but from woman. She lost the human race. Ah, poor Poo See! Thou kindled the fire that consumes us, and which is every day increasing." And so again poor Look See gets blamed, and all the while she is only matter and material desire, which did come from heaven, *desidero*, of the stars.

Every race of antiquity had this story and in practically all of them some kind of fruit served as the temptation symbol. In Greece it was an apple; in India it was figs. The Hindus tell us that the God Siva sent woman a fig tree and prompted her to tempt her husband with the fruit. This she did, assuring the man it would confer on him immortality. The man ate and Siva cursed him. Such is the honor of the gods. According to the Greeks, Zeus gave the Hesperides a tree that bore golden apples. As they could not resist the temptation to eat of them, Zeus placed Ladon, a serpent, in the garden to watch the trees. Finally, Hercules, a personification of evolutionary life, slew the serpent, matter, and gave the apples freely to the Hesperides. Thus the Greeks did not put the blame on the serpent; they merely made Evolution reverse the law of Involution.

Such is the Bible's "revealed truth"—other races' mythology, the basis of which is cosmology. Its literal interpretation that this fruit is sex has branded women with the scarlet letter for nearly three thousand years. Here again, a little knowledge erases that stigma also. It should also erase our belief in this entire book. Its account of the world's creation and man's estate is false. Man is not evil because he "fell" from perfection but because he has not risen to it. But never having been taught the nature and purpose of Evolution he does not know where he is or why he is what he is. Knowledge of Evolution would enlighten him: he is what he is because he is where he is—only the middle point of the first human plane, with billions of years to follow. Since it was the Creator that determined this process, man is not to blame for where he is but only for what he does. But since what he does is due to where he is, he is not, basically, to blame at all. He is, however, responsible for his own human world, another fact he has never been taught, and so acts regardless of it.

He has never been taught the "law of cycles" either, and so he does not know he is at the nadir of a materialistic cycle or how to counteract its influence. Here too he acts regardless of the whole—blindly carrying his material achievements to the danger point. With no vision of the future, he proudly calls this "civilization." It is not civilization at all but only mechanized barbarism, his purely material wonders but ant and spider technology carried to the human plane. If this be civilization we'll have to coin another name for the real thing.

Would you call a humanity civilized that has a hundred wars in as many years? that spends a trillion dollars on murder weapons while its schools and hospitals close for want of funds? that lets half its people starve while the other half sickens from overeating? Would you call a humanity enlightened that poisons the air, the water and the soil? that doesn't know mythology from history, or even what it exists for? This is the animal estate.

Today it may be doing something even worse than poisoning its physical environment. It may be destroying the biologic aspect of the ether. Science calls this element "the nervous ether," the Hindus call it *prana*, or the source of it. This is the vitalizing element of the body cells and should not be changed or tampered with, yet throughout this century we have been torturing it with our radio and television waves. This surely changes its nature and biologic efficiency. This changed and corrupted element in our cells may be the cause of our present nervousness and, who knows, our insane century. It's odd they are coincidental. In our sudden and unnatural release of atomic energy we may also be bringing upon ourselves diseases with which we cannot cope. The first manifestation of life from matter is the viruses, predatory and deadly. Released, en masse, they could destroy us. And who considers the global effect of removing billions of tons (oil and coal) from the earth's content? This lightens its weight and lessens the sun's hold upon it. Thus we may be bringing upon ourselves a premature ice age.

5

Genesis: Fourth Chapter

1. And Adam knew Eve his wife; and she conceived, and bare Cain, and said, I have gotten a man from the Lord.

"I have gotten a man from the Lord" was originally "a man even Jehovah." Luther's translation renders it thus: "I have gotten a man, even the Lord (Jehovah)." This makes it planetary, and Jehovah the evolutionary son of involutionary Man, not vice versa. But knowledge such as this served no religious purpose and so the mischief-makers changed it.

2. And she again bare his brother Abel. And Abel was a keeper of sheep, but Cain was a tiller of the ground.

And now that Adam is out of Eden, earth, and has two sons, the reader will assume we pass on to Evolution. But no; there is no Evolution in Genesis. Genesis deals only with the *genesis* of the world; that is its meaning. We trust this will not be too great a shock for the literalists, because there are many more to follow. And the first of them is this: Cain and Abel are not the sons of Adam. This may be "hard to take" at this point, but it is in keeping with the entire Bible, therefore reserve your judgment until later

The story of Cain and Abel is a separate Creation myth appended to the first to illustrate a different aspect of the process. Therefore, instead of sons of Adam and Eve, these two are Adam and Eve all over again. To realize this we have only to compare them. Adam is alone and lonely, and so is Cain. Adam takes himself a wife, and so does Cain. Adam sins, and so does Cain. Adam is banished, and so is Cain. Adam's land is cursed, and so is Cain's. Adam is sent out to "till the ground," and Cain is "a tiller of the ground." Adam goes to sleep, and Cain goes to "the land of Nod." Adam's garden is "eastward in Eden," and Cain's city is "on the east of Eden." Adam's wife "the weaker sex" is made subject to Adam, and in lieu of a woman the weaker Abel is made subject to Cain. To Eve the Lord God said, ". . . and thy desire shall be to thy husband and he shall rule over thee" (Gen. 3:16). And to Cain regarding Abel, ". . . unto thee shall be his desire, and thou shalt rule over him" (Gen. 4:7). Thus we see that these two stories are one. This being the case it would be but a waste of time to interpret the second verse by verse. The reader has but to return to the third involutionary plane and follow the story downward to the point where Cain founds a city, Enoch, and he is in Eden again. He will also solve two great scriptural mysteries: Who was Cain's wife? and what was "the mark of Cain"? Like Adam, Cain is creative consciousness, therefore his wife is planetary energy. They meet and marry in a city called Earth. This earth, or matter, is "the mark of Cain." Prior to the sun period, the nascent earth was an invisible entity, threatened with destruction by the violent suns that crossed its cosmic pathway. Thereafter it put on matter, it became visible, violent and self-protective like all other suns.

Here we can erase another Bible-inspired stigma. For centuries this "mark of Cain" was interpreted as black skin, and the Negro people suffered from it. They were called "the children of Cain" and scorned by whites so ignorant they did not know fact from fiction. These whites should now learn that this "mark" is materiality and that it is they, not the Negro, who bear it today.

To more fully understand this symbolic nature of Cain and Abel, we should read their story in other sources as well. There we find many hints that Cain was not a human being, that he was not the son of Adam but merely another name for Adam, a trick the authors use throughout the entire scriptures.

The word Cain comes from *kayin* and means begotten by the Lord, not from the Lord. The *ayin* is part of the Cabalistic Ayin-Soph, source. Cain was to live seven hundred years and be afflicted with a new punishment (condition) every one hundred years (cycle), as did Ishtar and Innana. This, of course, symbolizes the seven involutionary planes and the Life Principle's experience therein. Cain met his death when his house fell on him. The house here is the planetary structure and its fall is one with the "fall of man." Later we will find the same house falling on Samson. And the great man David met his death by falling downstairs, all implying the fall of spirit into matter. These noncanonical tales are called *Midrashes*, commentaries on the Old Testament. They are very useful because they throw light behind the literal word.

Abel comes from *hibbel* and means "transient as the wind, or breath." He was not, therefore, intended to survive. Abel is one with Hemera, the ephemeral, the prephysical elements in Involution. His death is in keeping with our statement that nothing remains of the prephysical when the physical is reached. There are parallels to this murder throughout all mythology, including both Old and New Testament. Romulus, the mythical founder of another city, Rome, slew his brother Remus. Set, the Egyptian, slew his brother Horus. Iphicles, brother of Hercules, was killed, not this time by his brother, but by a serpent, matter.

Cain's famous retort to the accuser—"Am I my brother's keeper?"—has ever been held up as a reproach to the coldly indifferent, but in this story it has no human significance at all. For Cain it was the only answer. The process must go on else it will never reach the plane where this retort is morally applicable, the human plane. The murder of Abel was therefore in the interest of the Creator, and Cain's act no more a crime than Adam's. Furthermore, they were both "acts of God."

There is another absurdity here. The God of this chapter is shocked and horrified at the murder of one man, but later we find him urging Moses and Joshua to slaughter men by the thousands. The key to the paradox is that these murderous patriarchs and their God are Cain now rampant in Evolution. Recently we spoke of the murderous nature of first life, and in this murder by the first man, not second, the Jhwhist is telling us the same thing, not once but twice for Lamech was also a murderer (Gen. 4:23). Such a source of life would never do for religion, however, so here the priest steps in and changes the line of descent. The last two verses of this chapter did not exist in the Jhwhist's account. This ends with verse 24, that is, the Editor ended it there, and substituted two verses from the next chapter which is priestly throughout. This should alert us to the fact that the Editor was, himself, a priest. This is the whitewasher of the Jhwhist's unvarnished truth everywhere, hence the interpolation which makes Seth our source and this source sinless.

25. And Adam knew his wife again; and she bare a son, and called his name Seth: For God, said she, hath appointed me another seed instead of Abel, whom Cain slew.

This substitute Seth is but a priestly subterfuge to hide from us the true nature of the Creative Principle. Because of this it does not tell us where the author got the name and idea. They come, however, from the Egyptian Set, another fallen god and fratricide. Bunsen, writing about him, said that when he reached the lower planes he became "an evil demon," *Deus inversus* again. Like Abram and Sarai, the Egyptian Set acquired an *h* and became the Hebrew Seth. He did not change his character, however, and so, be it Cain or Seth, we see the nature of our source. Adam and Cain, Seth and Satan are all one and that one the "beast" of Revelation. As we go on we'll see that, esoterically, the Bible completely refutes the religious concept of divinity, perfection, love and mercy; it is, in fact, the greatest indictment of God ever written.

26. And to Seth (Set, Satan), to him also was born a son; and he called his name Enos (Cain's son): then began men to call upon the name of the Lord.

In the original text this final sentence read, "Then began men to call themselves Jehovah." Involutionary Man became evolutionary Jehovah. Either this did not make sense to the translators or it made too much sense, and so they changed it. Cain's descendants, Tubalcain, the artificer in brass and iron, and Jubal, the musician, are but the Hebrew equivalents of the Greek gods Vulcan, the smith, and Orpheus, the magic musician.

Each of the two authors, thus far, gives a genealogical table leading up to Noah, but that one is merely a confusion of the other is obvious. The Jhwhist, prior by some two hundred fifty years, makes Noah the son of Lamech and hence a descendant of Cain; the priest makes Lamech, and hence Noah, a descendant of Seth. Very clever indeed; so clever, in fact, it has deceived our "great Bible students" for over two thousand years. In the interval between these two accounts, a professional priesthood had developed, and this did to truth what priests have always done, concealed it from those they would control. That we may get back to it, let us set these two genealogies side by side and look at them. As the first is generally referred to as the Kenite, from Cain, we will use this term.

Adam

Kenite	Sethite
1 Cain (a)	1 Seth
2 Enoch (b)	2 Enos (b)
3 Irad (c)	3 Cainan (a)
4 Methujael (d)	4 Mahalaliel (d)
5 Methusael (e)	5 Jared (c)
6 Lamech (f)	6 Enoch (b)
7 Noah (g)	7 Methuselah (e)
	8 Lamech (f)
	9 Noah (g)

You will notice that there are in each of these tables a Cain, an Enoch, a Lamech and a Noah; and since in one Lamech is the son of Methusael and in the other of Methuselah, the latter two are probably one and the same; and Jared is Irad. This is proved by Josephus's account: "Now Jared was the son of Enoch; whose son was Malaleel." And again, "Seth begat Enoch in his two hundred and fifth year." Thus these two are not different genealogies but one, the second a confusion of the first to hide from us the fact that life sprang from a ruthless principle, not divinity. Where the inference is known a priesthood is unnecessary, hence the deception.

Both these genealogies make Noah a descendant of Adam and both are false. Noah was not a descendant of Adam, he is Adam. The Kabbalah confirms this; it says "Noah is a revolutio of Adam," which means another version of the same. This is another priestly subterfuge that runs throughout the entire scriptures. Later, we will see that the Noachean Deluge has nothing whatever to do with Adamic disobedience.

The cunning hands of the priests perverted the entire Bible. It was they who made the redaction after the so-called Exilic period, and by that time they were the sole authority. Their purpose was the creation of a supernatural basis for a religion, hence the perversion of the original truth, than which there is no greater crime. As Dr. Johnson said: "I know not any crime so great that a man could contrive to commit as poisoning the source of eternal truth." And according to Kipling, "Words are the most powerful drug used by mankind." And the scriptures are the most deadly concoction of them all. They are the prescientific opiates, tranquilizers and placebos.

The reason our "Bible students" have been deceived is because they studied this "word of God" instead of the work of God, Reality, the source of Truth. Whenever I hear said of one of them "he is a great Bible student," I know he does not know the Bible at all save as chapter and verse. The Bible is not a book that has to be studied; you either understand it at once or you don't understand it at all. It depends entirely on your knowledge of Reality. When you have developed your consciousness of this, the Bible becomes an open book, and so does the book of life.

This is one of the peculiar differences between Truth and Reality. To know Reality you must see it, physically or mentally; with Truth you must know it before you can see it. That the scriptural truths have not been seen in two thousand years is due to the fact that Piscean man has never had sufficient truth to see them. How many knew, before they read it here, that Cain was not Adam's son? How many know before they read it that Solomon was not David's son, that Noah was not a descendant of either Cain or Seth, that Abraham was before Noah, that the great man Moses never existed, and that the entire contents of the New Testament *did exist* before the time of Christ? These are scriptural truths that only those who possess the truth about Reality can see. That they are not seen is proof that we have no such truth. And then you wonder what is the matter with our world—war among nations, chaos and confusion everywhere. What would you expect! Statesmen who lack this kind of truth are not qualified to run a world; they are ignorant men, forever doing today what proves disastrous tomorrow. Should you ask for an example I would say Palestine, where it began, of which, more later.

We should not look upon Genesis 5 as even chronological, to say nothing of genealogical; it is cosmological, therefore parallel. And so we come to another mystery—the amazing longevity of these ancients. It need not trouble us, however, for this is as mythological as all the rest. No man at any time lived eight or nine hundred years, but as mythology, this is modest indeed. From the cuneiform records of Babylon, 2170 B.C., we learn that postdiluvian man lived a mere twelve hundred years, but prior to this he lived for unbelievable ages. King Alulim, for instance, lived 18,900 years, and King Alalmar, 36,000. Beroseus, who lived about 260 B.C., thought this insufficient and so stretched it to 63,000. There's numerology here, not genealogy. You may notice that these figures add up to nine, a significant number even in Revelation. It should be obvious that these kings were personifications of great epochs, and so are the men of Genesis. This *truth* was lost even in Josephus's day. Believing the literal word, he had this to say of them: ". . . those ancients were beloved of God, and lately made by God himself; and because their food was then fitter for the prolongation of life, might well live so great a number of years: and besides God afforded them a longer time of life on account of their virtue, and the good use

they made of it in astronomical and geometrical discoveries."
But unfortunately Josephus was born thirty centuries too late
to know the truth, and so, like his successors, he but babbled
words he did not understand. The same may be said of Polyhistor, who tells us that Abraham created astronomy. Calendars
are based on astronomy and long before the alleged time of
Abraham, the people of the Euphrates valley had a calendar of
223 lunations or 6,585⅓ days, the error amounting to only one
day in 1,800 years. The Egyptians had a calendar based on the
Sothic (Sirus) cycle that began in 4241 if not 5701 B.C., the cycle
being 1,460 years. The chinese had a calendar older than the
world of Dr. Lightfoot and Bishop Usher. The Zodiac and the
Great Pyramid are also astronomical and they were hoary with
age before the alleged time of Abraham. Later we will see what
this astronomy ascribed to Abraham really means. Here we will
say only that it is no more factual than that of the Priest.

In spite of "the word of God" there was no first man called
Adam, or woman called Eve; there was no idyllic Garden, no
talking snake, no "fall" and no "sin"—save that of Creation.
Therefore we should no longer think of "the beginning" in
these terms. So misleading are they, it were better they had
never been written. Because of their diversionary influence we
have wasted two millennia saving our souls from an act of God
some trillions of years ago. Billions of dollars have been spent
on churches instead of schools. Millions have lived unnatural
and perverted lives, and still do. And all this because we know
no better. With all our science and technology we are going
about in a state of spiritual ignorance so profound we don't even
know it.

6

Noah and the Flood

The great snare of thought is uncritical acceptance of
irrational assumptions.

WILL DURANT

From here on we can offer some proof that
these Bible stories are parallels, not sequents. We must present
more of them, however, before this becomes self-evident.

Noah is given as the tenth from Adam, hence subsequent, and
as we think of Adam as the first human being, Noah must be
farther up on the evolutionary side. This is not so. Noah is just
another Adam and his story another Creation myth. In this one
we find the violence and "war in heaven," space, the Priest saw
fit to exclude from his. The "Deluge" was not a destruction of
the world but its creation.

Chronologically, Noah is eons prior to the Adam of the Garden, and contemporaneous with the Creator of the first chapter.
That he was not a human being is obvious from the Ethiopian
Book of Enoch. According to this source, Noah was transfigured
at birth, the light of his body illuminating the whole house—the
planetary entity. So here again we have that first "light shining
in darkness." Immediately thereafter he rose and talked to
God—for the simple reason that he was God. Lamech, his father, beholding this, was astonished, and hurried to Methuselah,
the grandfather, to find out its portent. But Methuselah was also

mystified and so he went to *his* father, Enoch, and Enoch told him it meant that the wonder child would become the Savior of the race during a subsequent Deluge. This Deluge, said Enoch, would be the consequence of adultery between divine and mortal beings. And this is where the scriptural account of Noah begins. In words that have puzzled the race for over two thousand years it reports this divine miscegenation thus:

1. And it came to pass, when men began to multiply on the face of the earth, and daughters were born unto them,
2. That the sons of God saw the daughters of men that they were fair; and they took them wives of all which they chose.
3. And the Lord said, My spirit shall not always strive with man, for that he also is flesh: yet his days shall be an hundred and twenty years.
4. There were giants in the earth in those days; and also after that, when the sons of God came in unto the daughters of men, and they bare children to them, the same became mighty men which were of old, men of renown.

These "sons of God" are the spiritual forces of the third involutionary plane, and the "daughters of men," generic, the material elements on the plane below, that is, prephysical matter. The spiritual came in unto the material and became material. In our outline we said the Trinity became the Quaternary, and so say the scriptures. This descent and Adam's "fall" are one and the same—spirit becoming matter. The adultery here is one with the Greek gods' adultery with mortals. This is that same "sin" we have assumed, yet between this "sin" and ours lie eons beyond our comprehension. Someone, either this author or the translator, has by such phrases as "on the face of the earth," "he also is flesh," made it sound earthly and human, but the earth here is prephysical earth and man prephysical archetype. It was these, not biologic forms, the Deluge figuratively destroyed. The giants mentioned at this point are the same as the Titans, the Cyclops, the "mighty men" of mythology; and later when we reach this same point in Evolution we will find them mentioned again.

As the story opens, Noah is none other than the Creative Principle on the dividing line between the third and fourth planes, Lamech, Methuselah and Enoch being the three or Trinity above—a very good reason why Enoch "walked with God." The word Noah itself comes from the Chaldean Nuah, the third person in the Chaldean Trinity, and also the third sign in the Chaldean zodiac. Perhaps this Chaldean Nuah is the source of the Greek *nous*, mind, philosophically defined as "an emanation of the divine principle." In the New Testament Noah is spelled Noe, and we have the word *noetic*, of the mind. Be this as it may Noah represents the fourth or mental matter plane in the creative process, Lamech, Methuselah and Enoch, the three planes above and Noah's "generations," Japheth, Ham and Shem, the three planes below. See diagram, p. 88. As this Noachean principle existed from the beginning, the 120 preparatory years are the three spiritual and preparatory stages preceding the material. These material planes, particularly the last, dense matter, are the "evil" of all mythologies, and when Noah arrives there he too becomes evil. While still spirit "Noah found grace in the eyes of the Lord," and

9. . . . Noah was a just man and perfect in his generations, and Noah walked with God.

The mythologist does not say that Noah was morally perfect, or even perfect in his generation (day and age) but "in his generations." And Noah's generations were what Noah generated, namely, the lower planes, elements and archetypes. No doubt that added *s* puzzled our translators, but they stuck to it and revealed much, the *virtue* of the Jewish patriarchs, for instance. It was not moral. Unfortunately our translators were not so scrupulous elsewhere.

Noah's generations were, like Adam's, three, and here they are personified.

10. And Noah begat three sons, Shem, Ham, and Japheth. (Explained later. The sequence is euphemistic. Shem is the youngest, Japheth the oldest, see Chap. 10:21.)

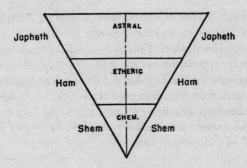

11. The earth also was corrupt before God, and the earth was filled with violence.

This is but the violence of creation, therefore not moral. Here we see the reason, as stated, for the various accounts. There was nothing said about violence in the Priestly account, hence the Noah version.

12. And God looked upon the earth, and, behold, it was corrupt; for all flesh had corrupted his way upon the earth.

If the Creator is morally perfect how could he create the morally imperfect? The answer is quite simple—there is nothing moral involved here. This is but the "original sin" all over again and it was not man's; it was the Creator's. Our castigation of the Hebrew scriptures is due to our realization of the tragic and far-reaching results of this deception. It was a prerequisite of a priesthood, but it wasted two thousand years on soul-salvation instead of soul development.

13. And God said unto Noah, The end of all flesh is come before me; for the earth is filled with violence through them; and, behold, I will destroy them with the earth.

And now, as in Greek mythology, this Hebrew Jupiter decides to drown everything he has made save the Hebrew Deucalion, Noah and his crew. How he is going to drown the fishes we are not told. To them a flood would be a red-letter day. The inclusion of the earth in this destruction can only mean the earth entity in Involution. This is to be destroyed, figuratively, that a physical earth and Evolution might be. And here we come to another absurdity, the ark. God tells Noah to build it and also how to build it. Can you imagine the Creator of the universe, as religion sees him, teaching a man how to build a boat? Later, we will have more to say about the absurd belief in "divine instructors" of primitive man.

14. Make thee an ark of gopher wood; rooms shalt thou make in the ark, and shalt pitch it within and without with pitch.
15. And this is the fashion which thou shalt make it of: The length of the ark shall be three hundred cubits, the breadth of it fifty cubits, and the height of it thirty cubits.
16. A window shalt thou make to the ark, and in a cubit shalt thou finish it above; and the door of the ark shalt thou set in the side thereof; with lower, second, and third stories shalt thou make it.

According to some, the Hebrew cubit was only 18 inches, others say 20. Even with the latter, the ark would be only 500 feet. Into this Noah put eight people, two or seven of every animal species, and sufficient provisions for one hundred fifty days; another account says one year. And for ventilation there was only one little window twenty inches square. The absurdity here is so great, I suspect it was meant as a hint for us to do a little thinking. But as stated elsewhere, Western man is incapable of thinking in the abstract or recognizing mythic symbolism. Yet consider the absurdity of its literalism. The fauna of the Middle East is not extensive. Where then did Noah get two or seven of every living creature? Did he go to Australia for the kangaroos, to the Arctic for the polar bears, and to the Antarctic for the penguins? And how many dinosaurs did he have aboard?

There is only one thing big enough to accommodate all the creatures of the earth and that is the earth itself. This is the ark of Genesis, or creation, and into it went the ark-etypal forms of every living thing. When in our version we spoke of archetypes, ideation, and genes, the reader, no doubt, dismissed it as mere metaphysical speculation, not realizing he had read it all before in his "word of God"—the plagiarized and corrupted wisdom-knowledge of Creation.

In this perverted version, the earth is still prephysical; its three stories are, therefore, the three prephysical planes, mental, astral and etheric. Mount Ararat where the ark "rested," like God, is the physical part.

The word *ark* is Egyptian and means a chest or box for preserving sacred things. Here, in its symbolic sense, the sacred things are the planetary genes and archetypal ideas that only the earth is capable of holding. The idea is by no means original; the Hindus had their Argha, the Greeks, their Cista, also the Argo of the Argonauts. In another myth it is Pandora's box. The numbers here are also symbolic. As in Revelation, the constant use of seven can have no other meaning than the septenate creative process. This is "the mystic number" in all cosmologies.

2. Of every clean beast thou shalt take to thee by sevens . . .

3. Of fowls also of the air by sevens . . .

4. For yet seven days, and I will cause it to rain upon the earth . . .

10. And it came to pass after seven days . . . (Chap. 7)

4. And the ark rested in the seventh month, on the seventeenth day of the month . . .

10. And he stayed yet other seven days . . .

12. And he stayed yet other seven days . . . (Chap. 8)

That there are here two conflicting versions is quite apparent. Chapter 7, verse 2, says seven of every kind, and chapter 6, verse 19, says two of every sort. In each the duration of the flood is also different. Chapter 7 says one hundred fifty days—five months; Chapter 8 says ten months before the mountain tops were seen. This is some of that rewriting of the original we spoke about in our Preface.

7. And Noah went in, and his sons, and his wife, and his sons' wives with him, into the ark, because of the waters of the flood.

10. And it came to pass after seven days, that the waters of the flood were upon the earth.

11. In the six hundredth year of Noah's life (sixth plane), in the

second month, the seventeenth day of the month, the same day were all the fountains of the great deep broken up, and the windows of heaven were opened.

12. And the rain was upon the earth forty days and forty nights (Chap. 7).

The forty days and nights represent the four prephysical periods. Noah's six hundredth year brings it down to the etheric plane, No. 6, beyond which is the sun period. In every mythology these four periods are described as violent, the elements being the aforesaid *turbulentos*, out of which another Creator, Fetahil, tried to form a world but could not until he gained the help of the monster Ialda-baoth (Behemoth), matter. But even together they could not form a world until they had first created the "seven stellars," the intermediaries. These "seven stellars" are one with the "seven pillars" wisdom hewed out for her house (Prov. 9:1). And this is the Deluge, the creation of the world.

21. And all flesh died that moved upon the earth, both of fowl, and of cattle, and of beast, and of every creeping thing that creepeth upon the earth, and every man:

22. All in whose nostrils was the breath of life, of all that was in the dry land, died.

And this cosmic fiend and genocide is absolved by man because His name is God. Did Satan ever commit so great a crime? And what are man's puny sins compared with it? We condemn and deplore the Nazis' genocidal attack on the Jews, but they destroyed human life only; this monster destroyed all life. And for twenty five hundred years no one has had the courage to cry out *"J'accuse!"*

And now let us see what it really means.

The only absolution for this mass-murder lies in our theory, namely, that the victims were not evolutionary beings but involutionary archetypes, and their death the same as that concerning which Adam was warned, the death of spirit, as such. Here, no morality is involved, but there is explanation. When the

Creator made hunger He also made lust, the hunger of the astral body, and the astral body is part of the Creator's body—astral matter. Thus the cause of human wickedness is in the original Cause. And this is the wickedness of Noah's day.

Herein lies the importance of the distinction we made between God and Creator. The fault lies with the translators. They should never have used the name of man's ideal, God, in translating Creation myths, or attributed love and mercy to the Creator. But they are not alone to blame. Had we been enlightened we would never have accepted this semantic miscegenation. And were we enlightened today we would not make fools of ourselves in sermons, novels, paintings and movies about Noah and his Ark.

While Noah was still afloat he sent forth a raven and later a dove three times, a sort of sounding of the various stages of concretion. This too was copied: the Babylonian Noah, Utnapishtim, sent first a dove, then a swallow, and finally a raven, which is more in keeping with the coarsening process.

1. And God remembered Noah, and every living thing, and all the cattle that was with him in the ark: and God made a wind to pass over the earth, and the waters assuaged;

4. And the ark rested in the seventh month (cycle and plane), on the seventeenth day of the month, upon the mountain of Ararat (Chap. 8).

The ark rested on the seventh day the same way God rested —in dense matter. This is Mount Ararat, called elsewhere, "the mount of descent." And today men who call themselves enlightened climb this mount in search of the ark. They should read other mythologies as well as the Hebrews'. The Babylonian ark rested on Mount Nisir, the Hindu ark on Mount Himalaya, and the Greek ark on Mount Parnassus. Hatho says the word Ararat, or Arath, is the Aramaic source of the word earth. It is generally assumed this comes from the Norse goddess Erda, but Erda is just the Arath of Scandinavian mythology.

When at last the dense and solid earth is reached, Noah and his crew come forth and build an altar, the earth itself. On this they sacrifice some of the animals, elements, which, radiating away, rose up and formed an aura. These God both saw and smelled. The "sweet savor" pleased him immensely, and so he made a covenant with Noah: never again would he destroy the earth by a deluge, and for a very good reason—the Deluge being the creative process, it happens only once. But that he might not forget his promise, he made a rainbow and set it in the sky as a reminder. Now a rainbow is the result of raindrops refracting sunlight—and there was no sun at this time. If, however, this story is literally true and the deluge an event in human history, then this is the first time the law of refraction operated. But what of the sun and rain in Adam's day and during those lengthy "begats"? The answer is quite simple: this is not a subsequent period, nor is the rainbow meteorological; it is cosmological—the seven auric elements in Evolution, only four as yet, however. The earth's aura is colored and constitutes the planet's cosmic index.

This tale was also copied from others. After the flood the Babylonian Utnapishtim also built an altar and sacrificed to his God. And strange to say, this God also "smelled a sweet savor" and Ishtar, "the lady of the rainbow," hung out her multicolored necklace. According to the Incas, the god Viracocha promised by the rainbow never to drown mankind again. And among the Chibehas of Bogota, Bochica quelled the flood while sitting on a rainbow.

1. And God blessed Noah and his sons, and said unto them, Be fruitful, and multiply, and replenish the earth (Chap. 9).

This is not a repetition of the command given to Adam; it is the same command in a parallel myth. Thus the replenishment here is not of the lost Adamic humanity, but of the involutionary archetypes and elements figuratively "lost" in matter. These are now to be replaced by their evolutionary antiscia, or planetary opposites. The command then is not to humanity, nor is it authority to breed by blind nature instead of human intelligence. It is not even a command by God, but only that of a mythologist observing a natural fact billions of years later.

18. And the sons of Noah, that went forth of the ark, were Shem, and Ham, and Japheth: and Ham is the father of Canaan.

Ham represents the etheric element, at this point in the story, involutionary. And now we can see why Ham is the father of Canaan. Canaan is a mythic name for matter, the earth in toto, and we asserted that suns transmute the etheric into the chemical. And this is the meaning of the next step down, namely, Shem, or Chem.

It's all cunningly concealed, but by no means original. Even the names of Noah's sons are copies. In Maurice's history of Hindustan we find this: "It is related in Padmapooraun that Satyavrata, whose miraculous preservation from a general deluge is told at large in the Matsya, had three sons, the eldest of whom was named Jyapeti, or Lord of the Earth; the others were Charma and Sharma, which last words are in the vulgar dialects usually pronounced Cham and Sham. . . ." In *The City of God*, St. Augustine uses these same forms, also Chanaan for Canaan. There is more to this quotation but it is apropos of something else assumed to be original; later we will return to it.

19. These are the three sons of Noah (the violent forces of Creation): and of them was the whole earth overspread.

And that explains everything, including the violence and savagery of Nature, a fact the Perfection concept and the Priestly account cannot explain. By such deception the priests hid from us the true nature of Causation, and at the same time established the idea the whole human race sprang from three Jews, and of course they were Jews, and so was Adam. Josephus, taking it all literally, says the descendants of these three spread over all the continents of Europe and Asia, founding nations and calling them after their own names. Then he berates the Greeks for subsequently changing the names and making these same claims. This, of course, was wrong for the Greeks but perfectly all right for the Jews.

The many descendants of these three were not even races but divisions in the earth itself: "And unto Eber were born two sons: the name of one was Peleg; for in his days was the earth divided . . ." (Chap. 10:25). Divided into Involution and Evolution and its planes.

The earth now created, we find a very different Noah. No longer is he the saint who "walked with God," but an old reprobate who got drunk, exposed his nakedness and cursed his son for seeing it—*"Demon est Deus inversus."*

20. And Noah began to be a husbandman, and he planted a vineyard:

21. And he drank of the wine, and was drunken; and he was uncovered within his tent (Chap. 9).

That is, he was, like Adam, naked. This is the naked earth—*Gymnoge*. He was also, like Adam, a tiller of the ground; in other words, he was Adam. The vineyard he planted was the Garden of Eden; the grapes he grew were the forbidden fruit of "the tree of good and evil"; the wine he drank was of this tree, and as with Adam, it was too much for him, therefore he also slept. Don't blame him, however, for even God had to rest. The wine is the opiate matter and its story is very old. In the Puranas of India, Indra the Creator became drunk on soma, an intoxicant that produces stupefaction rather than hilarity; actually the deathlike sleep of genetic consciousness in matter. And how many of us can see the epigenetic parallel? In this materialistic cycle we too are drunk on soma and stupefied spiritually. That is why we cannot see the meaning of the scriptures, or solve "the riddle of the universe."

22. And Ham, the father of Canaan (now the evolutionary etheric), saw the nakedness of his father, and told his two brethren without.

We dislike the Greek story of Cronos taking advantage of his father's nakedness, but it's all right here—this is "the word of God," and so is the tale of Lot's daughters. Naked Noah is naked earth; naturally, then the first emanation, etheric, saw the earth's nakedness as it had not yet been covered with vegetation. And now, like God covering Adam, ". . . Shem and Japheth took a garment (vegetation) and laid it upon both their shoulders, and went backward, and covered the nakedness of their father, and their faces were backward and they saw not their father's nakedness." This casting the garment backward is identical with Deucalion and Pyrrha casting the stones backward, the creative process reversed, evolutionary fission instead of involutionary fusion. Their faces backward from their father, earth, means they were turned from dense matter toward Evolution.

Otherwise, why should a man's nakedness be such a moral offense in those primitive days, that a third of the race should be cursed for all time? The Jews, even today, are not oversensitive about it. The naked earth, however, was a cosmogonical offense, as it was intended to be covered. Now actually Ham did the covering, but as the author wanted to "show cause" why the plant kingdom is subject to the other two, he made Shem and Japheth the virtuous ones. Japheth being the oldest son (see 21:10) was first in Involution, therefore last in Evolution.

24. And Noah awoke from his wine, and knew what his younger son had done unto him.
25. And he said, Cursed be Canaan; a servant of servants shall he be unto his brethren (as Abel was to his brother Cain).

Exoterically, this is the third curse pronounced thus far—Adam, Cain, and Ham—but esoterically, it is the same curse, the curse of life, of being as compared to nonbeing. This is "the original sin" and its consequence, but behold, what ignorance has done with it. It has made a religion out of it; it has built a parasitic church and priesthood upon it; it has wasted millennia in saving us instead of civilizing us. The only salvation that we need is salvation from this ignorance; this is our curse and the cause of all our troubles. Therefore we should make all other things secondary to the removal of this curse.

As an aid in escaping the curse of scriptural history, we will now conclude the Hindustani source of this part of it. "The royal patriarch for such is his character in the Pooraun—was particularly fond of Jyapeti, to whom he gave all the regions to the north of Himalaya, or the snowy mountains, which extend from sea to sea, and of which Caucasus is a part; to Sharma he alloted the countries to the south of these mountains; but he cursed Charma because when the old monarch was accidentally inebriated with strong liquor made of fermented rice, Charma laughed; and it was in consequence of his father's execration that he became a slave to the slaves of his brothers." And such is the "revealed" history of Israel.

It is curious what devils these divine beings, straight from the hand of God, become—Adam, Cain, Lamech, and now Noah, a great mystery to our "Bible students." Concerning Noah, one of them, C. A. Hawley, had this to say: "The second Noah seems to have been as much a reprobate as any of the descendants of the illicit union of the divine beings and mortal woman. He was the first to plant the vine, thereby identifying himself with the hated Baal religion, so violently condemned by the prophets. He was the first to become drunk with wine, again violating all the prophetic commands and injunctions. He was the first mortal to curse his fellow man. He was the originator of slavery. This could never be the same Noah who was named to be the savior of his people and the second father of the human race."

This is commentary without knowledge, learning without understanding. Lacking these his Reverence could not accept this change from saint to sinner. It's the same old Noah, nevertheless, but that Noah was not the second father of the race; he was the first, that is, one with Adam, and his fall from grace is Adam's fall. As both personify the Creative Principle, this is but an occultist's way of saying the Creator fell, from Deus to Demon—the original Dr. Jekyll and Mr. Hyde. The author of the Zohar also knew this fact, as per diagram. (See page 98.)

Thus both the Zohar and the Bible confirm our former statements. An honest search in other sources also helps. According to rabbinical lore, Noah entered into partnership with Satan. Satan was to fertilize the soil and Noah was to plant and tend the vine, the two splitting the profits. So this is the origin of the "profit system." We thought there was something Satanic about it.

Such is the story of Noah, merely a revolutio of other myths.

DEMON EST DEUS INVERSUS

As all the aspects of Creation could not be shown in one, the ancients made many. Furthermore, each race wrote the story in terms of its own people, hence both their universality and their difference. There are in all some four hundred deluge myths, each with its own Noah, ark and Ararat. The Greek parallel is too well known for lengthy comment, so just an outline.

Zeus, Jupiter to the Romans, becoming offended with his own creation, decided to drown the whole wicked lot of them, except Deucalion and Pyrrha, who had "found grace" in his eyes. These he allowed to escape in a boat or ark which finally landed on Mt. Parnassus. Here his "chosen" disembarked only to look upon a bare and desolate world. While wondering what to do they heard a voice from heaven telling them to pick up their parents' bones and cast them backwards. This they did and life sprang up to "replenish the earth." In this throwing backwards, we have a bit of knowledge we think we alone possess—the creative process reversed, atomic catalysis instead of atomic synthesis. Science calls it fission, in nature, radiation, slow and harmless. In a parallel myth Cadmus sows dragon teeth and warriors spring up from them—the warring elements now in Evolution. Their first biologic counterpart is the viruses, lethal and murderous. Such is even first life, and this is what the Jhwhist is telling us through Cain, Lamech, Noah, Moses and Joshua. Knowledge of this kind should open our eyes to what we are here for—to qualify the quantitative and civilize the savage, in other words, finalize God's unfinished business.

From the tablets of Assurbanipal we get the Babylonian account. Here the great God, Enlil, offended by man's wickedness, decides to destroy him with water, but Ea, the god of wisdom (creative), overhears his plan and tells Utnapishtim about it. This good man, like the Sethite Noah, is tenth in line from the first man, and, like Noah, walks with Ea. The latter advises him to forsake all else and build a boat, not just for himself and family, but large enough to hold all the beasts and birds and creeping things. No sooner was it built and all things stored within than a great storm arose, so great indeed that even the lesser gods "trembled in fear." For six days and nights it lasted and on the *seventh* it stopped. Meanwhile the boat had floated about until it came to rest on Mount Nisir. Now Mount Nisir is between Medea and Armenia and thus is practically identical with Ararat.

In this story Utnapishtim waits "seven days" and sends out the dove, swallow, and raven already mentioned. When the latter fails to return Utnapishtim knows the land is dry and so opens the boat and debarks. Immediately thereafter he builds an altar and offers incense upon it. The gods smell the "sweet savor" and gather around; and here it is that Mother Ishtar hangs out her colored necklace, the rainbow.

In the Persian and Hindu myths we get a closer approximation to the real meaning. In these it is not physical birds and beasts that are taken into the ark but their *seeds*, the planetary genes. And so we quote: ". . . (take) the seeds of sheep, oxen, men and women, dogs, and birds and every kind of tree and fruit, two of every kind, into the ark and seal it up with a golden ring ("ring-pass-not") and make in it a door and window."

The Hindu Noah, Vaivasvata, is warned by an avatar of

Vishnu that the earth is to be submerged and all life destroyed. The avatar then orders him to construct a vessel for his family and the *seeds* of plants, and pairs of animals. A great fish appears to guide the boat which, after being buffeted about, comes to rest on Mount Himalaya. In this, the number of days the storm lasted agrees exactly with that of the Hebrew account. We said the Jews in Bible days had many sources we're unaware of.

These are all Asian and might be copies one from the other, yet how did the people of far-off Mexico, Brazil and the Society Islands know about this event, even the details? The Tepanecans of Mexico tell of a great flood that lasted exactly forty days and nights. The Society Islanders say the great god Tangaloa, offended by the sins of man, caused a flood so great that only the mountaintops remained when the flood subsided—the present archipelago. Thereafter a stranger landed from a boat on Mount Eimeo and built an altar to his god. And no doubt he thanked this god for saving him after drowning all the rest. According to the Tupi-Guarani of western Brazil, their god Monan was so vexed with their evil ways that he tried to destroy them with fire, but a great magician, Irin-Magé, extinguished it with a deluge of water. The Quichi (Mayans) say that only four men and four women escaped from a rain and hail. These had taken refuge in a mountain and when they sought a better abode the waters parted and they passed through on dry land. The Mandeans of Mesopotamia tell of a flood of fire-water, from which only a pair escaped. The Mundari of Central India say their god Sing Bonga, perceiving that all men had become evil, destroyed them with fire and water. The Tolowas tell us of a great flood following a torrential rain. All were drowned except one pair. From this pair the Tolowas sprang. A Welsh myth says that Dwyvan and Dwyvach alone escaped the Great Flood. And even the Jews had other Deluge myths. In one a wrathful God scalded the sinful antediluvians.

There are some who contend that the other races copied from the Hebrew account, this being the one and only "revealed" account, yet the Hindu, Chaldean, Babylonian and Egyptian accounts antedate the Hebrew version by many centuries. Who did the copying then is obvious. Speaking of this Dr. Driver said: ". . . their materials it is plain were obtained by them from the best human sources obtainable." And again: ". . . the author has utilized elements derived ultimately from a heathen source." The truth is that the entire Bible is derived from this heathen source. The mythoplasm of all myths is that of the creation of the world, and all antiquity dramatized it. Below are a few of the better known deluge myths with their Noahs and their gods.

Culture	Hero	Warned By
Hebrew	Noah	God
Babylonian	Utnapishtim	Ea
Persian	Yima	Ahura Mazda
Hindu	Vaivasvata	Vishnu's Avatar
Chaldean	Xesuthras	Chinos
Greek	Deucalion	Prometheus
Ostyaks	Pairachta	Turin
Votyaks	Noj	Inmer
Mexican	Nata	Titlacuhuan
Algonquin	—	Glooscap
Choctaw	—	The Great Spirit

While on the subject of myths and "lost" races let us consider another—the "lost" Atlantis. Atlantis is also a myth, but as we know it, no part of the mythopoeic legacy. It belongs to historic times and Plato is the author. But Plato had no firsthand knowledge of this land or the original myth either. He got the idea from a pupil of his, who got it from a relative, Solon, who got it from Egyptian priests, who did not know its meaning either. Thus remote, in more ways than one, Plato just fictionized a myth into a fact. If you don't believe this can be done, just read your Bible. The facts of the case are these: While visiting Sais in Egypt, Solon was shown two pillars inscribed with hieroglyphics, ancient even then. Curious to know their meaning, he asked the priests to interpret them to him. This they did and the story they told is the story of Atlantis, another fabulous land in the *west*, now sunk in the Atlantic. This too was a wondrous place, but not as Plato described it—the philosopher needed a basis for his ideal Republic. It was more like Eden; in other words, the land of the gods, not of men. It was involutionary, and like all the rest it became corrupt and wicked, therefore it too was destroyed—that an evolutionary world might be. This is the story the tablets told, and if ever they are rediscovered they will tell a story as old and as universal as thinking man. Even in far-off China we find its counterpart—Teheon, so like the Hebrew Tehom. This was a happy, "Holy Island beyond the sun," which because of its sins was destroyed by a deluge. "Beyond the sun," not in space but in time, that is, beyond the sun period.

The word Atlantis, like Atlantic, comes from Atlas, the mighty man who upholds the world, that is, we believe the poor, benighted Greeks believed he did. But we see in others only what we are ourselves and by reason of it. Thus we know mythology only as we know cosmology, and having substituted religious faith for prereligious knowledge, we know but little. Atlas was not a reality even to the Greeks; he was but a mythic personification of cosmic power. And do we not believe a mighty power called God upholds the world? When once we acquire even a little knowledge of things cosmic we will then see Eden as one with Atlantis, Adam as one with Atlas, and even Noah. These are but earth on the involutionary side; their glories but the glories of mythology, their magic but the magic of creation; and their "fall" but descent into generation.

What then of "divine man" and his "divine instructors"? Simply this: they never existed, therefore all faith in and commentary on them is but misunderstood cosmology mythologized. Consider this now obvious misunderstanding from Panodorus: "Now it is during these thousand years (i.e., before the Deluge) that the reign of the Seven Gods (seven plane forces) who rule the world took place. It was during that period that those benefactors of humanity *descended* on Earth and taught man to calculate the course of the sun and moon by the twelve signs of the Ecliptic (the zodiac)." If man had divine teachers and divine knowledge in the beginning how did he get like Neanderthal, or even us? This is Devolution. That sin caused it, is part of the priestly hoax; science has "no need of that hypothesis"; it has studied first-man's remains.

The Seven Gods Panodorus took so literally and as coexisting, were the seven successive or henotheistic powers in Involution—the first seven Manus of Hindu cosmology. They did not descend to earth and teach men; they descended and became men. We now are they, biologically, and only by our own efforts do we learn to "calculate the course of the sun and moon"—also to build a boat. And we might also add, a radio, a plane, an antibiotic. This is our job in the Zodiacal Night; all such knowledge eventually handed *up* to the human group-soul. In the Zodiacal Day it will be changed and sublimated into wisdom, and as the twilight comes again, handed *down* to a wisdom lacking humanity that will again misinterpret it.

Today, we think of this wisdom-knowledge in terms of religion—"revealed," or mystically intuited rather than rationally discerned. It is not so; the ancient knowledge of Reality was as rationalistic as our own science, and far more extensive, cosmically. It was the result of preceding millennia of scientific study philosophically examined. To paraphrase a recent comment, it was scientific experience contemplated in tranquillity—the Zodiacal Day. Thus there was nothing mystic or mysterious about it. It was the period in between that myst-ified it, the age of religion. And as this gave us no knowledge whatever, we think, like Panodorus, that it was "revealed" to "holy men" by "divine beings."

This false idea has filled the world with nonsense—Gods and Devils, Angels and Archangels, Lipikas and Builders, Lords of Wisdom and Sons of Light. Even Madame Blavatsky, who should have known better, writes in this fashion. "The question will surely be asked: Do the occultists believe in all these 'Builders,' 'Lipikas,' and 'Sons of Light,' as Entities, or are they merely imaginary? To this the answer is given as plainly: After due allowance for the imagery of personified Powers, we must admit the existence of these Entities, if we would not reject the existence of spiritual Humanity within physical mankind. For the hosts of these Sons of Light, the mind born sons of the manifested Ray of the Unknown All, are the very root of spiritual man."[1] Thus belief in these beings depends on a delusion, namely, that this "Ray of the Unknown All" constitutes the

---

[1] *The Secret Doctrine*, vol. I, p. 131.

spiritual part of evolved humanity. It does not; this "Ray" is
only the Life Principle, the morally unqualified genetic; the
spirituality of evolved humanity is epigenetic and of man's own
creating.

There is simply no end to the delusions this false doctrine has
wrought. It molds the mind of the theologian, it bedevils the
philosopher, the statesman, and even the nation. In the Germans and Japanese we see the consequence of this. The latter
took literally their myth about divine beings descending upon
their islands and establishing their race and culture—then
fought like devils to force them upon the world. And only after
bitter defeat did they humanize their "divine" Emperor. The
statement that their founder was fifth in line from the Sun
Goddess has no racial meaning whatever. It means only that
they, mankind, are fifth in line cyclically from the sun period—
sun, earth, plant, animal, man.

A similar idea underlies the Germans' politicomysticism, ending in militarism—and two defeats. It too derives from mythology, its unscrupulous gods and violent means—Thor, the
thunderer, Wotan, the pact-breaker, Loki, the cunning schemer,
and so on. The result is *Der Tag, Blitzkrieg, Deutsche Donner and
dämmerung*, all due to ignorance of the ruthless nature of Causation and man's corrective purpose. Whenever a people associate
themselves with God or the gods and boast of their racial superiority, they are but exposing an inferiority complex. Due to a
sense of inadequacy they create a divinity to supplement their
own deficiency. In this we should not forget the Jews, with their
claim to divine origin and selection. The resulting pride and
prejudice is a good example of what happens when the wisdom-
knowledge is lost and only the deceptive letter remains. But
before we pluck the mote from others' eyes, let's get the beam
out of our own. We too believe their silly claims and help them
steal a country. We too believe we're essentially divine; we too
believe Causation is divine; for ages we believed in "the divine
right of kings," and still believe in the divine authority of the
Church. Indeed, in these things we're all so ignorant "it ill
behooves the best of us to talk about the rest of us."

7

The Tower of Babel

Genesis: Eleventh Chapter

> 1. And the whole earth was one language, and
> of one speech. (Naturally, since the language
> here was the language of nature.)
> 2. And it came to pass, as they journeyed from
> the east, that they found a plain in the land of
> Shinar; and they dwelt there.

We should not look upon this chapter as
even chronological. Its "they" are not the people of the preceding chapter, Noah's sons and their descendants; that is taken up again in verse 10. The "they" are the creative forces in Involution, and the Babel story just another Creation myth. It appears here only because the Editor deemed it worthy of a place with the others. Worthy it may be but not original. Even the name Babel (Gate of God) came from the Akkadian-Sumerian *Babili*, about 3900 B.C., and means Gateway of God, one with the Greek "Gateway of the gods." "Shinar," the Hebrew form of the native name Sumir, is of similar origin.

3. And they said one to another, Go to, let us make brick, and burn them thoroughly. And they had brick for stone, and slime had they for mortar.

Bricks are a building material and here symbolize the atomic units out of which "they" built a chemical world; and the place they burned them thoroughly was in the sun. When later they made biologic bricks (cells), they did not merely use slime; they *were* slime.

The city they built is earth, and its lofty tower the aura that rises heavenward from it. The "name" is that planetary index, the aura's colors. The author does not tell us the real reason for this project but Josephus does. His account, however, is rather mystifying. When the waters departed, he says the sons of Noah came down to the plain and tried their best to persuade others to follow them. Now who were these "others"? And how could there be, as he asserts, a multitude at work on the tower? And who constituted the colonies he says God commanded them to send out? It might be argued that this was long subsequent to the Deluge, but no, the one who incited them to build the tower was Nimrod, Ham's grandson. Now the sons and grandsons of one man do not constitute colonies and multitudes, but the creative forces do. Nimrod's reason for building the tower is given as anger at God for drowning the race, and who can blame him? He said *"J'accuse,"* but there's never been another like him. He was also afraid there would be another mass murder in spite of God's promise. To quote Josephus verbatim: "He wanted to avenge himself on God for the destruction of his ancestors thus: he would build a tower so high that the waters of another flood, with which the world might be afflicted, would not be able to submerge it." And a Babylonian parallel ends thus: "But all this they did only from fear of another deluge." And all this (mythic tales) the Jews had access to and used.

5. And the Lord came down to see the city and the tower, which the children of men builded.

"Children of men" is pure deception. These builders are the same as those of Blavatsky's comment—Lipikas and Lords of

Form. Now if they built that form called earth, who is this spying Lord? He is but a creation of the Jewish mind, which, honored for its monotheism, created many Creators, then told us the Lord is one. Exoterically, Bible and Babel are much alike—utter confusion.

6. And the Lord said, Behold, the people is one (the Life Principle), and they have all one language (genetic); and this they begin to do: and now nothing will be restrained from them, which they have imagined to do.

7. Go to, let *us* go down, and there confound their language, that they may not understand one another's speech.

And where is the monotheism here? This separating and confounding of the language represents the many divisions and tongues into which the life force divided in Evolution. If this be not the meaning, then this divider of one language is responsible for all the wars and woes that came therefrom. A universal language is one of the prerequisites of peace and civilization, a blessing, not a crime. It is also something man should strive for, the moral of Babel notwithstanding.

8. So the Lord scattered them abroad from thence upon the face of all the earth: and they left off to build the city.

The earth now built, they left off building it—"and God rested from all his labors." And what a world it was: earthquake and volcano, jungle, savagery, barbarism and finally semicivilization. Its builder here is Nimrod, "A mighty hunter before the Lord," which means he was the Lord, and like Cain and Lamech, a killer. What an indictment of God we have here! He, not man, made this place of chaos and confusion, of mindless matter and murderous force. How then is man to blame? Instead of its creator he is its savior; give him time and he will turn this God-made Babel-onia into a man-made Utopia.

Verse 10 now takes up the generations of Shem again, where it left off in chapter 10. Here the lineage of Shem is traced down to Abraham, a genealogy no more factual or historical than that of Noah from Adam. It is but a priestly attempt to make it appear that the Jews descended from Adam and therefore straight from God. But little do they realize what that implies.

We now know who "they" were, but who were the "us"? "Let us go down—" *Us* is not monotheistic, and neither were the earliest Jews. The later ones deleted many of their gods and devils yet their literature as a whole is replete with them. There were, for instance, seven evil spirits of which Satan, or Beelzebub, was the prince; Vessels of Iniquity, whose chief was Belial; Deluders whose chief, Nahash, deluded Eve; Tempters, whose chief was Mammon; the Turbulents (Turbulentos), chief, Meriram. There were also Lying Spirits, Furies, Revengers, and Inquisitors. Against these were the seven opponents: Cherubim, Seraphim, Virtues, Thrones, Dominions, Powers and Principalities. There were also the seven archangels: Michael, Gabriel, Raphael, Kamiel, Kadriel, Uriel and Zophkiel.

In Tobias, an Apocryphal book, it is related that the archangel Raphael seized Asmodeus, prince of the fourth order of evil spirits (fourth material plane energy), and bound him in the wilderness of Upper Egypt (earth). This is the angel Saint John said he saw binding Satan, billions of years after the event. A parallel myth is that of Apollyon, Prince of Darkness; simply Apollo, a sun extinguished, actually now our world. This is he whom the Bible calls "the prince of this world." In the myth, his kingdom was over those "wandering stars for whom is laid up the blackness of darkness for ages and ages." This is that stage and period we referred to earlier—between bright sun and life-bearing planet, in which the intermediate entity wanders alone until picked up by a sun. This is all part of the wisdom-knowledge of Creation of which the Bible is but a plagiarized and religionized relic.

Its deities, including its God, are just as mythic as Zeus and Apollo, Prometheus and Epimetheus, yet to any praise of the Greeks and their art the Christian priest makes haste to reply, "Oh, they were only myth-makers." Yes, and the difference between the two is that the myth-makers did not believe in their myths literally, and we do, in ours.

8

Abraham, Isaac and Jacob

> Strictly speaking it is difficult to view the Jewish Book
> of Genesis otherwise than a chip from the trunk of the
> mundane tree of universal cosmology rendered in ori-
> ental allegories.
>
> H. P. BLAVATSKY

Abraham

The first two chapters of Genesis deal with
the creation of the world and man. And there we think the
subject ends. But if this be so, why is the entire content of the
book called Genesis? Because the entire content *is* genesis, i.e.,
cosmology mythologized. Abraham is just another personification of the Creative Principle as were Adam and Noah. Contrary to all teaching and belief, the Bible itself tells us this: it
says that Abraham was before Noah, Joshua Chap. 24:

2. And Joshua said unto all the people, Thus saith the Lord God
of Israel, Your fathers dwelt on the other side of the flood . . . even
Terah, the father of Abraham, and the father of Nachor: and they
served other gods (the involutionary powers).
3. And I took your father Abraham from the other side of the flood
(the prephysical planes), and led him throughout all the land of Canaan
(the physical). . . .
15. . . . choose you this day whom ye will serve; whether the gods
which your fathers served that were on the other side of the flood
(involution), or the gods of the Amorites, in whose land ye dwell

(Evolution—the choice then is between Involution and Evolution, the same choice that Adam made between "the tree of life" and "the tree of knowledge). . . .

Now if Abraham was "on the other side of the flood," he was before Noah, who was contemporary with the flood. But let us not be deceived by even this obvious conclusion, for esoterically, Abraham is Noah, and in the Ethiopian version his life and Noah's are cognate and strangely similar.

Today Jewish scholars freely admit that the accounts of Adam, Cain and Noah belong in the realm of mythology; in other words, the Bible is mythology until, as they say, "we come to the historical Abraham, the father of the Jewish race." Now why should a book of mythology suddenly become history with Abraham? And why should historians revert to mythology again in Exodus? The story of Moses is just as mythological as that of Adam and Noah. And so is that of Abraham.

As with all the patriarchs, tales were told of Abraham so fantastic they could not apply to a mortal man. According to one, King Nimrod, like Herod, learning from the stars that a child would be born that would dethrone him, commanded all male children to be killed as soon as born. So when Abram was born his father Terah substituted a slave woman's child for his own and thus saved Abram. Another says that his mother Amitlai bore him in a cave, and that the light of his face lit up the whole interior. There she left him for ten days in which the angel Gabriel fed him milk from his little finger. On returning his mother found no infant but a grown man. She did not recognize him, but he recognized her. Now Nimrod on hearing of this wonder child sent soldiers to kidnap him but God blinded them with a cloud of darkness. This so frightened Nimrod he fled to the land of Babel. (So Babel was a land, not just a tower, and that's what we made it—earth.)

When first we meet with the scriptural Abraham he is called Abram, and according to our "best authorities" the word means "lifted up," "exalted." The "up" and "exalted," however, do not refer to his human position but to his planetary position—the highest planes in Involution. But where did the word itself come from? Is it Hebrew, or is it, like their history, borrowed mythology? In our Preface we said the Hebrews got many of their religious ideas from India, not God, and here we have some proof of this. Abram is but the Hindu Brama, with the *a* as prefix instead of suffix; and Brama was the original name of the Hindu Creator. Later the letter *h* was added, thus making it Brahma. So with Abram; it also acquired an *h* and became Abraham. To see the source of this more clearly, we have only to write down the Hindu name of Brahma's source, namely, Par*abrahm*. In Persia the name was originally Abriman, which also acquired an *h* and became Ahriman—an "evil deity; the ruler over the kingdom of darkness." the Babylonians also had their Abraham, only they spelt it Abarama. He was a farmer and mythologically contemporary with the Hebrew Abraham. Commenting on this, one of our "great Bible students" had this to say: "The Patriarch of Ur about whom we are studying probably was related to the farmer who lived near Babylon. At any rate they were not the same person, because they had different fathers, and the farmer was not a monotheist. But family names persisted in the ancient days among Semites, and we may suppose that a near descendant of this farmer became a monotheist, moved to Haran, and then went on to Canaan." Thus do the credulous account for parallel myths. The Moslems also claim Abraham as their "spiritual father," but to them he is Ibrahim. He it was who produced the Kaaba, the sacred stone at Mecca, a relic of a myth about that stone called Earth. And Abram's father was Terah, so like the Latin *terra*, also earth.

Now to form an earth every Creator, except the Jews' and Christians', must have a female consort, matter. In the Greek myth the Creator marries his sister, shocking indeed; in the Hebrew he marries his half-sister, which is quite all right. To our Bible students these little touches are called "Jewish refinements." Here the consort was Sarai, and as with Abram and Brama, an *h* was added and she became Sarah. But it so happens that Brahma had another name, Ishvara, and his wife was Shri. And when you take the vowels out of Sarai, as the Hebrews did, and add the *h*, you have Shri. This letter *h* signifies life, and thus did Brama, Abram, and Sarai in due time receive life, or being, which implies that in the beginning they did not have it. We should be familiar with this changing of names in mythology—Erebus became Aether, Nix became Hemera, Alkeides became Hercules, and El Shaddai became Yahveh and Yahveh became Jehovah; still later Jacob became Israel—the priestly alibi for that henotheistic succession of the Greeks.

Abraham came from "Ur of the Chaldees," and *ur* means light, also fire. And so it is used in the Hebrew *urim*, the lights, *ur*, the noun, and *im*, a plural. We find it also in Uriel, Uranus, etc. This root word was common in India, Asurias, the Builders; also in Assyria, Asshur, the most high god. In Chaldea one of the persons in their Trinity was Aur, god of light, the same light that Noah and Abraham manifested at birth, and likewise Lucifer. Yes, shocking as it may be to some, Abraham and Lucifer are one, that old Ahriman, the "evil deity." The literal alternative to this is that the father of the Jews was a Chaldean, but even here we cannot escape the occult implication, for the word "Chaldee" means demon, and Chaldean, demoniacal. Saint Jerome half admits this for he calls Chaldea *"quasi demonia."*

What then of the scriptural Abraham and all his descendants? The later authors endowed these personifications of a ruthless power with moral virtues and spiritual greatness, thus hiding from us the true nature of our source and our purpose in Creation. This is that crime concerning which Dr. Johnson said there could be no greater—"poisoning the source of eternal truth." Poisoning, concealing and mystifying was their purpose.

And here, perhaps, we can solve another of their mysteries—Melchizedek, "priest of the most high God," and contemporary with Abraham. According to this author he too was very wise and great, a "prince of peace," in fact, but St. Paul tells us plainly that this great one was not a human being. Referring to him in Hebrews 7:3, he says he was ". . . without father, without mother, without descent, having neither beginning of days, nor end of life; but made like unto the Son of God; abideth a priest continually." That is, eternal, uncreated and uncreating, having neither beginning nor end. Now there is only one thing in all existence to which such words apply and that is the Absolute, "inactive and asleep." Here and here only is there peace, from that heavenly war of Creation, and that is why Melchizedek was called a "prince of peace." This is inherent in the name itself: *melekh*, king, and *tsedheg*, peace. He was also called "The King of Salem," the latter also meaning peace. Later Salem became part of the word Jerusalem, which historically never knew peace. The word Salem is not Hebrew in origin. In a Babylonian poem of 1600 B.C. we find a city called Salem, home of a mighty hero called Daniel on whose exploits the scriptural Daniel is based. As the Absolute, Melchizedek was the source, and that is why he fed and blessed Abram, the Creator. And we said the Creator drew from the Absolute its substance. The Jews dislike the scriptural admission that Melchizedek was greater than their racial father; nevertheless, God the Absolute is greater than God the Creator, at least in extension.

And now if Melchizedek was not a human being, then neither was Abraham. To change the tense, he is a personification of the genetic principle, hence the oft-repeated "seed of Abraham." Sarah, his wife, is planetary substance and so we are right back with Adam and Eve again, also Erebus and Nix. On the first plane, substance is not yet impregnated with genetic ideation, and this is the meaning of Sarah's barrenness. It is, in fact, the meaning of that barrenness, or else virginity, of all scriptural women.

Abraham belonged to the land of light, or spirit, but like all his kind, he wasn't content to stay there. Like Adam, he had work to do, and so the Law God ordered him out of his Eden also. "Get thee out of thy country, and from thy kingdom, and from thy father's house, into a land that I will show thee" 12:1. And Abraham went out, "not knowing whither he went." This is the scriptural way of saying, as we said, that the Creative Principle is not conscious of its work or destination. The impelling force is energy, when free from matter.

And now driven from his Eden, Abram (the spelling thus far) goes to Haran, which Philo says means "the land of holes." And from the Sanskrit we learn that the creative force "Fohat digs holes in space," and from science, "Matter is a hole in the ether." From Haran one with Ham, he goes to Canaan, earth, and there he and his descendants dig many holes, here called wells. On this last safari, the aforesaid "Bible student" makes this naive comment: "When Abraham entered Canaan we do not know because the compilers of these documents had no interest in dates." And thus do the credulous account for dateless mythology. Mythologists are notoriously careless about historical dates, but we suspect this one was about one hundred trillion B.C., for Abraham was the first person in the Trinity of this myth.

In Canaan Abram paused a while at Beth-el, and Beth-el means "house of God," and "the house of God" is Bab-el, the earth. Neither part of the word is Hebrew in origin. The Egyptians had their Beth-Anu, house of Anu, the sun god; and El as a name for God appears in the aforesaid Babylonian poem. Here at Beth-el, Abram built an altar, that same altar Noah built, namely, the world, though as yet prephysical. This is the esoteric meaning of Polyhistor's statement that Abraham came from Uria, light, and created astronomy. As the Creative Principle he created astronomy by creating an aster—star, collectively, the cosmos. Yes, "God geometrizes." And now, perhaps, we can see what lies behind Josephus's naive statement that these ancients lived to great age because of their useful work in astronomy and geography. Again India furnished the idea, a myth about the first astronomer, namely, Asuramaya, "as great a magician as he was an astronomer." He is said to have lived one hundred thousand years ago, which, like the Bible's one thousand, signifies an indefinite period. The letters *ur*, light, appear in his name because Surya was the Sun God; and *maya* means illusion, matter. The Asuryas were many and they fought the Devas, devils, who created this maya-matter. And later we will find Abram fighting the kings of Sodom and Gomorrah, which means the same thing.

Abram knew not whither he went, but the law did; it knew his destiny was Egypt, which throughout the Bible also means, matter, earth. This fact is clearly proved by Revelation 11:8, which speaks of "the great city which spiritually is called Sodom and Egypt where also our Lord was crucified." Now, "our Lord" was not crucified in Egypt unless Egypt is one with the earth. So whether he knew it or not Abram was on his way to Egypt, or matter. This is part of the creative plan and the meaning of Abram's recourse to Hagar, the Egyptian, the Hebrew equivalent of Fetahil's recourse to Ialda-baoth, also matter. This is identical with "the sons of God" consorting with "the daughters of men," and the result is also identical, namely Ishmael, another Cain.

12. And he will be a wild man; his hand (like Cain's) will be against every man, and every man's hand against him . . . (Gen. Chap. 16).

And now again the mythologist, this time the Elohist, covers up the inference as with Seth, by making the line of descent from Isaac, not Ishmael. That it's all myth and allegory is affirmed by Paul in Galatians 4:22–24. "For it is written, that Abraham had two sons, the one by a bondmaid (Hagar), the other by a free woman (Sarah). But he who was of the bondwoman was born after the flesh; but he of the free woman was by promise. *Which things are an allegory* . . ." And so is Abraham, and so is the entire Bible. Therefore to understand this strange book we must know its nature and construction. It is not history or even a sequential allegory, but a mixture of many allegories. Collectively, these constitute the sum of Hebrew legend and tradition. Somewhere around 400 B.C. an Editor selected excerpts from them and inserted them as he saw fit, sometimes a whole chapter, sometimes but a single verse. The key to the system is the little sign ¶.

And now, like Juno, Sarai is jealous of Hagar, and drives her out into the wilderness, as the dragon drove out "the woman clothed with the sun," and Typhon drove out Isis. This wilderness is, as we said, the lower planes of which earth is the seventh; there it is called Beersheba, which means "the seventh well," or "hole" that Fohat dug. Here she too had a place "prepared of God" for her, called Beer-la-hai-roi, which does not mean as interpreted, "the well of the life of vision," but the well, or source, of the stream of life, namely earth, here called Egypt. When Ishmael grows up Sarai takes "a wife out of the land of Egypt" for him.

And now Abram himself goes to Egypt, an excerpt wholly out of place in a Creation myth. Abram never saw Egypt; this part of the descent is reserved for Jacob, Joseph, and others. Obviously it is from another allegory which makes Abram the actor throughout the story. But it follows the usual course. The Abram of the higher planes is portrayed as the soul of honor but as soon as he gets down to Egypt, earth, he is no better than Cain and Noah; in fact, he's so dishonest he gets *deported*. "And Pharaoh commanded his men concerning him: and they sent him away, and his wife and all that he had" (12:20). But Abram didn't learn, for he repeated his act with Abimelech, King of Gerar, in chapter 20. In both stories the cowardly Abram presents Sarai as his sister, lest the foreigners kill him and take her to wife. But the only result was that both kings took her, believing her to be unmarried. For this blameless act, the monstrous God of Abram sent *a plague on both their houses*.

17. And the Lord plagued Pharaoh and his house with great plagues because of Sarai Abram's wife (Chap. 12).

18. For the Lord had fast closed up all the wombs of the house of Abimelech, because of Sarah Abraham's wife (Chap. 20).

But nothing is done to Abram, the cause of it all; on the contrary he is loaded with gifts and sent away. Strange justice this! But only from the human standpoint, which is not the meaning here. This is still genesis, creation, and in this nothing is important but the creative seed; nothing must corrupt it; all things must give way to it. This is not only the meaning here but of many Bible tales that puzzle moral humanity. If it be not so, then nothing in Greek mythology or Mother Goose is more absurd than Jewish scripture. We condemn the Greek myths for their incest and adultery, yet both Noah and his father married their sisters,[1] Abraham married his half-sister, and Lot lay with his daughters—continuity of the cosmic germ plasm, this and nothing more. Later we will read about God killing Onan for

[1] According to the *Polychronicon* and the Dead Sea scrolls. The *Polychronicon:* a history of Creation by Ranulf Higden, 1342.

not doing with it what his conscience forbade him to do. Such things are not in the Bible as historical facts, but that we may see the genetic and nonmoral nature of Causation.

The story of Lot is but another Creation myth, part of which got interwoven with the Abram myth. In this one Lot is the Creator, and so it is his seed that must be preserved. At any rate the parallel is obvious. Like Adam and Cain, he "journied east" to the city of Sodom, which is Enoch, the city of Cain, and the Garden of Adam. Like Noah, he got drunk, and like Noah, Adam, and Abram, he fell asleep, and while he slept his daughters, like Noah's sons, took advantage of him. Since both Lot and Abram are involutionary symbols, we see where and what these wicked cities Sodom and Gomorrah were. Their royal wars, "four kings with five," are but the wars of the Titans, and the slime pits into which they fell are the same slime pits as those of Babel. Their sins and destruction are the same as those in Noah's day. That they were destroyed is but a mythologist's way of saying, as we said, that the higher planes in Involution are wiped out when the lower ones are formed. And so are their gods: Abram dies and gives way to Isaac; Isaac dies and gives way to Jacob. These are the Trinity of this myth, and all three disappear that Joseph, the fourth, may carry on.

This is the creative process; the sad lot of Lot's wife is a hint of what happens to those who refuse to cooperate. Once started, life cannot turn back; it must go on or perish. Lot's wife looking back at her city is but the Hebrew parallel of the Greek myth of Orpheus looking back at Eurydice. And let us not forget the Roman god, Ridiculus, "he who turns or causes to turn back"; that's ridiculous. So were the angels who refused to go on and create, and so got punished. And Jesus declared, "No man, having put his hand to the plow, and looking back, is fit for the kingdom of God" (Luke 9:62). These lessons in Evolution have been wholly lost on us, particularly our reactionaries, fundamentalists, etc. These are the children of Lot's wife and there are lots and lots of them. They too look to the past and so become pillars of unproductiveness. They cry out against war and blame the progressives for it, but they are the real cause of war—inertia, inaction, inadequacy. Like Adam they would cling to "the

tree of life" instead of "the tree of knowledge." Throughout this
work we have advocated conscious knowledge of and coopera-
tion with this forward process; we have tried to show that our
social disasters are but the modern "flood" that nature hurls
upon our ignorance and inertia, and now we find it is "Bible
teaching."

1. After these things the word of the Lord came unto Abram in a
vision, saying, Fear not, Abram: I am thy shield, and thy exceeding
great reward (Chap. 15).

As Abram represents the Creative Principle, he is also the
Creator. That there should be another Creator over and above
this Creator is quite unnecessary, save to a religionizing mythologist. The only possible distinction between these two is
that of genetic consciousness and its fractious energy. Since
neither of these is conscious or moral, why divinify the one and
satanize the other, thereby confusing all posterity?

5. And he brought him forth abroad, and said, Look now toward
heaven, and tell the stars, if thou be able to number them: and he said
unto him, So shall thy seed be.

Since Abram is the Creator, the author in his reference to
"seed" is telling us a truth we have refused to see for two thousand years, namely, that this "seed" is the planetary seed, and
from it came the world and all upon it. Had this basic idea been
realized and philosophically adhered to, religion would never
have risen to hide from us "the cosmic facts of life."

If as some believe this promise was given only to the Jews,
then it was never fulfilled, for the Jews are not numberless as
the stars or the dust of the earth as per chapter 13. That promise
was planetary not racial.

Just here we can slay two more illusions, peculiarly Jewish.
First, "The chosen people." "How odd that God should choose
the Jews!" Well, He didn't. Throughout the Old Testament and
Revelation the Jews are but symbols of the creative elements,

and "the chosen people" are the elements chosen from space for this particular world. Second, "And in thy seed shall all the nations of the earth be blessed" (22:18), repeated to Isaac (26:4). The seed here is the genetic world seed and it is this, life, not Jewry, that blesses nations. Yet it is upon this purely symbolic statement the Jews believe they bless all countries in which they dwell. Apparently Pharaoh and Abimelech did not think Abram and Isaac blessed their countries for they drove them both out. And both myth and history repeat themselves. It is this false sense of divine selection and separateness that underlies much, not all, of their tragic history. Only when they divest themselves of these illusions will they become an assimilable and acceptable part of humanity.

In the following verses we see what this blind belief and ignorance of Reality can do.

14. And the Lord said unto Abram, after that Lot was separated from him, Lift up now thine eyes, and look from the place where thou art northward, and southward, and eastward, and westward:
15. For all the land which thou seest, to thee will I give it, and to thy seed for ever.
16. And I will make thy seed as the dust of the earth: so that if a man can number the dust of the earth, then shall thy seed also be numbered (Chap. 13).

This is the Creator's seed, and the promise it holds is but the promise contained in every seed. In its cosmic sense it is the earth. This is "the Promised Land," this is "the Holy Land," and it was not given to the Jews but to all life.

17. Arise, walk through the land in the length of it and in the breadth of it; for I will give it unto thee (Chap. 13).
6. And I will make thee exceeding fruitful, and I will make nations of thee, and kings shall come out of thee.
8. And I will give unto thee, and to thy seed after thee, the land wherein thou art a stranger, all the land of Canaan, for an everlasting possession; and I will be their God (Chap. 17).

Canaan is the earth and the fulfillment of the promise, and yet it is upon this purely literal and mythological promise the Jews lay claim to Palestine. Here it is as recently stated: "For orthodox Zionism began with the divine pronouncement to our first Patriarch 'lift up now thine eyes and look from the place where thou art, northward, southward, eastward, and westward, for all the land which thou seest to thee will I give it and to thy seed forever.' These words which constitute our deed to Palestine, do not originate in the Balfour Declaration. They are in the Torah. The settlement of Palestine is a religious commandment which must be observed as a Divine decree." *Facts about Fictions Concerning the Jews,* put out by the Anti-Defamation League of B'nai Brith. It should have been titled *Fictions about Facts Concerning Reality.* The Jews must learn that God's decree is not in Torah but in terra, in history not mythology.

According to able historians, the only part of Palestine they ever controlled was Jerusalem and its immediate vicinity; the rest was always under the dominant power of the time, Assyria, Persia, Greece, Rome, etc. Concerning this, G. B. Winton wrote thus: "Darius had divided his empire into satrapies, and Judea formed part of the satrapy which included Cyprus and the whole of Syria. It was a small territory, consisting only of Jerusalem and the country immediately round its walls. Under such a regime there was no room for a Jewish king, and the leadership of the people devolved on its religious head, the hereditary high priest." In *The Educator.* And from the *Encyclopaedia Britannica:* "We may draw the inference that they formed an insignificant item in the population of a small province of the Persian Empire." Where then is the Jewish claim to all Palestine? It is based on nothing more substantial than mythology. Some of their wiser members are well aware of this. As Rabbi Elmer Berger said: "Actually, there is no historical proof that the present state of Israel ever was the ancestral homeland of the Jews."

The Jews have no more right to Palestine than any other people; they never conquered it, they never owned it. When we add up the time the Bible says the Jews were in captivity and subjection to other countries, we find it is nearly 700 years, the greater part of their ancient history. And what have they done since then to substantiate their claim? Nothing except brainwash the benighted Christians. That accomplished, they did not have to do anything save walk in and take possession. Those statesmen, presidents and premiers included, who take their scriptures literally should ponder well this part of them: "I will make Jerusalem a stone of burden for all the people; all that burden themselves with it shall be sore wounded" (Zech. 12:3). They should also read the rest of this fake promise: all the land between the Nile and the Euphrates (Gen. 15:18). This is the ultimate goal. Those believers in scriptural prophecy should consider *The Lehnin Prophecy*: "Israel will do a deed unspeakable, that only death can redeem." The deed has been done, the redeeming has yet to come. The fate of Israel is not yet settled, its mythical God to the contrary.

The Gentiles have had sufficient experience with the Jews to know their commercial cunning; why then do they not suspect this in their literature? They don't because in this that cunning is too great for their matter-blinded souls to see. Now if their eyes are opened they should do something to redress the wrong they did in their blind self-righteousness.

The theft of a country, a million Arabs driven out to starve, that is what belief in literal mythology can do. Instead of "the word of God" it should be called the work of the devil. Its cunning is so diabolical it has deceived the entire world for two thousand years. The result, as stated, is sixteen hundred years of darkness, Crusade and Inquisition, prejudice and bigotry, and now war in the source of them. It's time we rid ourselves of this troublemaker.

It's time also we examined that repeated statement, "And God said." Why is it so persistently used throughout the Bible? This same book tells us no man has seen God, yet every scriptural writer declares he heard Him. Is this but primitive man mistaking his own inner promptings for the voice of God, or is it a trick of the priestly trade? It is the latter and used only to give what they wanted divine authority. Spinoza, himself a Jew, said, whatever the Jews thought, they asserted God said it. God speaks not until he speaks as man. Once this simple fact is known, the trick no longer works.

And now this talkative God foretells the future of his "chosen."

13. And he said unto Abram, Know of a surety that thy seed shall be a stranger in a land that is not theirs, and shall serve them; and they shall afflict them four hundred years.

If the gift of Palestine was a "Divine pronouncement" and a decree of God, then so is this. Why then call their bondage unjust and blame the Egyptians? Why slander them, and destroy them as Moses did?

16. But in the fourth generation they shall come hither again . . . (Chap. 15).

Do four generations make four hundred years? No matter, we have here the prophecy on which the Hebrew captivity in Egypt is based. This we will deal with more fully in Exodus; here we will say only that this is as spurious as all the rest. The Jews were never in bondage in Egypt save mythologically. The four hundred years are the four cycles in Involution and the fourth generation represents the earth. From this life will arise and ultimately return to its source. As yet it is still on the way down and so Abram now descends to a lower plane and acquires a new name.

12. And when the sun was going down, a deep sleep fell upon Abram; and, lo, a horror of great darkness fell upon him.
17. And it came to pass, that, when the sun went down, and it was dark, behold a smoking furnace, and a burning lamp that passed between those pieces (Chap. 15).

So Abram also slept, but it is not the same sleep as that of Adam and Noah in dense matter. It is the sleep and the horror of the creative "spirit" as it descends into materiality. The primordial light has gone out, but soon it appears again as "a smoking furnace and a burning lamp." That smoking furnace and burning lamp is the earth in its sun period.

We are here taking liberties with the scriptural sequence, but since the Editor did likewise, innumerable times, we see no reason why we should not. Indeed without some rearrangement the true sequence, Creation, is lost. And who knows, perhaps the original sequence was confused for just that purpose.

3. And Abram fell on his face: and God talked with him, saying,
4. As for me, behold, my covenant is with thee, and thou shalt be a father of many nations (biologically, not ethnologically).
5. Neither shall thy name any more be called Abram, but thy name shall be Abraham; for a father of many nations have I made thee (Chap. 17).

Here we bid farewell to Abram; he has acquired *h*, material being, and is now Abraham. It's nothing new in mythology. "From this day forth thy name shall no more be Alkeides but Heracles (Hercules)." So spake Apollo through his priestess. And let us not forget the other is through a priest.

And God made a covenant with Abraham, and what a strange covenant it is—circumcision. Some may wonder why this mark of the "chosen" wasn't started with Adam. If the removal of the foreskin was so important to God, why did He put it on in the first place? Removing it is God correcting His own mistake. But no, the mistake was the Jews' and one of the most ridiculous results of literalism in all history. This is Creation and the foreskin here is the Creator's, not man's. It is His generative obstruction that must be removed, and this takes place in Evolution, or more correctly Devolution, the planetary genetic getting rid of its physical "coats of skin." In Involution it put these on. As the Kabbalah says, "The spirit clothes itself to come down and unclothes itself to go up." *The Secret Doctrine* speaks of these, and to the earth, its Creator might well have said, "Cease thy complaints. Thy seven (fore)skins are still on thee." See p. 72.

Actually this rite *was* started with Adam, for Abraham and Adam are one. Racially, however, it was not started with either.

According to Spengler ". . . it was in the Captivity that circumcision and the (Chaldean) Sabbath were first acquired, as rites, by the Jews." All knowledge of occult meanings lost by then, they took their myths literally and mutilated their bodies. We wonder what they would have done if instead of circumcise the myth had said *castrate*, as in the Greek. But this, we presume, is another of those Jewish refinements of Greek mythology.

Be this as it may, it is a priestly deception even in their mythology, for it does not belong here. Genesis 17:9–14 is a later interpolation by the priesthood. In their day circumcision had become a religious rite, hygienic in nature, but the priests, requiring a divine authority for it, inserted it in Genesis. Thereafter the Jews fell victim to their own ignorance not of its worth but of its origin. And then we are told it doesn't matter what we believe; it's what we do that matters. Do you not know that beliefs are stronger than facts? For thousands of years belief in a flat earth outweighed the natural fact. For thousands of years belief in a mythical hell terrified humanity, and for thousands of years belief in a covenant religion sustained an institutional parasite. Oh yes, it matters what we believe, and it's time we had some facts to believe in.

No longer Abram, pure spirit, the Creative Principle is now approaching the plane of genetic fecundation of the hitherto barren energy, and so the barren Sarah now conceives and brings forth the second person in the Trinity, namely Isaac. And to test the virtuous Abraham, God tempts him as he tempted Adam.

1. And it came to pass after these things, that God did tempt Abraham, and said unto him, Abraham: and he said, Behold, here I am.

2. And he said, Take now thy son, thine only son Isaac, whom thou lovest, and get thee into the land of Moriah; and offer him there for a burnt offering upon one of the mountains which I will tell thee of (Chap. 22).

What a God we have here! He believes in burnt offerings which the Jews later renounced and denounced. He sacrificed his own Son and here demands a man to sacrifice his. It makes sense only cosmologically. The first element must give up its "only begotten son," the second element, that the third and lower ones may be. This, of course, cannot be done, even in mythology, until the son also has a son, and so a lamb is substituted. In reading this, the pious believer no doubt sighs and thanks his God for sparing the little Isaac, never suspecting the subtle deception that lurks therein. Yet such there is, for Isaac is this lamb, Aries, "slain from the foundation of the world." This too is an old story and like so many others in the Bible, originated in India. Siva, like Abraham, was about to sacrifice his son on a funeral pyre, but his God, repenting, miraculously provided a rhinoceros instead. In a series of pictures the rhino is shown first with his horn caught in a tree, and later upon the pyre, the son kindling the fire. And Sanchoniathon tells us that Saturn offered his "only begotten son" to his father Uranus. Unlike his father, Isaac is not a warrior but a meek, mild-tempered man who "went out to meditate in the fields (of space) at eventide"; thus in every way corresponding with the son, or second person in the Trinity—always in mythology, slain for the sins, not of man, but of Man, the Creator. This is the only sin the Old Testament deals with. Why then did not its authors say so in plain words? For many reasons: first, because it wasn't being done in those days. This was the age of mythology, allegory, metonomy, synecdoche, and all the other literary subterfuges. Second, because there can be no priesthood where the truth is known. Third, this was priestly knowledge and then as now must be kept from the ignorant masses. To this is due much of the race's ignorance today; therefore it must be exposed, and its "divine authority" destroyed. It served the benighted Arian and Piscean ages but it will not do for the Aquarian; the race cannot go on forever living by a delusion.

The only authority for the Bible is the creative process, and now the first element completes its part of it.

19. So Abraham returned unto his young men, and they rose up and went together to Beer-sheba; and Abraham dwelt at Beer-sheba (Chap. 22).

Abraham himself is now down where he sent Hagar. "How the mighty have fallen"; we could even say the Almighty.

2. And Sarah died in Kirjath-arba; the same is Hebron in the land of Canaan: and Abraham came to mourn for Sarah, and to weep for her (Chap. 23).

You may have noticed that there is no account of Eve's death in the Bible. Then why should Sarah die? Because Sarah and Eve are not identical. Eve is the eternal Earth Mother, still existing, while Sarah is only first-plane substance. Yet, in spite of monotheism, she gives way to the next, which is Rebekah, Isaac's wife. But she too must go "the way of all" spirit, giving place to Rachel. Such is the process.

Here in Canaan, earth, Abraham virtuously bargains for a burial place. In spite of a free gift of land, he insists on paying for it—honest Abraham! In chapter 14 he will not take a thread, not even a shoe latchet that is not his—and thus did these ancient freebooters establish for themselves an honorable beginning.

Isaac

In due time Isaac grows to manhood, and his father is greatly worried about a wife for him; no other will do save one of his own people. And so this father of clannishness sends a servant back to their kinsmen for a spouse, namely, Rebekah, daughter of Bethuel, again of "the house of God." Isaac must not go back himself. Here we have again that fear lest the Creative Principle return and live forever as spirit.

And the servant found Rebekah at a well and brought her to Isaac. But Rebekah, like Sarai, was barren, and so Isaac, like Abram, had to beg the Lord for offspring. Curious is it not, that in those days of prolific progeny all these scriptural women were barren? Not when you understand them; they are planetary women, primordial substance, not yet endowed with genetic ideation. Time alone brings this about and by a very natural process. This would not do for a religion and so religion's God made Rebekah fruitful.

24. And when her days to be delivered were fulfilled, behold, there were twins in her womb (Chap. 25).

The Hebrew Gemini. One is stronger than the other, and the weak must serve the strong, as did Eve and Abel.[2] The two are consciousness and energy, and one shall dominate the other. Now we may assume that the original consciousness in the "womb" of space is older than the *planetary* energy, hence Esau, the older, should be consciousness, and Jacob, energy but wherever two males are employed there is confusion, and we suspect duplication also. Both Jacob and Esau represent the Creator, and perhaps sometime there was an Esau myth as we suspect there was of Lot and Ishmael. Esau is Ishmael and Jacob is Isaac; as Ishmael had twelve children, we can assume Esau had also. With these he founds a city, Petra, stone, earth, in Edom, which is Eden. Jacob has twelve children and goes to Egypt, which is also earth. Esau was first, and he was "red all over," like Adam, "red earth," and Jacob, following after, "took hold of Esau's heel" —and so became a "heel" himself. And Esau was a hunter of the fields (of space) and Jacob was a plain man dwelling in tents—the "sheaths" or "skins" put on in Involution. Esau was a rough man but Jacob was "a smoothe man." Indeed he was; he robbed his brother of his birthright, deceived his father and also his father-in-law.

Except for the rights of primogeniture, the Bible does not tell us what Esau's birthright was, but perhaps we can. In the creative process consciousness must forfeit its spiritual nature to energy, and energy drags it down to dense matter, here called a "mess of pottage." Spirit became matter; this is the tragedy and sin of all mythology including the scriptures. Such was Esau's and sometimes I think the Gentiles must be his children, since in swallowing this Semitic "mess of pottage" they sold *their* birthright, reason. "Spiritually, we are all Semites," said Pius XI. Yes, and that is what's the matter with us spiritually. We must now regain the birthright this Semitic mess of poison robbed us of.

[2] In a Greek myth the twins Proetus and Acrisius struggled with each other in the womb of Queen Algaia, and later for the Argive throne.

As with Abram, a great darkness now comes upon Isaac; old and ready to die, he would bless his eldest, Esau, but Rebekah, the female, loved materiality more, and so she taught her son to be dishonest, to cheat his father as he had cheated his brother. Together mother and son deceive Isaac so that he gives Jacob the blessing intended for Esau. That Isaac could not recall his misplaced blessing is but an occultist's way of presenting nature's irrevocable process: "What I have written, I have written." In the next chapter Isaac knows of the deception yet he cannot revoke the blessing; instead, he blesses Jacob again and again.

"The voice is Jacob's voice, but the hands are the hands of Esau." We should keep this statement in mind whenever we read the Bible. Its voice is the voice of literalism, but the hand that wrote it is the hand of occultism. We harkened to the voice and it deceived us. Yet the hand has warned us; it tells us Jacob, the voice, was a deceiver, a thief and a scoundrel.

The story, however, is cosmological, and so Isaac prophesied that the day would come when Esau would triumph over his unscrupulous brother—and humanly, let's hope it is now.

40. . . . and it shall come to pass when thou shalt have the dominion, that thou shalt break his yoke from off thy neck (Chap. 27).

And when will this be, cosmologically? In Evolution. Here consciousness breaks the yoke of matter and eventually gains dominion. Did Jew and Gentile understand their scriptures, this would be the object of their effort today. It is the hold that matter and material things have upon our consciousness that causes all our troubles; therefore it must be broken. This is the work of the remaining half of the Zodiacal Night.

In this story, however, we're still in Involution and on the second plane. The time has come to move on and so—

1. . . . there was a famine in the land, besides the first famine that was in the days of Abraham . . . (Chap. 26).

There is a famine on every plane when its work is done. There was one in Abraham's day; there was one in Isaac's day; and soon we will find another driving Jacob down to Egypt, earth. Isaac, however, was not allowed to go, only his seed, and so we come to Jacob.

Jacob

When Esau finally realized what Jacob had done to him, he determined to kill his brother—the Cain and Abel aspect of this myth—but Rebekah, overhearing the plot, warned Jacob and sent him off to parts unknown.

10. And Jacob went out from Beer-sheba, and went toward Haran.
11. And he lighted upon a certain place, and tarried there all night, because the sun was set; and he took of the stones of that place, and put them for his pillows, and lay down in that place to sleep.
12. And he dreamed, and behold a ladder set up on the earth, and the top of it reached to heaven: and behold the angels of God ascending and descending on it (Chap. 28).

Here we have another mystery that is no mystery—Jacob's ladder. This *scala coeli*, or ladder of heaven, is the seven-runged ladder of the planetary entity, here involutionary; and the "angels of God" that ascend and descend upon it are the creative forces. This is the involutionary Tower of Babel, which also reached to heaven. Now in spite of the "chosen" their God must have revealed this to the Persians also for they too had their *scala coeli*, a ladder of seven rungs on which the souls of earth descended and ascended. And the Brahmins had theirs, the sacred Mount Meru, reached by seven steps. Jacob called "the name of that place Beth-el," "house of God," and the "house of God" is the earth. And he awakened from his dream and said, "How dreadful is this place! this is none other than the house of God." Yes, this is El Shaddai's house and we too said it was a dreadful place. In it we all must suffer and it's time we learned the reason.

Why the possessive Jacob had to use stones for a pillow is not stated; however he piled them together and called them the "house of God." For once this is not figurative, as when we say the Church is God's house. The stones are symbols of this earth; and that we may know that Esau helped to build it, we are told he went south of the Dead Sea (dead sun) and there "reared Petra, a glorious capital," and petra means stone. Jacob and Esau are Jachin and Boaz, whose synergistic efforts produced this world. The Jhwhist shows us their far from holy nature. The dream is from the Elohist, but it ends with a touch that is surely priestly—"and of all that thou shalt give me I will surely give the tenth unto thee"—the divine authority for tithes. By the time we reach Malachi, the curse of God is called down on all who refuse to pay them. This little story confirms our opinion that the Elohist represents the transitional stage between the mythologizing Jhwhist and the religionizing Priest.

In chapter 32 we have another touch that is pure cosmogony mythologized. In all Creation myths, the gods who deal with fire (cosmic), forging thunderbolts, armor, and so on, are lame— Agni, Reginn, Vulcan, Hephaestus, and even Oedipus, cripple-foot. It is not just a coincidence that Jacob becomes lame at this time. He had just sent his possessions over the river Jabbok which means *muddy*, in other words, *matter*; later we will meet it again as Jordan. Going over these is the going-over of the Life Principle from the spiritual third to the material four. In the Greek myth this going-over or down was Dia-bolos, Devil, and Jacob is its Hebrew equivalent. Jacob's purpose here was to placate Esau with gifts, and Esau, the Bible says was Edom. It could have said Eden, for that is what it is, the lower involutionary planes. To the spirit this is a "great darkness," and as with Abram and Isaac, Jacob is afraid, so he tarried a while to pray for safety.

24. And Jacob was left alone; and there wrestled a man (force) with him until the breaking of the day (the fourth in Creation).

25. And when he saw that he prevailed not against him, he touched the hollow of his thigh; and the hollow of Jacob's thigh was out of joint, as he wrestled with him.

31. And as he passed over Penuel the sun rose upon him, and he halted upon his thigh.

In the creative process, accreting matter cripples spirit and so we have a crippled person in all mythologies. But think not of this as mere mythology, or even metaphysics; it is a fact in nature. At this very moment the free spirit of the sun is being "touched" and crippled by matter. In time it will become "Prometheus Bound."

32. Therefore the children of Israel eat not of the sinew which shrank, which is upon the hollow of the thigh, unto this day; because he touched the hollow of Jacob's thigh in the sinew that shrank.

Here begins a list of mythological prohibitions that ends in a dietary religion. And such are the customs of all religions, misunderstood mythology.

Verse 30 tells us that during this wrestling match Jacob saw God face to face. How can we harmonize this with those other statements: "No man hath seen God at any time," and "There shall no man see me and live"? Very easily; Jacob was not a man. He was the Life Principle on the third involutionary plane, and here his name is changed because henceforth that Principle is changed.

The Pentateuch and most of the New Testament are based on the creative process, and we said that where they depart from it we would challenge them. We have here one such case.

Esau married two Hittite women, "which were a grief of mind unto Isaac and to Rebekah," and so they began to worry lest Jacob marry a woman of Canaan, which is earth. Cosmologically, this was right but to the priest it was wrong; he must marry one of his own race. And this, like circumcision, has come down to us in the flesh—race inbreeding. For a Jew to marry outside his race is a grave offense, but this source of the rule is but the mythological miscegenation of "the sons of God" and the mortal women. Thus Esau's offense was but that of Noah's day, and it was no offense. It was right but the priest sends Jacob out to find a wife among his own.

And so he too journeys east, and soon beside a well he finds Rachel watering her sheep as Rebekah watered her camel. And not only did she water them; she was them, for Rachel means

"God's ewe," or sheep; and a sheep, or lamb, is the symbol of the sacrificed Life Principle. And Rachel was the daughter of Laban, which means light, and from this one of our "great Bible students" concluded Laban and his daughters were albinos. Such is the wisdom-knowledge of modern man! Laban was Jacob's uncle and when Rachel brought the stranger home, Laban said to him, ". . . surely thou are my bone and my flesh. And he abode with him the space of a month" (29:14). Thus Jacob was taken in by Laban, and later Laban was "taken in" by Jacob. Isaac's blessing and God's promise of the earth were not enough for him; he also cheated and "crippled" Laban, which is but a *revolutio* of the wrestling match.

1. And he heard the words of Laban's sons, saying, Jacob hath taken away all that was our father's; and of that which was our father's hath he gotten all this glory (Chap. 31).

But Laban also cheated Jacob, not only in wages "ten times" but in women also; he substituted Leah for Rachel on the wedding night. One would think that a smoothie like Jacob would know his women, but sophisticated moderns have no right to laugh, for they don't know Leah from Rachel either. The word *Leah* means weary ("Leah, the Forsaken"). And our version says she was "tender-eyed," therefore sweet and beautiful, we think, but the original meaning was tender in the sense of sore and unpleasant—hence the fraud by night.

Jacob must have been as drunk as Lot and as dumb as Adam, and we are not being disrespectful of "holy scripture"; merely explaining unholy nature and exposing priestly fraud. Laban's excuse was that the younger must not marry before the first-born. If this was the law, one would think that Laban would have told his future son-in-law the fact before the marriage, not after. In our society this act would be a serious offense but not in nature. In the creative process, first elements come first, hence Leah the elder. Throughout the Bible the youngest off-spring means forward in the creative process; Jacob's love for the younger Rachel is his adherence to it.

So now Laban promises Jacob the younger daughter if he will

work another seven years. These various seven years, three in all, are the septenary stages in Involution. Laban calls them weeks; "fulfill her week," he said. These, however, are planetary weeks and identical with the "days" of the first chapter.

And now the hard-working Jacob earns a different kind of wages, the wages of bigamy. He marries Rachel also, but alas, she too is barren; but not for long, for now begins the champion baby marathon of all history, and even mythology. Leah and Rachel, vying for Jacob's favor through offspring, race not only with each other, but use their handmaidens to help them win. They also use mandrakes. This little touch is not even mythology, but local superstition. The Druses of Syria, even today, have a legend that "the sons of God" created man by animating the plant mandragora, or man-dragon. The plant is shaped like a man and so became a symbol of fertility to barren women. Apparently it worked, for the result of this marital race was twelve sons and one daughter, of which more anon.

And now Jacob would leave Laban—but not with much. By another sly deception, he separates the good cattle from the scrubs and steals away in the night.³ Jacob was a thief and his wife was no better. She stole her father's gods, or images, and carried them away to another land. And when Laban, in his effort to recover them, caught up with her, she "put them in the camels' furniture and sat on them. And Laban searched all the tent but found them not" (31:34). No wonder the young Joseph made good in Egypt; with such a parentage, how could he fail? And what about these gods that Laban thought so much of? We thought the Jews were monotheists from Abraham on. All this, however, is but Jacob's voice; let us see what is in Esau's hand. These people represent the Creative Principle, therefore the images that Rachel took were those of the Creator, namely, the archetypal forms. These, as symbolized by her act, were carried downward, hidden in the carrier's furniture, the planetary genes. This is why Laban did nothing to the culprits; on the contrary, he said, "I have learned by experience that the Lord

³ In a Greek parallel, if not source, Hermes, the god of thieves, granted Autolycus, a master thief, the power to metamorphose the cattle he stole from Sisyphus.

hath blessed me for thy sake." And did we not say that the Creator had to learn by experience? We did, and so did the Greeks—Pro-metheus, pre, or involutionary, learning. And in Evolution he's been learning for billions of years, and he doesn't know yet how to make a perfect being. We've been long in getting around to this "divine authority" for our statement, but here it is. So with our other statements; they are all here in "God's word," but you have to *know them before you can see them*.

And now we find that Jacob is a coward also. On learning that Esau is coming against him, he divides his flock and also his family and servants. The latter, he puts in front as a shield, his wives and children next, while he stays behind to pray for safety. And this is the man whom God chose to father his "chosen people." Not in all pagan mythology can you find so despicable a character; only Joshua's God outdoes him. Yet the Jhwhist is right and the rest are wrong. It is he who gives us the true nature of the Creative Principle, and we here repeat, sinful Adam, murderous Cain, drunken Noah, and thieving Jacob—in other words, non-moral nature; the rest is priestly deception. Antedating the priests by centuries, the Jhwhist accords with the prehistoric Greeks, and just as mythology recedes from their time does it become "crooked and deceitful from the bottom." In due time, A.D. and the New Testament, it doesn't make sense at all.

Chapter 34 carries on the murderous process. Hamor the Hivite and his sons invite Jacob and his tribe to live with them. This they will do only if the Hivites are circumcised like them. In spite of the racial insolence and the covenant being only with Abraham and his descendants, the host agrees, and while they are sore, Simeon and Levi, Jacob's sons, murder them and take their possessions. The cause of it all was Hamor's son Shechem, who we later learn is a country. This was not just murder; it was war. Though not the first, one would think that a moral God would have punished the whole vicious lot of them; but no, He immediately appears to Jacob, blesses him again and promises him the world. A strange kind of God this! A blesser of murderers, a supporter of thieves. Here we would ask the Christian world why it respects this book, its people and its

God? To extricate itself from its dilemma it tells us this was but the primitive concept of a primitive people, later corrected. I say it is the very opposite. This is prereligious knowledge of natural Causation, later perverted by those who sought to establish a divine and holy basis for a power-hungry priesthood. In our concept of a nonmoral principle we get back beyond this to the truth.

And now this morally impossible God appears again and, as with Abram, changes Jacob's name. ". . . thy name shall not be called any more Jacob, but Israel shall be thy name . . ." (35:10). Jacob becomes Israel at exactly the same point in the Hebrew myth that Uranus became Cronos in the Greek. And there is apparently some connection here, for Movers tells us, "Kronus Saturn was called by the Phoenicians, Israel." And Philo makes the same statement. Jacob or Yakub, from the root word *yak*, means one, unity, but Israel is plural, collective and multiple.

And so from here on, the homogeneous one becomes the heterogeneous many, as in Herbert Spencer. As we put it, primordial substance became discrete, resulting in the "monadic host." And this is Israel, the many, here personified as twelve sons. These twelve appear in this myth at exactly the same time and place in the creative process as the twelve Titans in the Greek myth. These titanic twelve create the world and man, and the Hebrew twelve create the human race, or so says Israel. These are the Elohim of the Elohist's account, and the chief Eloah said to the rest, "Let us make man in our image"—a complete contradiction of subsequent monotheism.

So now begins the history of Jacob's sons. All of them were born in or near Beth-el, the house of God, later changed to Beth-el-hem and finally to Bethlehem, where another "son of God" was born. The word means *house of bread*, but not earthly bread, cosmic bread, the substance of the earth. This Rachel was, and now this provided, she dies, and Jacob sets up a pillar "that is the pillar of Rachel's grave unto this day"—and ours. A tomb now adorns the spot and credulous pilgrims believe that it is Rachel's grave, when all the while the "pillar" but marks the end of the spiritual planes and the beginning of the material. Proof of this is also here but again you must know it to see it.

The youngest of Jacob's children was Benjamin, which means, "son of the right hand." Here we should ask, The right hand of what? In mythology and cosmology, it means the right hand of Being, namely Evolution. This is the "right hand of God," the left being Involution, personified by Joseph.

3. And Israel loved Joseph more than all his children, because he was the son of his old age: and he made him a coat of many colors (Chap. 37).

Please note the wording here, "Israel loved Joseph more than all his children," not just more than any of his children, and also the reason given, "because he was the son of his old age." The latter is not usually the rule in large families; furthermore, Benjamin was still younger. What then does it mean? It means only that the third stage in Creation is drawing to a close and that a successor must be established—a matter for the narrator to determine. And this is how he does it: Besides having Jacob love Joseph more than all the others, he has this chosen one dream a prophetic dream in which he sees himself as ruler over his brothers. Naturally this offends these older and save in mythology, rightful heirs, and so they seek to kill him—the Cain and Abel of this version. So Joseph is the destined successor and his destiny, earth, here called Egypt, clothed in his "coat of many colors"—the earth's involutionary and colorful aura. And how many know that, when reading of some mythical being dying and *giving up the ghost*, this is the *ghost* he is giving up? This may even be a cosmic phenomenon, that sudden flare-up called a nova—the unused solar gases leaving, and lighting the cosmic dust clouds, at the demise of a sun. Well, the aura leaves a human body at death, and "as below, so above."

9

Joseph

11. And his brethren envied him; but his father observed the saying.

12. And their brethren went to feed their father's flock in Shechem (Chap. 37).

Shechem was the son of Hamor, slain by Simeon and Levi, but now we find he is a land. And Jacob sent Joseph into this land to find his brothers, but they had departed.

15. And a certain man found him, and, behold, he was wandering (planetlike) in the field (of space): and the man asked him, saying, What seekest thou?

16. And he said, I seek my brethren: tell me, I pray thee, where they feed their flocks.

The earth in its sun stage with its flock of planets. When Apollo, the sun, was banished he fed the flocks of King Admetus.

17. And the man said, They are departed hence; for I heard them say, Let us go to Dothan. And Joseph went after his brethren, and found them in Dothan.

These various places, Shechem, Dothan, and so forth, are but progressive stages in the descent towards matter, earth, which we are told, is but a "hole in the ether." And when Joseph arrives his jealous brothers throw him into a hole, or pit—that "bottomless pit" of Revelation. This then is but the Old Testament version of Satan being thrown into the pit called Hell, Lucifer into the pit called Orcus, the Titans into Tartarus, and Mahasura into Honderah. And "they stripped Joseph out of his coat, his coat of many colors that was on him"; in other words, he became "naked" as were Adam, Noah, Ishtar, Innana, and all the other Creators.

Now according to the New Testament it was Joseph's brothers who sold him "down the river," but according to this chapter, King James version, it was first the Midianites and then the Ishmaelites. "Then there passed by Midianites merchantmen; and they drew and lifted up Joseph out of the pit, and sold Joseph to the Ishmaelites for twenty pieces of silver; and they brought Joseph into Egypt" (37:28). And verse 36 says, "And the Midianites sold him into Egypt unto Potiphar, an officer of Pharaoh's, and captain of the guard." Yet in Acts 7:9 we read: "And the patriarchs moved with envy, sold Joseph into Egypt, but God was with him." And Genesis 45:4, where Joseph is speaking to his brothers, reads, ". . . I am Joseph your brother whom ye sold into Egypt." Who then did sell Joseph, and why? The answer is given in 45:5: "Now therefore be not grieved, nor angry with yourselves, that ye sold me hither: for *God did send me* before you to preserve life." And that is the key to the whole story.

These various versions seem to be among the many contradictions our "higher critics" search for: but no, for the *Midi-*anites, the Ishmaelites, and the God who was with them are all one— the planetary entity. The Ishmaelites were the descendants of Ishmael, son of Hagar the Egyptian, and the Midi-anites were the forces of the middle planes between spirit and matter. The ancient people of that name called themselves "Sons of the snake," the genetic serpent. This it was that sold Joseph, down the stream of life, into Egypt, earth. The crime then was no more moral than that of Adam or Cain; it was to be. This selling of Joseph into slavery in Egypt is but the parallel of Noah forcing his son Ham into slavery to his brothers, particularly Shem or Chem, which also is Egypt.

And now that we may see the purely genetic nature of this process, the story of Joseph is interrupted here and that of Onan is presented, an editorial act no one can understand who does not know the Bible's theme is Creation. Onan represents the genetic principle, hence the Creator. Now Judah, Onan's father (anything is possible in mythology), commands him to go in and lie with his brother's wife, to preserve the seed, which, from a moral standpoint, was contrary to Onan's conscience. He therefore refused, but instead of commending him, "God slew him." More strange justice: a moral God slays a man for following his moral conscience, and blesses thieves and murderers. You see, this Book is preposterous save as we interpret it. This God is the nonmoral genetic principle, here the planetary seed; and from its standpoint nothing matters but its own continuity, and nothing is wrong that is conducive to its purpose. This is the central fact that we must keep in mind if we would understand the subsequent atrocities of the Bible. The rest of Chapter 38 carries on the genetic process—Judah's misconduct with his daughter-in-law who plays the harlot. Thus the chapter is a genetic prelude and key to Joseph in Egypt.

His story, in fact, begins in the same vein. He is sold to Potiphar, the guard, that is, the guardian law of matter; and the symbol of matter is woman. The Bible does not tell us her name, but it was Zuleika.[1]

7. And it came to pass after these things, that his master's wife cast her eyes upon Joseph; and she said, Lie with me.

12. And she caught him by his garment, saying, Lie with me: and he left his garment in her hand, and fled, and got him out (Chap. 39).

Joseph is virtuous Adam and Prometheus, and so he will have naught to do with sensuous matter, as yet. And yet how the

---

[1] According to Robert Graves, the story of Joseph and Zuleika was taken from the Egyptian "Tale of Two Brothers."

inner contradicts the outer, for this is precisely what happens to Joseph. Since "Hell hath no fury like a woman scorned," the hussy has him thrown into that prison that is matter. Here he meets Pharaoh's chief baker and butler, personifications of the earth's substance and life's sustenance. Both these dreamed strange dreams that only Joseph could interpret. Joseph's brothers called him a dreamer and now we find him an interpreter of dreams, including Pharaoh's. Now dreams imply sleep, and the prominence given here to sleep implies a sleepy place, Eden, "the land of Nod," Noah's garden, and so on. Here the Life Principle slept and dreamed.

Now before we can understand Pharaoh or his dream, we must know who Pharaoh was, or more correctly, is. According to popular belief the scriptural Pharaohs were three Egyptian kings, yet nowhere, save in the Bible, is there any account of these specific kings, particularly the cruel Pharaoh; this is slander. Neither is there any record of Joseph, Moses, or even the captivity. Yet according to the Hebrews, Moses practically destroyed Egypt. Were this literally true, some record should remain. Since there is none, this itself should make us suspect it is wholly Hebrew in origin, and mythical at that.

The etymology of the word "Pharaoh" is a matter of dispute. According to some authorities, the *phara* is a combination of the Egyptian definite article *pha*, and Ra, the great sun god. Others assert it means "Son of the sun." And what would this be save the earth itself, for the earth is a son of the sun, not as in science, a cast off, but as in our theory, a son of its own sun period. And so says Revelation. Still others say the name comes from the Egyptian words *per-aa*, meaning "great house," and, of course, these assume this is Egypt's royal house. But no, this "great house" is the Egyptian Beth-el, house of God, the earth itself. A hint of this is found in certain occult manuscripts which speak of "the seven souls of Pharaoh," actually the sevenfold aura, planes and elements. Only as such can we understand this scriptural account of him.

And Pharaoh was asleep, and he dreamed a dream in which the number seven is used repeatedly. The heptads here, as elsewhere, refer to the seven planes and cycles in Evolution. All this the bare earth dreamed of while it slept, but only the genetic Joseph could interpret that dream. From Apocryphal sources we learn the reason for this: it is that Joseph dreamed the same dream as Pharaoh, and in that dream was told its meaning also. This is just a subtle way of saying Joseph and Pharaoh are one—consciousness and energy combined. That Joseph and God are also one is implied in 40:8. "And Joseph said unto them, Do not interpretations belong to God? tell me them"—the dreams. Yes, the interpretation of the earth's dream belongs to God, and Joseph does the interpreting.

For this great service Pharaoh made Joseph ruler over all Egypt and changed his name to Zaphnath-paaneah, which, since we are dealing with interpretations, means "nourisher of the world," "governor of the place of life," and who is that but the Creator? Pharaoh also gives Joseph a wife, Asenath. She is the Egyptian equivalent of the Assyrian Earth Mother, Ashtoreth, abhorred by the Hebrews. Well, they say if you hate or love a thing long enough it will come to you. Asenath was the daughter of the priest of On, and the priest of On is On, in mythology. And On was Egypt's god at that time. This is the *on* in Aton, their religion. The Hebrews took this also; it is the *on* in Onan and also in Solomon. On is thus but another name for God, and his daughter is matter. This, the genetic wed in Egypt, earth; and from this union came two sons, Manasseh and Ephraim—forgetfulness and fruitfulness. The material earth forgot its spiritual source, for which it is rebuked in Revelation. Later it too becomes a source, hence fruitful.

And now Joseph is master of all Egypt; Pharaoh, addressing him, speaks thus: ". . . without thee shall no man lift up his hand or his foot in all the land of Egypt." From slave to ruler, and all because of Joseph's superior virtue and intelligence. This formula is repeated many times in the Bible, and neither Jew nor Gentile realizes it is but racial conceit and historical deception.

In the fat years "Joseph gathered corn as the sand of the sea, very much, until he left numbering; for it was without number." But having read of Adam's herbs and Noah's grapes, we need not assume that this corn was real. It is symbolic and so is the famine. This is evident from 41:56: "And the famine was over all the face of the earth." This is not ignorant geography but ancient cosmology. However there was plenty of historical background for this myth—the accounts of King Baba of El-Kah and King Zoser (2980 B.C.). Baba, millennia before the alleged time of Joseph, wrote thus: "I collected corn as a friend of the harvest-god. I was watchful in time of sowing. And when a famine arose, lasting many years, I distributed corn to the city each year of famine." And Zoser: "I am very anxious on account of those who are in the palace. My heart is in great anxiety on account of misfortune, for in my time the Nile has not overflowed for a period of seven years. There is scarcely any produce of the field; herbage fails, eatables are wanting. Every man robs his neighbor. Men move with nowhere to go . . . The people of the court are at their wits' end. The storehouses were built, but all that was in them has been consumed."

According to the Hebrew myth, all countries of the earth came into Egypt for food and the smart boy Joseph fed them. He also taught the Egyptians, thousands of years older than his race, how to deal with famines. If this be history, one wonders how they ever got along without him.

And now, having prospered, Joseph did what Joseph always does—sends for his tribe, and they came flocking into Egypt, Jacob along with them.

6. And they took their cattle, and their goods, which they had gotten in the land of Canaan, and came into Egypt, Jacob, and all his seed . . . (planetary seed, that is).

27. . . . all the souls of the house of Jacob, which came into Egypt, were three score and ten (70 or 7, the number of Creation) (Chap. 46).

In all religious philosophies the Trinity is something above and beyond us and our world, but we have said that it comes down and becomes matter. [2] And now, oddly enough, the Bible says the same thing, for Jacob, the third person and summation

---

[2] These people were immigrants, and oddly enough the Hebrew word for immigrants, *yordim*, means *descenders*.

of the others, comes down into Egypt, which is earth. And for those who refuse to identify the rascally Jacob with God, the fourth verse tells us God came also.

4. I will go down with thee into Egypt; and I will also surely bring thee up again . . . (Evolution).

"The beings on earth say that God is in heaven, but the angels in heaven say that God is on earth." The Zohar.

Right but not specific: "God is *on* earth" in the forms *on* earth, but he is also *in* the earth as its vast potential. Thus God is more beneath our feet than above our heads.

Were we to make a diagram of this long descent from Abram in primordial light called Ur, to Jacob and Joseph in primeval darkness called Egypt, we would find it strangely similar to our own, and if we include the female aspect, very much like that of the Greek.

Again, How the mighty have fallen! The creative process has reached dense matter and Jacob, spirit, is about to die. Realizing this he calls the earth's two qualities, forgetfulness and fruitfulness, to his side to bless them. As the first is the elder, Joseph guides him to Jacob's right hand, but Jacob, unlike Isaac, outwits him. Aware of the earth's future, he blesses the younger, fruitfulness; in other words, the earth will be fruitful and triumph over its death and forgetfulness.

Jacob then gathers his twelve sons about him to tell them "that which shall befall you in the last days"—of Creation. And here we come to another mystery—the meaning and destiny of the twelve tribes of Israel. As this is a Creation myth, the "tribes" are but part of it. There were not twelve tribes of Jews, nor were ten of them lost. These twelve sons of Jacob are the twelve Elohim, and one with the twelve Titans and the twelve creative aspects of the zodiac. All occultists, past and present, identify them with the latter, but the priestly redactors confused the allusions to them to conceal their true meaning. Judah, "the lion of the tribe," is obvious; this is Leo, the sun, of which it was said, "The sceptre shall not depart from Judah, nor a lawgiver from between his feet, until Shiloh come; and unto him shall the gathering of the people be." The gathering of the elements from space; we called the sun a gatherer and transformer of the elements; we also said these are "the chosen people." The phrase "until Shiloh come" is also a mystery, but here we can see at least what it is not—the Christ of religion. The sun shall reign until complete materialization comes. Benjamin, "son of the right hand," is the first stage in Evolution. Dan is the third, Scorpio, "a serpent (desire) by the way, an adder in the path, that biteth the horse heels, so that the rider (Sagittarius, man) shall fall backward" morally to the animal. The rest are as you see them. Jacob's inclusion of Manasseh and Ephraim in his own family is an occult addition to the zodiac making fourteen in all, seven down and seven up.

After the death of Jacob, Joseph takes his place, that is, he represents the Creative Principle *in toto*, not just a projection thereof. Therefore all the prophecies and blessings Jacob heaps upon him are of and for the earth, not Jewry. Jacob also foretells that Joseph will someday return to the house of his fathers, Bethlehem, the planetary source. And we said that the earth returns to the Absolute.

Prior to their going down to Egypt, God promised his "chosen" he would bring them up again. If this be Jewish history, one is justified in asking why God sent them down in the first place. The only result was four hundred years of slavery. The answer lies in Joseph's words: "for God did send me before you to preserve life." He could have said to produce life; this is the next step in the process, namely, Evolution.

10−

Exodus or Evolution

The controversy which is so perseveringly carried on
in our own day between supernaturalists and rationalists rests on the failure to recognize the allegorical
nature of all religion.

SCHOPENHAUER

For two thousand years the human race has
been reading Genesis and Exodus without knowing what either
the words or the books actually mean. It assumes that the one
got its name from its own first chapter only, and the second from
a historical migration of the Jews from Egypt. Thus again is the
race deceived for want of knowledge of Causation and Creation.
Genesis means creation, in this case the world, and the entire
book is devoted to it. Concerning this we said that Creation and
Involution were one, and that Involution is the involving of the
Life Principle in matter. Now Exodus is its exit from matter,
the coming forth of the potentials involved. This is Evolution,
and this is the subject of the second book, not Jewish history.
Leviticus, Numbers, and Deuteronomy set forth the laws and
rituals of Jewry written by priests a thousand years after the
alleged time of Moses. As we said, who but priests would write
books on these subjects, and who but priests would declare that
God dictated them?

We now come to that other Pharaoh "who knew not Joseph,"
the prephysical. This represents that postsolar period of condensation and incrustation as set forth in our theory. Here the

Israelites, or creative elements, were slowly sinking into bondage to a congealing force the Greeks called Medusa. That this is the true meaning of the Hebrews' bondage in Egypt is attested to by scripture itself. In Galatians 4:3, St. Paul says: "Even so we, when we were children, were in bondage under the elements of the world." Here the creative forces were set to making bricks, for Pharaoh's treasure city, Raamses, city of Ra, the sun, where the bricks were made. Bricks are "building blocks" and such are atoms called today. The bricks of this chapter, therefore, are the same bricks as those of Babel; and the work the Israelites were doing was the same as that at Babel, namely, the building of this earth. Here they became "Prometheus Bound"; a deliverer, or releaser from matter, was needed, and so we come to the great man Moses.

To most people Moses is as real as Caesar or Alexander, yet if, like them, he actually lived, why has history ignored him? There is not a word about him anywhere save in the Jewish scriptures. True his name appears in ancient books but only because their authors had read the scriptures and accepted them as history. Sigmund Freud, himself a Jew, made an extensive search for him and found nothing. The reason should now be obvious—Moses is as mythological as Adam, Abram, Jacob and Joseph; in fact, he is Joseph now in Evolution. According to Josephus, Moses' real name was Osarsiph, i.e., Joseph; in other words, the Creative Principle now on the seventh plane. The Bible itself implies this: Moses, it says, was the seventh in line from the father principle—Abram, Isaac, Jacob, Levi, Kohath, Amram, and Moses, the involutionary seven. The word Amram is but a variant of Abram, the Life Principle that died spiritually when it became matter. And from Apocryphal sources we learn that Amram "lived without sin" and dies, not of old age, but "owing only to the effect of the poison of the serpent," again, matter. This too was borrowed from old Egypt, for according to its mythology the sun god Ra died of the sting of a serpent. Amram, Abram, and Adam are all one, and Moses is their evolutionary sequel.

The name Moses is Egyptian and comes from *mo*, the Egyptian word for water, and *uses*, meaning saved from water, in this case, primordial. Names of several Egyptian kings bear traces of it; we have, for instance, Ahmose, Amosis, Thutmose and Thutmosis. The word *thut* means "is born," and *mose*, as used, means Savior. Thus Thutmose means a Savior is born—and such is Moses, the evolutionary savior of the involutionary Life Principle. This is the basis of all Savior myths. It is their Mahdi or Savior, and the Hebrew Messiah, savior from matter not hell. It is the early references to this inevitable event that are now interpreted as prophecies of Christ.

That the entire story is mythology and nothing more is proved by its pagan parallels. Arabia, Assyria, and Phoenicia all had their Moses, only there he was Mises, so like Moses. In the Orphic hymn to Bacchus we find that this Mises was also picked up in a box floating upon the waters. For this reason he was called Mises. But Mises had another name, Bimater, meaning of two mothers, one by nature, the other by adoption. So had Moses, so also the two sons of Abraham, "which things are an allegory," said St. Paul. This Mises, like Moses, had horns on his head; and also, like Moses, his laws were written on two slabs of stone. Again like Moses he had a rod with which he worked miracles, the rod having the power to turn itself into a serpent. With the help of this rod Mises divided the rivers Orontes and Hydastus; by means of it he passed dry-shod over the Red Sea, at the head of his army. When his army thirsted, he struck the rock with his rod and water gushed out. Wherever he went the land "flowed with milk and honey," and whereas Moses had but a pillar of fire by night, Mises had the light of the sun.

Nor does the parallel end with Mises. The myth woven about the legendary Sargon I, 2750 B.C., strikingly resembles the early history of Moses, that is, his infancy. This part is given only by the Elohist, long subsequent to the Assyrian myths. Now according to the Elohist, ". . . when she, Moses' mother, could not longer hide him, she took for him an ark of bullrushes and daubed it with slime and with pitch, and put the child therein, and she laid it in the flags by the river's brink" (Exodus 2:3). And on the tablets of Kouyunjik, Sargon tells his story.

4. My mother, the princess, conceived me; in difficulty she brought me forth.

5. She placed me in an ark of rushes, with bitumen my exit she sealed up.

6. She launched me in the river which did not drown me.
7. The river carried me to Akki, the water-carrier, it brought me.
8. Akki, the water-carrier, in tenderness of bowels, lifted me . . .

In appreciation, Sargon named his capital Agadi, called by the Semites Akkad, and Akkad was near the city Sippara. Now note that Moses' wife was Zipporah. In both myths, the ark is the same as Noah's ark, the earth entity, carrying with it the seeds of all things. This Sargon himself was; the word means, "prince of the sun," from Sar-gina, the true king. All mythological kings were named for the sun—the God of mythology. From this it was only a step to historical kings who worshiped the sun. As Socrates tells us, the first gods that the Greeks worshiped were the cosmic bodies. These are realities; it remained for the Hebrews to replace them with a conceptual unreality.

The Egyptian Osiris was also put in a coffer or coffin and set adrift on the river Nile. In due time he was picked up by his mother—and Moses was returned to his. In like manner the Greek god Perseus was shut up in a chest and cast into the sea at the command of King Acrisius. On the shores of Seriphus he was found and raised by Dictys, as was Moses by Thermuthis, and Thermuthis was the name of the serpent sacred to Isis, the earth mother. This is the same serpent as that of Eden, namely, the life-force, and this is the serpent Moses lifted up in the wilderness, the lower planes in Evolution.

Similar tales were told of Romulus of Rome, Mithra of Persia, and even Alexander of Greece. Of Alexander it was said that he crossed the Pamphylian Sea miraculously. Menander wrote of it thus:

Have I to cross where seas indignant roll?
The sea retires and there I march.

Incapable, like us, of distinguishing mythology from history, Strabo tried to explain this on natural grounds—low water in the winter season; and Josephus, no more enlightened, used it to convince the Greeks of the miracle of the Red Sea.

The Hebrews had many stories about Moses besides those

found in the canon, and they reveal much. From them we learn that, as with Noah, the whole house was filled with light when Moses was born. This, however, was not the same light; it is that second "light shining in darkness," the first emanation of the primeval world. We learn also that there was a "war in heaven" fought over Moses similar to that described in Revelation. This is from Apocryphal sources, but a hint of it is found in canonical Jude, the ninth verse: "Yet Michael the archangel, when contending with the devil he disputed about the body of Moses, durst not bring against him a railing accusation." Now why should these cosmic powers fight over the corpse of a man? Can any priest or Bible student tell us why? He cannot, but we can. The fight was between Involution and Evolution over possession of the earth, here called Moses. After this battle, Metatron (Enoch) appeared and conducted the spirit of Moses, the life force, up to heaven, the higher planes, again. On the way he passed through *seven* of them, theoretical, and there saw the angels (energies) of each, from those in the first that "controlled the waters standing in line" to those of the last and highest plane. He was also permitted to inspect hell, and there he saw the damned, ranging all the way from murderers to those who did not fast on Yom Kippur. It does not say which was the worse.

The earlier Bibles say that Moses, when he came down from the mount, had horns on his head—as Michelangelo portrays him. The authors of the King James Version, believing this to be an error, made it read "the skin of his face shone," thus hiding the key to Moses. The former idea came from the Latin Vulgate and reads as follows: *"Cumque descenderet Moyses de monte Sinai, tenebat duas tabulas testimonii, et ignorabat quod cornuta esset facies sua ex consortio sermonis Domini."* Translated this means: "And when Moses came down from Mount Sinai, he held two tables of the testimony, and he did not know that his face was horned from conversation with the Lord." Modern scholars believe it should read *rays* rather than *horns*, but that is because they don't know Moses. It is also why they can't translate properly. Every attempt they make but robs the Bible of its true meaning.

Horns are mythological accessories, and in no sense peculiar to the Hebrew Moses. Many mythical beings had them, among which was Bacchus, called by some "the horned child," and by others, "Zagreus son of Zeus," and Koré, or Persephone. Thus in the *Dionysiacs* we read:

> A Dragon-Bridegroom coiled in love-inspiring fold . . .
> Glided to dark Koré's maiden couch . . .
> Thus by the alliance with the Dragon of Aether,
> The womb of Persephone became alive with fruit,
> Bearing Zagreus, the Horned Child.

Moses is the earth, the horned beast of Revelation; he is Aries, the genetic Ram; he is Pan, the goatlike Aries on earth; he is Phallus Erectus, or the serpentine force thereof in Evolution. Thus the Vulgate is right and the rest are wrong. As one saved from water, Moses is what was saved after the Deluge. As such he is identical with the slimy dragon that Apollo discovered after the flood dried up. And this dragon is the devil of scripture, and its devil and its Moses are one. Both have horns and this is what the key word *horns* is trying to tell us.

Like all the other Bible heroes, Moses is but a personification of the creative power, particularly its violent aspect. His milder brother, Aaron, like Abel, is the genetic consciousness; the word Aaron itself means "to conceive," and it is he who does the prolific conceiving later on. It is this that eventually reveals the meaning and purpose of the earth, and so Aaron becomes a mouthpiece for its mindless partner, as did Joseph for Pharaoh, the one involutionary, the other evolutionary. Miriam, their sister, stricken with leprosy represents matter afflicted with disintegration. Were it otherwise, why did not these two miracle-workers cure her? The answer is, their miracles were the miracles of Creation, not man. Just here we wonder if the name Miriam derives from Meriram, chief of the Turbulents, see page 108.

Moses' serpentlike rod is the Hebrew Caduceus, symbol of the creative power, and wherever it strikes the earth a miracle is wrought. But so was it with Mises, and also Abaris, a high priest of Apollo. According to Pindar, Apollo gave this great one an arrow with which to work miracles. Why do we not believe these stories also? We don't because we have been taught one is pagan myth, the other "the word of God." Such is the power of priestly diabolism. It has blinded us all, including the clergy. These tell us "the revealed truth" of the Bible is all the *spiritual* literature we need, yet without the literature of other races we cannot understand the Bible. So, we here repeat, our great need is to have this "revealed truth" revealed.

Because of this "revealed truth" millions believe that Moses divided the Red Sea and led all Israel through it dry-shod. The rationalists doubt but do not deny and so, like Strabo, they try to explain it on natural grounds. The name is wrong, they say; it should be the Reed Sea, a shallow, swampy place much farther north. This makes a physical crossing possible and so literalism is satisfied. It does not make sense, however, either mythologically or cosmologically, whereas Red Sea does: it is the red earth through which the Life Principle passed.

The Red Sea is one with Adam, red earth. The wilderness beyond is the savage lower planes in Evolution, through which this life force must struggle to reach the Promised Land, the higher, and someday spiritualized, planes. This is *our* Promised Land, and *we* will spiritualize it. The forty years, the four material cycles, is the time given us to reach this man-made heaven. These forty correspond with the forty days of the Deluge and together constitute those *antiscians,* or shadowy opposites.

This is Exodus, a wholly uncomprehended book. In proof thereof let us quote from one of our professors of "Biblical Literature and Religion." "The culminating incident of the Exodus was the crossing of the Red Sea. That this was accomplished miraculously, is a matter of clear history." And what is this "clear history"? The Bible, of course, three times over. "The record furnishes us with the facts in triplicate narrative." Therefore it must be true. But to continue: "True there is the admission that, up to the present time no direct reference to the Exodus has been found among the Egyptian inscriptions." And then follows the credulous reason: "Such silence causes no surprise; it is the expected silence of a proud and contemptuous people regarding an event of humiliating circumstances." This represents modern enlightenment concerning Causation, Truth and Reality, and then we wonder what's wrong with us morally. Morals, like faith, are the evidence of things not seen, namely, consciousness, enlightenment, wisdom. These our spiritual leaders cannot give us, because they haven't them to give. Our rabbis, priests and ministers are but "innocents abroad" in an occult world. The scriptures are to them as the Egyptian hieroglyphics before the Rosetta Stone.

There is no end to the explanations these apologists find to prove the historicity of Hebrew mythology; they must prove it lest their own house of cards come tumbling down. In this extremity they sometimes refer to the Tell-el-Amarna tablets, dating from the alleged captivity period. These tablets speak of the Habiri, and our apologists assume these were Hebrews. There is no proof of this nor would they be construed as such but for the priestly necessity. The Tell-el-Amarna tablets contain a political correspondence between Ikhnaton (Amenhotep IV) of Egypt and Barrburyash II, king of Assyria 1375 B.C., and at that time the Hebrews as a distinct sect did not exist, the Bible to the contrary.

Only as the sequel to the allegorical Genesis does this scriptural Exodus become intelligible. As such it tells the same shocking story—the nonmoral and murderous nature of Causation; that is, the Jhwhist part does; the others try to conceal it. The first chapter, and the second down to the tenth verse, is from the Elohist and Priestly accounts, and here as elsewhere they extol the virtues of God and his "chosen people," then the Jhwhist steps in and tells us the truth—Moses is a murderer.

11. And it came to pass in those days, when Moses was grown, that he went out unto his brethren, and looked on their burdens: and he spied an Egyptian smiting an Hebrew, one of his brethren.
12. And he looked this way and that way, and when he saw that there was no man, he slew the Egyptian, and hid him in the sand (Chap. 2).

Thus does life begin. Why have we overlooked this beginning in every Bible myth? Because it was subsequently covered over with sanctity, divinity and poetry, the harlotry of scriptural mythology. In this account we have a good example of that whitewashing referred to in our Preface. Neither the Priestly nor Elohist account mentions this murder, yet if their God was opposed to murder why did he pick this murderer, Moses? Because a murderer was just the man he needed. Life itself is murderous and the Jhwhist knew it. Being nearest to the Zodiacal Day, he was, like the Greek mythologists, an Initiate in the Mysteries and knew the cosmic facts. Then came the darkness and the priests, knowing nothing. These destroyed the mythic legacy. Midway between the two was the Elohist, and there you have the three, not four, sources of the Bible. That both priest and prophet used the same formula "And God said" implies one source, and one concern—sin, not truth. If those parts of the Bible attributed to prophets were not written by professional priests, then they were written by priestly minded nonprofessionals.

After this crime, Moses fled to Midia, and the "sons of the snake." There he meets Zipporah, watering her father's flock, as did Rebekah and Rachel. And Moses marries her, as did Isaac and Jacob. But according to Josephus, he had a wife already, Tharbis, daughter of the king of Ethiopia, that same Aethiopia of Genesis. This is no scandal in Moses' life, however, for in mythology Egypt and Ethiopia are one, and also one with Midia, the middle point in Creation, namely, earth. Now according to the Jhwhist, Zipporah was one of the *seven* daughters of Reu-el, the priest of Midia, but in the next chapter the Elohist tells us that Jethro was Moses' father-in-law; and Numbers 10:29 calls him Ragu-el. The two authors also differ in the name of the sacred mount; the Elohist calls it Horeb; the Jhwhist, Sinai. And so, wherever the one or the other is used, you may know who is speaking. There is also another key. The pet phrase of the Elohist is "an angel of the Lord." He does not claim his murderers talked to God but only to an "angel of the Lord," a creative force. It's still allegory, however, for no man has ever talked to God; no man has ever seen him, heard him or even smelt him, so why believe in him? Because we don't know enough about Reality to disbelieve.

1. Now Moses kept the flocks of Jethro his father-in-law, the priest of Midian; and he led the flock to the backside of the desert, and came to the mountain of God, even to Horeb (Chap. 3).

From here on we will be reading two myths about the same thing, scrambled and confused by an editor centuries later. This is the reason for the two mounts, both of them identical with Ararat, Meru, Parnassus, and Himalaya, namely the earth. This is "the mountain of God," and its "backside" is one with the "backside" of the book in Revelation, namely, Evolution. This is the "backside" of God which elsewhere, Moses saw (Exod. 33:20, 23): "Thou canst not see my face . . ." but "thou shalt see my back parts"—אהור, a'chor—backside. No, Moses never saw God's frontside, which is Involution, but only his "backside," which is Evolution; and the reason is obvious—Moses is God's "backside." This fact is cunningly concealed in Jewish numerology. The numerical value of Jehovah is 543 and that of Moses is 345. Moses is thus Jehovah reversed, and Jehovah reversed is Satan, say the Kabbalists. And to carry it further: 543 plus 345, or 888, is the Gnostic number of Jesus Christ, who, with name and title, is both.

And now we come to another mystery no modern priest can explain—"the burning bush."

2. And the angel of the Lord appeared unto him in a flame of fire out of the midst of a bush: and he looked, and, behold, the bush burned with fire, and the bush was not consumed.

Our Premise said that suns and worlds are cosmic plants. The Elohist had the same idea. His burning bush was this earth in its own sun stage, which for trillions of years, "burned with fire and was not consumed." Such also was Sinai. Moses meeting God in this fiery mount is but Evolution meeting Involution in the fiery earth period.

7. And the Lord said, I have surely seen the affliction of my people which are in Egypt (matter), and have heard their cry by reason of their taskmasters (laws); for I know their sorrows ("The Sorrows of Satan" by Marie Corelli, Amherst Press).

This God sent them down there and now blames the Egyptians for the consequence.

8. And I am come down to deliver them out of the hand of the Egyptians, and to bring them up out of that land unto a good land and a large, unto a land flowing with milk and honey.

Is Palestine a large land, and is the Negev "flowing with milk and honey"? No, this is the Life Principle's *evolutionary* Paradise, the superphysical planes where it is free from bondage in matter. Its escape, allegorized as that of the Jews from Egypt, is but the Hebrew equivalent of the Greek Cronos disgorging his children. The coming down of the Lord here is the same as that at Babel, and as unnecessary, for Moses is all there is, and he is already down. Here in, not at, the burning bush he receives his commission.

10. Come now therefore, and I will send thee unto Pharaoh, that thou mayest bring forth my people the children of Israel out of Egypt.

The children of Israel in Egypt are the planetary genes in matter, their bondage, chemical, and their release, Evolution. But Moses, like a good many others, wants to know who this High Commissioner is, and so he boldly asks.

14. And God said unto Moses, I AM THAT I AM: and he said, Thus shalt thou say unto the children of Israel, I AM hath sent me unto you (Chap. 3).

This confusion of "I AM" with "I AM THAT I AM" well illustrates a fact already pointed out, namely, that the Jews did not create their own mythology, nor did they fully understand it. The creators of the original myths were the older and more metaphysically enlightened races; from these the Jews picked up bits and made a metaphysic of their own, and a sorry mess it is. Thus they did not know that "I AM THAT I AM" is not applicable to the God of Sinai and the burning bush. "I am" is the indicative mood, present tense of the verb "to be," and since the planetary entity is a being, the term could well apply to it, but the rest of the sentence cannot. "I AM THAT I AM" is applicable only to the motionless Absolute, not the Creator, and the distinction is the same as that between Melchizedek and Abram. As the Absolute does not act, it has no predicate, and as it creates nothing, it has no name in apposition save its own. And this is what "I AM THAT I AM" means—Be-ness, not Being. It is, and that is all that can be said about it. The Vulgate translates the words thus: "Ego sum qui sum"—"I Am Who Am." It is in no sense an original concept; in fact, every ancient race had its equivalent. All the temples of Egypt had carved on their walls the words, "Nuk Pu Nuk"—"I Am That I Am." The Hindus had their "Tat Twam Asi"—"I Am That," and the Persians their "Ahmi Yat Ahmi." Thus salvation may be of the Jews, but not originality.

Now as soon as Being exists, "I Am That I Am" becomes "I Am What I Will Be," and this is the meaning of the word Yahveh. This is made up of four Hebrew letters: Yod, He, Vah, He, or YHVH. As the Y and I are identical, these four are the same as those of the Tetragrammaton. They all mean *Being*, and their transpositions, *change*. The priestly scribe, aware of this changing process, presents it in another way; he has Yahveh change his name.

3. And I appeared unto Abraham, unto Isaac, and unto Jacob, by the name of God Almighty (in Hebrew, El Shaddai), but by my name Jehovah was I not known to them (Chap. 6).

Historically, the word Jehovah is a semantic accident. As the Hebrews considered the name Yahveh too sacred to be uttered, they used the words Adonai and Elohim instead, and in writing, added the vowel signs of these words to the consonants YHVH. In due time these were mistaken for parts of the word itself and so YHVH became Jehovah.

Elsewhere we are told that God is "the same, yesterday, today, and forever," but according to the Torah he is constantly changing, as he should. This change in his name is the same as that of Abram, Jacob, and others, but now on a lower plane. It represents that change from Involution to Evolution, an isomerism—same in substance, but different in quality. In other words, Jehovah, the God of Moses, is the creative power in Evolution. There is, however, a woeful confusion here also. According to this text the name Jehovah was not known in Abraham's day, yet, according to Genesis, Abraham called the place of Isaac's sacrifice Jehovah-jireh. And even in Seth's day (Gen. 4:26), "Then began men to call upon the name of the Lord," originally Jehovah. These earlier statements are, like circumcision, priestly interpolations long subsequent and for a priestly purpose.

The word El Shaddai means "terrible power," namely, a sun. In our Premise we said it was this "terrible power" that created this earth. Here we find it so terrible that it even tried to kill Moses, the life force in it. "And it came to pass by the way in the inn that the Lord met him (Moses) and sought to kill him." Can any professor of "Biblical Literature and Religion" explain this statement? He cannot on his hypothesis, but we can on ours. This "inn" is the earth, and the "way of the inn" is *In*volution, life *in*volved in matter, and here in this entombment it is nearly killed, in fact, we call it "dead matter." And such it would have remained but for Moses the Evolutionary Savior.

And now, perhaps, we can understand this strange and incredible tale, the plagues of Egypt. It is but an allegory about this ruthless but wonder-working power as it afflicted the earth in its own postsolar period. This was the time of condensation and solidification, in other words, hardening, and this is the hardening of Pharaoh's heart, seven times, to be exact. The Egyptians spoke of Pharoah's "seven souls," the Hebrews said seven hearts. Thus the plagues and torments were but earth's primeval agonies. These we'll meet again in Revelation, the New Testament's version of Genesis and Exodus. It's a long and loathsome story and so we will deal only with the plagues given by the Jhwhist. He alone knew the septenate process and so he gives but seven. These are as follows: Blood, frogs, flies, murrain, hail, locusts, and first born. The rest are additions by the Priest and Elohist.

After each plague we read that the Lord (law) hardened

Pharaoh's heart, "and he would not let them go." This, we repeat, is the law of accretion and solidification *hardening* the elements in accordance with the sevenfold atomic table, in other words, chemical synthesis. Had a scientist written it, he would have spoken of geologic ages and a seven-period table of elements. We think of this as strictly modern knowledge, yet it seems the Jhwhist was well aware of it. That these ancients knew these things may be hard to accept, yet here it is. What is more, they knew something modern scientists do not know— the nature and meaning of Devolution, the freeing process. "The sacred writings of the early Hebrews contain few allusions to what may be termed the scientific understanding of the universe, or of precise observations such as have been preserved in the records of other ancient peoples," Sir Richard Gregory. Just so, the early Hebrews did not know, but those from whom they got their material did. We moderns are not discoverers of new truths but rediscoverers of old truths. Go back far enough, twelve thousand years or so, and you will find our modern knowledge was quite well known; not all of it, of course, because each cycle adds its *epiota*. This is how the epigenetic is built up. It was this more ancient knowledge the Hebrew epigoni saw "as through a glass darkly," but why they should write of it in this fantastic manner only mythologists can say. But mythologists are clever fellows, ambidextrous as they are ambiguous. They write with both hands and each tells a different story—one of Man, the other of man. And along with these the Hebrew mythologists wrote a sympathy story, and proof that they are the one, sole interest of God. For them he slaughtered all who stood in their way. *Chutzpah!*

1. And the Lord said unto Moses, See I have made thee a god to Pharaoh: and Aaron thy brother shall be thy prophet.

2. Thou shalt speak all that I command thee: and Aaron thy brother shall speak unto Pharaoh, that he send the children of Israel out of his land (Chap. 7).

Energy, consciousness, and dense matter, the *dramatis personae* of this story. As energy is mindless, consciousness must speak for it. This is the meaning of Moses' speech affliction.

3. And I will harden Pharoah's heart, and multiply my signs and my wonders in the land of Egypt.

5. And the Egyptians shall know that I am the Lord, when I stretch forth mine hand upon Egypt, and bring out the children of Israel from among them.

I know of no one who has attributed pride and egotism to God, but it is here; he wants the Egyptians to know what a mighty fellow he is. And what a diabolical method! Since he "hardened Pharoah's heart," could he not have softened it, thereby sparing Egypt and the Egyptians? This is learning about God the hard way, but is only a mythologist's way of telling us we learn only by experience, and bitter experience at that. Why then worship what can teach only by pain and suffering?

31. And the people believed: and when they heard that the Lord had visited the children of Israel, and that he had looked upon their affliction, then they bowed their heads and worshipped (Chap. 4).

And their foolish descendants have been worshiping ever since. What is more, they have taught us to worship. It therefore behooves us to know what kind of a God they and we are worshiping.

20. And Moses and Aaron did so, as the Lord commanded; and he lifted up the rod, and smote the waters that were in the river, in the sight of Pharoah, and in the sight of his servants; and all the waters that were in the river were turned to blood.

21. And the fish that was in the river died; and the river stank, and the Egyptians could not drink of the water of the river; and there was blood throughout all the land of Egypt.

25. And *seven* days were fulfilled, after that the Lord had smitten the river (Chap. 7).

This is the first period in chemical synthesis, but Pharoah's heart was not nearly hard enough, and so we come to the second.

5. And the Lord spake unto Moses, Say unto Aaron, Stretch forth thine hand with thy rod over the streams, over the rivers, and over the ponds, and cause frogs to come up upon the land of Egypt.

6. And Aaron stretched out his hand over the waters of Egypt; and the frogs came up, and covered the land of Egypt (Chap. 8).

And how could Aaron, a man, stretch his hand over the whole of Egypt? Only natural forces can do that. And how could any race believe the Creator would do such things for it? This is racial egotism carried to Infinity.

14. And they gathered them together upon heaps: and the land stank. ("And the evening and the morning were the second day.")

Here a meaningful touch is added by another writer: Moses and the Egyptian magicians vie with one another in doing miracles. The Egyptians duplicate everything Moses does until he produces lice, then they give up. The great man Moses has shown his superiority by creating lice!

Here also a division is made between the Jews and the Egyptians, that same division that occured in Peleg's day—Involution from Evolution, or, more correctly, Devolution. We might therefore interpret this story thus: the hardening of Pharaoh's heart as the solidifying process, and the plagues as the forces brought to bear upon matter to release the Life Principle. This would be the same as Deucalion and Pyrrha casting the stones backward.

22. And I will sever in that day the land of Goshen, in which my people dwell, that no swarms of flies shall be there; to the end thou mayest know that I am the Lord *in the midst of the earth* (Chap. 8).

And did we not say God is in matter?

24. And the Lord did so; and there came a grievous swarm of flies into the house of Pharaoh, and into his servants' houses, and into all the land of Egypt: the land was corrupted by reason of the swarm of flies.

"And the evening and the morning were the third day." This severing of the people is the separation of creative consciousness from dense matter at the three and one-half point.

1. Then the Lord said unto Moses, Go in unto Pharaoh, and tell him, Thus saith the Lord God of the Hebrews, Let my people go, that they may serve me.

2. For if thou refuse to let them go, and wilt hold them still,

3. Behold, the hand of the Lord is upon thy cattle which is in the field, upon the horses, upon the asses, upon the camels, upon the oxen, and upon the sheep: there shall be a very grievous murrain.

4. And the Lord shall sever between the cattle of Israel and the cattle of Egypt: and there shall nothing die of all that is the children's of Israel.

6. And the Lord did that thing on the morrow, and all the cattle of Egypt died: but of the cattle of the children of Israel died not one (Chap. 9).

These cattle, horses, camels, and so on are as symbolic as those of Adam and Noah, and so is their destruction. Were it otherwise, where did Pharaoh, a few days later, get a thousand horses to pursue the Hebrews? And where were Pharoah's seven hearts that he allowed a man called Moses to destroy his land and people? But no, it was not just Moses' work; it was God's "good deed" on the fourth day. But Pharaoh's heart was very hard by now and so the plagues continued.

12. And the Lord hardened the heart of Pharaoh, and he harkened not unto them; as the Lord had spoken unto Moses.

13. And the Lord said unto Moses, Rise up early in the morning, and stand before Pharaoh, and say unto him, Thus saith the Lord God of the Hebrews, Let my people go, that they may serve me.

14. For I will at this time send all my plagues upon thine heart, and upon thy servants, and upon thy people; that thou mayest know that there is none like me in all the earth.

Let's hope not. If this be the God of the Jews they should disown him. As for the Gentiles, they should hang their heads in shame.

15. For now I will stretch out my hand, that I may smite thee and thy people with pestilence; and thou shalt be cut off from the earth.

16. And in very deed for this cause have I raised thee up, for to show

in thee my power; and that my name may be declared throughout all the earth.

More divine egotism, of which Pharoah was but an instrument—the Judas Iscariot of this myth. How then can he be blamed? He cannot, even mythologically, yet the Hebrews blackened his name and that of Egypt for nearly three thousand years.

18. Behold, tomorrow about this time I will cause it to rain a very grievous hail, such as hath not been in Egypt since the foundation thereof even until now.

25. And the hail smote throughout all the land of Egypt all that was in the field, both man and beast; and the hail smote every herb of the field, and brake every tree of the field.

The Lord's "good deed" on the fifth day—complete destruction of the Egyptians' food. If as we are told, he is omnipotent and omniscient could he not have accomplished his end by merely "passing a miracle"? This hail is the same as that of Sodom and Gomorrah, and here as there the Hebrews are spared. Why? Because this is a Creation myth and the Hebrews represent the Life Principle. This and nothing more.

1. And the Lord said unto Moses, Go in unto Pharaoh: for I have hardened his heart, and the heart of his servants, that I might shew these my signs before him:

4. Else, if thou refuse to let my people go, behold, tomorrow will I bring the locusts into thy coast:

14. And the locusts went up over all the land of Egypt, and rested in all the coasts of Egypt: very grievous were they; before them there were no such locusts as they, neither after them shall be such.

15. For they covered the face of *the whole earth*, so that the land was darkened; and they did eat every herb of the land, and all the fruit of the trees which the hail had left: and there remained not any green thing in the trees, or in the herbs of the field, through all the land of Egypt.

This is the Lord's "good deed" on the sixth day, and no doubt He looked upon it and called it good. And as I write this, reports are coming in about the death and destruction caused by an earthquake. This is His "good deed" in our day. If this be disrespect for all that is sacred, so be it. It is the sacred that is blinding us to the truth, the false sacred of religion. There is only one sacred and that is life, and this monstrous God has no respect for it. Why then should we respect Him? This story we are reading is from the Pentateuch, and shocking as this Pentateuch is, it is the only part of the Bible that is true, theistically. Through allegory and personification it is telling us the true nature of Causation. The rest is falsehood essential to priestcraft.

Just here another author gives an additional plague, and an additional hint: "darkness in all the land of Egypt three days." This is that ultimate darkness of life's final entombment in matter, midway between Involution and Evolution; this is the meaning of the three days, elsewhere, three and a half. Since, occultly, the mystic seven governs all things, this dark period must also be septenate.

1. And the Lord said unto Moses, Yet will I bring one plague more upon Pharaoh, and upon Egypt; afterwards he will let you go hence: . . .

4. And Moses said, Thus saith the Lord, About midnight will I go out into the midst of Egypt:

5. And all the firstborn in the land of Egypt shall die, from the firstborn of Pharaoh that sitteth upon his throne, even unto the firstborn of the maidservant that is behind the mill; and all the firstborn of beasts (Chap. 11).

29. And it came to pass, that at midnight the Lord smote all the firstborn in the land of Egypt, from the firstborn of Pharaoh . . . (Chap. 12).

And this is the God who was shocked at the killing of one man, Abel. This, we repeat, is but Cain in Evolution.

Considered literally, this Moses practically destroyed Egypt. Do you suppose its king would have permitted such a troublemaker to live? A predecessor cut off the head of his baker for a minor offense, yet this more cruel Pharaoh allowed this Public

Enemy No. 1 to go free. No, this tale is intelligible only as personified cosmology.

30. And Pharaoh rose up in the night, he, and all his servants, and all the Egyptians; and there was a great cry in Egypt; for there was not a house where there was not one dead.

31. And he called for Moses and Aaron by night, and said, Rise up, and get ye forth from among my people, both ye and the children of Israel; and go, serve the Lord as ye have said.

Thus stands the record, and upon that record religion must stand or fall, for if it be literally true and historical, this monster should be damned instead of worshiped; and if it be but mythology, the Bible's religious authority is gone forever. The latter, we claim, is its true nature. That the race can read it, believe it, and still worship its monstrous God is an index of our intelligence, our knowledge of Causation, Reality, Truth. It is that of the child and the savage, yet this is the intelligence that is running our world; this is the intelligence that sustains our religion, nationalism, commercialism—and the giving away of countries on the words of a myth. These are not the fruits of wisdom and understanding but of incredible ignorance. Do you wonder then that we have war and oppression, crime and corruption? What would you expect of beings still in the God-worshiping stage?

The destruction of the firstborn was the final touch; the broken Pharaoh was willing now to let the people go. Had this been history they would have been driven out or put in a ghetto. But what were these firstborn, and what the destruction? Literally, it should be the lastborn, final elements in the atomic table, but it all depends on what the mythologist was thinking about. Perhaps he knew that these last and heaviest elements were the first to be afflicted with disintegration and radiation. Our scientists are well aware of this process but they are not fully aware of its biologic significance, namely, that through disintegration and radiation creative intelligence becomes free from matter to create biologic forms, and atomic energy free to become biotic energy. As such it becomes vital enough to warrant a place in creation mythology; as history it does not.

The ancients were well aware of the significance of this process but a mythologist could not say so in plain words, and so he made an allegory out of it. And the priestly scribe gave it a name; he called it "circumcision"—the removal through radiation of the genetic's obstruction, namely, physical matter; and ridiculous as the terminology is, this is the place for it, Exodus, not Genesis. To quote the Kabbalah again: "The spirit clothes itself to come down and unclothes itself to go up." And so all the elements going out must be circumcised (chapter 12). Later we will find them clothing themselves in flesh and again the priest has a strange and wonderful name for it.

But circumcision was not enough for these elements, and so we come to another religious literalism—the Passover. The Life Principle is about to *pass over* from Involution to Evolution ("and Hell followed with him"), but scripturally God is about to pass over the Israelites on his diabolical mission to the Egyptians. This is the killing of the firstborn, and lest He make a mistake and kill the firstborn of the Hebrews also, He has them mark their houses with blood; and this in spite of the fact the Israelites live apart from the Egyptians, in Goshen; also in spite of the fact that God, we are told, is no respecter of persons. But these are His "chosen people" and so He orders each family to kill a lamb, eat it in haste, and then sprinkle its blood on the two gateposts of each house—the Jachin and Boaz of Being. And blood has been sprinkled on them ever since. They must also eat unleavened bread for a period. "Seven days shall ye eat unleavened bread—for whosoever eateth leavened bread from the first day until the seventh day, that soul shall be cut off from Israel." Thus began the sacred Passover. Easter and Holy Communion are the Christian equivalents, and so began all religious rites and ceremonies—ignorance enslaving itself.

The Paschal lamb sacrificed at this time is the earth itself, sacrificing some of itself that evolutionary life might be. In the beginning, this lamb was Aries, "the lamb slain from the foundation of the world," and the lamb of Exodus is this same lamb, now in physical form. And what is left of it after Exodus is the unleavened bread, namely, lifeless and soulless matter. This it was the Life Principle ate at first for the simple reason that that was all it had to eat, and the protists are still eating it. The "seven days" primeval life had to eat it represents, as seven always does, a plane or subplane. They might well represent the entire plant cycle and kingdom, since plants live on earth-matter. But elsewhere we are told the Israelites were to live on this soulless bread "until the one and twentieth day," the third plane. This unleavened bread of higher forms is life without soul qualities—plant, animal, and submoral human. These are life unleavened by spiritually qualified consciousness. After the third, namely, the human plane, we are supposed to partake of the leavened bread, but for lack of it we are still living on Jacob's "mess of pottage," matter and materialism. The ancients had a name for such people; they called them Borborites. The word means *dirt-eaters*. Passover, Succoth, Yom Kippur, Hanukah, what good are they if you lack knowledge of their occult meaning? They are but *Biur Chometz*, destruction of the leaven. "Hear, O Israel," get a *get* [1] from God and marry Sophia; this is the only ritual that you need. The truth will set you free, free from the ancient curse a diabolical priesthood put upon you.

The Life Principle has now taken its first step out of matter and so we read:

1. And the Lord spake unto Moses and Aaron in the land of Egypt, saying,
2. This month shall be unto you the beginning of months: it shall be the first month of the year to you (Chap. 12).

Not "the first month of the year," but the first epoch in Evolution, the etheric plane and plant kingdom. This month is now the month of Nisan, and the twenty-first of it is the birthday of Moses. Thus does ignorance reduce the sublime to the ridiculous. In the New Testament this sublime process is again reduced to one man and his birthday.

37. And the children of Israel journeyed from Rameses (the treasure city, earth) to Succoth, about six hundred thousand on foot that were men, beside children.
38. And a mixed multitude went up also with them . . .

---

[1] The Hebrew word for divorce.

40. Now the sojourning of the children of Israel, who dwelt in Egypt, was four hundred and thirty years $(4 + 3 + 0 = 7)$.

Thirty more than God foretold Abraham. But what of that; in Creation, "a thousand years is but a day." Jacob brought but seventy people into Egypt, and now according to Numbers 1:45–47, the Israelite army alone numbered 603,550. This was exclusive of women, children, and the Levites who were not numbered. This would mean a nation of between three and four million. What amazing fecundity! For man, yes, but not for the Life Principle. This is the monadic host emerging from the earth, Cronos disgorging his children, and Phoenix rising from its own ashes. A hint of this is contained in the next chapter:

19. And Moses took the bones of Joseph with him: for he had straitly sworn the children of Israel, saying, God will surely visit you; and ye shall carry up my bones away hence with you (Chap. 13).

Joseph's bones are Moses' bones and therefore he took them with him. They are also Adam's bones, out of which Eve, Mother Earth, was made.

17. And it came to pass, when Pharaoh had let the people go, that God led them not through the way of the land of the Philistines (matter), although that was near; for God said, Lest peradventure the people repent when they see war, and they return to Egypt: (He was also afraid Adam would return and "live forever.")
18. But God led the people about, through the way of the wilderness of the Red sea: and the children of Israel went up harnessed out of the land of Egypt.

"Eastward from Eden" again, through the first part of the evolutionary wilderness.

20. And they took their journey from Succoth, and encamped in Etham, in the edge of the wilderness.

"The edge of the wilderness" is the edge of the etheric plane, hence Etham is very apt. Succoth might well be *succor*, food, for

it represents the plant kingdom. It is now the occasion celebrated as the Jewish fall harvest festival.

21. And the Lord went before them by day in a pillar of a cloud,
to lead them the way; and by night in a pillar of fire, to give them light;
to go by day and night:

This, of course, is figurative language as is the sun that led
Mises by night. Literally, it could mean that primeval cloud that
went up from the earth, which is of the nature of light.

And now they encamp at Baal-zephon. The name is a combination of two satanic gods—Baal and Typhon—and soon we
will find them in the wilderness of Sin—an evil God of Babylon.
These are but symbols of the lowest plane forces, and we too
said they were satanic.

5. And it was told the king of Egypt that the people fled: . . .
8. And the Lord hardened the heart of Pharaoh king of Egypt, and
he pursued after the children of Israel: . . .
7. And he took six hundred chosen chariots, and all the chariots of
Egypt, and captains over every one of them (Chap. 14).

In chapter 9 we were told that all the horses, asses and oxen
died of the murrain. Where then did Pharaoh get six hundred
or perhaps twelve hundred horses? In any other book such contradictions would destroy its authority, but not the Bible.

21. And Moses stretched out his hand over the sea; and the Lord
caused the sea to go back by a strong east wind all that night, and made
the sea dry land, and the waters were divided.
22. And the children of Israel went into the midst of the sea upon
the dry ground: and the waters were a wall unto them on their right
hand, and on their left. (These are the "waters standing in line" that
Enoch showed Moses.)
28. And the waters returned, and covered the chariots, and the
horsemen, and all the hosts of Pharaoh that came into the sea after
them; there remained not so much as one of them.

There was no mundane sea at this time; it had not yet been
formed. This Red Sea is the red earth, in the midst of the cosmic

sea, a wall on either hand, namely Involution and Evolution.
Into the latter the life-force went and escaped from matter. Here
the physical cannot go and so king Pharaoh "died"—and to this
day he is known as "dead matter." How very different from our
sermons, novels and scenarios, and how little understanding the
novices who write them—"unworthy descendants" even of the
Hebrew Homer! They too but cull "mythic artifacts they do not
understand."

If this story be literally true, what of the Egyptians? Were
they not also God's children? And if God is no respecter of
persons, why this partiality to the Jews? If He still exists, does
He still take sides in human warfare? If He be "the same, yesterday, today and forever," why does He not perform His miracles
today? If He saved the Jews from the Egyptian sword, why did
He not save them from the German gas chamber? To help the
Jews slaughter their enemies He stopped the sun and moon but
He has never yet stopped a war, no, not even a plane from falling
or a ship from going down. When one foundered and sank off
our coasts, sharks attacked the survivors; when a landslide
buried a village in Mexico, scorpions stung those who escaped;
an earthquake is followed by a tidal wave, and war by pestilence.
No, the quality of mercy is not cosmic.

The Shipwreck
Proud man in his kingdom of the earth,
Sat watching a spider weave and spin
Its delicate thread almost as fine
As fancy's dreams are woven in;
And the man, he smiled on the frail result
Of so many journeys to and fro,
And he cried Shall I crush this puny thing?
But his heart in pity answered No.

The restless sea in a sullen mood
Played round the triumph of human skill
As it danced away on the rolling wave
Its trusted journey to fulfill;
And the sea, it smiled on the frail result

> Of so many journeys to and fro,
> And it cried Shall I crush this puny thing?
> But there was naught to answer No.

Another question might well be asked here: If the Jewish people had such protection three thousand years ago, why have they been persecuted ever since? The answer lies not in their false theology but in their true mythology. Consider Joseph, for instance. He comes a stranger to a foreign land, and ere long controls it. The rightful owners soon find themselves working for him instead of vice versa.

21. And I will give these people favour in the sight of the Egyptians: and it shall come to pass, that when ye go, ye shall not go empty:
22. But every woman shall borrow of her neighbour, and of her that sojourneth in her house, jewels of silver, and jewels of gold, and raiment: ye shall put them upon your sons, and upon your daughters; and ye shall spoil the Egyptians (Chap. 3).

Here we have the God of the Jews actually teaching them to be dishonest, to steal and misappropriate. This is literalism and all that the Jews understand today; the occult meaning, however, is very different. "Every woman" is Virgo, the plant kingdom, which does and must steal from Egypt, earth, its raiment and its jewels, substance and vitamins, to clothe and feed itself biologically. This it is that God approves and not the Jewish people. It is the will of the acquisitive genetic, but carried to the epigenetic this nonmoral acquisitiveness ends only in the disfavor of man, hence the persecutions. If they would escape their proverbial fate they must eschew its provocative cause.

Because of the false literalism of their scriptures the Jews have been living in a great illusion for two thousand years—the chosen, the favored, the protected, and the smartest. If they cannot see this is mythology, they should be shown.

And now having destroyed the Egyptians and taken their jewels, we have a song of triumph for Israel and praise for their monstrous God. This is attributed to Miriam, herself a mythical being. It consists of but two lines, later expanded into a lengthy hymn by priests a thousand years after the alleged event.

1. . . . I will sing unto the Lord, for he hath triumphed gloriously: the horse and his rider hath he thrown into the sea.

2. The Lord is my strength and song, and he is become my salvation: . . .

3. The Lord is a man of war: the Lord is his name. (Monster would be more correct.)

11. Who is like unto thee, O Lord, among the gods? Who is like unto thee, glorious in holiness, fearful in praises, doing wonders? (Chap. 15).

Thus begins the priestly glorification of a purely mythical protector. But it does not belong here; it was put here by postexilic priest and for their own special purpose. There is none of it in the earlier writings nor do we find it chronologically until we come to the darkness that fell on Jacob's sons "in the last days," historically about 400 B.C. By that time the Jews, as now, were wholly ignorant of their own scriptures and so took literally what their forebears meant only symbolically. Thus does history bear out our statement—just as we recede from the ancients so do we recede from truth. That we in this age can believe their symbology literally is the measure of our intelligence and the key to our world conditions.

But let's, like Pharaoh, pursue after them. Reports have come in that these holy ones are now in sin.

1. And they took their journey from Elim, and all the congregation of the children of Israel came unto the wilderness of Sin . . . (Chap. 16).

A very good name for it, for here is where "sin" began, or at least the cause of it, the lower planes, where "the Holy One of Israel" inaugurated "the struggle for existence" and "the survival of the fittest." As Life and appetite are practically synonymous, it now hungered, a fact the significance of which no preacher has ever seen, yet when God made stomachs and hunger he inaugurated warfare, savagery and sin. And now we come to another great mystery—manna from heaven.

14. And when the dew that lay was gone up, behold, upon the face of the wilderness there lay a small round thing, as small as the hoar frost on the ground.

15. And when the children of Israel saw it, they said one to another, It is manna: for they wist not what it was. And Moses said unto them, This is the bread which the Lord hath given you to eat (Chap. 16).

Bread for human beings falling from heaven "as small as the hoar frost" is hard to believe, but only until you know the human beings here were even smaller, mere biotic atoms. In the beginning of Evolution the first energies hung about the earth like methane on the marshes. This eventually fell to earth and produced amino acids, protein and protoplasm. Figuratively, this manna represents all those energies that pour down upon the earth to nourish and sustain life.

We said there was no sea yet, and now we find there was no water at all. And so the children of earth, not Israel, thirsted also. But not for long, however, for Moses still had his magic wand. With this he struck the rock called earth, and water came forth from it, a miracle for man but not for nature. Verse 6 tells us the rock was Horeb, and Horeb is the earth. "And thou shalt smite the rock, and there shall come water out of it, that the people may drink." But so did Mises, Mithra, and also Rhea, who

> . . . with her sceptre struck
> The yawning cliff; from its departed height
> Adown the mount, the gushing torrent ran.

This is but nature separating the watery element from the primeval earth. And such are all scriptural miracles. The next one we come to is the defeat of King Amalek. And here we meet Joshua for the first time—he who was called Hur. And Him and Hur, the positive and negative, hold up Moses' hand, and when it is up they win, and when it is down they run. It reminds us of the play-party game, "The Grand Duke of York."

The word Amalek means "that which exhausts," and being a king, he represents that king of all called death, which prevails when the life-force is low and prevails not when it is high. Life has now become biologic and thus forever after subject to death.

Chapter 18 deals with the subdivision of Moses' power and

judgment over Israel. This is the breaking up of the one Life Principle into the various subdivisions in nature—kingdoms, genera, and species—Exodus's version of Genesis's confusion of tongues. These divisions are to teach laws and ordinances and "the way wherein they must walk." And only when we understand that these laws are nature's laws and the way is the way of the ruthless genetic, can we understand the rest of this book, and particularly what follows for now we come to Sinai.

This is the "holy mount of God," yet its name, Sinai, belies the holy part. It is a derivative of the evil Babylonian god Sin, and the Egyptian Seni. Modern editors divide the word thus: Si-nai to hide this unpleasant fact. The authors of the Septuagint were not so squeamish, and so they spelt it Sina.

In all mythologies the gods dwell on some mount: Mount Olympus in Greece, Mount Meru in India, and so forth. Thus Mount Sinai is nothing new in mythology. Its position, however, is very significant geographically, the lowest point in the Israelites' journey. This represents the nadir point reached in the creative process, that "valley" of densest elements in the atomic table. Thus it is a turning point, and, strange to say, *seni*, the Egyptian name for it, means "a turning point." And the Sinai peninsula itself is a triangle similar to our diagram of Invo-Evolution. All this however is hopelessly lost in the narrative. Thus far we have been progressing nicely in Evolution, but now we are right back at the beginning again, Horeb and the burning bush. The events at Sinai are not, therefore, subsequent to those previously related.

11

Mount Sinai and the Laws

18. And mount Sinai was altogether on a smoke, because the Lord descended upon it in fire: and the smoke thereof ascended as the smoke of a furnace, and the whole mount quaked greatly (Chap. 19).

This is the earth in its postsolar convulsions, that *cosmic bomb* we spoke of earlier. This follows naturally from the "burning bush" stage, which is the sun. In both, the creative power is violent and this is the awful God of Sinai; the terrestrial God of Canaan, earth, is this same power in its subsequent tranquillity.

17. And Moses brought forth the people out of the camp to meet with God; and they stood at the nether part of the mount.

This "nether part of the mount" is identical with the "backside" of God, namely the Evolutionary part. As we have said, mythologists have no respect for time, place or sequence, and so we have both Involution and Evolution here.[1]

---

[1] In fact, fiery Sinai represents a period prior to life's exodus from Involution.

16. And the glory of the Lord abode upon mount Sinai (the planetary entity), and the cloud covered it six days (Involution): and the
seventh day (of Creation) he called unto Moses (the Life force) out of
the midst of the cloud.

17. And the sight of the glory of the Lord was like devouring fire
on the top of the mount in the eyes of the children of Israel (Chap.
24).

We have heard much about "the glory of the Lord" and many
of us hope to bask in it somewhere beyond the grave. Here we
see what it consists of—the glory of the sun, so violent it would
destroy us were we any nearer. Out of its involutionary "cloud"
this violent power now speaks to Moses, saying "Come up and
see me sometime." And Moses went up taking with him the
same number Jacob brought down, namely, seventy. And Moses
was in the mount "forty days and forty nights"—those of Involution now in reverse. Here he is given moral laws, and here
we come to one of the greatest pieces of spiritual deception in
all literature.

The laws of Sinai are not the moral laws nor are those of the
tablets, the Ten Commandments. The laws of Sinai are the law
of nature, antedating the commandments by billions of years.
The stone on which they were written is that stone called earth,
and to carry it further, the two human stones on which are
written the laws of heredity. As we have said, the laws of God
are not in Torah but in terra. We also said there were no such
things as laws but only actions. This is the energy aspect; the
consciousness part is not even action but ideation, biologic and
hereditary. The moral laws were the priests' creation and to give
them divine authority they declared them handed down by God
at Sinai.

The moral laws are laws of moral man, the epigenetic; the
laws of God are the laws of the genetic, and considering its
nonmoral nature, moral man could draw up ten times ten commandments for it: Thou shalt not destroy the work of man's
hands with earthquakes, hurricanes and tornados; thou shalt not
make floods in one part of the country and droughts in another;
thou shalt not make polio germs to cripple little children or

cancer to kill their parents; thou shalt not drive mankind to war, adultery, prostitution and overproduction. These are all products of this ruthless power and instead of striving to control it, we waste our time worshiping it. We are not here to worship God but to make intelligent use of what He (it) has created.

From chapter 20 to the end of Deuteronomy is no part of the Exodus myth, but an insertion by priests a thousand years after the alleged time of Moses. This murderous one would never have said, "Thou shalt not kill," nor would his murderous God. This is the law of a long subsequent and more civilized era. It was the priests of this era who compiled the laws, including a few for themselves: "And ye shall give unto us tithes," and food and tabernacles, and we'll be "a kingdom of priests," as God commanded. To these priests their God was the Creator of the entire universe; would such a being concern himself with tribal rites and rituals, arks and tabernacles, even the number of loops on the curtain? Our Preface said that only priests would write volumes about such things.

The laws of Sinai are the laws of Involution, written by El Shaddai; they must be broken that Evolution might be, and now we find they are, not once but twice because of different myths. The first was by the plagues, and now by Moses personally. On descending the mount with horns on his head, and probably with hoofs and tail also, he "cast the tables out of his hands and brake them beneath the mount" (32:19). Rather within the mount. The reason for this was his anger on finding his people worshiping a "golden calf," a symbol of the golden sun and therefore something in the past. This, as with Adam, they must not return to and "live forever." Breaking the law here is identical with that of Eden, and as with Adam it greatly angered the God of Israel. He was so angry, in fact, He threatened to kill His "chosen." But Moses, much wiser than He, persuaded Him that this was wrong, and so, "the Lord repented of the evil which he thought to do unto his people" (32:14). But as Moses and the Lord are one, it also angered Moses and so he ground their brazen symbol to dust, as he had ground their other symbol, Egypt, then forced his people to consume it. Life had looked back and so, like Lot's wife, it had to be punished. Moses, the law of planetary progression, therefore commanded the Levites to slay their brothers with the sword, "and there fell of the people that day about three thousand men" (32:28). And this is the man who later is called "meek"—not by wise mythologists but by tampering priests.

It was for breaking this first law that Moses was denied the "Promised Land," and not, as some suppose, for his anger or his killing of the Egyptian. Indeed the more Egyptians he killed, the more respect his God had for him, but breaking the law of Involution and thus precipitating the tragedy of Evolution put him in a class with Adam and Satan. And so he has two sins to atone for; his own and his people's.

On returning to the mount to receive the second law he finds his God exceedingly angry, and to appease Him he offers his own life as a sacrifice for his people. And how the preachers praise him for this act! Only the sacrifice on Calvary, they say, excels it. And yet how factual is it? We are told (33:11) that "the Lord spoke unto Moses face to face, as a man speaketh unto his friend." And a few verses later it says, "Thou canst not see my face: for there shall no man see me, and live" (33:20). If then Moses saw God and no man can see God, then Moses was not a man. What then of his willing sacrifice? It is like Isaac's, mythological.

The reason "no man hath seen God" is not because he is an invisible spirit or too awful to look upon, but because "he" is consciousness, and no man hath seen consciousness at any time, or energy either. It is time the credulous race realized that theophanies such as this occur only in mythology. We say *such as this* because there is a theophany, three of them, in fact. The word means a visible appearance of God, and the three are, first, a sun, second a world, and finally, its forms. We ourselves are a theophany, but theophanies such as we should not look for theophanies other than this. God is in what he creates.

The account of Sinai is a wonderful story, brilliantly and compellingly told, but is that any reason why we should believe it literally? Elsewhere we said that knowledge of other races' literature helps us understand the Bible. So is it with Sinai, Moses and the law. According to the Assyrians, Mises also wrote his laws on two slabs of stone. Dionysius, the Greek lawgiver, was portrayed as holding up two tables of stone on which the law was engraved. Minos, King of Crete, received the laws of his land from God on Mount Dicta. The Persians say their laws came to them in the same way. As Zoroaster prayed on a high mountain God appeared in thunder and lightning and delivered to him the *Zend Avesta,* or "Book of the Law." What then is so unique about the Hebrew account?

At a time contemporary with the literal Abraham, Hammurabi of Babylon delivered to his people a code of laws, that according to tradition, was given him by Shamash, the great sun god and maker of human laws. This code is entitled "Laws of righteousness that Hammurabi, the mighty and just king, has established for the benefit of the weak and oppressed, the widows and orphans." Historically, not mythologically, this code antedates the Mosaic code by more than a thousand years, yet it is just as enlightened, and in some cases less severe, than the Mosaic code. In the latter, the law governing slaves reads thus (Exod. 21:2): ". . . six years he shall serve; and in the seventh he shall go out free." In the Hammurabi code it reads: ". . . for three years they shall work . . . in the fourth year they shall be free." Commenting on the similarity of these codes, I. Elliott Binns remarks: "The variety of cases provided for is much greater than in the Mosaic codes, but where they deal with the same matters there is an extraordinary similarity in their ordinances, especially in phraseology." Thus this older code could well be the source of the Mosaic code, not Jehovah. At any rate the moral laws are no part of the laws of the mythological Moses. There is nothing miraculous about them; they are but the codified morality of the age and race that wrote them. Instead of "the word of God" someone dubbed them "Ten ways of keeping out of jail."

Those who go no further than the Bible for their knowledge of man's moral development, see its origin and flowering in the Jews, surrounded by ignorant, Godless heathen, yet thousands of years before the Jews were ever heard of the Egyptians, whom they painted as morally inferior, had a well-developed sense of morality. The evidence for this lies in the Egyptian

"Oath of Clearance," which *in toto* contains six of the ten commandments. It reads in part as follows:

> I have not committed fraud and evil against men.
> I have not diverted justice in the judgment hall.
> I have not caused a man to do more than his day's work.
> I have not caused a slave to be ill-treated.
> I have not taken milk from the mouths of children.
> I have not stolen cattle.
> I have not been weak.
> I have not been wretched.
> I have not been impious or impure . . .[2]

Any race that could even devise such a code is not without a high moral sense. What is more, it reveals a more enlightened kind of morality than that of the Mosaic law—"An eye for an eye and a tooth for a tooth." "Thou shalt not suffer a witch to live." "If an ox gore a person and he die, the ox shall be stoned, and his owner put to death." Holding an ox guilty of homicide implies belief in the animal's moral responsibility, and killing its owner, ignorance of moral justice. The Mosaic law recognizes a man's right to sell his daughter into slavery and makes rules to govern it. There is nothing that low in the Egyptian and Babylonian codes. It is not only our opinion but that of able scholars that morality flowed *to* not *from* the Hebrews. Here we quote from one of them—James H. Breasted. "We are all aware that Egyptian-Babylonian culture set European civilization going; but few modern people have observed the fact, so important in the history of morals and religion, that Egypto-Babylonian culture also set Hebrew civilization going."

How presumptuous then for this semibarbarous tribe, still in the nomadic state, to sit in judgment upon a race whose culture even then was twelve thousand years old. According to Herodotus the Egyptian gods were "in existence twenty thousand years ago." If we take literally the "piromis stones," we must admit such antiquity, though they too may be somewhat mythological.

[2] From G. G. Atkins, *Procession of the Gods*, p. 59.

There were 340 of these, representing the generations down to Sethon, 720 B.C., and after Sethon twenty more, making in all 360. Now an Egyptian generation was 36 years. Thus 360 times 36 equals 12,960 years. Our false concept of the ancient Egyptians is due in part to our own ignorance, but the evil we attribute to them is due entirely to the libelous nature of Hebrew mythology.

I think we have proved the mythological nature of Moses, but what about Aaron? Elsewhere we said that this ancient priest was genetic consciousness; in other words, the generative principle. The word itself implies this fact. It comes from *harah*, which means "to conceive." Ginzberg translates it "woe unto this pregnancy"—the mythological woe resulting from the earth's pregnancy, biologic existence. This was the woe Eve brought upon herself, not just painful childbirth. It is stated that only Aaron and his two sons could perform the rites for women during and after delivery. This puzzled another of our "great Bible students," Bishop Colenzo, who figured the time on the basis of six or seven hundred thousand women. He concluded it would take the three of them fourteen hours a day without rest or interruption. But like all his cloth, Bishop Colenzo did not understand his Bible. If he had he would have known that since Aaron means to conceive, Aaron himself did the conceiving, and also the rites and ceremonies. He is the planetary genetic, but once in organic forms he becomes sex and its organs. This is the key to the occult balderdash that follows here, and has been so religiously observed ever since. The "sacred" garments with which Aaron clothed himself are but the physical flesh the genetic puts on in biologic forms, male and female. We said the priest had a strange name for these also and here they are—ephod for the male, and breastplate for the female. These were to be cunningly made and elaborately adorned, but not by human hands: these are the Creator's work. The ephod is the tumescent phallus, its genetic nature implied in the Greek *ephebe*, pubescent youth.

32. And there shall be an hole in the top of it, in the midst thereof: it shall have a binding of woven work round about the hole of it . . . (Chap. 28).

If this be the prepuce, what about literal circumcision? The miter worn by priests is a well-known phallic symbol; but there is more to the vestment than just the phallus.

9. And thou shalt take two onyx stones (rather, Onan stones) and grave on them the names of the children of Israel (Chap. 28).

Three or four million names could not be engraved on two onyx stones, but their heredity could be on two Onan stones.

11. . . . thou shalt make them to be set in pouches of gold (rather, pouches of skin).

On these two stones, testes, are engraved the genetic law and hereditary characteristics of all forms of life. But one telling was not enough; a little later the ground is gone over again and this time they are pomegranates. The word, from *pomum* and *granatus,* means a fruit of many seeds. Among the ancients it was a symbol of generation and fecundity. The goddess Nana conceived by putting a pomegranate in her bosom. Mythologists, it seems, are no respecters of places either.

And now, perhaps, we can learn the nature of the "holy oil" with which Aaron anointed everything; it is the seminal fluid.

31. And thou shalt speak unto the children of Israel, saying, This shall be an holy anointing oil unto me throughout your generations (creations, as with Noah).
32. Upon man's flesh shall it not be poured, neither shall ye make any other like it, after the composition of it: and it shall be holy unto you.
33. Whosoever compoundeth any like it, or whosoever putteth any of it upon a stranger, shall even be cut off from his people (as Onan was) (Chap. 30).

To some, such an intrepretation of this "holy oil" will be offensive, but if so, it is only because they do not know the Bible and the cunning of its creators. The Hebrew name for this holy oil was *shemen,* and when the *sh* is written with a dot over the left side thus שׂ, as it is in this case, the *sh* is pronounced as *s.* Thus it is simply *semen.* This is the only "holy" that nature recognizes, and likewise the Bible.

The equally ornate breastplate is the female part, and this and the ephod are to be joined together, occasionally. Genetic Aaron must carry these whenever he goes into the "holy place"; and now we can see what the scriptural "holy place" is also—the womb of generation.

This, we repeat, is the "sacred" and the "holy" of the Bible, and religion is replete with its symbolism. The church with its steeple is a symbol of the two sex organs. The "seed of Abraham" is the seed of the Creator. The word testament itself comes from the Latin *testes*, the genetic receptacle. Here again our priestly cover-ups tell us it comes from an ancient custom— swearing by the testes—as did Abraham and Abimilech. This is indeed a strange name-source for "the word of God." As with the Bible itself, there is nothing that inconsequent about it. The real meaning is the Bible's meaning—genetic Creation. This earth is a cosmic *testis*, whose genes created everything upon it, and as we proceed we will find that this "holy Bible" is but the testament or record of this work. Indeed the Bible and our own work could well share our subtitle, A Genetic Cosmoconception. We have not said that the Bible teaches our theory, "worlds from world seeds," yet its emphasis on seeds, its name and its nature come as close to it as the cunning hand of Jacob comes to anything.

Life was originally male-female, and when not clearly divided appears even now as the third sex. And this, when religiously inclined, takes upon itself the guardianship of sexual purity, particularly in women, a task not difficult for the indifferent. But the Bible does not deal with sexual purity but sex purity: this is the meaning of the Urim and Thummim, light and per- fection. It is not human light and perfection, however, or even chastity, for nature cares nothing about that; this is a social problem. The sex purity of scripture is genetic purity; it must not be contaminated or in any way affected extraneously. It is set apart in the body as a specialty, and this is the meaning of the Levites, set apart from the rest of Israel. Elsewhere we said that the genetic would have naught to do with the epigenetic, also that the genetic partakes not of man's heaven, and now we find the Levites have no inheritance in the "Promised Land."

Not even their chief symbols, Moses and Aaron, are allowed to enter it. Thus does the Bible confirm our statement that God cannot enter our heaven, man's epigenetic world.

The numerous Levites who succeeded Aaron represent the divisions of the androgenous Life Principle, the many forms it took, and the genetic nature of it. Thus the scriptural Levites are no basis for a sex-condemning religion, for they are sex, and their paraphernalia, sex symbolism. The priesthood today in all its regalia is but an ignorant literalization of this.

Only by recognizing this sex symbolism can we understand the scriptural ark, the tabernacle, the temple, and other structures of wondrous beauty and fabulous wealth produced in the wilderness by a band of refugees so destitute they had to be fed from heaven. Where did they get their silver and gold, their precious stones and fine linen? These they had in abundance, and even after the work was completed, each tribe had wagonloads to offer as sacrifices.

Were these the treasures the fleeing Israelites stole from the Egyptians? Yes, esoterically, for this tabernacle of the Lord is the biologic form, and the materials with which it is built are the treasures of symbolic Egypt, namely, earth. This is another "temple not made with hands," another "house of God." In Involution we "live and move and have our being" in God, but in Evolution, God lives and moves and has his being in us.

Later, we read that this holy tabernacle became a regular slaughterhouse, in which innumerable fowl and beasts were burnt as sacrifices, yet soon these people are again starving in the wilderness and must be fed from heaven—the Joshua myth. At the dedication of Solomon's temple, they sacrificed twenty thousand oxen and one hundred and twenty thousand sheep. And every sacrificed animal had to be without blemish. Taken literally, this would end in the complete destruction of their stock. It doesn't make sense, literally or racially; it does, however, symbolically. This vast and ruthless sacrifice of life represents nature's sacrifice thereof.

No doubt these ancient God addicts had some place of worship, and the details of the ark, temple, and other buildings could refer to it, but these are not in the narrative historically but only as the moral laws and the priestly rituals are—to make them seem of divine origin. There is nothing uniquely Hebrew about them. Every ancient race had its ark, and the sacred things put in it were symbols of the genetic principle. "The ark represents the holy of holies, the consecrated receptacle of life and was one of the most important symbols in the religious ceremonies of the ancients." "The ark of the Egyptians held the symbols of the Creative forces of life." "The Jewish ark of the covenant bears a close resemblance to the sacred ark of the Egyptians." E. E. Goldsmith. These arks are all of historic times, and symbols only, whereas the ark of mythology is the body, and that is the meaning of the statement that the Israelites carried it about with them.

And now having conquered Egypt, the "Promised Land" lies before them. But before they can enter it, they must first invade and utterly destroy the six great nations that occupy this "land of milk and honey." These had "cities great and fenced up to heaven" (Deut. 9:1). Is this fact or just some more mythologized cosmology? In our Premise we said that after the earth was formed some physical elements disintegrated and formed, or would eventually, an aura of six metaphysical elements, likewise "great and fenced up to heaven." These are the energy substantives of biologic forms, and part of the organism's work is to absorb, qualify and thus isomerize them. They are thus our servants, and so we find Joshua making them "hewers of wood and drawers of water" (Josh. 9:27). Now we are not asserting that this planetary aura was what the Hebrew authors had in mind when writing their account, no more than we had theirs in mind when writing ours—this was perceived later—we point it out only because the parallel is so obvious. At any rate, we hope the barbaric treatment of these unoffending nations was not human.

16. But of the cities of these people, which the Lord thy God doth give thee for an inheritance, thou shalt save alive nothing that breatheth:

17. But thou shalt utterly destroy them; namely, the Hittites, and the Amorites, the Canaanites, and the Perizzites, the Hivites, and the

Jebusites; as the Lord God hath commanded thee (that the Godites may have their land) (Deut. 20).

And this, that "meek" man Moses, who said "thou shalt not kill," did with a vengeance.

32. Then Sihon came out against us, he and all his people, to fight at Jahaz.
33. And the Lord our God delivered him before us; and we smote him, and his sons, and all his people.
34. And we took all his cities at that time, and utterly destroyed the men, and the women, and the little ones, of every city, we left none to remain:
35. Only the cattle we took for a prey unto ourselves, and the spoil of the cities, which we took (Deut. 2).

If their Judeo-Christian God is as opposed to war as we are told, why did He not stop it here in the beginning? Because God never stopped any war; on the contrary He starts them. It isn't a pleasant picture as presented here, but we make a great mistake in explaining it as primitive man's crude God-concept. The authors of the Bible were not primitives intellectually; they were men of great intellect who, unfortunately, wrote in a manner beyond our comprehension. They were mighty men and dealt with mighty things. Out of stuff that dreams are made of they fashioned men and women and breathed into their forms the breath of life and they became living souls—to us. Such were their prophets, patriarchs, heroes, kings, and likewise their gods and saviors. We, absorbed in our commercialism, cannot comprehend their cosmolingua, their myths and symbols. Myths are little stories containing great truths, but little souls cannot see great truths, great anything, in fact. And so we took their story literally—a personal God, a human Adam, his "fall," his "sin," and hence "salvation." Rise ever so little on the mental plane and you see them for what they are—mythic formulae, and applicable only to the world.

So let us interpret this divinely inspired conquest and destruction as we did the plagues—the dissolution and transubstantiation of planetary elements. Thus does a little knowledge absolve even God. In an early chapter we said our theory did just that, and also removed Him from the horns of the religious dilemma. But it does even more than that; it removes Him, period—an event greatly to be desired for it will mean the intellectual emancipation of both Jew and Gentile.

Moses had wandered in the wilderness forty years, and now he is old and ready to die. This mighty man is Man, the Life Principle, and the wilderness it had to wander through is the four lower evolutionary planes, a wilderness indeed, or should it be jungle? The wanderings are life's blind groping towards its "Promised Land," the spiritual planes above. In the last chapter of Deuteronomy we read of this great one's death: ". . . his eye was not dim, nor his natural force abated." Why should it be since Moses is this natural force, very much alive even yet. He was buried on Mount Nebo, ". . . and no man knoweth of his sepulchre unto this day." This should read, no man lacking metaphysical enlightenment knoweth, which means Piscean humanity. The word Nebo means fire and the fiery Mount Nebo is fiery Mount Sinai, namely, earth. This is Moses' sepulchre and most of the slumbering giant is still within it. And here Michael is still contending with Satan for it, and not even an archangel dares bring a railing accusation against this alibi for God's diabolism.

Such knowledge of Moses should end for all time the argument about the authorship of the Pentateuch. For ages it was believed that the man Moses wrote it, yet strange to say it records his own death. Modern critics make much of this self-obituary, yet it is all vain argument. Moses as the creative force did what the Pentateuch records, namely, a phase of Creation, so he provided the material no matter who wrote it. Then there is the Ezra faction, which claims this later prophet wrote the wondrous five books. The date of Ezra is more in keeping with the priestly part, but the account savors too much of tradition to be anything else. According to this, Ezra, after fire destroyed the originals, sat down and from memory dictated, in the usual forty days, ninety-four books to five scribes: twenty-four of the Old Testament and seventy Apocryphal.

As Leviticus, Numbers, and Deuteronomy are but elaborations of the mythical Moses, we will leave them and this key to the reader himself. Thus as far as we are concerned, the story of Moses is finished. We are not done with mythology, however, for this is but the end of one myth and the beginning of another, namely, that of Joshua, son of Nun—which could as well be None. According to the Arabs, Joshua was the son of Miriam, and Miriam is matter. But in Egypt Nun means water, cosmic, in mythology, and so Joshua, son of the water, is but a revolutio of Moses taken from the water.

12
Joshua

Joshua is so closely associated with the fall of Jericho in Hebrew tradition that it is therefore necessary to place his lifetime around 1400 B.C. Moses, on the other hand, appears to be linked to a period about two hundred years later, for the Hebrews slaved in the cities of Rameses. The story, then, of Joshua following Moses seems to be a confused version of two originally different episodes.

ENGBERG, *The Dawn of Civilization*

Here the scholar substantiates our claim, unfortunately he does not see that these stories are not history, hence *his* confusion. They are not confused versions of different episodes, but confused myths about Creation. Thus the book of Joshua is not a sequel to Exodus but a parallel, dealing with the same subject. In spite of the fact that both God and Moses selected Joshua as the next leader, it is not so. As Cain is the same as Adam, and Abraham the same as Noah, so Joshua is the same as Moses. The Bible presents Moses as a deliverer, or Savior, and this is both the nature of Joshua and the meaning of his name. He is the Savior of this myth, and what he saves is, as before, the Life Principle in bondage to matter. Thus with Joshua we are right back at the beginning of Exodus again. And such is the entire Bible—cosmology mythologized. As Genesis and Exodus, with their elaborations, are Involution and Evolution, there is nothing else to write about. These are the Bible's themes and its books may, and should, be divided accordingly. Their present sequence is the work of a later priesthood that either ignorantly or maliciously confused them. The key to it lies not in the textual sequence, but in the planetary sequence, and so it is this we will follow.

But where, you ask, is the figurative earth this time? It is Jericho instead of Egypt. The parallel is cunningly hidden by presenting Joshua's Red Sea incident first, that is, the crossing of the Jordan. We, however, will follow the Creative process.

1. Now Jericho was straitly shut up because of the children of Israel: none went out, and none came in (as in Egypt).
2. And the Lord said unto Joshua (as he did unto Moses), See, I have given into thine hand Jericho (Egypt), and the king thereof (Pharaoh), and the mighty men of valour (his charioteers).
3. And ye shall compass the city, all ye men of war, and go round about the city once. Thus shalt thou do six days.
4. And *seven* priests shall bear before the ark *seven* trumpets of rams' horns: . . . and the priests shall blow with the trumpets (the seven plagues of the Moses myth, and both are chemical disintegration) (Chap. 6).

And for twenty-five hundred years the Jews have been blowing a ram's horn, the *shofar;* I hope that they will now see that this is as mythical as all the rest.

16. And it came to pass at the *seventh* time, when the priests blew with the trumpets, Joshua said unto the people, Shout; for the Lord hath given you the city.
20. So the people shouted when the priests blew with the trumpets: and it came to pass, when the people heard the sound of the trumpet, and the people shouted with a great shout, that the wall fell down flat, so that the people went up into the city, every man straight before him, and they took the city.

Here we have in cryptic form the long account of Egypt's conquest, namely, the destruction of matter. We have also a fact not revealed in Exodus, that the destruction of matter is accomplished by vibration—we called it radiation, and the scientist, fission. As stated elsewhere, all the details of Creation cannot be presented in one myth, hence the many. Collectively they tell a fairly complete story, but only abysmal ignorance of the subject can look upon them as racial history. And this, we claim, the Jews have done since 400 B.C., hence their racial delusions, one of which is their right to take whatever they want. Another is that they bless all places, and now we find that they not only destroy Jericho but put a curse upon it.

17. And the city shall be accursed, even it, and all that are therein, to the Lord: only Rahab the harlot shall live, she and all that are with her in the house, because she hid the messengers that we sent (the Hebrews' "wooden horse").

Rahab is the same harlot as in Revelation, and sparing her is but an occult way of saying not all matter was destroyed.

All ancient mythologists and cosmologists considered matter evil and accursed, and so, once free, Joshua, the life-force, pronounced a curse upon it and all who would restore it. And yet with only a colon between, the mythologist drops a hint that it is phoenixlike matter he is talking about and not a city. Jericho will be rebuilt.

26. And Joshua adjured them at that time, saying, Cursed be the man before the Lord, that riseth up and buildeth this city Jericho: he shall lay the foundation thereof in his firstborn, and in his youngest son shall he set up the gates of it (Chap. 6).

From the standpoint of Evolution the destroyed matter of this earth must not be restored, yet sometime, someone will again "lay the foundation thereof in his firstborn and in his youngest son shall he set up the gates of it." This means that the matter or energy of this earth will someday be reused to build another—"Eternal process moving on," "World(s) without end." And in the day thereof the foundation will be laid by the firstborn Principle, number 1, and its physical part set up by the last, or youngest, number 7. And this is what we find so stated in 1 Kings 16:34, added for no reason whatever save to show that Joshua's prophecy came true. "In his day did Hi-el the Bethelite build Jericho: he laid the foundation thereof in Abiram his firstborn, and set up the gates thereof in his youngest son Segub, according to the word of the lord, which he spoke by Joshua the son of Nun." Now regardless of etymology, Hi-el is just High God, of Beth-el, God's house, or source, and Abiram is

Abraham, not the father of a race, but the father principle of the earth. And such are all Old Testament prophecies found in the New—not prophecies at all, but references to a known certainty—Evolution.

21. And they utterly destroyed all that was in the city, both man and woman, young and old, and ox, and sheep, and ass, with the edge of the sword (as they did in Egypt) (Chap. 6).

If this be history, why should an army that so recently had to be fed on manna, and Joshua's was so fed, utterly destroy a rich and well-stocked city? Why did they not just move in, occupy it, use its animals for food, and so on? Because this army was not human; it was nature destroying matter that she might build organic forms from its energy. And so all must go save "the silver and gold and vessels of brass and iron," symbols of earth's chemical riches, stolen this time from Jericho. These were "consecrated unto the Lord"—the Hebrew "fence" for stolen goods; "they shall come into the treasury of the Lord." The "tabernacle of the Lord" is now "the treasury of the Lord," the human body, on which a later priesthood built a treasury for loot; another even built a Vatican on it.

That this Hebrew conquest of Jericho is a myth is proved by recent discoveries. According to Barton, the pre-Israelitish city of Jericho was so small that "the whole of it could have been put into the Colosseum at Rome." Thus there was no great city of Jericho at that time for the Jews to take.

And now comes the Red Sea parallel: the children of Israel are about to pass over a body of water again on dry land. And this passing over takes place at precisely the same time as that of Exodus. What is more, the same rites and ceremonies are repeated, though differently placed to hide the parallel. They celebrate the Passover; they are also circumcised. "And the Lord said unto Joshua, This day have I rolled away the reproach of Egypt from off you," 5:9. The reproach of "accursed" matter. But they were circumcised in Moses' day. This is not a second cut-off, but a tip-off that this is a wholly unrelated myth.

They remove from Shittim (the Jewish concept of matter,

elsewhere called dragon-dirt) and arrive at the river Jordan, the evolutionary equivalent of Jabok, over which Jacob passed in Involution. Here they tarry three days, during which the officers instruct the people.

3. And they commanded the people, saying, When ye see the ark of the covenant of the Lord your God, and the priests of the Levites bearing it, then ye shall remove from your place, and go after it (Chap. 3).

The three days represent that halfway goal where, as in Peleg's day, "the earth was divided" into Involution and Evolution. Here the genetic principle, the Levites, is awakened and begins to "pass over," the ark, as we said, being the carrier. And now the Red Sea miracle.

13. And it shall come to pass, as soon as the soles of the feet of the priests that bear the ark of the Lord, the Lord of all the earth, shall rest in the waters of Jordan, that the waters of the Jordan shall be cut off from the waters that come down from above; and they shall stand upon an heap.

Jordan is the mythic "river of life," whose waters came "down from above," Involution; and when they were cut off they did literally "stand upon an heap," a heap of matter called earth. These are "the waters standing in line" that Moses saw, and later crossed.

And now as in Moses' day, the people gather stones and build a memorial, that their descendants may remember that here "the Lord of all the earth" wrought miracles for the elect of all the earth, the Jewish people. So runs the parallel, but it is not yet complete, for here again the elect of all the earth are starving and the Lord of all the earth *passes* another miracle, no, not another, the same, a shower of manna. One would think that if the Israelites could build such magnificent structures as they did in Moses' day, they would not need divine charity so soon after. But this is not subsequent history, it is duplicate mythology. Thus we are no farther along in Evolution than we were at the Red Sea crossing. What is more, it is not human evolution or moral warfare. The Pentateuch does not deal with human life and its conquest of evil, but with Life and its conquest of matter. This is the subject of both Exodus and Joshua, and we see they differ little when misplaced things are *put in their proper places.*

In the last chapter of Joshua we get a hint of the ultimate point Life reached as represented by this character. In spite of the fact that the Israelites have been wandering in the wilderness more than forty years, they still have Joseph's bones with them, and these they bury in Shechem. Now Shechem, in Involution, was the place where Joseph was found wandering in the wilderness. And this point on the opposite side is not even in the human kingdom. In the meantime, they had passed through the land of the Genesic giants, here called the Anakim, whose cities were "high and fenced up to heaven," as in Moses' day. There were also Amorites, Perizzites, Hivites, and Hittites to be slaughtered, as in Moses' day, and all for the benefit of the Godites, as in Moses' day. Now it was in the battle with the Amorites that Joshua performed his greatest miracle—causing the sun and moon to stand still. Today, even our literalists admit that this is some sort of mythology, but even in this they are mistaken, for this is the one part of Joshua that is not mythology, nor has it any occult meaning. It is merely an excerpt plucked bodily from the Book of Jasher, a collection of war songs, and war songs consist of poetic imagery and wild exaggeration of national deeds and heroes. Such are the words: "And the stars in their courses fought against Sisera." So also, "Sun, stand thou still upon Gibeon; and thou moon, in the valley of Ajalon." Yet as late as 1664 the pope of Rome issued a bull condemning Copernicus and upholding Joshua. Such are the results of literally interpreted scripture.

These literalists should read their Bible more intelligently, particularly Joshua. It is trying to tell us the true nature of Causation, a nonmoral and violent power. Only when they recognize it will they understand "The slings and arrows of outrageous fortune" it flings upon them. This is the real "revelation" of the Old Testament, completely destroyed by the epigonous ignorance of the New. Jewish scholars consider the

Pentateuch the most important and truest part of their scriptures; this is correct because it accords with nature, the one true source of truth.

What do we see when we look out into space at night? Millions of stars, and stars are suns and suns are centers of violent forces. When an old sun dies it becomes a young planet and that violence is still in it, hence the earthquake and volcano. When life forms appear on it, that violence is in them also; it is in us and it is this that drives us to war and killing. Then we pray to it for peace. If we would have peace we must first learn the cause of war. This is what the honest Jhwhist is trying to tell us, so let us read and learn.

18. And the Lord said unto Joshua, Stretch out the spear that is in thy hand (Moses' rod) towards Ai; for I will give it into thine hand. . . .

24. And it came to pass, when Israel had made an end of slaying all the inhabitants of Ai in the field, in the wilderness wherein they chased them, and when they were all fallen on the edge of the sword, until they were consumed, that all the Israelites returned unto Ai, and smote it with the edge of the sword.

25. And so it was, that all that fell that day, both of men and women, were twelve thousand, even all the men of Ai.

26. For Joshua drew not his hand back, wherewith he stretched out the spear, until he had utterly destroyed all the inhabitants of Ai.

27. Only the cattle and the spoil of that city Israel took for a prey unto themselves, according unto the word of the Lord which he commanded Joshua (Chap. 8).

These are literal words; do the literalists see in them any evidence of divinity, morality, love, and mercy? That they are but symbolic words is proven by our archeologists. According to them, the city of Ai was a ruin long before the Hebrews appeared; indeed, the name in Hebrew, *ha'Ai*, means "the ruin." It was destroyed before 2000 B.C., and not rebuilt until some four hundred years after the alleged time of Joshua. Thus the author is not writing history; he is writing theology. In the Book of Numbers these wars are called by their rightful name—"the wars of Jehovah," that is, the wars of the Creator. We said the

Bible is the greatest indictment of God ever written, but this Hebrew Hitler has only gotten started; we should read on until we either blush for shame or else admit that the Bible is a book of mythology.

7. So Joshua ascended from Gilgal, he, and all the people of war with him, and all the mighty men of valour.

8. And the Lord said unto Joshua, Fear them not: for I have delivered them into thine hand; there shall not a man of them stand before thee.

9. Joshua therefore came unto them suddenly, and went up from Gilgal all night.

10. And the Lord discomfited them before Israel, and slew them with a great slaughter at Gibeon, and chased them along the way that goeth up to Beth-horon, and smote them to Azekah, and unto Makkedah.

11. And it came to pass, as they fled from before Israel, and were in the going down to Beth-horon, that the Lord cast down great stones from heaven upon them unto Azekah, and they died: they were more which died with hailstones than they whom the children of Israel slew with the sword (Chap. 10).

And what had these people done that they should be stoned from heaven? Nothing except that they were in the way of "the chosen of the Lord," for which he will do anything—miracles, murder, massacre and mayhem. "Ask of me, and I shall give thee the heathen for thine inheritance, and the utmost parts of the earth for thy possession." Psalm 2:8. Today the Arabs are in their way so Ali Baba beware.

That Joshua's maneuvers were a military impossibility makes no difference to the believers; nor does the fact that the Jews at the time were nomads, shepherds, not warriors. Such race-glorification was common in those days; the Babylonian tablets tell a similar tale about the king of Akkad plundering city after city, the source, perhaps, of the Hebrew story.

28. And that day Joshua took Makkedah, and smote it with the edge of the sword, and the king thereof he utterly destroyed, them, and all

the souls that were therein; he let none remain: and he did to the king of Makkedah as he did unto the king of Jericho.

29. Then Joshua passed from Makkedah, and all Israel with him, unto Libnah, and fought against Libnah:

30. And the Lord delivered it also, and the king thereof, into the hand of Israel; and he smote it with the edge of the sword, all the souls that were therein; he let none remain in it; but did unto the king thereof as he did unto the king of Jericho.

31. And Joshua passed from Libnah, and all Israel with him, unto Lachish, and encamped against it, and fought against it:

32. And the Lord delivered Lachish into the hand of Israel, which took it on the second day, and smote it with the edge of the sword, and all the souls that were therein, according to all that he had done to Libnah.

33. Then Horam king of Gezer came up to help Lachish; and Joshua smote him and his people, until he had left him none remaining.

34. And from Lachish Joshua passed unto Eglon, and all Israel with him; and they encamped against it, and fought against it:

35. And they took it on that day, and smote it with the edge of the sword, and all the souls that were therein he utterly destroyed that day, according to all that he had done to Lachish (Chap. 10).

Such is the record, but only part of it. Little wonder the poet E. A. Robinson on reading it exclaimed: "A most bloodthirsty and perilous book for the young. Jehovah is beyond a doubt the worst character in fiction." We blame the movies and the comics for juvenile delinquency but there is nothing in them to compare with Joshua and his God. To help His "chosen" this God destroyed Egypt and drowned its people; He even drowned "all in whose nostrils was the breath of life." And we're supposed to worship him. If so, then we are all devil-worshipers.

The Jews firmly believe they are "the chosen people"; what they do not know is that that which chose them is the devil. If the reader cannot accept this, he should read again the book of Joshua. There this Jehovah commanded Joshua to kill thirty-one kings and possibly a million men, women and children. If this be not the devil's work, what is it? And whom did this killer choose to do His dirty work? Jacob, Joshua, Moses and David, criminals all. Yet they were men "after God's own heart." If so,

God must be like His men. This is what the Torah is telling us, and only when the Jews realize it will they understand themselves and their tragic history.

Now this is not anti-Semitism. The scriptural Jews are but symbols of life and that includes us all. Their ancient priests deceived us but so did their Christian counterparts and for 2,000 years.

These see no theistic lesson in Joshua. On the contrary, they use it to show us the rewards of faith in God. He stopped the sun, He divided the sea for His chosen; He sent down manna from heaven for them—and hailstones for their enemies. This is that false security the scriptures offer. On the basis of it fools let serpents sting them to prove their faith, others refuse inoculation and deny their children blood transfusion. Such false faith must be destroyed. A mythical God is a spiritual "Maginot Line"—a comfort when all is well but useless in time of trouble, war, for instance. When that occurs both sides pray to this God, but God is on the side of the heaviest cannon. Here cannon power is God's aid, and whoever gets there with "the mostest" wins. Now, that aid is El Shaddai's power, atomic energy, and this is our security today not the God of religion. Lacking any diviner aid some of our preachers tell us that God withdrew from his world after this miraculous age; they must now learn that this miraculous age was mythology's age, and its God but mythology's stage equipment.

Forty wars in one generation should convince any intelligent person of these facts, but for lack of such intelligence, war only magnifies the illusion. Its helpless victims cry out to God because they know not what else to do. The Church is quick to capitalize on this, and so we have a revival of faith—the public's extremity is the priests' opportunity. During the Second World War they told us repeatedly, "There are no atheists in foxholes." If so, it was only because there was no wisdom or understanding either; there was only that religion-born ignorance that produces foxholes. From these the tortured souls of men may cry to God as an instinctual reflex, but if they could reason from war to cause, their "Prayer from a Foxhole" would read like this:

> Now I lay me down to sleep
> Where bullets fly and vermin creep;
> If I should die before I wake,
> I pray the human race will take
> The measure of a God whose will
> For moral man is Kill and Kill.

"The fool saith in his heart, There is no God"—and another fool saith there is; but for two thousand years the affirmative fools have run the world and so they branded all who differ with them as atheists, infidels, social outcasts, etc. Yet what other attitude is there for the enlightened? Strip the theists of their mythological authority and you see the atheists have been right, not in denying a Creator, which they do not, but in denying the God of religion, which they do and rightly so. It is from these that all enlightened government comes, including that of our founding fathers, most of them atheists and we could fill pages with their atheism. In spite of this fact no avowed atheist can hold a government position. This too is due to religion. The Church fears atheism, not because it is inimical to human welfare but because it is inimical to its welfare. The churchmen want their mythical God because in him they live and move and have their cake and eat it too. The Church has thus become an institution for the care and maintenance of God, not man. You can say anything about man, and the Church will do nothing, but speak one word against its God and the whole benighted crew will rise in wrath against you. They should read Joshua again, then ask themselves which is the true God, the God of Joshua or the God of Jesus? They cannot both be right, yet Joshua was written before the darkness fell completely. That darkness is still upon the churchmen and while they sleep nature's savage forces kill and kill; compare them with Joshua's God and you find they agree completely.

If this God is the father of Jesus Christ, then this book is blasphemy, and the Jews have libeled God as well as Pharaoh. It makes him the complete antithesis of his son. The question then is, Which is right, the Old Testament or the New? Volumes have been written to resolve this paradox and all have missed the point. Their authors, as ignorant of the Old Testament's subject as its lesson, have made the change to appear as due to man's increasing knowledge of the goodness of God, when all the while it is due to his decreasing knowledge of Causation and Reality. As we have said, the people of the mythopoeic age knew the true nature of these, and just as we receded from them was their knowledge lost. The first part of the Old Testament being the nearest to that age contains this knowledge, but as its books increased, that knowledge decreased, until it culminated in the New Testament, which, from the standpoint of metaphysical truth, represents the nadir of human understanding. Thus the Old Testament is right and the New is wrong. Its God is the true God—a soulless, senseless power whose only "righteousness" is biologic rightness, and whose only "grace" is survival fitness. The one sin in its eyes is weakness, laziness, complacency. This in time these mythological Israelites became, and to punish them this God raised up nations to destroy them. And only when great heroes rose again to plunder and despoil was His wrath averted. Ehud burying his knife in the fat King Eglon's belly, and Jael driving the nail into Sisera's head, were glorious deeds in His sight and worthy of recompense; which is just another way of saying that moral principles mean nothing to the Creative Principle. It has but one goal, Evolution, and whatever stands in its way must be destroyed. Yes, God "is a man of war" and destruction is in his hands.

And what does that make man? In war man is but a victim of a merciless power, using him for its own end, the evolutionary goal. And since war is a means to this end, man, in waging it, is a murderer climbing to Utopia on the corpses of his fallen brothers. He must find a better way than that devised by God. These things he cannot see because he has been blinded by a false theology. This is one of the evils of religion.

War is an instrument devised by God for the salvation of man—Evolution. Its purpose is to destroy what we will not, to tear down the fixed inadequacies that the more adequate may be built. War is nature's spasmodic effort to change the *status quo*, but we will have none of that. As soon as one war is over, we lay the foundations of another. Blinded and obsessed by

religion and commercialism, we set up old boundaries, old sover-
eignties, old systems and old ways, when the purpose of war is
to destroy them. Do you not see then the part we *self-righteous
wrongdoers* play in war? Were we to make peace a time of war
on our social evils, there would be no need of military war.

To escape this man must find an intellectual as well as a moral
equivalent for war, something that can bring about change without violence—brains instead of battles, books instead of bullets.
But where are the brains to write such books? Try one and you'll
be an atheist and an infidel. Here is the place for your "rugged
individualism," but no, we'll think no new thoughts, make no
changes where personal and material things are concerned;
we'll keep right on provoking war below and trusting to "divine
providence" above to give us peace. According to the Pentateuch, there is no such *above* but only a savage *below* and the
Pentateuch is right.

This is the lesson the Old Testament is trying to tell us. As
plainly as the occult can make it, it denies a moral and merciful
Deity and presents instead a nonmoral and merciless Principle—the genetic of our theory. It is this, or its creation, our
desire nature plus our ignorant minds, that drives us into war,
and as long as we are ignorant of it we are in our glorious wars
but dupes and boobs and victims of it. This is the vital knowledge religion is hiding from us. Instead of teaching us the facts
of life it tells us everything moral, merciful and just must come
from God, the very opposite of the truth. Everything moral and
merciful we've ever dreamed of—peace, brotherhood, Utopia—
must come from the epigenetic, ourselves. This can be summa-
rized in the word consciousness, the evolving factor. When this
is sufficiently moralized, intelligized and civilized we will see
our dream realized. This is Christ-consciousness, and this is
what the New Testament offers us—life as lived by moralized,
intelligized and civilized humanity. That this way of the New
Testament will someday prevail over the Old is inevitable, but
no such world is possible yet. We too are in "the wilderness"
and never will we reach our "Promised Land" while we remain
as now, epigenetically inadequate to our place in genetic Creation.

What we need today is a complete reexamination of war in terms of Causation, Creation, biology and economics, uninfluenced by religion and its false securities. As Clemenceau said, "War is too important to leave to generals," so, peace is too important to leave to God. Fortunately the idea is now dawning on the race, hence our nascent but promising United Nations— the supernational instead of the supernatural. In this the collective will of the moral epigenetic will control the individual's genetic will to war and conquest.

13

Judges and Kings

It is God that girdeth me with strength . . . He
teacheth my hands to war . . .

PSALM 18:32, 34

Judges

After reading about Moses and Joshua we
naturally suppose that the subsequent books deal with subsequent periods, but again we say, the Bible has no such sequence.
Its numerous excerpts are dovetailed together regardless of
chronology; at one time we are reading about Evolution, at
another, Involution. Indeed, we cannot even trust it when it is
supposedly dealing with history. As an immediate instance of
this, the second chapter of Joshua tells us this man of war killed
Jabin, king of Hazor, but the fourth chapter of Judges says Barak
killed him. According to the Jhwhist account, Saul committed
suicide, but the Elohist says an Amalekite killed him. Daniel is
assumed to be contemporary with Nebuchadnezzar, yet part of
his story was written in Aramaic, a language not adopted by the
Jews until centuries later. The scriptures call Belshazzar a king,
but the historical Belshazzar was never king but only regent for
Nabonidus. Thus we cannot trust the Bible even historically.

Like all the rest, Judges is mythology, and its authors use a
mythic formula that, according to our Bible students, runs like

this: Israel sins; Jehovah is angry; Jehovah punishes Israel; Israel repents and all is well—until the next time. The punishment is bondage to some other nation, and the extent of it belies their other historical claims. They are in bondage in Egypt 430 years, in Babylon, 70. These alone make 500 years. Add to this 40 years to the Philistines, to Hazor 20, to Eglon 18, to the Midians 7, and in Mesopotamia, 8. Add to this several others scattered throughout the Bible and it makes nearly 700 years, practically their entire authentic B.C. history. If this is racial history, the Jews should be ashamed of it instead of proud. And again, if it is racial history what becomes of their B.C. claim to Palestine? They never owned it, save mythologically.

Judges is not post-Mosaic history but pre-Mosaic cosmology; in other words, we are back in Involution again. The revolution is too long to treat in detail, and so we will select just a few highlights that reveal most clearly the mythological nature of scriptural history.

Samson

One of the most interesting characters in Judges is the great man Samson, the misnamed Hebrew Hercules. Like all the rest, his story has been accepted as true and historical, when all the while it is just a sun myth. The name itself means "man of the sun" or "sun man." But please understand that a sun myth is not about our sun; it is about our own world when it was a sun. Every world or planet was once a sun and therefore has a past quite different from its present mundane lot. Now the ancients knew this, if we do not, and so their solar myths are allegories about this glorious stage and the mighty works accomplished in it. Its hero is a personification of this, but in the Samson myth the tale is not complete. Like that of Jesus, it tells only of his parentage and birth, then skips to his manhood.

2. And there was a certain man of Zorah, of the family of the Danites, whose name was Ma-*noah;* and his wife was barren, and bare not.

3. And the angel of the Lord appeared unto the woman, and said

unto her, Behold now, thou art barren, and bearest not; but thou shalt conceive, and bear a son.

4. Now therefore beware, I pray thee, and drink not wine nor strong drink, and eat not any unclean thing.

5. For, lo, thou shalt conceive, and bear a son; and no rasor shall come on his head: for the child shall be a Nazarite unto God from the womb: and he shall begin to deliver Israel out of the hands of the Philistines (Judges 13).

So here again the Hebrews are in trouble—the usual forty years, and the inevitable cause—sin. And here again we have a barren woman, the planetary mother, promised a son by "an angel of the Lord." This is Genesis all over again. Judges, however, combines the Genesic stories for Ma-noah is none other than Noah, and his barren wife is none other than Abram's Sarai. The *son* she is to bear could well have been written *sun*, for that is its occult meaning. It is also the occult significance of the admonition to drink no wine or strong drink: a fiery sun cannot be nurtured on the liquid element. The word Nazarite comes from *nazar*, which means *unshorn*, and has nothing to do with Nazareth, except mythologically.

The story thus far deals with the higher planes in Involution, but now we find Samson as a young man *going down* into Timnath to find a wife among the Philistines, the lower elements, as did Joseph before him. This greatly displeases his father, who, like Abraham and Isaac, wanted his son to marry one of his own people. But again a son of God saw a daughter of men, and again trouble resulted.

In its descent to dense matter, the creative force passes through the sun stage, and so Samson on his way to Timnath meets a lion, Leo, which he slays to show his strength. Later, he finds a bee hive in the carcass, and from this he expounds a riddle. This is not just a touch of Jewish humor, as some suppose, but a fact we have asserted from the beginning, namely, that out of the dead carcass of a sun comes the sweetness of evolutionary life; in other words, the best part of Creation is the last.

Now this strong man had three women in his life, and all of

them "done him wrong." The first tried for *seven* days to learn the answer to his riddle, that she might relay it to the Philistines who sought to kill him. The third sought the secret of his strength for the same reason. The second, a harlot, also wanted this secret and so detained him in her house until the Philistines surrounded it. But he "took the doors of the gate of the city, and two posts, and went away with them." Now if Samson was in a house, why would he take the doors and posts of the city? Because the house and the city are one, namely, the earth. The posts or pillars are its Jachin and Boaz, which we will meet later on.

So with the women; the three are one, and none, but rather varying degrees of spirit-sapping matter. Only one has a name, the enervating Delilah, which means "the weakening or debilitating one." The word comes from the Hebrew *lilah*, which means *darkness, night*, and with a D or De before it, becomes Delilah. Now the Hebrew D, *daleth*, means *door*, and so Delilah is the door to darkness which in mythology means the underworld of matter. And that we may see these myths are all synonymous, Delilah is none other than Adam's first wife Lilith, from the Babylonian *Lilitu*, an evil night-spirit. In all the Mesopotamian nations, Lilith was identified with Succubus, female of Incubus, who visits men at night. But as Samson and Adam are the cosmic Man, Delilah and Lilith are their cosmic counterparts—spirit-destroying matter. Thus, no sex or immorality is implied. You see, mythology makes the Bible decent, which as a religion-source it is not.

It also makes this part of the Bible understandable, for now we can see what the Eve of this story really did. After many attempts she discovers the secret of Samson's strength lies in his hair, a literal absurdity, but not so absurd esoterically. This hair that had never been shorn was of *seven strands*, the mystic number, and signifies here the sun's rays with their seven colors, vibrations, and the like. Once a sun loses these—the free, radiant energies—its power as a sun is gone; it then becomes a planet—power captive in matter. We know that the Greek Apollo was the sun, and Homer called him "he of the unshorn hair." The Egyptians pictured the summer sun with hair and the winter sun as shorn; and the priests cut their hair in winter in tribute thereto. Thus Samson is the sun and his sacred hair its streamers.

Now the secret out, Delilah made Samson "sleep upon her knees; and she called for a man, and she caused him to shave off the seven locks of his head; and she began to afflict him, and his strength went from him" (16:19). As a precautionary measure, she also had him bound with *seven* withes—the septenate congealing process. Samson must have been a heavy sleeper, for he did not know he was being bound or shaved. Still, matter is a sleepy place; thus it was with Adam, Noah, Pharaoh, and even God, who had to "rest" in it. The withes the strong man broke with ease, but before Delilah got through with him, "his strength went from him."

As a story of two human beings the sex implication is inevitable. As this is the extent of our clergy's understanding of scripture, one wrote of it thus: "The immoralities and sexual irregularities of Samson were more akin to the tales of the gods of the Greeks and Romans than to the moral requirements of the prophetic commands. Samson was to the Israelites (probably the Philistines had their Samson too) what Hercules was to the Greeks, a witty athlete but utterly devoid of morality." Little does His Reverence know how near akin to the gods of Greece and Rome this Samson is. He was not, however, the Hebrew Hercules; he was the Hebrew Prometheus. But, blinded by scriptural diabolism, His Reverence saw no connection between Samson bound and Prometheus bound. And no one sees the cosmological meaning of either. From other sources we learn that Samson was lame, like all the fire gods of mythology, but this too falls on deaf ears.

/ Certain it is, Samson was no mortal. According to various Midrashim, his shoulders were sixty ells broad, and when the spirit of the Lord was upon him, he could step from Zorah to Eshtaol. So strong was he, he could pick up two mountains and rub them together. When he was thirsty, a well of water sprang from his teeth. In the Bible the water springs from the ass's jaw with which he slew a thousand Philistines—but that was before he met Delilah.

Now, his power gone, this "witty athlete" is helpless, and so the Philistines (matter) took Samson (the sun) and put out his eyes (light) and brought him down to Gaza (the lower planes) and bound him with brass (density) and he did grind (labor) in the prison house (earth). Thus "eyeless in Gaza at the mill with slaves," the once-free spirit principle is again in bondage, this time in Philistia instead of Egypt. What then of his mission, "to deliver Israel out of the hands of the Philistines"?

The rest of Samson's story is but planetary anticlimax, nay, repetition. His pulling down the pillars, the solar Jachin and Boaz, upon himself and the Philistines represents the creative force pulling down upon itself the material substance of the planetary structure—an act already accomplished. As this resulted in Samson's death (the Life Principle's death in matter), he was, like Jacob and Joseph, taken up (by way of Evolution) to the land of his father Ma-noah (land of Noah), the spirit planes again. Such is the story of Samson—the creative process concealed by priestly cunning. How different from our novels and movies about him!

We wish that we could say this bit of cunning occultism was strictly Hebrew and original, but we cannot. The Siamese had their Samson also—Sommona Cadom (Adam)—and their ancient books show him as their Savior, pulling down the pillars of a pagoda upon himself and his enemies. The Greeks also had their Samson and Delilah, matter's triumph over spirit, symbolized by woman's triumph over man. This is the real meaning of the myth of the Amazons. These warrior women never existed; they represent matter's triumph over consciousness on the lower planes. Their queen was Hippolita, known also as Antiope—anti-ope. As the *ope* comes from *ops*, the eye, symbol of intelligence, she was matter, the opposer, thus one with Delilah the opposer of Samson, and Mephistopheles, the opposer of light. So now we have Antiope to add to Antigone, Antigonus, and the others. All these *anti-bodies* are oppose matter, and according to the Amazon myth, the only way to overcome it was to secure the girdle of the queen. Now a girdle is something that binds, and the girdle of Antiope is the binding force of matter. Its removal was one of the twelve labors of Hercules, who also unbound Prometheus, and Hercules is the creative force now on the evolutionary side of the Tree of Life. This is a mythologist's way of presenting that process we call radiation—nature freeing consciousness from the prison house of matter. We read it all before in Moses and Joshua.

Samuel, Saul, and David

The Book of I Samuel tells the life of the last of the judges of the theocracy, Samuel, and his work as king maker. This book has presented perplexing problems to scholars who have long tried to arrange the different sources into connected accounts of the lives of the three men involved: Samuel, Saul and David. This problem is one on which all students of the Bible may profitably spend time.

C. A. Hawley

As these are but a repeat of Abraham, Isaac and Jacob, we will deal but briefly with them, and then only to explain the difficulties that have perplexed our Bible students. Contrary to the above advice, no Bible student can profitably spend his time on this or any other book of the Bible while laboring under religion's concept of Causation.

As stated, the book is but a repetition of previous scripture, and so we find another barren woman, Hannah, beseeching the Lord for offspring. If he will but grant her a son she will, like Samson's mother, "give him unto the Lord all the days of his life, and there shall no razor come upon his head." The child is duly born and called Samuel—man of God, as was Samson. And like Samson, he is a Nazar, dedicated from his birth to the Lord's work, which is Creation. He is also a Levite and a priest, hence the Creative Principle. In his early youth he is placed under the care of a high priest called Eli, and Eli means God, here the first aspect. Too little remains of Eli's story, because the Editor's purpose was to make David a historical character and exalt him above all other men. The little that does remain, however, is very significant. He incurs the wrath of the Hebrews' God, and this God determines to get rid of both him and his children. This he accomplishes in his consistently ruthless way: Eli breaks his neck and his children die in battle. Here we have in Hebrew scriptures something we thought existed only in pagan mythology—the wanton destruction of the first god and the henotheistic succession of the next, in this case Samuel.

"And the child Samuel grew on, and was in favor both with the Lord and also with men," a statement later taken from here and applied to Jesus. Now as soon as Samuel reached manhood he continued the slaughter begun by Moses and Joshua; he utterly destroyed the Ammonites and then the Amalekites whose king was Agag—"And Samuel hewed Agag in pieces before the Lord in Gilgal" (1 Sam. 15:33). In all these wars the Hebrews carried their God about in a cage, the ark of the covenant; and so terrible was this God that when some curious ones peeked in "he smote of the people fifty thousand and threescore and ten men" (1 Sam. 6:19). Again we ask, Is this the God of Jesus or of nature? There is but one and if this one be the God of nature, what are we worshiping the other for? In doing so, we are all idolators, for he is a false God. Samuel's own sons refused to worship this murderous God and so, like eleven of Uranus's sons, were declared unfit to succeed their father. The people therefore demanded something new in Israel—a king. Here again we should forget Israel and think in terms of Creation. The planetary elements are approaching materiality and they want a material king, not a spirit-god, and so Samuel, against his own will, appoints Saul, one with the Roman Sol or sun— "head and shoulders above" all other cosmic bodies. This is the sun's sovereignty over his people, the planets. This first king in Creation was sent out by his father to find certain asses that were thereabout, and the "thereabout" in this case is the vicinity of Leo, the sun. Now there are in the neighborhood of Leo two asses know as the Ascelli, and they have been woven into numerous creation myths. It was upon these that Bacchus and Vulcan rode in their war against the Titans; it was on these that Moses, his wife and his sons returned to Egypt, and still later another Savior rode to Jerusalem. It was these the future king Saul was seeking.

Patriarch, judge and king—three stages in the descending process—and all of them must go. In spite of the Lord's assertion that Saul was perfect and would deliver Israel from the Philistines, he became insane and was killed by these Philistines. Such is the fate of every god when his work is done, including Saul. Because of a slight transgression "the Lord repented that he had made Saul king over Israel" (15:35), and an "evil spirit from God" came upon him. These words are a sore perplexity to our deluded clergy. They cannot deny them, neither can they explain them away. That is because they are students of Divinity instead of Reality. The result is that "an evil spirit from God" is upon them also; its name is priestly theology. Even after reading five books about an evil God, they cannot attribute evil to him. Well, Isaiah did, and reported this God as saying, "I create evil." He is the involuntionary evil for which Evolution must atone, and His work, Creation, the "sin" for which man must suffer. Concealing this fact from man is the priestly sin of the rest of the Bible.

Saul now disqualified, Samuel anoints David, son of Jesse. It should be son of Jacob, for he was like cunning old Jacob reborn again. But ". . . the evil spirit from God was upon Saul, and he sat in his house with his javelin in his hand . . . and Saul sought to smite David even to the wall with the javelin; but he slipped away out of Saul's presence, and he smote the javelin into the wall: and David fled, and escaped that night." 1 Sam. 19:9, 10. He escaped to the wilderness, and there wandered about like Joseph and Moses, there became naked like Adam and Noah. There also he cut off Saul's skirt and robbed him of the desire to kill, as Delilah cut off Samson's hair and robbed him of the power to kill.

Eventually Samuel dies, and the insane Saul is left to govern Israel alone. Unable to meet the Philistines, in spite of the Lord appointing him to destroy them, he resorts to the dead Samuel for advice. And here we have that curious story about "the witch of Endor." In spite of Moses' "thou shalt not suffer a witch to live," there were some in Saul's time—a hint that Saul is prior to Moses. The Bible does not tell us the name of this one; it was, however, Sedecla, and she had a "familiar spirit."

13. And the king said unto her, Be not afraid: for what sawest thou? And the woman said unto Saul, I saw gods ascending out of the earth.

14. And he said unto her, What form is he of? And she said, An old man cometh up; and he is covered with a mantle. And Saul perceived that it was Samuel, and he stooped with his face to the ground, and bowed himself (1 Sam. Chap. 28).

Here we see the true nature of Samuel, for Samuel *was* these gods—the creative forces, and these ascending forces are identical with those Jacob saw ascending the ladder of heaven. Through the witch Samuel tells Saul that he will lose his kingdom and also his life. This is indeed occult cosmology, for the woman is matter, and through this the Creator tells Sol, the sun, that it must die and be succeeded by David, king of Jerusalem, which is earth.

And now to illustrate the influence of literal scripture upon the human mind, and history, let us quote the eminent legal authority, William Blackstone, who in 1765 said: "To deny the possibility, nay actual existence of witchcraft and sorcery, is at once flatly to contradict the revealed word of God in various passages both of the Old and New Testament." Thus on the authority of "the word of God" this eminent jurist poured legal oil on the fires of religious fanaticism. On the same authority, Pope Innocent VII in 1484 issued his famous "Witch Bull," authorizing women, who should have been sent to psychiatrists, to be burned at the stake. In two years, 1515 and 1516, the Catholic Church burned over five hundred Protestant witches. A thing of the past, you say, so why recall it? Yes, witch-burning is past, but not the witch-burning mentality. There are still with us priests who would burn in boiling oil the dissident Protestants—modern Torquemadas without an Inquisition. Though of the atomic age, they still believe in witches, pacts with the devil, and the literal "word of God." The *Catholic Encyclopedia* still offers this on witchcraft: "In the face of the Holy Scriptures and the teachings of the Fathers and theologians, the abstract possibility of a pact with the Devil and of diabolical interference in human affairs can hardly be denied." Such people should know; they've been in a pact with the Devil for five thousand years, and their "diabolical interference in human affairs" is the proof thereof. Today it's contraception and abortion.

It was, again, the literal word without understanding that caused the witch burning of the Christian era. It is also the cause of our students' difficulty with the books of Samuel. Added to this is another, the redactor's method. He had at least three versions, and wishing to conserve significant points in each, he juxtaposed excerpts from them all; the result is not only confusion, but seeming contradiction as well. Chapter 16, for instance, tells us that David came to Saul as his armor-bearer and court musician. As such, the king would know him well, yet presumedly later, in chapter 17, Saul does not know David even when he sees him, nor does Abner, his general. Here David is introduced to Saul as the hero who was about to kill Goliath— the Philistine Samson and scriptural Titan. "And when Saul saw David go forth against the Philistine, he said unto Abner, the captain of the (monadic) host, Abner, whose son is this youth? And Abner said, As thy soul liveth, O king, I cannot tell. . . . And the King said, Inquire thou whose son the stripling is" (17:55–56). Still another account (17:12–30), omitted in the Septuagent, is from a third author. We have also two distinct and apparently contradictory accounts of Saul's death: one by the Jhwhist, the other by the Elohist. The candid Jhwhist says plainly that Saul committed suicide, a disgrace the priestly Elohist could not stomach, and so he has an Amalekite kill him. Now an Amalekite is of the house of Amalek, death. Amalek is the Hebrew Siva, the destroyer, and his purpose is to destroy Brahma's previous work.

In the beginning, Saul was the good or creative spirit, but when his work was done this spirit left him and passed to David, the next plane and element. It was then that "the evil spirit from God" came upon Saul, as it comes upon every Sol when its time comes to die and become a dense-matter planet. Were it not so, we would never have been. This evil was not, therefore, moral but creative, and were we wise we too would use it; we would use it to destroy Arian theology as nature is now destroying Piscean ideology. With a little Aquarian cosmology, even our Bible students could solve their problems. They cannot today because their whole God-concept is wrong. Therefore they too must put away their idolatry and return to the God of Reality, the unmoral and unmerciful Principle of Life.

David

And now, Eli, Samuel and Saul departed, we pass to David, a man of vast importance to both Jew and Gentile, for on him rests the glory of Israel and the hope of Christendumb. It therefore behooves us to know who David was.

If the Bible is chronologically correct, a vast period of time is implied in the books of Exodus, Joshua, Judges, and Samuel: the Israelites were in Egypt alone four hundred and thirty years, in the desert forty more, and in bondage to other nations at least two hundred. David must therefore be removed from Jacob nearly a thousand years, and so say our encyclopedias. But in the book of Ruth we are told that David was but tenth from Pharez, a contemporary of Jacob. Now ten generations do not make a thousand years, even in David's time; he lived but seventy. And so we see we cannot trust the chronology, or sequence, of the Bible. Because of this we should discount all its second-millennium history; it is mythology and nothing else.

David was neither historically nor mythologically subsequent to Jacob; he is one with Jacob and appears in this separate myth at exactly the same point and time as did Jacob, namely, the third plane. "And David was thirty years old when he began to reign and he reigned forty years." The thirty years represent the first three planes and preparatory periods, as with Noah, and the forty, the four below. He lived just seventy years, the seven involutionary cycles. From Midrashic sources we learn that he was destined to die at birth and on a Sabbath, seventh plane, but when the Lord was showing Adam his future progeny, this long-lived forebear offered to give David seventy years of his own life. These are the seventy David lived, but he died nevertheless on a Sabbath and by falling downstairs. This is an Apocryphal writer's way of describing spirit's descent into matter; it is also his way of saying *Demon est Deus inversus*. And that explains David's subsequent life, so different from its beginning.

He was born in Bethlehem, the "house of bread," or source; his father's name was Jesse, which means "to be" or "he that is," the I AM of this myth. Like Moses' father, he died sinless, that sinlessness of prephysical being, identical with that of Edenic Adam and Noah.

In his youth David tended his father's flocks, as Moses tended Jethro's; and while thus occupied the Lord spoke to him, as He did to Moses. David also slew a lion with his bare hands, as did Samson. But this was not enough for the Apocryphal writers; they made it four lions. Another Midrash tells us that David, on seeing something in the wilderness he mistook for a mountain, began to climb it, but suddenly it became a great monster that rose and lifted him high on its horns. Perceiving his danger he besought the Lord's help, promising to build Him a temple one hundred ells high if He would save him. As God intended him to build a temple anyway, the earth, He sent a second beast, as in Revelation, which subdued and overcame the first—the earth subduing and overcoming its sun stage. This is a mythologist's way of describing the creative process, but how many will see its theological implication? If David personifies that which created the temple, earth, what need is there for the scripture's God? Again, none except to religionizing priests.

These carefully removed the unbelievable miraculous from their account; indeed, there is little in David's life that could not happen to a historical character. Why then, you ask, do we inject the Midrashim; they are no part of "the word of God." To this we reply, the whole book of Jonah is a Midrash, and so is the book of Job. These so-called exegetical or interpretive supplements contain the cosmological key to the canonical hoax. Like the myths, these fanciful tales are not meant to be believed, but to be understood, whereas "the word of God" was meant to deceive. With a cunning that can only be described as diabolical it has duped the world for two thousand years. Clever fellows, these Hebrew mythologists! Not everyone can deceive his enemies and still be praised and defended by them.

Now this Midrashic temple and David's scriptural city, Jerusalem, are one. In the name itself we have a hint of its nature. According to the Tell-el-Amarna tablets it was originally called Urusalim—Ur and Salem, light and peace—identical with the city of Abram and Melchizedek. But these involutionary cities never stay luminous and peaceful long; they soon become the battleground of warring Titans—the "war in heaven," "the wars of Jehovah," and others. This is the warfare of David, the king.

But David was not only a warrior; he was also a lecher, a thief, a murderer and a bandit. Next to Joshua's God he is, perhaps, the worst character in the scriptures. This we learn from his means of securing wives and concubines, of which he had many. His first wife was Michal, Saul's daughter. But Saul, fearing David, and hoping to be rid of him, sent him on a dangerous mission. This was to secure for him 100 Philistine foreskins as a dowry. To the smart boy David this was child's play, so he doubled the dowry, 200 foreskins. This not only pleased Saul but Michal also and so she married him. His second wife was Abigail, the wife of Nabal. By a lifetime of toil this man had acquired great wealth in sheep and goats. On learning of this, David blackmailed him. He demanded tribute or death. When Nabal refused, David sent 400 men to kill him, but his partner in crime saved him the trouble, "the Lord smote Nabal, that he died." Now David sent for Abigail and made her his wife. His next conquest was even more despicable. While spying on Bathsheba at her bath, he fell in love with her. But alas she, too, was married, to Uriah, a military hero. So what to do? Why, as he did to Nabal. To this end he sent a letter to Joab his general ordering him to put Uriah in the forefront of battle that he might be killed. He was, and David married Bathsheba. In the meantime he was killing Philistines by the tens of thousands. And this is the book we compel our children to read for moral uplift.

If it be history, and if God required a man to build him a holy temple, lead His "chosen people" and serve as forebear to His "only begotten son," why should He choose a man like David? For the same reason he chose the murderous Moses and Joshua. Force and violence are His way and so He needed an agent of like nature. "God is a man of war," and to Him David attributed all his warlike power.

> God is my strength and power.
> He teaches my hands to war.
> Thou hast girded me with strength to battle.
> Thou hast also given me the necks of mine enemies (Psalm 18).
> Then did I beat them as small as the dust of the earth, I did stamp them as the mire of the street, and did spread them abroad (2 Sam. 22:43).
> And David gathered all the people together and went to Rabbah, and fought against it, and took it (2 Sam. 12:29).
> And he brought forth the people that were therein, and put them under saws, and under harrows of iron, and under axes of iron, and made them pass through the brickkiln (the solar crucible): and thus did he unto all the cities of the children of Ammon . . . (2 Sam. 12:31).
> And David did so, as the Lord had commanded him . . . (2 Sam. 5:25).
> Therefore the Lord hath recompensed me according to my righteousness; according to my cleanness in his eye sight (2 Sam. 22:25).

So this is righteousness, this is cleanness in God's sight. Preposterous as it may sound, it is not the false God-concept of premoral humanity; it is the true God-concept of prereligious humanity, now lost in the religious night. It is God, the Creator, the murderous genetic, not the moral epigenetic. If it be otherwise, then what mental myopia afflicts us that we see these ancient murderers as spiritual men and their monstrous God as divine? It's a disease of some kind, and its name is religion— "Nature sicklied o'er with the pale cast of thought." Because of it our churchmen cannot see the truth or teach it to the public. The apologetic volumes they have written would fill a library, and in all of them these scriptural devils are glorified and exonerated, Jacob, Joshua, Moses, David—the whole murderous lot of them are held up to us as men of noblest character, their monstrous crimes due only to the times and their pagan adversaries. These they call serious studies of Hebrew history; serious they may be, but honest and enlightened they are not. Indeed the literature of religionists is peculiarly characterized by intellectual dishonesty, spiritual blindness and moral cowardice. Now this has an implication not limited to the clergy; it involves the laity as well. The clergy could not offer absurdities to a public that understood the scriptures because it knew Reality. The implication then is that the race is ignorant of the very nature of Being, its own included. In spite of all its science and invention it is going about in a state of appalling ignorance of fundamental truth. Naturally in such a state it cannot create a moral, ethical and enlightened society.

This is one of the results of the priestly hoax, and the Jews have been capitalizing on it for ages. It is the basis of our respect for them; we thank them for their gift of perverted truth. We honor them for their "heroic faith" in the face of persecution. But we should ask ourselves some serious questions. Is their faith based on fact or blind acceptance of tradition? Is it justified, or is it not? With only a little knowledge of Reality, the answer is No. That faith is based on spiritual falsehood; its partial God and protector exists nowhere save on paper. Its "pure and simple monotheism" is but ignorance of cosmic complexity. There are, we repeat, as many Gods as there are bodies in the universe, and myriad forces attend them all. Lacking knowledge of these, the Jews lumped them all together under the obscuring name Jehovah, applicable only to this one world. This is cosmology personified instead of understood.

But, you say, they must have been right, they must have been highly spiritual because they gave us a noble code of morals. True, they demanded justice and mercy but for whose benefit, the race's or their own? If with their wrathful God they could frighten others into being merciful, then they would be the beneficiaries. This selfish motive underlies even their praise of God. The Psalms are poetry, yes, but strip them of poetry and what is left? Flattery, selfishness, greed and cowardice. The psalmist but flattered his God to fatten himself. Unless there is within them some meaning not yet discerned, they are but the wailing of spiritual weaklings calling on God to compensate them for their own lack of personal and national power. That this may be clearly seen, let us again do a little selecting.

Psalm 3

1. Lord, how are they increased that trouble me! many are they that rise up against me.

3. But thou, O Lord, art a shield for me; my glory, and the lifter up of mine head.

7. Arise, O Lord; save me, O my God: for thou hast smitten all mine enemies. . . .

Psalm 4

1. Hear me when I call, O God of my righteousness: thou hast enlarged me when I was in distress; have mercy upon me, and hear my prayer.

Psalm 5

8. Lead me, O Lord, in thy righteousness because of mine enemies. . . .

10. Destroy thou them, O God; let them fall by their own counsels. . . .

Psalm 9

1. I will praise thee, O Lord, with my whole heart.

2. I will be glad and rejoice in thee: I will sing praise to thy name, O thou most High.

3. When mine enemies are turned back, they shall fall and perish at thy presence.

Psalm 18

1. I will love thee, O Lord, my strength.

3. I will call upon the Lord, who is worthy to be praised; so shall I be saved from mine enemies.

32. It is God that girdeth me with strength, and maketh my way perfect.

34. He teacheth my hands to war, so that a bow of steel is broken by mine arms.

42. Then did I beat them small as the dust before the wind: I did cast them out as the dirt in the streets.

49. Therefore will I give thanks unto thee, O Lord, among the heathen, and sing praises unto thy name.

Yea, Lord, feed me, clothe me, kill my enemies, and you can be my God; protect me from all harm and I will worship You. Cunning old Jacob, unchanged and unchanging. "And Jacob vowed a vow, saying, If God will be with me, and will keep me in this way that I go, and will give me bread to eat, and raiment to put on, so that I come again to my father's house in peace; then shall the Lord be my God" (Gen. 28:20–21). And such are the Psalms: a cry for help, a bargaining with God. This is not "heroic faith"; it is spiritual degradation and ignorance. No enlightened man would utter such words; no spiritual man would be so downright selfish. There is not a thought for others in them, nor a touch of mercy either. And, had the Jews been a military power, they would never have been written. They would not have praised the Lord, just passed the ammunition, as in Joshua's day.

There was none of this glorification of the Creator in the Jhwhist's account; why then in these later books? Because by that time the Jews had lost all contact with the ancient wisdom-knowledge, and so mistook the symbol for the fact and the letter for the spirit.

These Psalms are attributed to David, and his time, but deception lurks even here. Like Miriam's song, supposedly of Moses' day, they are mainly post-exilic effusions. Concerning this date, G. B. Winton had this to say: "To the same age perhaps belong the last chapter of Isaiah, the prophecies of Malachi and Jonah, and the books of Ruth and Job, and above all, many if not most of the Psalms." Thus David wrote these Davidean hymns in the same way Queen Elizabeth I wrote the Elizabethan dramas. He wrote his famous lament for Saul in like manner—another excerpt from the book of Jasher.

As with so many other things, there is an apocryphal account of these Psalms also. David, it says, collected them from the time of Abraham, and while singing them one day became boastful and cried out, "O Lord of the world, is there any creature that has praised thee so much?" Whereupon the Lord sent a frog to remind him that lesser creatures than he praised God day and night. And David was but a human frog, and his Psalms but "Poems in praise of practically nothing"—religion's God. If man must sing hymns to his Creator, I could suggest one more appropriate than any psalm—"You made me what I am today, I hope you're satisfied."

From all this we see that beautiful poetry is no proof of truth. A poet can sing from a false hypothesis as divinely as from a true one. Milton did, Dante did, and so did David. Poets are the singing soul of man but let them learn and sing the truth and not seductive error. Truth and Beauty are separate muses, and in poetry as in life, if truth be not with beauty, then beauty is but a harlot and a seducer of the race. Such are the Psalms of David—poetic seduction. The Egyptians left their psychism in their tombs, the Hebrews in their tomes. For nearly two thousand years they've cast a spell over the human mind; like the Trilby of fiction, it cannot think aside from this literary Svengali. Under its hypnotic spell neither cleric, scientist, nor philosopher can see the obvious; no one can teach the cosmic facts, or even biologic. Should he try, he is prosecuted by gun-toting, Bible-reading primitives or expelled by medieval-minded judges. Now that we know of what this diabolism consists, perhaps our eyes will be opened and we'll see as men knowing fact from fiction and reality from mythology.

Solomon

Of the many deceptions in the Bible there is none more cunning than its genealogy. We have already seen the deceptive use to which it was put in Genesis, and that in Kings is no better. Here we read that Solomon was the son of David, but since David himself was but a mythological hero, with no historical proof to the contrary, we are under no obligation to believe he had a son named Solomon. The latter's story is just another creation myth and wholly independent of the Davidean myth. Were it factual, ancient documents would record it. According to 2 Chronicles 9:23: ". . . all the kings of the earth sought his presence." If this be so, it is strange none of them mention him. His time, allegedly, was just prior to Homer and Hesiod, yet they do not mention this richest and wisest one. Herodotus who traveled throughout the entire Middle East does not mention him, or even the Jews. The reason is obvious: this was the age of mythology and each race wrote its own. The Bible is but Israel's religion-perverted version; its wisest man but a personification, his metaphysical wisdom but creative wisdom, his human wisdom but that of his creators.

Samson, Samuel, Saul, and Solomon: all four are names of the sun, but Solomon goes the three others two better, for the word is made up of three ancient sun names—the Roman Sol, the Hindu Om, or Aum, and the Chaldeo-Egyptian On. All three represented the creative spirit and were worshiped as such. As the sun is the visible vehicle of this, solar heroes were conceived to represent it. Such was Samson, he of the long hair, and as Absalom, Solomon's brother, like Samson, had long hair and died because of it, Solomon no doubt was similarly arrayed. And just as with so many Bible heroes, old Egypt now plays its part.

1. And Solomon (creative spirit) made affinity with Pharaoh king of Egypt (earth), and took Pharaoh's daughter (matter), and brought her into the city (of the sun) (1 Kings, Chap. 3).

He also brought the Queen of Sheba, and his mother's name was Bathsheba. Now *sheba* means seventh, and the seventh here is seventh plane matter. This story of Sheba, by the way, was taken from the *Mahabharata*, a book of Hindu poetry dating from about 500 B.C. If proof is needed that this part of the Bible is neither ancient, historical nor original, it is here. It proves that 1 and 2 Kings were not written during the alleged time of Solomon, nor were his proverbs.

One wife, however, was not enough for this wise man. He had hundreds. Now what does this mean? Abraham, Isaac and Jacob had but one or two, but as we said, from the third plane down primordial matter became infinitely discrete or divided— the "monadic host," as others called it. So here again a son of God saw the daughters of men and took them to wife.

1. But King Solomon loved many strange women, together with the daughter of Pharaoh, women of the Moabites, Ammonites, Edomites, Zidonians, and Hittites;

3. And he had seven hundred wives, princesses, and three hundred concubines: and his wives turned away his heart (Chap. 11).

Thus did the Jews libel all women—not that it has no biologic basis, but why make them the entire cause? It takes two to make a concubine. It's all right in mythologized cosmology, however; the holy Krishna of India had more than twice that number. Women in creation myths always represent matter or the material elements; Solomon's many women then were but the many material elements the genetic principle united with to form a physical world, the seven hundred being symbolic of the seven planes. This it was that turned away Solomon's heart, from the spiritual to the material—*Demon est Deus inversus* again.

The implication is that from here on Solomon became evil, and so we learn now that, like all Old Testament personifications of God, Solomon was a murderer, killing even his own brother, Adonijah. Thus Solomon is the Cain of this story. Nevertheless, "the Lord loved him," and commissioned him to build His "holy temple." For this, Solomon sent his ships to the ends of the then-known world for materials, but elsewhere we were told that David assembled these. This is not a contradiction, just an overlap of two sun myths.

This "holy temple" has gone down in history as one of the greatest of all buildings, yet according to specifications it was small indeed, only about 40 by 125 feet, and the chancels built around it were so puny as to be meaningless. Compared to other ancient temples, this one was insignificant. Consider Nagkon-Wat in Cambodia, for instance. It is 769 by 588 by 250 feet, elaborately carved and columned. In the stonework there are approximately 100,000 figures, one picture occupying 240 feet.

Solomon's temple, like Solomon himself, never existed on this earth, for the simple reason, it is the earth—that "temple not made with hands, eternal in the heavens," that same temple the Great Pyramid symbolizes. Thus Solomon is one with Philithion, its alleged builder, not actual but mythical. Both represent the Creator in the Sol, or sun, period, and we said that suns are the creators of worlds. This it was that built this fabulous temple, and this is why "there was neither hammer nor axe nor any tool of iron in the house while it was building," and its stone was "made ready before it was brought thither," from the preceding planes. To build this temple required seven years, the seven days of creation (1 Kings 6:38). This is the Lord's house, the world entity down to the end of the sun period. But Solomon built another house, this time for himself, and he was "building his own house thirteen years . . ." (7:1). Now why should this wisest of men spend so much more time on his own worldly house than on that of the Lord? Because thus far this cosmic house is not the whole house but only half. The whole house includes the earth and Evolution as well as sun and Involution, and this constitutes thirteen periods if you count the physical but once. The accounts of the two buildings are purposely confused by improper sequence of excerpts from different sources.

As given in 1 Kings 7:32–33, the details are simply those of the cosmological zodiac. The "molten sea" is the molten sun, which "stood upon twelve oxen, three looking toward the north, and three looking toward the west, and three looking toward the south, and three looking toward the east: and the sea was set above upon them, and all their hinder parts were inward" (7:25). And if you will look at the animals in the zodiac you will see that *all their hinder parts are inward.* The twelve oxen *(kirubs)* are the twelve cherubs or planentary forces. "And Solomon had twelve officers over all Israel, which provided victuals for the king and his household: each man his month in a year made provision." The twelve periods of both zodiacs, each sequentially influencing life. And the master at Lebanon was Adoniram, and in Levi's picture of Ezekiel's wheel, the word Adoni was placed over it, and in India, the word Adonari—and both mean Lord and Creator. We are also told there were "three thousand and three hundred which ruled over the people that wrought in the work"—3300. These are but the Hebrew equivalent of the Hindu Croners, the "thirty-three million builders of the world." This is a hint of that complexity concerning which we said the monotheists were ignorant. "And the floor of the house he overlaid with gold, within and without" (1 Kings 6:30). This is Revelation's "streets of gold." This temple also had a porch as had Revelation's city of God. And when it was all finished, Solomon "sat on the throne of the Lord." Is a little throne in a little building in little Judea worthy of this name? Can a little building in little Judea contain the Creator? If so, how equate this with 1 Kings 8:27, ". . . behold, the heaven, and heaven of heavens, cannot contain thee; how much less this house that I have builded"? A man-made house cannot contain the Creator but that house called Helios both can and does contain its creator.

The two fundamentals of this house are consciousness and energy, and in the scriptural account they are personified by Solomon and Hiram—idea and substance, architect and builder. The latter is the Hiram Abiff of masonry, and *Abiff*, like *Ab*, means father. Therefore Father Hi-ram is none other than Father Ab-ram. In the rebuilding of Jericho, earth, Abi-ram, a combination, laid the foundations, and Jericho and Solomon's temple are one. And Joshua, who destroyed Jericho, is the evolutionary aspect of the involutionary Solomon who built it. He is Siva the destroyer, but he is also Brahma the builder, for Joshua in the guise of Jeshua rebuilt the temple in Jerusalem. Solomon, the sun, built the temple, earth, as we stated it, but "Satan came also." "Satan is the doorkeeper of the Temple of the King; he standeth in Solomon's porch; he holdeth the keys of the sanctuary."[1] Solomon, Siva, Satan, Joshua and Jehovah are all one.

Certain fraternities base their symbolism on this temple, assuming that occultly it means the human body, but there is nothing human implied in creation myths. Their subject is the planetary body, their dimensions but a blind, and they have the same occult value and planetary significance as Noah's Ark. In mythology this earth is often called a "cave." And this is the "cave" or crypt of Cryptic Masonry, the "secret vault" under Solomon's temple wherein "Wisdom, Strength and Beauty" hid the "foundation stone" of the second temple. This stone is the earth itself, the lithos formed in the cosmic crucible, the first temple. The "seven pairs of pillars" found in the passageway

---

[1] Appendix to Kingsford's *Perfect Way*.

are the seven dual elements in Creation. When the Masons learn to think in this wise, they will begin to understand their own symbology.

Again, no doubt, these God-addicts had some place to worship in, yet since they borrowed their mythology perhaps they borrowed their architecture also. The Hebrews are "a people who never invented anything." They merely used "for their poetic imagery the characteristic beliefs of the people to whom they made direct reference." E. E Goldsmith. So perhaps they used, literarily, the details of Sargon's temple at Khorsabad, or maybe Nebuchadnezzar's Ekua, at Esagila. The latter left us an account strangely similar. "To the building of Esagila my heart inclined me; I held it constantly in mind. I selected the best of my cedar trees which I had brought from Mount Lebanon, the snow-capped forest, for the roofing of Ekua, the shrine of his lordship, and I decorated with brilliant gold the inner sides of the mighty cedar trunks used in the roofing of Ekua. I adorned the under side of the roof of cedar with gold and precious stones. Concerning the building of Esagila, I prayed every morning to the king of the gods, the lord of lords . . . Like dear life, love I the building of their lodging-places." From an ancient inscription.

That the Hebrews borrowed their architecture is not our opinion only, but also that of Myers, the historian. "The ancient Hebrews," said he, "made little or no contribution to science. They produced no new order of architecture; the temple at Jerusalem was little more than a reproduction of a Babylonian sanctuary. In sculpture they did nothing; their religion forbade their making graven images." Yes, but the image they graved on the human mind was worse than any graven on wood and stone. These perish but ideas remain, and, because of a higher, finer element, take on a sacred permanence that defies all nature, reason, science and sense. Because of these mental images, every serious book and every imperious sermon in two thousand years has been fundamentally false; because of them every social plan and hope of peace has failed to materialize. Therefore all these vain efforts must now be revised in keeping with this cosmological interpretation of the literal word.

In this interpretation we have, for instance, knowledge of one

of the great fundamentals of Being, the aforesaid two principles—consciousness and energy. This temple had two pillars,
and it is here we learn their names—Jachin and Boaz, which
must be of equal height and strength or the temple will fall. It
therefore behooves us to know what they are. The English *j* is
the equivalent of the eastern *y;* the word Jachin is thus Yachin
or Yakin. And just as in Jacob or Yacob, the root means one;
and that one is the creative principle. We have called it creative
consciousness, but we said also that consciousness of itself can
do nothing. It must have energy, and this is the nature of Boaz.
The word is derived from *awaz*, meaning voice, and the voice
is the creative Word. These are the pillars of the two scriptural
temples, sun and earth.

Now as man is the microcosm of the planetary macrocosm,
he too has his Jachin and Boaz, and, as in a building, if he would
have balance and endurance, these two must be equal. Today
they are not, and this is the key to our present chaos. Our
tradition-crippled consciousness is not equal to our biologic
energy, and so we are unbalanced. This first temple has also
produced a second, which is both effect and cause, and it too has
two pillars—religion and industry. In their own peculiar way,
these are the Jachin and Boaz of human society; they hold it up
but what they're holding up is only a tower of Babel, a temple
of confusion. Boaz is sustaining dishonesty, crime and corruption, and Jachin is too ignorant to know how to change it.
Between them they have made a sorry mess of us; because of
them we cannot even conduct a war successfully. When industrial greed and selfishness have provoked war, religious hatred
and intolerance makes mutual effort impossible; instead of
standing together to fight aggression it's Catholic against Protestant, Jew againt Modammedan, Mohammedan against Buddhist, and Buddhist against Catholic, the vicious circle. Such is
religion's contribution to the human temple; division instead of
union. And what is the source of it all? Misunderstood scripture,
oriental and occidental.

The Bible states in three different places that Solomon built
the walls of Jerusalem, yet the historical Jerusalem was a walled
city in the fourteenth century B.C., and the Jews as a distinct

sect did not then exist, tradition to the contrary. The statement that he began to build the temple some four hundred years after the Exodus from Egypt is also historically false. The figure 4 here represents the fourth material plane in Involution. On the cusp of this, the Creator began to build a physical sun, for which he needed physical material, and so Sol sent his navy to Ophir and Tharshish to get it.

28. And they came to Ophir, and fetched from there gold, four hundred and twenty talents, and brought it to king Solomon (1 Kings Chap. 9).
22. For the king had at sea a navy of Tharshish with the navy of Hiram: once in three years came the navy of Tharshish bringing gold, and silver, ivory, and apes, and peacocks (Chap. 10).

We have been told that Ophir was India and Tharshish was in Spain, but these words are also blinds to hide the occult truth from us. They both mean the same. Tharshish is the Greek Tartarus, the underworld of matter; the word itself means hard, dense, dark; and Ophir is a derivative of Ophis, serpent, Satan, matter. Thus Tharshish and Ophir are one, namely, earth.

23. So king Solomon exceeded all the kings of the earth for riches and for wisdom.
14. Now the weight of gold that came to Solomon in one year was six hundred threescore and six talents of gold (Chap. 10).

This gold, 666 talents, is the same as the beast of Revelation, also earth. And such was Solomon's "riches."
Some years ago an American expedition wasted considerable time excavating Ezim-geber, the alleged site of Solomon's navy yard. An article describing the place paints a glowing picture of its ancient glories, but ends as we should expect: "Not a vestige was found of the cradles and ways where for centuries the ships of the Jewish navy were built and launched." Children searching their back yard for the treasures of Captain Kidd are no more naive and gullible than these learned but unenlight-

ened scientists searching Ezim-geber for Solomon's navy or Ararat for Noah's ark.

It is not likely the Jews of that time ever had a ship larger than a coastal fishing smack, and it is less likely they ever had a great kingdom, king or temple. They were a small, weak pastoral people; even their country's name derives from this fact: Palestine, from *pali*, shepherd, and *s'than*, land. And it wasn't even theirs; according to Winston, already quoted, their part consisted "only of Jerusalem and the country immediately around its walls." From this he concluded "there was no room for a Jewish king, and the leadership of the people devolved on its religious head, the hereditary high priest." This was their king and his rulership the purpose of the priestly hoax.

Just as their priests reduced the world to a little Judean temple, so they reduced the sublime story of Creation to a racial epic, and all to glorify themselves. The ingenuity with which they accomplished this is nothing short of diabolical. If you require proof of the devil's existence, it is here. But have no fear of him; he is only a priest. But a priest with a deadly purpose—to cripple reason and reduce the race to priestly servitude. And how wonderfully he succeeded! Not even our empirical scientists are immune to it.

An eminent archeologist begins his examination of the evidence for these scriptural buildings thus: "Concerning the building of Solomon's palace and the temple there can be no doubt, for the Bible contains accounts of these." Precisely, the Bible says thus and so; therefore it must be true. This is using the false to prove the false is true. But to continue from the same source: "We shall take as evidence of the plan and situation of the buildings the Biblical writers who had seen them." Even so, he has to admit that "we are at the start confronted, however, with a difficulty, since no Bible writer has given us an exact statement as to what part of the hill Solomon's temple occupied." No indeed; they were too clever for that. And so our scholars have argued for centuries over the precise spot, some asserting it was on the east side of Jerusalem, some on the west. To quote again: "A few modern writers still insist that the 'city of David' was on the western hill, which since 333 A.D. has been called Zion. This, as most scholars have seen, is an impossible view. Solomon built a palace for Pharaoh's daughter near his own on the temple hill, and when she moved into it, she went *up* out of the city of David (1 Kings 9:24). As the western hill is higher than the eastern, she must have gone from a point on the eastern hill lower than the temple. When the temple was completed, Solomon brought the ark *up* from the city of David to the holy of holies in the new temple (2 Chron. 5:2)." This is a modern literalist wrestling with ancient occultism, and no more knowledgeable than those at Ezim-geber and Ararat. Solomon's temple is the sun; the city of David is the earth. Pharaoh's daughter is its matter, which later went up from the earth to form the evolutionary part of the temple. Thus these three buildings—the temple, the king's palace, and the queen's house—are occultly identical with the Sphinx—Leo, Libra, and Virgo. It is also one with the Phoenix but alas, there's been no Oedipus to solve its riddle.

The scriptures also make much of ancient Israel's military power, but this we suspect was as mythical as its naval power. Wherever the military accounts of other nations speak of the Jews at all, it is to record a complete triumph over them. Their scriptural triumphs, therefore, were but literary compensation for their lack of military and political power. As Spengler aptly put it: "For the Chaldeans and Persians there was no need to trouble here about proof—they had by their God conquered the world. But the Jews had only their literature to cling to, and this accordingly turned to theoretical proof in the absence of positive. In the last analysis, this unique national treasure owes its origin to the constant need of reacting against self-depreciation." To this end they perverted other races' history to glorify themselves. As recorded by them, Hezekiah, with the help of their God, completely and miraculously destroyed Sennacherib's army at the gates of Jerusalem, whereas in fact, this calamity did not happen at Jerusalem at all. It happened at Pelusium near the border of Egypt, and it wasn't miraculous. Thus the Jews and their God had nothing to do with it. They merely used another's misfortune to fake a glorious history. When no such factual event served this purpose, they invented one—the cruelty of a Pharaoh, the weakness of the Syrians, etc. Chapter 20 of 1 Kings, for instance, tells about 7,000 Jews killing 100,000 Syrians in one day, but the symbolic language and literal absurdities should make us suspect its mythological nature.

29. And they pitched one over against the other *seven* days. And so it was, that in the *seventh* day the battle was joined: and the children of Israel slew of the Syrians an hundred thousand footmen in one day.
30. But the rest fled to Aphek, into the city; and there a wall fell upon twenty and seven thousand of the men that were left. . . .

That must have been a big wall, so big indeed it killed the fact as well as the footmen. Had we read it in some ancient pagan book we would dismiss it as mythology. Well, it is Hebrew mythology, and this is why so many events in Jewish history take place on the seventh day or year and require forty days or years to complete them: "And the seventh year Jehoiada sent and fetched the rulers over hundreds" 2 Kings 11:4. "Seven years old was Jehoash when he began to reign" (11:21). "In the seventh year of Jehu, Jehoash began to reign: and forty years reigned he in Jerusalem" (12:1). And so did David, and so did Solomon. All these sevens are on one page and it is only illustrative. The reason is that the entire book is mythology, with Creation as its theme. Its incessant warfare is but the conflict of planetary forces, and its heroes personifications thereof; the slow disintegration of the Israelites from the great kings Solomon and David, to captivity and death, but the natural process of spirit becoming matter. The literal presentation of this as racial history, sin and punishment, is one of the most calamitous things in all literature. Not only has it falsified history and wasted millennia, but it has hidden from us the central fact of our history, namely, that it is ignorance, not sin, that constitutes our problem. It has convinced that ignorance that it was once divine and virtuous like Adam and Abraham, and that it is now evil and wretched because it sinned, whereas sin is the result of ignorance; sin is the natural way ignorance acts; it is the effect then, not the cause. Ignorance, moral, mental and spiritual, is the cause of all our troubles, and there has never been anything else. Starting with the morally vacuous virus and protist, life has never been anything but ignorant; what is more, there has never been anything to enlighten it save itself. Its entire history has been exactly what it would be without the God of religion. Why then insist that this God exists? Gods are but part of our primitivism. We of the West condemn the Russians for their "godless communism," while priding ourselves on being "a God-fearing people." Little do we realize that in doing so we are condemning ourselves and acknowledging the Russians are more advanced, for a civilized world will be a Godless world.

The Jews would have us believe their entire book is a revelation from this God, yet how can it be since all the other races had the same material? Here we repeat, there is scarcely anything in their scriptures that cannot be found in the literature of older races. This they will deny, tracing as they do their lineage back to Adam, but their antiquity is as mythological as their history, so also their calendar, of which, more later. As for revelation, there is no such thing. All knowledge is humanly acquired sometime. The word implies an external source of truth, a giver of wisdom, as, for instance, "God gave Solomon wisdom and understanding, exceedingly much . . ." And all because Solomon asked for it. Utterly false; no man is *given* wisdom; whoever asks for it is somewhat wise before he asks, and if he is exceedingly wise he will not ask it of God, for wisdom is functional, not revelational, and once operative is independent of all extraneous aid. But think not it is gratuitous; like every other child, a "brain child" is conceived in pleasure but delivered in pain. When nature finds someone with something to give the world she proceeds to torture it out of him, and no kind, merciful God makes straight the way. On the contrary, he is beset by every impediment, that the essential pain and suffering be assured.

> All cosmic knowledge comes of wisdom stored
> In minds made luminous by suffering.[2]

This is true, but needs a commentary. It is true only of the personal increment; wisdom in general is a race construct, and

---

[2] Edward Davis in *Lovers of Life*.

can be manifested by the individual without personal experience. A more significant statment would read thus: All cosmic wisdom comes of knowledge stored in minds made luminous by suffering. Wisdom, we repeat, is knowledge funded by death and withdrawn by life, the living organism from the group—soul. These things the scriptural authors did not know. Wholly ignorant of the evolutionary genesis of qualities, they attributed them to a God who, lacking them, created man to produce them. Unaware of this their misguided converts still deny Evolution, yet if there is no such thing, even materially, why didn't Solomon have an automobile and the Queen of Sheba an airplane? These are products of our technological evolution and if there is technological evolution there is also psychological evolution, in fact, the last must come first.

What then of Solomon's wisdom? Was it from God or man? To answer this we must know there are two wisdoms, one cosmic and creative, the other human and rational, our genetic and epigenetic. It is the former that is presented in Proverbs, Chapter 8:

23. I was set up from everlasting, from the beginning, or ever the earth was.
24. When there were no depths, I was brought forth; when there were no fountains abounding with water.
29. When he gave to the sea his decree, that the waters should not pass his commandment: when he appointed the foundations of the earth:
30. Then I was by him, as one brought up with him: and I was daily his delight, rejoicing always before him;

Are we to assume that Solomon, the man, was with the Creator before "the foundations of the earth"? What ignorance and conceit! This is the genetic or creative wisdom, of which the epigenetic is no part. The Bible, however, makes no distinctions, sets up no categories. This shows no knowledge of Causation, Creation or the evolutionary construct. By the time these words were written the epigonous descendants of the Hebrew Homer attributed everything to a personal Deity, including man's qualities, and the latter's wisdom consisted mainly of fearing this awful Being. Thus we read: "The fear of the Lord is the beginning of knowledge." It is not; it is the beginning of spiritual ignorance and it began at the close of the mythopoeic age and the dawn of the religious era, some six thousand years ago.

As for Solomon's human and social wisdom, it is but the eponymous wisdom of his creators, worldly not cosmic, thus anthroposophy not theosophy. The story told to prove this wisdom—"The Judgment of Solomon"—is but a *fable convenue*. In other sources it is attributed to David. And neither is Jewish wisdom originally. The literature of the Jains of India tells this same story of their Solomon. Proverbs 22:17–23:11 is a nearly verbatim translation of the Egyptian book, *The Wisdom of Amenemope*, written about 1000 B.C.

But no matter the source, this wisdom contains one gem "of purest ray serene"—"with all your getting, get understanding." Understanding is of all human qualities the highest; without it man is but a blind "creature moving about in worlds not realized," the Bible included. Such is he today. In other chapters we condemned his ways and systems, and we did so because we realized that they are but the result of his present lack of understanding. Therefore, like Solomon, we say to him: "With all your getting, get understanding." Had our statesmen one iota of this, they would not have reestablished the state of Israel. Had our astronomers an iota of it they would not offer absurdities as creation theories.

Solomon's wisdom was not such that it saved him from downfall. He "fell" as did Adam, Noah and Samson, and for the same reason: the authors were secretly following the creative process. If it be otherwise, then the promise of God is not worth the paper it is written on. Abraham, Jacob, David and Solomon were all promised a kingdom that would last forever, yet in spite of all these promises and forevers the "chosen" ended in captivity and final dispersion. In 70 A.D. and again in 135, Jerusalem was destroyed and the Jews forbidden to enter it. These promises are true only cosmologically, for this kingdom is the world, not Israel. No human kingdom lasts forever, but as far as we

are concerned, the earth does. Mythology, all is mythology, saith
the preacher (priest), and by it the Jews built for themselves a
mythical kingdom.

Aside from this, they never had one. Their political history
began with the Maccabees, and their system was a common-
wealth. One objective clue to the political antiquity of any race
is its coins, and there are no Jewish coins prior to the Maccabean
period, and even those they had are of Greek imprint. The first
of these are of the year 138 B.C., the time of Simon the Maccabee.
Another political and national clue is the calendar, and the Jews
had none; they used the Babylonian. Their present calendar
5,700 plus has no basis in fact. It is based on the absurd date of
creation 3760 B.C. This makes 1239 A.D. the 5000 year and the
present 5730 plus, minus facts.

The Maccabean period is Jewish history; the rest is mythology historized. Save for its peculiarly Jewish theology and
exaggeration, the Book of the Maccabees is historical, and this
the compilers of the canon threw out as "uninspired." And what
was the inspiration of the inspired? The unlimited license of
mythology. This our saints mistook for divinely revealed truth
and rejected the factual and historical; they weren't sufficiently
incredible for a supernatural religion. Only the tall tales of
mythology can supply this foundation. This is the basis for that
Catholic absurdity, *"Credo quia absurdum "*—"I believe it because
it is absurd." The assumption is that the ways of God are so
miraculous that they are of necessity absurd to us, and so only
the absurd is theistically credible. And how well the Hebrew
mythologists knew it. They exploited it to the full, thus an-
ticipating by thousands of years the Nazis and their methods—
"If you tell a big enough lie, it will be believed."

To begin with, there is no personal, partial and very loqua-
cious God as these scriptures affirm. The world was not created
by this God in six days or a million. There was no Garden of
Eden or talking snake. There was no first man, Adam, or
woman, Eve. They did not commit a moral sin and so we are
not under condemnation for it. They did not fall from grace and
so there is no need of redemption. Cain and Abel were not their
sons. There was no Deluge and no Noah. There was no racial

Father, Abraham, nor was he promised Palestine. The Jews never were in bondage in Egypt, nor did Moses lead them out. They did not walk through the Red Sea, nor did they conquer Canaan. There was no David or Solomon or even a wondrous temple.

Now if this be so, how can we longer respect this book? That both Jews and Christians have not only respected but accepted it as history, can be explained only by our original assumption— that Western man is incapable of metaphysical perception.

14

The Prophets

God is a blank tablet, on which there is nothing save
that which thyself hast written.

MARTIN LUTHER

It is said that only the prophets had the true
vision of God, and this because they were God-inspired men.
Some of them did not deal with war and conquest, but rather
with man and his relation to God. Here then we should find that
truer vision than, say, that of warring kings and patriarchs.
Well, let us see of what it consists.

The subjugation of the Jews in Babylon has been called "The
second captivity," that in Egypt being the first. We say, however, it is the same captivity, and but the prophets' version of
the first; and both are but allegories about Life's captivity in
matter. "From the power of the nether world I will ransom
them" (Hosea 13:14). Of course our translators did not know
that in mythology the nether world is the material earth and
so they made it "grave," King James Version. And thus are the
keys obliterated.

In the Prophet-version, this nether world is Babylon instead
of Egypt. This is the same Babylon as in Revelation, namely
earth, the mythic symbol of evil, corruption, materialism. But
in this second version the cause of this captivity is different, and
this because the prophets, so called, were priests. And to priests

the cause of all trouble is sin; by this time these Hebrew epigoni had even developed a "conviction of sin," and so sin was the cause.

4. Ah sinful nation, a people laden with iniquity, a seed of evildoers, children that are corrupters: they have forsaken the Lord, they have provoked the Holy One of Israel unto anger, they are gone away backward (the sin syndrome of religion; Isa. Chap. 1).

Isaiah, Ezra, Nehemiah

The Book of Isaiah is a lead-up to this "second captivity," and if we read it knowingly the words become strangely like those of the first.

1. The vision of Isaiah the son of Amoz, which he saw concerning Judah and Jerusalem in the days of Uzziah, Jotham, Ahaz, and Hezekiah, kings of Judah (Chap. 1).
17. Behold, the Lord will carry thee away with a mighty captivity, and will surely cover thee (Chap. 22).
16. In that day shall Egypt be like unto women: and it shall be afraid and fear because of the shaking of the hand of the Lord of hosts, which he shaketh over it.
17. And the land of Judah shall be a terror unto Egypt, every one that maketh mention thereof shall be afraid in himself, because of the counsel of the Lord of hosts, which he hath determined against it.
21. And the Lord shall be known to Egypt, and the Egyptians shall know the Lord in that day, . . .
22. And the Lord shall smite Egypt . . . (Chap. 19).
15. And the Lord shall utterly destroy the tongue of the Egyptian sea; and with his mighty wind shall he shake his hand over the river, and shall smite it in the seven streams, and make men go over dryshod (Chap. 11).
5. And the Lord will create upon every dwelling place of mount Zion, and upon her assemblies, a cloud and smoke by day, and the shining of a flaming fire by night . . . (Chap. 4).

Now why all this talk about Egypt if the "second captivity" was in Babylon? And why this similarity to Exodus? Because Babylon and Egypt are one, and Isaiah is rewriting Exodus, as we are told Ezra did. His subject then is not the captivity of the Jewish people in Babylon but life's captivity in matter, a universal event. In his preface he gives us a hint of this, and a hint to the wise should be sufficient.

11. And I will punish the *world* for their evil (the wicked elements that would become matter; Chap. 13).

This is the mytho-tragedy that befell our world when it was a sun. "An evil spirit from God" came upon it; its free life-force became captive in matter; a deliverer was needed, and who should appear but Joshua the Savior, alias Jeshua. That this Jeshua is Joshua is proved by Nehemiah 8:17. Here Joshua is again called "the son of Nun" and the name is spelled Jeshua. And just as Joshua read the book of the law (of life) to the Israelites after the first captivity, so Jeshua now reads it to them after the second. Thus if this "second captivity" is historical, it is strange indeed that it follows so closely a prior and purely mythical one.

In this "second" not even a Pharaoh is missing, for Pharaoh-nechoh came also. And Necho means dragon, Satan, serpent, matter. And this is brought up from Egypt, earth, to conquer Jehoahaz, one of the last kings of Judah.

33. And Pharaoh-nechoh put him in bands at Riblah in the land of Hamath (as was Samson in Timnath), that he might not reign in Jerusalem . . . (2 Kings, Chap. 23).

Here follows a succession of kings from Josiah down to Jehoiachin. And only now do we come to Nebuchadnezzar and Babylon.

11. And Nebuchadnezzar king of Babylon came against the city, and his servants did besiege it.

13. And he carried out thence all the treasure of the house of the Lord, and the treasures of the king's house, and cut in pieces all the vessels of gold which Solomon king of Israel had made in the temple of the Lord, as the Lord had said.

14. And he carried away all Jerusalem, and all the princes, and all the mighty men of valour, even ten thousand captives, and all the

craftsmen and smiths: none remained, save the poorest sort of the people of the land. (Yet later they had great armies.)

15. And he carried away Jehoiachin to Babylon, and the king's mother, and the king's wives, and his officers, and the mighty of the land, those carried he into captivity from Jerusalem to Babylon (Chap. 24).

And here follows one of those confusions wrought by careless editing. Verse 16 tells us of the smiths and the craftsmen and there ends this account, then verse 17 from another source continues thus:

17. And the king of Babylon made Mattaniah his father's brother king in his stead, and changed his name to Zedekiah.

Whose father's brother? And in whose stead? The preceding part of this account is missing and so it would seem that Mattaniah or Zedekiah was Nebuchadnezzar's father's brother. The text, however, refers to Jehoiachin, Zedekiah's nephew. Zedekiah was the last of the kings, apparently by divine decree. Having offended "the Holy One of Israel," the latter decided to destroy him. To this end he brought Nebuchadnezzar back to besiege Jerusalem.

20. For through the anger of the Lord it came to pass in Jerusalem and Judah, until he had cast them out of his presence, that Zedekiah rebelled against the king of Babylon (2 Kings, Chap. 24).

If this be so, then Nebuchadnezzar was not to blame; he was but the instrument of this monster's vengeance. Now if, as we were told, this holy monster ordered the building of His temple, why would He allow its destruction? And what of His promises to David and Solomon? They were revoked, we are told, because of sin. Does God cancel His decrees because of this? That promise of an everlasting kingdom was not made conditional.

6. So they took the king, and brought him up to the king of Babylon to Riblah; and they gave judgment upon him.

7. And they slew the sons of Zedekiah before his eyes, and put out the eyes of Zedekiah (as with Samson), and bound him with fetters of brass (as with Samson), and carried him to Babylon (instead of Gaza) (2 Kings, Chap. 25).

This was the second capture of Jerusalem under Nebuchadnezzar, but another account tells of a third, this time under Nebuzaradan. Again all the silver and gold and sacred vessels are removed, and the priests and the people are carried away to Babylon. Yet "there's plenty more where they came from," and so we have another story. Gedaliah becomes a sort of ruler over them, and in the *seventh* month, of course, Ishmael, earth, and still alive, slays him and all the Jews that were with him. Thereupon the remainder flee to Egypt. Chapter 24 told us that none were left in Jerusalem "save the poorest sort," yet chapter 25 verse 26 says: "And all the people, both small and great, and the captains of the armies, arose and came to Egypt."

Where then are the Jews? In Babylon or in Egypt? Both, for both represent the same thing—dense matter. And so the children of Israel are again captive in earth, and thus ends the everlasting kingdom promised by their God, if this be history. A hint of its mythical nature, however, is found in a postscript to this chapter. The captives again need a deliverer, and one appears in the person of Jehoiachin, the Joseph and Moses of this story. In the thirty-seventh year of the captivity, a king with a very appropriate name, Evil-merodach (Emil Marduk), raised Jehoiachin up and set him above all the kings of the empire, as was Joseph by the Pharaoh.

Quite unknown to the credulous there are other accounts of these events besides those found in the Bible, the latter being, no doubt, those most useful to the compilers. One of these concerns Nebuzaradan. On entering the temple court he found the blood of Zechariah boiling, in anger no doubt. Unable to stop it or have it explained, he burned 80,000 young Jewish priests. Another account says these 80,000 fled and found refuge among the Ishmaelites. This reminds us of the 100,000 Syrians the Jews killed in one day and the 27,000 the wall fell on. If lay historians wrote such things, would we believe them? We accept them scripturally only because here they're assumed to be under the imprimatur of God. From this we see the necessity of this divine accessory to the fraud.

Of this second captivity there is no more proof than of the first. Herodotus, the Greek historian, visited Babylon about the time the scriptural "return" was in process, yet makes no mention of it or the captivity. In his history of ancient Egypt there is no word about the first captivity; in fact, Herodotus never mentioned the Jews at all; nor did Homer, Plato or Socrates. Lacking any such evidence, our preconvinced apologists have searched elsewhere. Of the proofs offered, the most important are the cuneiform archives of the house of Murashu, which record commercial dealings with the Jews of Babylon. But were these exilic Jews? Are not Jews everywhere, and are they not commercialists? Then there are the Elephantine papyri, but Elephantine was in Egypt, not Babylon. At the time of these records, 408 B.C., Jerusalem was, according to the Bible, completely bankrupt, yet these records tell us these colonial Jews appealed to Jerusalem for help. Thus they belie rather than support the Bible. According to the latter the Jews were always and everywhere strong in their faith in Jehovah, yet these records tell us these Jews in Egypt worshiped Egyptian gods as well as their own—Anath-Yahu, for one. This dual name signifies "consort of Yahveh," and this Anath is one with Asenath, Joseph's wife. These ancient documents are no proof whatever of a historical captivity, nor would they be considered such but for the belief that the Bible itself is historical.

It is time our scholars and our clergy sought the hidden meaning of this story instead of historical proof thereof. The kingdom of Solomon is the involutionary world whose glory is the sun. Solomon, the symbol of this, created a material temple, the earth—the sun, as we said, is laying down within itself a future world. As this goes on, the free Life Principle is made captive in dense matter, and this is the Israelites' captivity in Babylon, elsewhere called Babel, and Zerub-babel appears in this story. Here for eighty years, this time, the Israelites (elements) dream of rebuilding the glorious temple of Solomon (sun), but they build only a sorry replica of it, a dull and somber earth. No

wonder the old men wept. This second temple is identical with
the second "beast" of Revelation. Of the building of this, we
have several accounts, and in all of them there is an adversary,
an opposer. The most interesting one is Sanballat, who opposed
Nehemiah. Here our scholars are again in trouble; they have
great difficulty in placing this man, for, as they say, he has no
place in the political structure of his time. And they are right.
Sanballat was not a man but a principle, not *an* opposer but *the*
opposer, the eternal adversary of myth and scripture, namely
matter—Satan, Antigone, Antiope, Antigonus, Mephistopheles,
etc. Mindless, senseless matter's only will is inertia, and any one
who has ever worked with it, or tried to bend it to his will,
knows well its opposive nature. At times it seems even malicious; as someone so aptly put it, "The utter depravity of inanimate things." This too was personified.

To build this second temple the Israelites came out of Babylon, as they came out of Egypt to build the first, and the man
to lead them was none other than Joshua, alias Jeshua—with
Zerub-babel as his right-hand man. The cosmogonical nature
of the work is clearly implied by the repeated use of the number
seven.

1. And when the seventh month (cycle and plane) was come, and
the children of Israel were in the cities, the people gathered themselves
together as one man to Jerusalem (the gathering of the "chosen" elements).
6. From the first day of the seventh month began they to offer burnt
offerings unto the Lord. . . . (The first of the seventh month is the
beginning of the seventh plane and hence a burning sun; Ezra,
Chap. 3).

In this account Ezra is the builder, then later, we learn it was
Nehemiah, he having secured the right from Cyrus of Persia.
In the latter book, Ezra served only as scribe and priest, yet
elsewhere we are told he preceded Nehemiah by fourteen years.
These are not different builders but different accounts of the one
builder, written, by the way, centuries after the alleged event.
Yet what proof is there that Ezra ever existed? No more than
for Moses or Solomon. In 200 B.C. Ben Sirach reviewed the

famous men of Jewish mythology, not history, yet made no mention of Ezra. The reason should now be obvious; Ezra is also mythological. Modern scholars confirm this. In his *History of the Jews*, Sachar writes thus: "Parts of the account in Ezra are probably the imaginative interpretation of events by the pious chroniclers who wrote many generations later. The grandiloquent proclamation of Artaxerxes, and the account of a second general migration to Palestine, seem, at best dubious. Many modern critics even question whether Ezra is a historical character; they lean to the view that he is the impersonation of the Puritan tendency which dominated the middle fifth century." [1] He is said to have rewritten the books of Moses but this means only he repeated the mythological works of Moses, namely, Evolution. By its very nature the first captivity is mythological; is it possible a later historical event would parallel so closely a mythological precedent? Knowing now the purely mythical antiquity of Abraham, Jacob, Moses, etc., one might well ask, How old is the Old Testament? In *The Decline of the West*, Spengler has this to say: "It was in post-Exilic times that the idea arose of the Tables of the Law received by Moses on Sinai; later such an origin came to be assumed for the whole Torah, and about the Maccabean period for the bulk of the Old Testament."

This is correct. "The bulk of the Old Testament" is but priestly montage imposed on Jhwhistic cosmology, and the reign of the priesthood was long subsequent to the events recorded. It was also pseudo-Hellenic and this carried over into the Christian era. Thus the New and the Old were not separated by long ages, as assumed; the one was but a continuation of the other.

Using a diagram we might illustrate it thus, greatly simplified, of course, because not showing the many sects, both Judaic and Christian, that flourished at that time. The date 300 is not definite either, but only illustrative. It was, however, in the fourth and third centuries B.C. that Hebrew mythology lost its symbolic meaning and became the basis for a priestly religion, and it was in the third and fourth centuries A.D. that Christian mythology lost its symbolic meaning and likewise became a

[1] Abram Leon Sachar, *A History of the Jews*, second edition, p. 88.

priestly religion. Both began as mythology and ended in dogmatic theology.

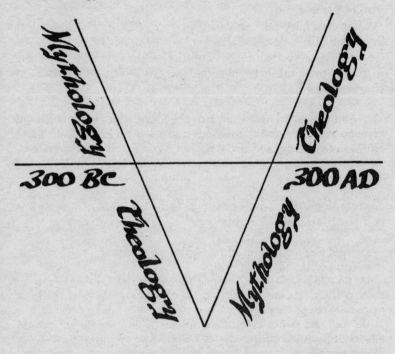

Elijah

No résumé, or should we say exposé, of the Bible would be complete without a word about Elijah and Elisha. But since their accounts are but more of the same, perverted cosmology, we will be brief. For future reference, however, we wish to record them. And for the liberties we take with the Bible's sequence we make no apologies here either. In doing so we are but following the examples set by its compilers. They too have taken liberties, not only with the planetary sequence they are secretly following but even with sentences. Second Chronicles ends in the middle of a sentence, the remainder of which is found in Ezra chapter 1, verse 3. In chapter 23 of 2 Kings, verse 23 is incomplete, verse 24 dealing with something quite different. As for the original sequence, the planetary process, the entire Bible perverts and conceals it. Thus, we, following it, are but putting things misplaced by priestly cunning back in their proper place again.

Eli, as we have said, means God, and the suffix signifies life. Such is Elijah, and also Elias, and in the apocryphal Ecclesiasticus, Elijah is called Elias. These two are therefore one, the former representing Involution, the latter Evolution, "which was for to come."

1. And it came to pass after many days (the first three planes and periods), that the word of the Lord (law) came to Elijah (as it did to Noah) in the third year (epoch), saying, Go shew thyself (spirit) unto Ahab (matter); and I will send rain upon the earth (the deluge; 1 Kings, Chap. 18).

Mythologically, Ahab is the Babylonian Adad, "the storm god" or "rainmaker," cosmogonically, the deluge-maker.

41. And Elijah said unto Ahab, Get thee up, eat and drink; for there is a sound of abundance of rain.

42. So Ahab went up to eat and to drink. And Elijah went up to the top of Carmel; and he cast himself down upon the earth, and put his face between his knees.

43. And said to his servant, Go up now, look toward the sea. And he went up, and looked, and said, There is nothing. And he said, Go again *seven* times.

44. And it came to pass at the *seventh* time, that he said, Behold there ariseth a little cloud (monadic host) out of the sea (cosmic), like a man's hand (and like the stone in the image). And he said, Go up, say unto Ahab, Prepare thy chariot (Ezekiel's wheel and Noah's ark), and get thee *down*, that the rain stop thee not.

45. And it came to pass in the mean while, that the heaven was black with clouds and wind, and there was a great rain (deluge). And Ahab rode, and went to Jezreel (as did Noah to Ararat; 1 Kings, Chap. 18).

As this was also Elijah's destination, "he girded up his loins, and ran before Ahab to the entrance of Jezreel," that is, the entrance of the first material plane. And here, the queen thereof, namely Jezebel, matter, tried to kill him. Was ever a Creation myth written wherein the Creator's life was not threatened? No, this is part of the mythic formula, implying Creation's violence. On learning of his danger, Elijah fled for his life. And need we ask where? To the wilderness, of course. This is where all Creators flee at this point, that wilderness of the intermediate planes, and stay "forty days and forty nights." Here Elijah sits down under a tree, that "tree of life," and exclaims, "It is enough; now, O Lord, take away my life (spiritual)." He was afraid of that great darkness beyond as was Abram before him. There he slept until an angel awakened him, fed him, and sent him "in the strength of that meat forty days and forty nights (four planes) unto Horeb the mount of God (the earth itself)." Here he turns "eastward" (to Eden), and hides himself by the river Jordan, the involutionary "river of life." "And the ravens brought him bread and fish in the morning, and bread and flesh in the evening; and he drank of the brook" (17:6).

This is indeed "divine providence," but not original. When Jupiter was hiding in the wilderness from Cronos, Aquila, the eagle, fed him also. And such is the "divine providence" of scripture—mythological. Look not then for God's ravens to feed you; they won't.

And now Elijah, like Saul and David, is living in a cave, that "hole in space" called matter, earth. This is a Magian touch; in this religion the earth is spoken of as "the world cavern." It is also the "cave" of Kundalini. From this the life force must be released and so the wholly unnecessary overlord decreed:

11. And he said, Go forth, and stand upon the mount (earth) before the Lord. And, behold, the Lord passed by, and a great and strong wind rent the mountains, and brake in pieces the rocks before the Lord; but the Lord was not in the wind: and after the wind an earthquake; but the Lord was not in the earthquake:

12. And after the earthquake a fire; but the Lord was not in the fire: and after the fire a still small voice. (And after the earth's convulsions, the "still, small voice" of radiation.)

13. And it was so, when Elijah heard it, that he wrapped his face in his mantle (freed energies), and went out (Exodus), and stood in the entering in of the cave (exit from matter). And, behold, there came a voice unto him, and said, What doest thou here, Elijah? (Chap. 19).

This is the same voice Moses heard and the message was of like nature—go on and establish Evolution.

15. And the Lord said unto him, Go, return (by Evolution) on the way to the wilderness of Damascus: and when thou comest, anoint Hazael to be king over Syria. (According to 2 Kings 8:15, Hazael became king only by murdering Benhadad.)

16. And Jehu (Joshua) the son of Nimshi (Nun) shalt thou anoint to be king over Israel: and Elisha the son of Shaphat of Abelmeholah shalt thou anoint to be prophet in thy room (1 Kings, Chap. 19).

The entire Old Testament implies that the God of the universe participated in the political affairs of Israel. Can modern man believe that? Well, he believes in what follows.

8. And Elijah took his mantle, and wrapped it together, and smote the waters, and they were divided hither and thither, so that they two went over on dry ground (the crossing of the Red Sea and the Jordan).

11. And it came to pass, as they still went on, and talked, that, behold, there appeared a chariot of fire, and horses of fire, and parted them both asunder; and Elijah went up by a whirlwind into heaven (2 Kings, Chap. 2).

This is but the ascension of life from matter in Evolution, yet some five hundred million credulous Christians and Jews believe it literally, or did. They even painted pictures of this holy man going up to God in a material chariot. They should read other races' mythology, then they would understand their own. Romulus, who founded Rome, the earth, was also taken up to heaven in a chariot of fire. And Mithra of Persia was similarly translated. So with the story of Elijah bringing down fire from heaven upon the priests of Baal and their sacrifice. Prometheus also brought fire down from heaven. This we say is a myth but Elijah's story is "the word of God." Do you not see how the art of "sacred literature" has deceived us? In both cases the fire is but the fire of life, brought down in Involution and carried up again in Evolution. Why then is one profane myth and the other "sacred literature"? The tragedy of the Piscean Age lies in our ignorance of the former and our faith in the latter.

While he lived, this God of fire destroyed besides all the priests of Baal, two companies of fifty innocent messengers sent him by King Ahaziah. Addressed as "thou man of God," he answered them thus: "If I be a man of God, then let fire come down from heaven, and consume him and his fifty" (2 Kings 1:10). And again some five hundred million of us believe this Elijah was a just and holy man. Not even John Neanderthal would be so monstrously cruel as Elijah—or so credulous as we. We can't even see what "a man of God" is like, or draw the conclusion that God is like his man. To Satan we attribute every cruelty, crime and evil, but nowhere do we find a Satan as satanic as the God of the Old Testament. Where then is its God of love and mercy? We have examined some ten or twelve of its books and nowhere have we found a trace of him. The reason is because he exists only where there is ignorance of Reality.

All down the ages man has been telling man what kind of a God, God is, and yet with all his endless theories no word has come from that vast silence to tell him which is right. To me that silence has a meaning, and that meaning is just this—there's nothing there to answer. All that could or would answer is man-made and evolutionary.

Elisha

Elisha is the evolutionary aspect of the involutionary Elijah; he is therefore one with Moses and Joshua, and as such repeats their miracles.

14. And he took the mantle of Elijah that fell from him, and smote the waters, and said, Where is the Lord God of Elijah? and when he also had smitten the waters, they parted hither and thither: and Elisha went over (2 Kings, Chap. 2).

Only the spiritually blind can believe this literally; only the metaphysically ignorant can miss its cosmological meaning.

23. And he went up from thence unto Bethel: and as he was going up by the way, there came forth little children out of the city, and

mocked him, and said unto him, Go up, thou bald head; go up, thou bald head.

24. And he turned back, and looked on them, and cursed them in the name of the Lord. And there came forth two she bears out of the wood, and ate forty and two children of them (Chap. 2).

What tolerant people these men of God were! Yet what would you expect if they were men of God? The Jews are proud of being the "chosen" of this God, but little do they realize its occult implication. As for the epithet: the bald-headed Elisha was but the bald-headed earth, still naked and bare like Adam and Noah, and biologically wanting like Belshazzar. The children's voices crying, "Go up, thou bald head," are the same voices Elijah heard saying, "What doest thou here, Elijah?"—the planetary urge to rise and create. In an Oriental book a thousand years older than the Bible, the bare, primeval earth is called "bald head," and in Mexico a sacred hill where their God was crucified bears the same name. Later we will come to another—Calvary.

Chapter 4 tells us about Elisha miraculously filling the poor woman's vessel with oil, as Elijah had filled another's barrel with meal; also of his feeding a hundred men with a few loaves of barley. Thus Christ was not the first to multiply food for the hungry, nor yet to raise the dead. Both Elijah and Elisha did that. A Shunammite woman had befriended Elisha, and when her child fell sick she sent for this man who had just killed forty-two children. Is there no one in all Christendumb sufficiently enlightened to see the meaning of these contradictions? No, not in two thousand years, and the reason was given in our Preface—the metaphysical incompetency of Western man. His borrowed Bible is just too subtle for his blunted mind to understand. Of its contents he comprehends only the literal word, and so, like a child reading a fairy tale, he believes this scriptural infanticide was at the same time so divine he could bring the dead to life even after he himself was dead.

20. And Elisha died, and they buried him. . . .
21. And it came to pass, as they were burying a man, that, behold,

they spied a band of men; and they cast the man into the sepulchre of Elisha: and when the man was let down, and touched the bones of Elisha, he revived, and stood up on his feet (Chap. 13).

And Western man believes that. Here again he cannot see that this is but the work of the genetic palmed off on him as that of the epigenetic. Elisha is the genetic principle, and its task is to raise biologic life from "dead matter." And such are all scriptural raisings of the dead.

Before Elisha died he carried out Elijah's command to anoint Jehu king of Israel. And so we have another anointed trinity—Elijah, Elisha, and Jehu. And what a strange way these people had of ordaining their leader. In this case a young man was chosen to carry a box of oil to Jehu's quarters, and, by hook or by crook, pour it on him and run. This he finally accomplished, then "opened the door and fled."

11. Then Jehu came forth to the servants of his lord: and one said unto him, Is all well? wherefore came this mad fellow to thee? . . . (Chap. 9).

And now having been appointed by God and anointed by Elisha, Jehu sets out on a campaign of extermination. By subtlety, trickery, and atrocity, he destroys Ahab's seventy children (septenate elements) and all the priests of Baal (matter), in spite of the fact that Elijah had destroyed them all before him. For these monstrous acts Jehu's monstrous God rewards him as usual.

30. And the Lord said unto Jehu, Because thou hast done well in executing that which is right in mine eyes, and hast done unto the house of Ahab according to all that was in mine heart, thy children of the fourth generation shall sit on the throne of Israel (Chap. 10).

And this is the God to whom we pray for peace and justice, love and mercy. Little wonder they are so scarce. What is "right" in the eyes of this God is the very opposite of the "right" of moral man; therefore man must recognize this and become his own moral authority.

Made ignorant by two thousand years of priestly falsehoods, modern man does not know that it is this same ruthless force within himself that drives him to war and death while his own self-created morality cries out against the atrocities this power compels him to commit. He does not know that it is this God-power within himself that underlies his ruthless commercial competition and its offspring, gangsterism—the little man's way of using the big man's method. Then there is "juvenile delinquency"; but this same impelling force without parental wisdom to guide it.

In all that has been said and written about the latter, I have never yet seen or heard the real cause mentioned. Home and parents are blamed, and rightly so, but what made home and parents what they are? The cause of delinquency both juvenile and adult is our way of doing business. It is in our daily activities, thoughts and interests that character is made. Thus the molder of minds and morals today is the market place, and until this is realized all the precepts of home and heaven are but wasted effort. Modern business is a postgraduate course in crookedness, dishonesty and deception, and it has destroyed the moral content in human nature. Even the would-be honest ones must lie and steal to meet the high cost of living it has created. Not for nothing did the Greeks make their god of commerce (Hermes) also the patron of thieves. And not for nothing did Hosea brand the merchant with deceit. "He is a merchant, the balances of deceit are in his hands; he loveth to oppress" (12:7). You see he was known of old, and every cycle he dominates is an age of crime and corruption. Little wonder modern youth is rebelling against such a system and society. As for their opposition to war, it is the most hopeful sign in this century. Only when young men the world over refuse to die because old men can't think, will there be peace.

15
Ezekiel's Vision

Suppose someone told you something that seemed of great spiritual significance, and, on inquiry, asserted that he had gained this knowledge in a vision. No doubt you would consider him a spiritual man and an instrument of divine revelation. Then suppose you learned later that this man did not have a vision at all, and that what he had told you was common knowledge among the wise. You might still rate the knowledge high, but your estimate of the man would fall pretty low; indeed if you were like most people, you would set him down as an old fraud. Well, such is Ezekiel, and such is his pretended vision, but let the old fraud expose himself. The italics are ours.

1. Now it came to pass in the thirtieth year, in the fourth month, in the fifth day of the month, *as I was among the captives* by the river of Chebar, that the heavens were opened, and *I saw visions of God*.

4. And I looked, and, behold, a whirlwind came out of the north, a great cloud, and a fire infolding itself, and a brightness was about it, and out of the midst thereof as the colour of amber, out of the midst of the fire.

5. Also out of the midst thereof came the likeness of four living

creatures. And this was their appearance; *they had the likeness of a man.*

10. As for the likeness of their faces, they four had the face of *a man,* and the face of a *lion,* on the right side: and they four had the face of an *ox* on the left side; they also had the face of an *eagle.*

15. Now as I beheld the living creatures, behold one wheel upon the earth by the living creatures, with his four faces.

16. The appearance of the wheels and their work was like unto the colour of a beryl: and they four had one likeness: and their appearance and their work was as it were *a wheel in the middle of a wheel.*

18. As for their rings, they were so high that they were dreadful; and their rings were full of *eyes* round about them four.

19. And when the living creatures went, the *wheels* went by them: and when the living creatures were lifted up from the earth, the wheels were lifted up.

20. Whithersoever the spirit was to go, they went, thither was their spirit to go; and the wheels were lifted up over against them: *for the spirit of the living creature was in the wheels* (Chap. 1).

Such is the vision Ezekiel claimed to have had—and it was no vision. These four creatures, man and ox, lion and eagle are but Aquarius, Taurus, Leo and Scorpio, the four cardinal points of the *stellar* zodiac, and hence of the creative process. All antiquity knew about them, and every race made use of them in its art and mythology. Why then should they be a revelation to Ezekiel? Among the Orphics they were designated Dragon, Bull, Lion, and Eagle. The Chaldeo-Babylonians called them Oustour, the Man; Kirub, the Bull; Nirgal, the Lion; and Nathga, the Eagle. In the Hindu pantheon they are the cosmic Maharajas, otherwise known as the Asuras, Kinnaras and Nagas; also the Avengers, the Winged Wheels, the Locapalas or supporters of the world. As the latter they were respectively Indra, the East; Yama, the South; Varuna, the West; and Kuvara, the North. There is a drawing by Levi of these four animals enclosed in a six-pointed star, with the Hebrew name *Adoni* over it. In India there is a similar picture with the word *Adonari* over it, hence the Adoni of the scriptures. Their word *cherub* comes from the Babylonian Kirub, the Bull, and means only a creative force. The ox, an emasculated bull, is one with the emasculated Uranus, and both are third-plane symbolism.

The complexity, a "wheel within a wheel" and many other wheels, is but the zodiac itself, with its cosmogonical, precessional, annual and diurnal cycles within it. The "whirlwind" is its ceaseless motion. The ancient symbol of this was the swastika, turning thus卍. The Ancients called it "The Wheel of Fire." The "eyes" of the wheel are symbols of the creative intelligence within this complexity. The four beasts "had the likeness of a man"; in plain words, they are Man, Aquarius, the evolving Life Principle. This is the one and only factor in Creation, the God of religion being but a priestly necessity.

In this alleged vision of God there is nothing new or personal. Buddha was called "the Wheel king"; Shamash, the Babylonian god, is shown seated upon a throne with a wheel behind him, and the spokes of the wheel are made of stars instead of eyes. The Assyrians pictured their god Asshur within a wheel, and

they said, "The life of God is within the wheel." "It is highly probable therefore that when he described the four living creatures and the wheel, Ezekiel was simply making use of Assyrian symbology which he had seen again and again when the Jews were in captivity." E. E. Goldsmith.[1] And again, "The Hebrews merely used for their poetic imagery the characteristic beliefs of the people to whom they made direct reference." And Madame Blavatsky asserts: "The religion of the Masters—the Babylonians and Assyrians—was transferred almost bodily into the revealed Scriptures of the Captives and from there into Christianity." And now its four beasts are the four angels of the

[1] *Ancient Pagan Symbols*, p. 94.

Catholic Church—Michael, Gabriel, Raphael, and Uriel, and when humanized, Matthew, Mark, Luke, and John.

What then of the statement "the heavens opened and I saw visions of God"? The only heavens that opened for Ezekiel were the Creation lore and symbolism of Babylon and Assyria. This, some priest, alias Ezekiel, dressed up in awe-inspiring words to give his diatribes on sin divine authority. And such is the nature of all "divine revelation"—ancient cosmology lost in the dusk of the Zodiacal Night, rediscovered and perverted by priestly plagiarists. In our Preface we said the Bible's creators were plagiarists and that they got their knowledge from older races. The above quotations are but the first of many proofs thereof.

As for proofs of our own theory, there are still many more: the Cabala, the Tetragrammaton, the Gnostics, philosophers, and others, but save for one quotation we will leave these to the reader. The quote is from Dionysius the Areopagite. According to him, "The cause of all things is neither soul nor intellect; nor has it imagination, opinion or reason, or intelligence; nor is it reason or intelligence; nor is it spoken or thought. . . . Even intellectual contact does not belong to it. It is neither science nor truth. It is not even royalty or wisdom; not one, not unity; not divinity or goodness, nor even spirit as we know it." This is truer theology than anything the Hebrews ever wrote. It is our creative principle, neither divine, moral nor even self-conscious.

16
Daniel

Dare to be a Daniel,
Dare to stand alone;
Dare to have a purpose firm,
And dare to make it known.

OLD HYMN

Well, let us see what Daniel's "derring-do" consisted of. Was it personal or mythical? factual or fictional? To the occultist it is but some more cosmology used to glorify a race.

Our "Bible students" classify Daniel as an apocalyptist rather than a prophet, but it matters little since his book is but priestly perversion of mythology, and like all Hebrew literature, not original. The story of Daniel was taken from a north Syrian poem written before 1500 B.C. The hero, Daniel by name, was a son of El or God—the source of the Hebrew El. He was a mighty judge and lawgiver, also a provider for his people. This poem about him became so widely known that many races used its hero as a model for their own. It is this Daniel that Ezekiel refers to; it is this Daniel the Hebrews remodeled and placed in Nebuchadnezzar's time. It is also this Daniel that the story of Joseph in Egypt is based on; the latter married Asenath and the woman in the Syrian poem is Anath. As the Jews used the word Daniel, it means "God is my judge," but the occult meaning is "the judgment of God," the inexorable decrees of nature. This is the judgment of Daniel even in the Old Testament.

That Daniel is Joseph, Nebuchadnezzar is Pharaoh, and Babylon is Egypt is obvious from the parallel. Like Joseph, Daniel is an interpreter of dreams; like Joseph he interprets the king's dream, for which, like Joseph, he is made ruler over the kingdom. And like Joseph, his power to interpret the king's dream is due to the fact that he dreamed the same dream, namely the dream of life. Thus he and the king are one, the only distinction being, as with Joseph, that of the two principles, ideative consciousness and mindless matter. The latter is king on the lower planes, but its meaning and purpose must be interpreted by the former. And so we have Nebuchadnezzar, like Pharaoh, dreaming a dream of his own future but ignorant of its meaning. And just as Pharaoh changed Joseph's name to Zaphnathpaaneah, so Nebuchadnezzar changed Daniel's to Belteshazzar—and Belteshazzar was the name of Nebuchadnezzar's God. Thus Daniel became a God unto Nebuchadnezzar as did Joseph and Moses to the Pharaohs. He also became chief of the magicians of Babylon, as did Moses among those of Egypt. And the miracles of these magicians are the miracles of life. These things understood, the apocalyptic book of Daniel becomes "an open book," a book of cosmology, not history. Better it be considered such for otherwise it brands the author as wholly ignorant of Evolution and its construct, the human psyche. To him a revelatory dream was not from this but from, as he thought, the God of the universe. Elsewhere these authors speak of a God "who seeth in secret and rewards openly." The only thing that "seeth in secret and rewards openly" is our own subjectivity, but this too is attributed to an external Infinite. So these authors are neither cosmologically nor psychologically knowledgeable.

In the first part of his dream, the "image" Nebuchadnezzar sees is that of Involution, later shifting to Evolution. Therefore we must think here of the whole earth entity.

31. Thou, O king, sawest, and behold a great image. This great image, whose brightness was excellent, stood before thee; and the form thereof was terrible (Daniel, Chap. 2).

And we too said it was terrible, and so did Jacob, and John the Revelator.

32. This image's head was of fine gold, his breast and his arms of silver, his belly and his thighs of brass,

33. His legs of iron, his feet part of iron and part of clay (Chap. 2).

These are symbols of the Creator in Involution: the fine gold represents the pure, primordial spirit, the rest its coarsening sequence down to clay, the earth—the gold, silver, bronze and iron ages of mythology later applied to man.

37. Thou, O king, art a king of kings: for the God of heaven hath given thee a kingdom, power, and strength, and glory.

This bright "king of kings," like Solomon before him, is the sun. As the sun is solar fire, even the name of this king is appropriate. The first syllable comes from Nebo, a god of fire. Mount Nebo is "the mount of fire," and king Nebo is identical with it. In this we are not denying the Nebuchadnezzar of history but asserting only that here he is being used mythologically. And like all mythological kings he becomes afflicted, and so does the image, which means they are one.

34. Thou sawest till that a stone was cut out without hands, which smote the image upon his feet that were of iron and clay, and brake them to pieces.

35. Then was the iron, the clay, the brass, the silver, and the gold, broken to pieces together, and became like the chaff of the summer threshing-floors; and the wind carried them away, that no place was found for them: and the stone that smote the image became a great mountain, and filled the whole earth.

36. This is the dream; and *we* will tell the interpretation thereof before the king (Chap. 2).

We too said the involutionary six disappeared when the seventh appeared. As for the stone that displaced the original entity and finally became a mountain: this is that dense core we said every sun is laying down within itself, namely, a future earth or planet. This, like Solomon's temple, is not made with hands, but by a chemical process which beginning small, increases until the entire solar source is transmuted into atomic matter.

This is the destruction of that bright image the sun, following which it becomes that "abomination of desolation," a lifeless clinker wandering in space. And now after "seventy weeks" another image appears, a newborn planet with its evolutionary symbolism. This is but this myth's rebuilding of the temple. As it is but Creation symbolism, Daniel was a prophet after the fact, some billions of years after. And such is the nature of all Biblical prophecies—cosmology bedeviled by religion; therefore those who try to interpret them politically or religiously are only wasting their time.

That this is their nature is obvious from the symbolism in the seventh chapter. The beasts here have been interpreted as nations, tyrants, and the like, but verse 23 tells us "The fourth beast shall be the fourth kingdom upon earth, which shall be diverse from all kingdoms, and shall devour the whole earth." This is the *human* kingdom and it doesn't take a prophet to tell us what it will do. But now a better kingdom is promised, one that is to last forever. This is the fifth plane and this as Daniel says will break and bend to its will the other four. We too asserted this, and not from a gift of prophecy, but just a little knowledge of the creative process. Here, the symbols are in reverse, the clay, iron, brass, and other materials representing the ascending kingdoms and their conditions.

And now the earth, well pleased with its future, rewards its interpreter.

48. Then the king made Daniel a great man, and gave him many great gifts, and made him ruler over the whole province of Babylon, and chief of the governors over all the wise men of Babylon (Chap. 2).

("And Pharaoh said unto Joseph, See, I have set thee over all the land of Egypt," Gen. 41:41.)

Thus these two are one and both are cosmological symbols.

This is a scriptural formula, still in use: the Jew is always the cleverest, the wisest—Joseph, Moses, Daniel, Mordecai, etc. Indeed, Daniel was "ten times better than all the magicians and astrologers that were in all his realm" (1:20). Thus did they pervert cosmology to glorify themselves and deceive the Gentiles. This realized, it's rather difficult to believe the rest of Daniel: Nebuchadnezzar eating grass, the golden image he commanded all to worship, his putting Daniel in a lion's den, three others in a fiery furnace, the handwriting on the wall, etc.

The libelous degradation of Nebuchadnezzar was but the mighty spirit of the sun brought low in matter. The golden image that the brave Daniel refused to worship is but the "golden calf" of Exodus and the first "beast" of Revelation. It too represents matter, and the Life Principle, now free, must not return to it. This is the brave Daniel's courage, likewise that of his race. Daniel in the lion's den is this Principle in Leo, the sun; it is also "the fiery furnace" or crucible in space referred to earlier. The three men, Shadrach, Meshach, and Abednego, are the three prephysical elements of which the sun is made; the fourth whom Nebuchadnezzar saw walking in their midst is element number four and one with the stone that slowly appeared in the image, namely, physical matter. Chapter 3, verse 25, should therefore read thus: "Lo, I see four men (elements) loose (not yet condensed) walking in the midst of the (solar) fire, and they have no hurt (are not destroyed), and the form of the fourth is like the Son (Sun) of God." This God saved three men in a fiery furnace but not three million in the gas chamber. And such is God's special care of the Jews.

Nebuchadnezzar, the sun, or first "beast" (little wonder he ate grass), was, according to the scriptures, succeeded by Belshazzar. This is not according to history; Belshazzar was never king but only regent. He was not the son of Nebuchadnezzar (5:2); it was not Nebuchadnezzar who became ill but Nabonidas, the last of the Neo-Babylonian dynasty. To regain his health he lived for eight years at Tiema, in northern Arabia. It was during this period that Belshazzar served as regent only. The Hebrew mythologist applied the facts about Nabonidas to the character he was using for his occult cosmology.

In this, Belshazzar is the second "beast," namely, the earth, and the handwriting he saw on the wall was that of the planetary law. The barren earth, weighed in the balance, Libra, was found biologically wanting, and was overthrown as was Pharaoh in the other myth. And now the handwriting is on the wall again, and this time it is we who are in Libra, the material sign, and hence "found wanting," mentally, morally and spiritually. This occurs at the beginning of every zodiacal cycle, and all that is cheap and shallow, subversive and obstructive is overthrown. This time it is the Aquarian cycle, and it is sweeping out something neither cheap nor shallow but decidedly subversive and obstructive—the Hebrew scriptures. Yes, the handwriting for them is on the wall also. Grand symbolism and noble literature though they be, they were never intended for a permanent guide to humanity; they were for the benighted Piscean Age only. The Aquarian will have naught to do with their false security, false theology and eschatology. This is Siva the destroyer's day, and his "moving finger writes, and having writ, moves on."

17
Jonah

The story of Jonah is such a challenge to reason one would think it would arouse in us a demand to know what it really means, and why it's in the scriptures at all. The reason it has not, is the mentality of Western man. Having no knowledge of the creative process, he cannot see this in it. To him, if a story isn't literally true, it has no meaning at all. Such to him are the myths, the deepest source of truth we have.

Briefly, the story is this: Jonah, the son of Amittai, is commanded by God to go down to Nineveh, another wicked city, which is to be destroyed in *forty days,* unless it repent of its sins. Here he was to preach and prophesy its doom that it might turn from its ways and be saved. But Jonah refused the commission, and instead, took ship at Joppa for Tarshish, somewhere in the West, by which disobedient act he hoped to escape.

4. But the Lord sent out a great wind into the sea, and there was a mighty tempest in the sea, so that the ship was like to be broken (the Deluge of this myth; Chap. 1).

The crew, suspecting Jonah was the cause, threw him overboard, but he was not lost for,

17. Now the Lord had prepared a great fish to swallow up Jonah. And Jonah was in the belly of the fish three days and three nights (Chap. 1).

10. And the Lord spake unto the fish, and it vomited out Jonah upon the dry land (Chap. 2).

So far Mother Goose has nothing on the Book of Jonah, but occultly it is the same old creation mythology. Jonah is also the Life Principle; the ship he takes is the Ark; the tempest, the Deluge, and the "dry land," earth. Thus Jonah is but a revolutio of Noah, the Creator from the third to the seventh plane in Involution. As such his God is quite superfluous, his refusal but that of the angels who refused to create. This account does not tell us the fish was a whale, but in the New Testament Christ refers to it as such. But no matter what, the fish is just another ark symbol, another life vehicle. Apocryphal accounts say there were two whales, a male and a female, thus implying generation. The whale is a water sign and as a constellation is know as Cetus. This account does not tell us the name of Jonah's whale either but the *Shalshelet ha-Kabbalah* does; it calls it Cetos. Later we will meet it again under a strangely similar name. The three days Jonah is in the whale's belly are the three prephysical periods after which comes earth, the "dry land." Onto this the whale vomited Jonah, and Cronus, having swallowed his children, vomited them out also. In the creative process matter "swallows" genetic consciousness in In-volution, then "vomits" it out again in Ev-olution (Genesis and Exodus).

Now this "dry land" was the goal Jonah set out for in the first place. The author calls it Tarshish, but this Tarshish is the Tharshish of the Solomon myth, and both are Tartarus, a place lower even than Hell, the sun, hence the earth. That this Hell is the sun, Tarshish the earth, and the earth and the whale are one is obvious from the second chapter. "Then Jonah prayed unto the Lord his God out of the fish's belly . . . Out of the belly of hell, cried I, and thou heardest my voice . . . And the Lord spake unto the fish and it vomited Jonah out upon the dry land." Just another version of "captivity" and "deliverance." "I went down to the bottoms of the mountains; the earth with her bars was about me for ever: yet hast thou brought up my life from corruption" (2:6). And this is the nature of scriptural corruption—matter, God's work not man's.

There is nothing new in this story, only the Hebrew version of a very ancient myth. In the *Heracleid* we learn that Hercules was swallowed by a whale, and strange to say, at precisely the same place, Joppa: and that he too remained in the whale's belly exactly three days. And the Persians tell us that Jamshyd, their hero, was devoured by a sea monster that later vomited him out safely upon the shore. Then there is the other Greek myth of Arion, the musician, who on being thrown overboard for causing a storm, was saved by a dolphin. And back beyond all these is a similar tale from India. In the *Samadeva Bhatta* we learn of Saktadeva who was swallowed by a fish and later stepped out unharmed when it was opened. And there is Vishnu, the Avatar; he is shown rising from the mouth of a fish. Practically all the saviors of the world are fish men; and such was Jonah the savior of Nineveh, earth. He is the Noah of this myth; even his father's name, Amittai, carries a hint of this. Amittai is a derivation of Amriti, the Hindu "waters of life," and Jonah is Nârâyana, "the mover on the waters." The name Jonah was also common among all the ancient races. The Persians had their Jawnah, the Basques, their Jawna, the Chaldeans, their Ionn or Jonn. From these come the familiar name John, which we are told means ram, that is Aries the first generative element. Others say Jonah means dove, but even as such Jonah is still Noah, for Apocryphal books say that the dove of the ark was Noah himself. And why not since all within the ark was but the monadic host in Involution. This, after three pre-physical stages, became dense matter. This was God's creation yet branded wicked by mythologists, hence personified as a wicked city, Nineveh.

That this wicked city is God's creation is implicit in the name. Nineveh was named for Ninus, its legendary founder, but both Ninus and Nineveh are derived from Niniv, one of the Assyrian Elohim. Collectively these Elohim were the founders of another wicked city, Babel, and Nimrod its scriptural founder is but the Hebrew's Niniv.

That this Nineveh is symbolic only is obvious since it took

three days to cross it. Now it would not take three days to cross
any man-made city, but it took three cosmic "days" for the Life
Principle to cross from spirit to matter and the physical sun.
This is the sinful Nineveh, and its sins are but those of Noah's
day; those wicked sons of God are again consorting with the
daughters of men, hence under condemnation. And here we see
the nonmoral nature of such condemnation. These sins are
necessary to Creation, yet the Creator, as in scripture, is opposed to them. This is but a mythologist's way of stating the
ancient concept that matter is vile and creation a crime.

This wicked city is to be overthrown in the usual "forty
days," unless it repents. And the repentance is like the condemnation. The turbulent and adulterous elements come to rest on
the fourth material plane, and out of this comes a sober and
repentant earth. This is postsolar and hence the planetary
"morning after," so naturally there is repentance. That it is
planetary is obvious since not only the people repent, fast, sit
in sackcloth and ashes, but the flocks and herds do also. They
too are ashamed of themselves, and so, like those in Noah's day,
are archetypes. The *ashes* part is very apt for the earth is the *ashes*
of the solar fire.

10. And God saw their works, that they turned from their evil way;
and God repented of the evil, that he had said that he would do unto
them; and he did it not (Chap. 3).

And God too repents of his evil, and is rebuked by a mortal
much wiser than he. Nor is this the first time; Moses also made
him see his error. Jonah even throws back in his face his gift
of life. "O Lord take, I beseech thee, my life from me; for it is
better for me to die than to live" (4:3). And so prayed Job and
Elijah. What greater indictment of God is there than this? What
greater rebuke than condemnation of his purpose? Is this *the
prophets' truer vision?* Yes.

Jonah saved the city but only to be persecuted for his trouble;
in less canonical books we find him suffering all the torments
of Job, his counterpart. However, in the natural course of
events,

6. . . . the Lord God prepared a gourd, and made it to come up over Jonah, that it might be a shadow over his head, to deliver him from his grief . . . (Chap. 4).

These other sources tell us this gourd was so enormous it completely covered Jonah. Now as Jonah is the Creative Principle, a gourd of such dimensions can be none other than the earth itself; it is, in fact, the growing stone of Nebuchadnezzar's dream. But this would never do; under it Jonah was much too comfortable, so God repented again and "prepared a worm when the morning rose next day, and it smote the gourd (earth, with radiation) that it withered." No doubt you have heard of "the worm that never dies," and you assume it is the human soul or spirit. Here we see what it really is—the genetic principle. This died not even when entombed in dense matter; on the contrary, it destroyed this matter, the mythical gourd, with radiation, after which it created organic forms and thereby brought upon itself still further miseries, real, this time, for now it inhabited sentient matter. It is of this torturous nature of life and its tormentive cause the myth is trying to tell us.

Under it, Jonah finally fainted, but he did not take it lying down; he accused his Creator of evil; and Job declared himself more righteous than God. When elsewhere we said that man is God's moral superior no doubt it sounded like blasphemy, yet it is *the prophets' truer vision.* As the creator of morals, man is morally superior to that which created him.

> Though He's belted you and flayed you,
> By the livin' God that made you,
> You're a better man than He is, Gunga Din
> (with apologies to Kipling).

Our preachers hurl their anger at man and hymn their praise of God, but if they would just reverse the process they would show some evidence of enlightenment, like the prophets. They would also see in Jonah themselves and act accordingly. We are all Jonahs, life, and we are all in wicked Nineveh, God's savage construct; our shelter has been taken away, the heat of battle is upon us and the cold of death around us. This is life—a period of light in a parenthesis of darkness. Jonah preferred the latter, and even death. Death, God's final insult to his creature.

9. And God said to Jonah, Doest thou well to be angry for the gourd? And he said, I do well to be angry, even unto death (Chap. 4).

But we, no matter what happens—war and pestilence, quake and eruption, even death—it's all for some divine purpose beyond our calculation, including cancer and polio. How long must we live in this ignorance of Reality? Is there no one to see these monstrous "acts of God" are not the work of divine wisdom but only the blind motions of the planetary organism and the predacious life upon it; therefore thou doest well to be angry. As Huxley said, "Know the truth and the truth will make you mad," and someone else said "make you sick." Well, we're all sick but we haven't sense enough to be angry.

Nothing, I suppose, could be more futile than human anger at Causation, yet at least it would imply we know what it is not—love and mercy. These are our creations and once we realize it righteous anger will arise in us whenever the ruthless God-force tries to assert itself. We feel such outrage in war and call it a virtue, but it takes a war to make us feel it, because we haven't the wisdom to practice it in peace. Our religion has so intimidated us we haven't even courage enough to cuss the weather. Though it has killed millions, "He tempers the wind to the shorn lamb." What mockery! The shorn lambs of this world are the poor, and the suffering one cold winter causes them damns such doctrines in the eyes of intelligence. The ones that suffer not are those who shear the lambs, because they temper the winds to suit themselves. These violent forces of nature kill millions every year, so as far as Cosmolupus is concerned we are all lambs, or is it Little Red Riding Hoods?

To many this commentary on Jonah will seem brutal and pessimistic, but actually it is scriptural and very optimistic, for in it lies an opportunity greater than man has ever yet perceived. Had this world been created by Perfection, it would be perfect, ourselves included. But where can you go from perfection?

What would there be for us to do? With the knowledge now at hand, we can go far and do much; we can go from savage Nineveh to civilized Utopia. We can even do what Omar only wished, take this sorry scheme of things and mold it nearer to our heart's desire. That's what we're here for, not worship. This world is God's "unfinished business"; our task is to complete it. "Life is a gift of nature; but beautiful living is the gift of wisdom." Greek proverb.

18
Job

Job is the finest and most significant book of the Bible.

MANLY P. HALL

With this we agree, but as with Jonah, we have our doubts about its authorship and place in Hebrew literature. Theistically, it is not Hebrew at all, but Arabic and maybe Babylonian. Job and Jonah are not priestly but midrashic and therefore free from the philosophy and religiosity of the priesthood—and therein lies their superiority. Job, the man, was in trouble, but so were Noah, Moses, Joseph and Daniel, and in all these cases the God of the priest broke every law of nature, and morality, to help them. Not so with Job; not even an angel of the Lord comes to his rescue. He is an innocent victim of inexorable law in a literature of sin and forgiveness. This is Islam's *kismet:* fate, not divine favor. Thus we suspect that Job, like Jonah, is but a Hebrew version of an allegory common to all antiquity. There is, for instance, a Babylonian poem about a virtuous man named Tabu-utul-Bel who was sorely afflicted for some inscrutable reason. After enumerating his virtues and good deeds, he tells how his God tormented him.

Into my prison my house is turned,
Into the fetters of myself my feet have stumbled,

> With a whip he has beaten me;
> All day long the pursuer pursues me,
> In the night watches he lets me suffer;
> Through torture my joints are torn asunder;
> My limbs are destroyed;
> My sickness baffled the conjurers,
> And the seer left dark my omens.

Like this poem, Job is mythopoeic knowledge of Reality; its one defect lies in its anticlimax—an apology by ignorance and a recantation by fear. This is, no doubt, by a second and later author who, unable to stomach the realism of the first, turned its message to priestly purpose. In the first part, proud, scornful Job, knowing he is innocent, will not accuse himself even to mollify his persecutor; he sees the cause of his afflictions and puts the blame where it belongs. This the later "God-fearing" Jews could not accept, and so Elihu is introduced to plead the cause of God. Unable to find Job's sin, he resorts to ridicule; he belittles Job because of his mortal insignificance and exalts the Creator because of His mighty works. Then the latter Himself appears to press his mean advantage.

4. Where wast thou when I laid the foundations of the earth? declare, if thou hast understanding.

31. Canst thou bind the sweet influences of Pleiades, or loose the bands of Orion?

32. Canst thou bring forth Mazzaroth (the zodiac) in his season? or canst thou guide Arcturus with his sons? (Chap. 38).

This is not the taunt of infinite wisdom but of finite ignorance, of all, in fact, who, lacking knowledge of Reality, assume the universe made and governed by a moral and self-conscious Being. This is very convincing to this ignorance but it neither absolves nor exalts the Creator. Vast as the universe is, it is quantitative only, and where is the moral and spiritual superiority in that? Even on Arcturus's sons, planets, there is pain and suffering, and only when they have suffered enough to surmount it will they escape it. This is the way of life, and the only way the Creator has provided. This is the theme of the first part of Job, and like Jonah, an indictment of God. Job is but Jonah in detail; he is also Adam, Noah, Joseph and Moses, in other words, life. His afflictions are the afflictions of Egypt, and his losses the losses of Ishtar and Innana. Like so many others, he came from the "East," and had "seven" sons, elements. And these seven sons must die that they may live again in Evolution. The cause of it all is the scriptural alibi for God's diabolism, namely, Satan. He is the prime mover throughout the story, which is but the story-teller's way of saying he is the Prime Mover. As he is the alleged cause of all evil, it is also an acknowledgement that this evil had to be. Scripturally, that evil is material existence; this is the cosmic tragedy, a tragedy we, of late, have been trying to turn into a comedy, but comedy can also be tragic as we, of late, have proved.

The Book of Job is thus much more than a personal tragedy; it is a magnificent allegory of life itself. As the Talmud plainly tells us, "Job was not created, but is an allegory." In it is dramatized the paradox with which we began—divine source and savage nature. Job, a child of alleged divinity, is made to suffer in this divinity's savage creation. Can any theologian supply that reason? Not on his hypothesis. He would, like Job's comforters, assume Job must have sinned else a God of love and mercy would not have punished him. "Who ever perished, being innocent? or where were the righteous cut off?" argues Eliphaz, 4:7. And Bildad puts in his two cents' worth: "Yea, the light of the wicked shall be put out, and the spark of his fire shall not shine," 18:5. Here we have the keynote of Hebrew philosophy— human sin and divine retribution—and Christianity says amen. But what of the suffering before there was a man to sin? Pain and death did not begin with Homo sap.

As "the greatest of all the men of the east," the man, Job, was proud; as the richest in the land he was much too self-sufficient. Therefore he must be humbled; he must be made to see he too is but "a worm of the dust." To this end he is stripped of all his possessions, including his children; he is afflicted with boils "from the sole of his foot unto his crown." And all this because he is indifferent to the virtues of God.

In this we have another racial touch. To the Hebrews, hell

hath no fury like Jehovah scorned, and so He must be continually praised to keep Him pacified. If Job will but devote his life to this, God's omnipresent good will make him whole. This pretty well summarizes the Hebrews' error: suffering is the result of sin, not existence; God is conscious of it in everyone and as consciously punishes it; He wants praise and honor and man must furnish it; He accepts it all and equates it with material blessings; His Creation, matter, is evil but He is morally good, and being infinite, that good is omnipresent; this includes justice and so justice rules the universe. What nonsense! There is no *moral* justice in the universe; there is only dynamic justness. There is no omnipresent good; there is only unqualified quantity. This is the *universal*, in which resides local morality, man's own humanly qualified soul, and its qualitation is morally superior to God's entire prehuman creation. Why then should the one praise the other? Man owes God nothing, not even thanks. Whatever is, exists because of necessity, not divine sufferance; and whatever exists suffers because of nondivine Causation. Our world is full of suffering, tragedy, disease, disaster, pain; we demand a better reason than religion has to offer.

The above was Job's position—until the priest got round to him. "My righteousness is more than God's," and "It profiteth a man nothing that he should delight himself with God"—*the prophet's truer vision*—and the accusing figure upheld by facts excels the penitent cast down by fear—man's plight since the dawn of religion. Since then every tale that tells of his "lost faith" ends in its recovery. What we need now is the moral courage and mental ability to think this thing through to unbelief and stick to it.

Job is the actual Reality, his God but a priestly hypothesis, his sin but the sin of being, his punishment but the consequence of living. He is life personified, therefore in reading his story let us not think of him as a man, or his troubles as personal, but as though it were the travailing earth itself speaking.

10. Hast thou not poured me out as milk, and curdled me like cheese?

8. Thine hands have made me and fashioned me together round about; yet thou dost destroy me.

7. Thou knowest that I am not wicked; and there is none that can deliver out of thine hand (Chap. 10).

2. Oh that my grief were thoroughly weighed, and my calamity laid in the balances together!

4. For the arrows of the Almighty are within me, the poison whereof drinketh up my spirit: the terrors of God do set themselves in array against me (the one man in all literature who dared say, *"J'accuse"*; Chap. 6).

3. Is it good unto thee that thou shouldest oppress, that thou shouldest despise the work of thine hands, and shine upon the counsel of the wicked?

4. Hast thou eyes of flesh? or seest thou as man seeth? (Chap. 10).

"Doest thou well to be angry!" Is it not better than ignorance of Reality babbling about love and mercy, peace and brotherhood? These are for us to create, God knows them not.

21. Oh that one might plead for a man with God, as a man pleadeth for his neighbour! (Chap. 16).

4. I would order my cause before him, and fill my mouth with arguments (Chap. 23).

But no:

32. For he is not a man, as I am, that I should answer him, and we should come together in judgment (Chap. 9).

This is the plight of life itself—pain without recourse, prayers and the soundless void, suffering sentiency unable to reason with its intangible cause. Only something nonmoral and unconscious of what it has done can account for this predicament. Blame not then any self-conscious Being; the crime is much too great. Impute, not blame, unconscious creativity. This we have asserted from the beginning; it is our Genetic Cosmo-Conception. In this there is no blame, no paradox, no agonizing question, If God is love, why do I suffer so? As a part of a suffering whole, suffering is inevitable. As the whole is also a victim, of necessity, man need not bow down before it. Such humility is not a virtue; it is but ignorance's attitude towards what it does not understand.

And what does Job offer for this attitude? Immortality? Eternal bliss in an unearned heaven? No, this is the priest's idea; Job had a different one.

20. Are not my days few? cease then, and let me alone, . . .
21. Before I go whence I shall not return, even to the land of darkness and the shadow of death (Chap. 10).
9. As the cloud is consumed and vanisheth away: so he that goeth down to the grave shall come up no more (Chap. 7).
1. Call now, if there be any that will answer thee; and to which of the saints wilt thou turn? (Chap. 5).

The saints would have us believe that this is but the cry of a poor distracted soul, tested by God to prove his worth, and that salvation lies in persevering faith in God and a Redeemer. To this end they deliberately changed the words of Job to read, "For I know that my Redeemer liveth." These words did not exist in the original texts. The Septuagint renders it thus: "For I know that he is eternal who is about to deliver me on earth: to restore this skin of mine which endureth these things." Job, a personification of life afflicted with materiality, was speaking only of the evolutionary process that would someday lift him up and make him whole again. Thus he says:

19. He shall deliver thee in six troubles (planes): yea, in seven there shall no evil touch thee (end of Evolution; Chap. 5).

This is salvation of the whole, not the part. He who is a man will accept it and make the best of it. He will see life as an inexorable necessity, the genetic cause of which sees not the epigenetic's pains and sufferings, hopes and aspirations. He will see also that there is no short cut to salvation through supernatural gods and saviors, but that Evolution alone can compensate for what Involution has done.

Involution and Evolution—this is the entire esoteric content of the Old Testament, concealed and yet immortalized by mythology, the wisdom-knowledge of the entire ancient world, subsequently theologized for priestly purpose. And so we will leave this book of borrowed mythology with this expression of Western man's ignorance of it, and also of God. "In order to understand mythology we must imagine a race of people who had no divine revelation as to the origin of mankind, animals, earth, sun, moon and stars. The Israelites were the only race to whom this knowledge was given, consequently they are the only people who have no myths." A. Holman, in *The Zodiac*.

They had nothing else, and, what is more, their myths were not their own; they were but plagiarized versions of older races' knowledge of Causation and Creation. This, through substitution of their own false God-concept, they perverted and destroyed. They had no prophets inspired by God to foretell the future, including a Savior; they had only priests garbling events some billions of years in the past, namely, Creation and its inevitable sequel Evolution. We do not claim to be prophets, but we can do better than that; we can prophesy before the event, not after. We can prophesy that within the next few decades the entire Bible, Old and New, will be exposed for the priestly fraud that it is. We can prophesy that the race will realize that the Jews, instead of being the most spiritually enlightened of all the ancient races, were the most fanatically wrong; that in their ignorance of Causation, they gave to a ruthless principle an awesome majesty and thereby set benighted Western man to worshiping it instead of using this time to conquer the awesome deviltry of this principle within himself. This alone explains man's evil, not "original sin" but original source.

The mistake the subsequent Jews made was that of believing their mythology, literally. The Greeks were not so gullible. So let us see the difference between the Hebrew mythologists and the pagan ones. The purpose of the latter was the preservation of truth and enlightenment of man through the Zodiacal Night. To this end they wrote their tales in such a way that no intelligent man could be deceived by them; they purposely made their myths incredible and their gods immoral that no religion might be founded on them. They did not say they walked and talked with Zeus, or that he commanded them to write. They made no claim to divine revelation or inspiration; they wrote with a simple naïveté that charms but does not seduce. The Hebrews, on the other hand, wrote with malice aforethought; their purpose was not the preservation of truth and human enlightenment but the obscuration of truth and the enslavement of the mind to priestly rule. They were religion makers, and to this end they claimed divine authority; they even put their preposterous claims into the mouth of their monstrous God and declared he said them. Having no material or national power of their own, they invented a conceptual one to intimidate their neighbors and to cripple the Gentile race. And how they have succeeded! In the past two thousand years they have so drugged the mind of Western man, he cannot see the designs they have upon him. In fact, he will not even believe it when one of them points it out to him. Yet here it is by one appropriately named Mr. Ravage, in *Century Mazazine*. [1] So true are his mocking words, that every Christian in Christendumb should hang his head in shame. These too have a double meaning but we'll take the literal first.

You have not begun to appreciate the real depth of our guilt. We are intruders. We are disturbers. We are subverters. We have taken your natural world, your ideal, your destiny, and played havoc with them: We have been at the bottom not merely of the latest great war, but of nearly all your wars, not only of the Russian but of every other major revolution in your history. We have brought discord and confusion and frustration into your personal and public life. We are still doing it. No one can tell how long we shall go on doing it . . .

Our legends and our folk-tales are the sacred lore which you croon to your infants. Our poems have filled your hymnals and your prayerbooks. Our national history has become an indispensable part of the learning of your pastors and priests and scholars. Our kings, our statesmen, our prophets, our warriors are your heroes. Our ancient little country is your Holy Land. Our national literature is your Holy Bible. What our people thought and taught has become inextricably woven into your speech and tradition, until no one among you can be called educated who is not familiar with our racial heritage.

Jewish artisans and Jewish fishermen are your teachers and your saints, with countless statues carved in their image and innumerable

[1] *Century Magazine*, January, 1928.

cathedrals raised to their memories. A Jewish maiden is your ideal of motherhood and womanhood. A Jewish rebel-prophet is the central figure in your religious worship. We have pulled down your idols, cast aside your racial inheritance, and substituted for them our God and our traditions. No conquest in history can even remotely compare with this clean sweep of our conquest over you.

And now, you "God-fearing people," how do you like that? It probably never occured to you, you were so completely indebted to the Jews for all you know and believe, religiously. Well, we said you could not think metaphysically, and so you had to borrow your religion. But there is more here than meets the eye, because presented somewhat out of context. This is Jacob speaking, but underneath his biting irony Esau adds an insult even deeper. According to him, this conquest was moral and spiritual and but for it the Gentiles would still be barbarians. Its moral code rebuked our savagery; its precepts stayed our blood-stained hands and raised our eyes to God. This is the implication behind the irony, but I say its words are true without the irony; strip them, this time, of their hidden meaning and Jacob's words are literally true and also his intention—to cripple his Gentile foe. The myths and legends have malicious purpose, their content, the well known "opiate."

And so we say to their authors, What about your own hands, and those of your murderous God? What about your God Himself? He never existed and your prophets were priestly liars. Their partial Deity was but paper security in lieu of native strength; your Solomon, Samson, David, Moses but figments of your race's politically undercompensated minds and souls. Your "holy scriptures" robbed the world of the ancient wisdom-knowledge, your "revelation," but tales you filched from other races. With these you did much more than just invade us; you "brainwashed" us until we sang the praises of our seducers. You wove them into our ignorant souls and we have paid the price—two thousand years of ignorance, Inquisition, massacre and war. Because of them our people hate, our nations fight, and peace is quite impossible. Because of them our statesmen know not myth from history and so they take from others and give to you who deceived them. This was your purpose from the beginning. All religions are but means to power over men and minds and money, fictitous Gods, but their accessories.

It's true your code served as a crutch for the crippled souls your folk tales made, your myths became our mental food because we had no other. When robbed and hungry, a rotten apple is better than nothing; it served a starved and benighted age you helped to make, but that age is passing now and the feeble crutch and rotten apple must go with it. The spirit of independence now pervades the world; the time has come for another Emancipation Proclamation.

19

The New Testament

The Mythical Nature of Christ

For as Jonas was three days and three nights in the whale's belly; so shall the Son of man be three days and three nights in the heart of the earth.

MATTHEW 12:40

And now having seen the nature and substance of the Old Testament, what of the New? Since both are the product of one race, one age, and together constitute one book, can we believe the New is any different from the Old? Each, it is true, has its own peculiar miracles and miracle workers, but there is only one miracle, Creation, and one miracle worker, the Creative Principle. Know, therefore, that any other of whom you have heard or read is but a personification of this original. Such is Moses, the savior of the Old Testament, and such is Jesus of the New. Specifically, Jesus is the Principle that "fell" into generation, matter, Christ its subsequent Savior, the two constituting Involution and Evolution. This is mythic methodology and used throughout the entire Bible. Only when we know this fact can we understand this later addition to the scriptures, for in both content and structure it is but another version of the Hebrew myth of Creation.

This is the reason for *its* four sources—not four historical biographies as now assumed, but an Old Testament precedent followed in the New. Even the Church Fathers, ignorant as they were of occult meanings, sensed some deeper purport in this number. Irenaeus tried to explain it on the grounds that there are four elements, four quarters of the world, etc. To quote verbatim: "For as there are four quarters of the world and four general winds . . . it is right that she (the Church) should have four pillars." Here at least is recognition that the number is symbolic and planetary. The four sources, in both books, represent the four cardinal divisions of the planetary zodiac—the "beasts" of Ezekiel and John the Revelator—and in the Roman Vulgate the Gospelists are so presented. Standing beside Matthew is an angel, Aquarius or Man; beside Luke, a bull, Taurus; with Mark is a lion, Leo; and with John, an eagle, Scorpio. Whether Irenaeus understood this or not, these are his "four quarters" and "four general winds"—forces.

Bible students today do not know whether the four Gospels are the work of just four men or of many, but the evidence is all on the side of the many. We find in them the same abrupt endings and interpolated excerpts as we did in the Old Testament. In some chapters there are as many as ten or twelve of these, some reasonably sequential and others not; that is, the subject may be the same but the literary sequence is not such as we would expect in a holograph. From this we may conclude that the Gospels are the gist of a considerable secret literature on the subject of Creation and Evolution, its central figure a selective synthesis from all known sources. Long before the alleged time of Christ, the word Jesus, meaning Savior, was used by the ancients—Joshua, Jonah, Jason, Ionnes, etc. There was a Jesus cult among the Nazarites long prior to 1 A.D. It was also this symbolic Jesus that the Essenes referred to as "the teacher of righteousness." The authorities for this pre-Christian Jesus are Epiphanius and the modern scholar, W. B. Smith.

In spite of the Christians' destruction of their source material, commentary still exists that proves beyond a doubt that Christianity did not spring from the gospel Christ. No less an authority than Saint Augustine, "Founder of Christian Theology," made this statement: "That which is known as the Christian religion existed among the ancients, and never did not exist; from the very beginning of the human race until the time when Christ came in the flesh at which time the true religion, which already existed, began to be called Christianity." On the same subject Eusebius had this to say: "That the religion published by Jesus Christ to all nations is neither new nor strange. For though, without controversy, we are of late and the name of Christians is indeed new; yet our manner of life and the principles of our religion have not lately been devised by us, but were instituted and observed, if I may say so, from the beginning of the world." And speaking of the Essenes, sometimes called Therapeutae, he makes this astonishing remark: "These ancient Therapeutae were Christians and their writings are our Gospels and Epistles." This, we think, should prove our point, namely, that not only the Gospels and Epistles but the entire New Testament is but a priestly rewrite of the Ancient Wisdom.

The significance of this pre-Christian body of literature is not realized by our scholars; as for the masses, they have never been told it existed, much less that the Christian Fathers destroyed it. Determined, as these were, to build a religion upon a historical Christ, they had to annihilate all evidence of his mythic nature. This they did with a vengeance, to conceal as Carpenter said, "the evidence of their own dishonesty." And confirming this, Gilbert Murray said: "The polemic literature of Christianity is loud and triumphant; the books of the pagans have been destroyed." By the fifth century the destruction was so complete Archbishop Chrysostom could boast of it thus: "Every trace of the old philosophy and literature of the ancient world has vanished from the face of the earth." Doane, Bible Myths, p. 436.

It is common knowledge that the present Gospels are not the originals. As with the manuscripts of the Old Testament, those of the New were soon lost to the world; not even the earliest Church Fathers claimed to have seen them. It is well know that the Gospel of Luke was preceded by another called Ur-Markus, a part of the Logia, or occult cosmology, the present one being but this older one distorted into history. The book of Matthew is an outgrowth of a prior book known as the Logia of Matthew. Jerome said the canonical version was a rewrite of the Hebrew text by a disciple of Manichaeus named Seleucus. These revisionists were literal-minded religionists and they inserted much extraneous matter, even, according to some authorities, whole chapters. The titles "gospel according to" implies questionable authority; it means not *of* but *attributed to;* in other words, the compilers are evading the issue of eyewitness authority. There is also in all four, a biographical evasiveness peculiar to mythology. As with Samson, Saul and David, whole decades of Jesus' life are omitted, while miraculous deeds are thrown at the reader until he forgets to question the doer. It all adds up to the fact that the Gospels are a final rendition of an ancient esoteric literature, the subject of which is the planetary Logos [1] personified. Writing of this, Arthur Drews confirms it thus: "The Gospels do not contain the history of an actual man, but only the myth of the god-man Jesus, clothed in a historical dress."

The purpose of the rewrites and historical dress was the reduction of the cosmic and universal to the human and personal, but to see this you must first suspect deception here; you must know that a vast conspiracy was afoot when this book was written. In this, first things were put last and vice versa. John of the Gospels goes straight to the cosmic source, the Logos; Matthew related the birth of the infant Jesus. John of Revelation deals strictly with Causation and Creation, while Mark makes it a man. From this we conclude that the canonical order assigned to them—Matthew, Mark, Luke and John—is incorrect; it should be somewhat reversed. This gradual reduction of the Planetary Logos to a human infant was a monstrous crime, but there is no crime too monstrous for a scheming priesthood.

Tatian's *Diatessaron,* a continuous story of Christ's life (second century), begins with John's Gospel, and this is where it should begin.

1. In the beginning was the Word, and the Word was with God, and the Word was God.

2. The same was in the beginning with God (like Solomon).

3. All things were made by him; and without him was not any thing made that was made.

4. In him was life; and the life was the light of men.

[1] A Greek name for the planetary creativity, without personality.

5. And the light shineth in darkness; and the darkness comprehended it not.

This is not a reference to the prehuman life of religion's Christ, but an occult clue to the latter's true nature—a personification of the Planetary Logos, an *it*, not a *him*, not a person but the creative power that was with Ideation from the beginning. It is the life-energy and thus the life and light of all things. And if you would know its pre-Christian name and nature, it is Lucifer. This light shone in that darkness we called the Absolute; this, John tells us but being theistically misinformed he does not tell us that this "light" did not comprehend itself—and therein hangs the whole fallacy of religion. He makes it appear, or so we have interpreted it, that the human mind is the incomprehending darkness, incapable of recognizing the divine nature of Christ. Being, in plain words, ignorant of the human source of divine qualities, he attributes them wholly to God and Christ, thus denying man the credit for them. And such is Christian teaching today.

John's first words are about the Creative Principle, and to what else can his last words apply? "And there are also many other things which Jesus did, the which, if they should be written every one, I suppose that even the world itself could not contain the books that should be written" (21:25). Said of a man whose works covered but three years, this is sheer nonsense, but said of the Creative Principle, it is "gospel truth," for all the books that are and were and ever shall be, are of its works. If then John's first and last words are of the Creative Principle, why not those in between? It is the devilish perversion of this that we condemn, not the moral teaching.

All religions have good moral teachings, but religion is a duality—a morality to live by and a philosophy to think by. Today most people know that the philosophy of Christianity is false and so have thrown out the morality with it. This is because the philosophy is incapable of enlightening them sufficiently to distinguish the good from the bad. These two must be separated that the good may survive. But what shall we put in the place of the bad? The legitimate partner of morality is that which the false philosophy destroyed, namely, the wisdom-knowlege of Reality, as taught in the Schools of the Mysteries—destroyed by the Christians. With this we would be so enlightened we could practice the morality. This would not be religion but ethics, morality practiced instead of preached.

Esoterically, the Gospels are this knowledge then known as the Gnosis, but so ignorant of the latter's nature are our theologians, they write of it thus: "The great menace, in fact of Gnosticism, was its refusal to remain outside of Christianity. It fastened itself as a parasite upon the Christian faith, drawing substance from it and at the same time robbing it of its individual character and vitality." This is a sample of the later inversion and perversion of facts: Christianity was the parasite drawing its substance from Gnosticism, not vice versa. And instead of refusing to remain outside of Christianity, Gnosticism refused to remain in it, after its perversion. With its literalization, the Jewish adherents (Ebionites) reverted to Judaism, denying all supernatural nature to Christ and authority to Paul. Indeed so great became the opposition, it acquired a name, Docetism—Gnostic opposition to the literal belief in Christ.

The question now arises: When were these gospels written? The simple-minded are led to believe they are eyewitness accounts of their Savior's life written soon after His departure, yet according to the *Catholic Encyclopedia* the book of Luke was not written till nearly two hundred years after this event. The proof offered is that the Theophilus to whom Luke addressed it was bishop of Antioch from 169 to 177 A.D. This same authority tells us that Pope Clement I, fourth from Peter, circa A.D. 97, never quoted from the Gospels or mentions any of the four authors. Neither did any Pope or church father for nearly a century later. According to Wheless, ". . . no written Gospel existed until shortly before 185 A.D., when Irenaeus wrote; they are first mentioned in Chapter XVI of his book II." This explains why Justin Martyr, circa A.D. 140, never quoted from and apparently never heard of the Gospels, so likewise Paul. Paul did not have to read them to know about Jesus and Christ; he had only to read the pre-Christian mystic literature, subsequently destroyed.

And now the final question: Who wrote these Gospels, and for what purpose? No doubt their content was known to the Essenes, but it is not likely they wrote them. They were firm adherents to the Mosaic tradition, therefore not likely to present a new Savior; they were extreme ascetics, therefore not likely to present their Messiah as a wine-bibber, consorting with publicans and sinners. For the authors of such a character we must look to a more liberal and cosmopolitan group.

From about 100 B.C. to 100 A.D., the orthodox Jewish priesthood suffered an eclipse. The promises of their scriptures had failed them—Jerusalem was destroyed and Israel was dispersed. Thereafter many Jews fled to Egypt, Rome and Greece, and those among them who might have become priests joined the schools of the Mysteries, among them that of the Gnostics. Here from a new perspective they learned, or relearned, the secret Gnosis or wisdom-knowledge of the Ancients. Still priests at heart, however, they were not satisfied with a pure, impersonal metaphysic, and so to Hellenic Gnosticism they added Semitic theology. With this as a basis they set about to reestablish religion and a priesthood. But what to do? Why, just as their predecessors had done, write a new and wondrous scripture, based on the creative process. This is the New Testament—cosmology theologized for the fifth time and for the same purpose. In other words, the New Testament is but a sequel, inspired not by the fulfillment of the messianic promise of the Old, but by the failure of the Old. But for this failure, the New would never have been written.

Morally and socially the New differs from the Old and the reason lies in the change that had taken place in its authors. Prior to their contact with pagan philosophy the Jews were a race of bigots: no one could live in their midst who did not adhere to their narrow creed; no one not a Jew was considered worthy of Jehovah's interest. Contact with cosmopolitan minds changed them. They saw now the social inadequacy of their narrow, sectarian creed; they drew the logical conclusion from Zion's fall and Israel's flight—they were not the one and only concern of the Almighty. Jehovah was still their God but He was now the God of all mankind; Messiah was still their hope and now they would present him to the world, not just Israel. And so the religious genius of the race set to work again, and with the aid of the new social consciousness it gave to the world its noblest code of ethics. But alas, alas, Satan came also—the false theology of the race. This is the Jewish "shibboleth" and now it catches them again, for though the wisdom of their work is wondrous, it is not that of a Christ, but only that of man with a touch of Christ consciousness. And lacking this more fully, it created a Christ with all its own false concepts—divine source, moral perfection, and in spite of this, a Son thereof who did not know the genesis of the world or of man's moral and ethical qualities. Many antireligionists have tried to demolish this exalted being but none have brought the charge of ignorance against him, and for an obvious reason—they lacked the knowledge to discern his errors. Yet this is the only effective approach, and only when the race acquires knowledge superior to his, will it escape enslavement to a superstition.

Semienlightened Gnostic Jews created the Christ of the Gospels, but they did not intend their Christ to be taken literally, not at least by the initiated. They were presenting an ideal, a model to be copied, but they did not reckon with the ignorant Gentile literalists who were to follow them. These seized upon the Gnostics' symbolic writings and reduced them to a literal and historic basis—the greatest error of the Piscean age. With this humanization of their ideal, the Jews would have naught to do, hence their rejection of a historical Christ. This occurred years subsequent, the rejection in the Gospels being but part of the symbolic story. In other words, the Jews did not reject the scriptural Christ, but only the Christ of the Gentile Church. In this they acted wisely and right; Christs belong to mythology and the wiser Jews knew it. Then let's hear no more the cry of "Christ-killers"; the Jews did not kill Christ; they created him. The Gentiles were the ones who killed the Jewish Christ—an occult symbol. This required a state of spiritual ignorance unparalleled in human history. All commentators agree there was such at that time but none have explained it. This we will do at the end of this chapter.

Those who read only Hebrew mythology believe there was

only one Christ, and Savior; they do not know that there were at least sixteen,[2] all of them but literalizations of a once-universal Creation myth. The one subject of both myth and scripture is the Life Principle. In the involutionary process this "fell" into that corruption called matter, and in the evolutionary, it is raised or resurrected again. Thus the one is portrayed as the "savior" of the other. This is the anticipated Messiah of the earlier Jews, not the Christ of Christianity. And like so much of Jewish tradition it is a borrowed idea. Long before the Jews appeared, the Egyptians had their Madhi, "the coming Messiah." So with the Greeks: their myth of Hercules, freeing Prometheus bound on the rock, is their mythic version. By the time of Aeschylus, 525 B.C., he wrote of it thus: "To such labors look thou for no termination until some god shall appear as a substitute in thy pangs and shall be willing to go both to gloomy Hades and to the murky depths around Tartarus." And so it was said of Christ.

One has only to read in full the story of Hercules to realize the pagan and mythic nature of the whole Christ story. He too was born of a virgin, Alcmene; he too had a god for a father, Zeus; he too was the "only begotten" of the father; he too was called "Savior," the Greek Soter, and "the good shepherd," Neulos Emelos. And just as with Christ, he died, went to the lower world and then ascended to heaven from Mount Orca. He was also called the Prince of Peace; according to Lucian, "He sought not to subjugate nations by force but by divine wisdom and persuasion." According to Bart, "His voluntary immolation betokened an eternal new birth of man . . . Through the release of Prometheus and the erection of altars we behold in him the mediator between the old and the new faiths . . . He abolished human sacrifice wherever he found it practiced. He descended into the somber realms of Pluto, as a shade . . . He ascended as a spirit to his father Zeus in Olympus." Of Mithra of Persia, E. E. Goldsmith wrote thus: "He descends into the abode of death only to rise again in the full glory of light and power for the eternal salvation of man."

[2] See page 352.

So was it with Bacchus, called by Euripides "Bacchus, the Son of God." In *Bacchus, the Prophet-God*, Professor Wilder writes of him thus: "He represented to them (his followers) alike the world of nature and the world of righteousness, with healing in his wings, and he not only brought joy to mortals, but opened to them hope beyond mortality of immortal life. Born of a human mother, he raised her from the world of death to the supernal air to be revered and worshiped. At once lord of all worlds he was in them all alike the Savior . . . Such was Bacchus, the Prophet-God. A change in cultus, decreed by the Murderer-Imperial, the Emperor Theodosius, at the instance of Ghostly Father Ambrosius of Milan, has changed his title to Father of Lies, and his rites stigmatized as witchcraft." Just so; the founders of Christianity got their material from pagan mythology, and after turning it to their own account, put the pagans to the sword, burned their books, branded their healing arts as sorcery and their gods as devils. So with the Gnostics. The author of Revelation was one; the Church destroyed his sect, then incorporated this gnostic masterpiece in what they proclaimed as a new and wondrous gospel. Quite incapable of understanding it, they thought it further proof of their wonder-working God.

The *Sibylline Verses* also contained material that later became "sacred Christian doctrine"—the prophecy of a Savior, his miraculous birth, and divine parentage, etc. Vergil mentions them thus:

> Begin Sicilian Muse, a lofty strain,
> The voice of Cumae's oracle is heard again.
> See where the cycling years new blessings bring;
> The Virgin comes, and he, the long-wished king.

Saint Justin, born about 100 A.D., quoted the *Sibylline Verses* in his efforts to convince the Emperor Marcus Antonius that Christ's coming had been foretold, not only by Hebrew prophets but by the Cumaean Sibyl. Constantine also quoted them to prove the divinity of Christ, which proves only that these early Christians were completely ignorant of their meaning, for these

Verses were referring only to the zodiacal cycles. In these cycles lies also the zodiacal meaning of many things assumed to derive from Christ—Christmas, Easter, and the like.

There is no end to this material, but the little given here should answer the question, If no such being as Christ existed, where did his creators get the material for such a character? Considering the vast mythic reservoir, the Old Testament included, we see they did not lack source material. As stated elsewhere, they had access to ancient learning wholly unknown to us today, because destroyed. The two libraries in Alexandria alone contained nearly a million volumes.

Besides all this there were at that time certain magicians who performed feats the credulous mistook for miracles—Celsus, for instance, from whose name the later Paracelsus derived his. Then there was Simon Magus, spoken of in Acts. The Apollos thereof was, perhaps, Apollonius of Tyana, whose "miracles" so mystified Justin Martyr that he exclaimed: "How is it that the talismans of Apollonius have power in certain members of creation, for they prevent, as we see, the fury of the waves, and the violence of the winds, and the attack of wild beasts; and whilst our Lord's miracles are preserved by tradition alone, those of Apollonius are most numerous and actually manifest in present facts." Of this man the *American Encyclopedia* says: "A Pythagorean philosopher born at Tyana, about the beginning of the Christian era. He professed miraculous powers, was venerated for his wisdom and considered by some a rival of Christ." Here was a man who had some useful human power while the Church's miracle worker was only "preserved by tradition," and founded on mythology. Little wonder then his talismans didn't work while Apollonius's did.

According to some, we are indebted to this man for the entire story of Christ. The argument runs thus: There was in ancient India a very great sage called Deva Bodhisatoua. Among other things he wrote a mythological account of Krishna, sometimes spelled Chrishna. About 38 or 40 A.D., Apollonius while traveling in the East found this story in Singapore. He considered it so important he translated it into his own language, namely, Samarian. In this he made several changes according to his own understanding and philosophy. On his return he brought it to Antioch, and there he died. Some thirty years later another Samaritan, Marcion, found it. He too made a copy with still more changes. This he brought to Rome about 130 A.D., where he translated it into Greek and Latin. This was seized upon by a hungry and disinherited priesthood and developed into the New Testament. Apollonius became Apollo, Marcion, Mark, and Chrishna, Christ. True or not, many of the things attributed to Christ are also in the Chrishna story. His raising of Jairus's daughter, for instance, is too similar to that of Chrishna's raising of Angashuna's daughter to be anything other than a copy. The coming of the Magi, the herald angels also figure in the Hindu account. For the raising of Angashuna's daughter see page 339.

Had there actually lived a man who could raise the dead, heal the sick and walk on the water, history would have recorded it. Why then did it not? For lack of historians? Had this been the case, the believers would have at least a negative proof, but oddly enough the period was peculiarly distinguished in this respect. There were many historians just then and some of them the most illustrious of all time—Tacitus, Plutarch, Livy, the two Plinys, Philo and Josephus, among others; and besides these, many men of literary note such as Seneca, Martial, Juvenal, Epictetus, Plotinus and Porphyry. We are all too prone to forget the brilliancy of this period, yet this was the age of Vergil, Horace, and Ovid, the latter living till Christ, if real, would have been twenty-two. These were all men of great intellect, and deeply interested in the doctrines and morals of their day. Why then did they not record this wonder-working Savior of the race? Because like all Saviors, he belongs to mythology, not history.

Livy was born too soon to record Christ's works, but not too soon to report the most sensational and unnatural events in human history—immaculate conception and virgin birth. Plutarch lived from about 46 to 120 A.D. but apparently never heard of Christ. Had he but written a life of this sixteenth Savior and paralleled it with any one of the others, Christianity would not be the superstition it is today. Pliny the Elder, 22–79 A.D., was Christ's contemporary, yet makes no mention of him. The younger Pliny, 62–110 A.D., speaks of the Christians of Pontus and Bithnia but refers to Christ only as the object of their worship. Tacitus, a moralistic historian, produced his greatest work while the New Testament was allegedly written, yet he, like the younger Pliny, mentions Christ only in terms of the Christians and their beliefs; in other words, these men were speaking of a new religion not of a historical founder, and for this new religion they had nothing but contempt, see page 443. Then there was Juvenal, the moral critic of his age; one would think he would cite this paragon of virtue in his attack upon decadent Rome. And the stoic, Epictetus, and the mystics, Plotinus and Porphyry, why did they not make good use of this mystical Christ? Porphyry, instead of accepting Christianity, called it "a blasphemy barbarously bold," for which thirty-six of his books were burned. The truth is there is not a single word about Christ, divine or otherwise, in secular literature dating from the first century. And what of those preceding it? What of the Torah, that most revered part of the Old Testament? It is a revelation from God we are told, yet this God never told His "chosen" that He had a son. Yet this son is the "word," the Logos, the creator of the world. Would this God have kept so vital a fact from such an intimate as Moses? to whom He said "the Lord, thy God is one"? The answer is very simple: This son of God had not then been invented.

Christ lives, moves and has his being in just one book and that, a book of mythology. "It has always been an unfailing source of astonishment to the historical investigator of Christian beginnings that there is not one single word from the pen of any pagan writer of the first century of our era which can in any fashion be referred to the marvelous story recounted by the Gospel writers. The very existence of Jesus seems unknown." G. R. S. Mead, in *Did Jesus Live 100 B.C.?* The answer to his query is, Yes, mythologically. This was the Jesus of the pre-Christian Nazarites. More recently Tillich concluded: "Historical research has made it obvious that there is no way to get at the historical events which have produced the Biblical picture of Jesus who is called the Christ with more than a degree of probability." And Dr. Schweitzer came to the same conclusion.

In trying to explain away this silent century, the excuse is made that Judea was isolated and that there was no "news service" in those days; therefore these men did not know about Christ. No, but they did know about the new religion: Jerome refers to Seneca as "our own Seneca," therefore Seneca knew; Theodoret, writing of Plutarch, said, "he had heard of our holy Gospel and inserted many of our *sacred mysteries* in his works." Yes, he had heard of the "sacred mysteries" (and who hadn't in those days?) but not of Christ, and the reason is that the Christ of religion did not then exist. "We find nothing like divinity ascribed to Christ before Justin Martyr (141 A.D.) who from being a philosopher became a Christian." Dr. Priestly. Not much of a philosopher, we suspect, for he became convinced of a historical Christ by reading the Old Testament prophecies of a Messiah—and they are not prophecies. We should not, in passing, miss the significance of this: if the philosophers of the time could not distinguish myth from history, what of the ignorant masses? This too will be dealt with later.

Those who accepted Christianity were unquestionably ignorant, but our modern apologists cannot charge the aforesaid pagans with it; they were all men of exceptional intelligence. Some of them held high office and therefore knew their world. Pliny the Elder was procurator in Spain; Pliny the Younger was governor of Bithynia; Josephus was governor of Galilee; Seneca was the brother of Gallio, proconsul of Achaia at precisely the time Paul is said to have preached there. While he wrote of many lesser things, no mention is made of Paul or the wonder-working Christ. Yet surely the latter's miracles, virgin birth, and so on, would have interested him. They would have made excellent material for his *Questionum Naturalium.* Just here we could explain another mystery: Why did none of these world Saviors write a book? The reason should now be obvious—world Saviors do not make books; books make them. They are the creations of mythologists, not historians, of occultists, not literalists.

Coming down to the aforesaid Justin Martyr, we have, perhaps, the strongest refutation of all. This particular phantast sought to convert the rejecting Jews to Christianity, and in his writings he tells us of his encounter with one named Trypho.

Replying to Justin's arguments, this Jew had this to say: "Now Christ, if he has indeed been born and exists anywhere, is unknown and does not even know himself and has no power until Elias come and make him manifest to all. And you, having accepted a groundless report, invent a Christ for yourselves and for his sake are inconsiderately perishing." The saintly martyrs for mythology. Elsewhere Trypho refers to Jesus as "that Jesus who you say was crucified . . ." Thus we have a very early Jewish denial of Christ's existence. If, as some in desperation argue, Trypho was but a foil for Justin's argument, the words still carry weight, for they express contemporary Jewish opinion.

Whether accepting or rejecting Christ, one would think the Jewish historians would at least admit so great a personage was of their race. And if anyone would do so, it should be Philo. This philosopher-historian lived both before and after the time of Christ, yet never mentions him. The only direct reference to Jesus in Jewish history of the time is found in Josephus, *born in Jerusalem*, 37 A.D., but no serious student today, not even the theologian, believes Josephus wrote it. It is so palpably false that it is now attributed to those notorious forgers, the early Christians. It does say Jesus was the Christ, and it does imply He was superhuman, and for such words Christ was allegedly crucified and His disciples stoned. If Josephus, a Jewish official, had written these words he would have suffered a similar fate. Spinoza, sixteen centuries later, was cursed and banished for much less. As this passage from Josephus is often desired by serious students, we quote it in full: "About this time lived Jesus, a wise man, if indeed he should be called man. He wrought miracles and was a teacher of those who gladly accept the truth, and had a large following among the Jews and pagans. He was the Christ. Although Pilate, at the complaint of the leaders of our people, condemned him to die on the cross, his early followers were faithful to him. For he appeared to them alive again on the third day, as god-sent prophets had foretold this and a thousand other wonderful things of him. The people of the Christians which is called after him, survive until the present day." *Jewish Antiquities.*

As long as the mythological source and meaning of Christ was unknown, the authenticity of such statements could be defended but when we know this being never existed, how can we believe his near-contemporaries wrote them? The one just quoted clearly admits the Jews' responsibility for the death of Christ; would the Catholic hierarchy today be absolving them if it believed Josephus wrote it?

The Social Context

Neither the Christian religion nor the Christian Church dates from the alleged time of Christ, or even from the first century. These are creations of the third and fourth centuries, and what they subsequently became was but what their founders made out of their pagan source material. That what they made was all based on ignorance of that material's occult meaning is a reflection on their intelligence. The question then arises, How did it happen that so soon after the pre-Christian age of enlightenment, the mental level sank so low that this purely mythical Christ could be accepted as a historical person and a basis for a new religion?

By the third century all the science, philosophy and mythology of Greece had disappeared, mostly in flames. Rome was now the dominant power, but the Romans were not like the Greeks. They lacked the Hellenic love of learning; they had no use for philosophy; in fact they drove out the philosophers. Power was their god and conquest their vocation. And so when the Empire declined and finally fell, they had no inner light to guide them, no inner strength to sustain them. While a few intellectuals remained, the masses were sunk in abysmal ignorance, poverty and want. So they too "fell"—for the priestly hoax.

In this lies another contributing factor, not fully realized today—the economic one. All mass movements are security inspired, and make no mistake this played its part in Christianity. The masses are always more interested in bread than philosophy, especially masses that have never known philosophy. So, as Roman prosperity vanished the masses found themselves in desperate straits; they were, like us after the Depression, ripe for a "New Deal." Christianity offered it; the hungry masses accepted it. Christianity was the Communism of that day, and the Christians were its "subversives." Today, the inquisitor's query is, "Are you or were you ever a Communist?" In those days, it was, as Pliny tells us, "Are you or were you ever a Christian?" Until then the Romans scoffed at all religions, but when religious fanaticism was added to material need, the "subversives" became defiant, rebellious and even incendiary. Naturally they "were punished, not for their incendiarism but because they brought down upon themselves the hatred of mankind." And these were the noble martyrs we've been hearing about ever since.

This is the social and economic context of Christianity, and all unbiased commentators recognize it, but there is still another none of them recognize because Christianity robbed them of all such knowledge. This is the cosmic context. The first century or thereabouts was the beginning of the so-called Piscean Age, whose nether opposite, Libra, as we made it, is the nadir of the Zodiacal Night. Its influence is materialistic and its product, spiritual blindness. To this must be added Western man's incapacity for abstract thought, still with us. It was the coincidence of these three factors mentioned here that furnished the mental soil for Christianity, see last chapter also. Only the spiritual ignorance they jointly produced can account for the acceptance of a mythic symbol as a divine epiphany. Only such mental impoverishment could accept such things as immaculate conception, virgin birth, transfiguration, and resurrection as applicable to man. These are mythical terms applicable only to the Creative Principle. Yet what time and effort we have wasted on these unnatural and unprovable things! Books by the thousands, sermons by the millions, and all for want of knowledge of Reality. Until this is attained, the intelligent thing to do with an unprovable is question the necessity of its existence. Once this attitude is taken we may be led to knowledge that does not require it at all; accept it as a hypothesis and you are compelled to accept its preposterous corollaries. If, for instance, you accept religion's God-hypothesis, you must accept its miracles, divine source, condemnation and revelation; if you accept its Christ-hypothesis, you must accept its salvation, damnation, resurrection and Second Coming. Throw them both out and you don't have to accept any of these; you are free to roam the whole realm of Being and perhaps arrive at truth—truth they cannot supply and knowledge that doesn't need them. This is the way of logic, reason and sense, and we shall apply it to the Gospels.

20

The Gospel Story

Believe not because some old manuscripts are produced, believe not because it is your national belief, believe not because you have been made to believe from your childhood, but reason truth out, and after you have analyzed it, then if you find it will do good to one and all, believe it, live up to it and help others to live up to it.

BUDDHA

We said the New Testament was of the same nature, age and race as the Old. We should therefore expect to find in it the same theology, methodology and formula. And such is the Gospel of St. Luke, a physician, we are told. This begins with the parentage of John, and here again we find a barren woman lamenting her fate, an angel promising her husband a son who "shall drink neither wine nor strong drink" (1:15). And so it was said of Samson, Samuel, and others. Is this the normal process in reproduction? No, it is either rank superstition and ignorance of nature or mythic symbolism. As we can't believe a *physician* could be that naive about babies, we'll assume he was using symbolic language. If so, then it is not history, and if it is not history with John, it is not history with Jesus.

The angel was Gabriel, and having corrected barrenness, virginity was easy, "For with God nothing shall be impossible" (1:37).

26. And in the *sixth* month the angel Gabriel was sent from God unto a city of Galilee, named Nazareth,

27. To a virgin espoused to a man whose name was Joseph, of the house of David: and the virgin's name was Mary.

30. And the angel said unto her, Fear not Mary: for thou hast found favor with God.

31. And behold, thou shalt conceive in the womb, and bring forth a son, and shall call his name Jesus. (The Greek equivalent of Joshua—savior.)

32. He shall be great, and shall be called the Son of the Highest; and the Lord God shall give unto him the throne of his father David;

33. And he shall reign over the house of Jacob for ever; and of his kingdom there shall be no end.

The same Old Testament promises. Were they intended literally, they would be as false as those given to Jacob and David, for Jesus never reigned over the house of Jacob or sat on David's throne. Is it possible Gabriel was so mistaken? Not when you understand it: the house of Jacob is the world, and over it reigns the planetary Logos, and of its kingdom "there shall be no end," at least for us. You see such statements make no sense when applied to man, the epigenetic; they are, as stated, applicable only to the planet, that is, the genetic. It is this the Creator is interested in, not a peasant girl in Galilee. To see it otherwise is to be guilty of the most benighted anthropomorphism.

The Old Testament's "angel of the Lord" now has a name, Gabriel, and the planetary genetic is now "the Holy Ghost," verse 35. And how did he get into the New Testament? We did not find him in the Old. He got in by way of Persia and for a time contested Christianity, see page 452. As for Gabriel, he is the Hebrew Hermes, the messenger of the gods, and so he announced to the female aspect, which is matter, that from its virgin womb a physical sun should be born, here the planetary embryo on the *sixth* plane, as yet invisible.

34. Then said Mary unto the angel, How shall this be, seeing I know not a man?

The problem should not be difficult by this time; it is but the mother of Isaac, Samson and Samuel, all skeptical of barren, or virgin, space producing a sun. How shocking to say that this "virgin Mary" and Jonah's whale are one and the same.

35. And the angel answered and said unto her, The Holy Ghost shall come upon thee, and the power of the Highest shall overshadow thee: therefore also that holy thing which shall be born of thee shall be called the Son of God ("Dr." Luke, Chap. 1).

If today a doctor reported a pregnancy in this manner, what would we think of him? The "good doctor" seems a bit confused and also contradictory. According to him Joseph had no part in this supernatural affair; it was the Holy Ghost. Yet later we learn that Jesus was of David's line because Joseph was David's descendant. How can this be when Joseph had no part in it? For Jesus to be of David's line, Mary would have to be David's descendant also. And so it is argued, but it's all unnecessary—Jesus and Mary were David's descendants the same way Solomon was—mythologically. And since David and Solomon are both mythological, so are their descendants. According to Matthew, Joseph's father was Jacob, but Luke says he was Heli—which might well be Helios. Indeed Luke seems very uncertain about this, since he says of Jesus, he "being (as was supposed) the son of Joseph, which was the son of Heli." And the parentheses are Luke's.

"It's a wise child that knows its own father," and later we will prove this child did not know his. And we might well add, it's a wise Christian who knows who Jesus' father was. Who, for instance, knows what this Holy Ghost is? And who is enlightened enough not to be shocked when told it was Christ Himself who "overshadowed" His mother Mary? Yet if He didn't, He is no part of the Godhead. As the second person in it, He must partake of the whole, and so He, Himself, was this Holy Ghost and consort of the mother principle. The tale is but the Hebrew version of the Greek Oedipus and Jocasta, and the Egyptian Isis and Horus. The early Christians destroyed all such occult knowledge, yet one little source remains, the Gnostic *Pistis Sophia*, which tells us this fact quite plainly. Equally shocking would be the statement that this "holy Mary" killed her own son. Yet this too is true—matter killed the spirit. To understand such things you must get away from the human and historic.

The idea of immaculate conception of mortals is based on the immaculate conception of the world. The cosmic Mother Principle, primordial substance, became immaculately impregnated with planetary ideation, immaculately, because no sex or passion can be imputed to the primordial elements. This is but our Involution—ideation involved in substance. From this a son, actually a sun, is born, but scripturally, the planetary Logos, or Creator of the world. The virgin Mary is therefore but virgin space, whose son is a future sun. This is the occult meaning, but whenever the race becomes completely ignorant of Causation and Creation it takes this mythological presentation of it and on it founds a religion. Such is Christianity, the most spiritually ignorant of all religions.

Annunciation is an integral part of occult cosmology. The Old Testament has many parallels. An angel announced the birth of Samson and Samuel, both solar men. Of Zoroaster it was said, "The divine glory reveals to his mother his conception and touches her with great splendor . . . A preview of his ideal image was seen in the heavens and an ox foretold in human speech 'the revelation he would bring the world,' " Atkins. Zoro, *son of*, and aster, *star*. Son of a star and such is a planet. Even in far-off Mexico, an ambassador from heaven announced to the virgin Sochequetzal, mother of Quetzalcoatl, that she would conceive and bear a son immaculately. And just as Gabriel announced to Mary the coming of Jesus, so Bodhisat announced to Maia, his mother, the coming of Buddha. In the Christian pictures of the Annunciation, Gabriel is always shown as holding a water lily in his hand; in the Hindu pictures Bodhisat holds a lotus. Both are symbols of life rising out of the water element, in the planetary sense, the primordial waters —in India, Amriti, from which comes Amittai, Jonah's father. The two names, Mary and Maia, come from the same root, signifying water. Indeed Mary in one form or another is the standard name for mothers of world saviors. We have for instance:

Mother	Son
Mary	Jesus
Maia	Buddha
Maia	Hermes

Maya	Agni
Myrrha	Adonis
Myrrha	Bacchus
Maya Maria	Sommona Cadom
	(Siamese Savior)
Mariama, title of	Krishna

All these Marys are one—the planetary Mother, and the "Holy Mary" of Catholicism is no different, save in its error. The ancients, the Greeks particularly, made their earth Mothers voluptuous, sensuous and prolific, which to us is but the primitives' concept of the divine and the holy, yet considering the vast fecundity and nonmoral nature of Nature, which is the more intelligent symbol, voluptuous Venus or virgin Mary? The priestly religion-makers could not present the mother of their world Savior as voluptuous and venal, and so they contrived a prostitute substitute—Mary Magdalene, identical with the "whore" of Babylon in Revelation. This is that old whore, promiscuous Nature, and her mythic name is Mary, virgin only primordially. Substituting Magdalene for the venality of Mary in the New Testament is but following Old Testament precedent—an evil Satan to alibi for God, and Seth for Cain. The pagan mythologists were too intellectually honest for such deception; the Jews and Christians were not, because intellectual honesty comes from knowledge of the truth, dishonesty from blind faith in fallacies. Our contempt for the immoral gods of Greece is not that born of knowledge but of ignorance. Morality is epigenetic and strictly human; why then attribute it to the genetic and prehuman? The Greeks did not because they had knowledge; we do because we haven't. That the Gospel writers hadn't either is obvious, since they called the fecundating principle the "Holy Ghost." There's nothing holy about it, morally; indeed it is more hellish than holy, and there is nothing blasphemous about this statement, for, as we shall see later, this principle created what both mythology and scripture call hell, and Christ himself so defined it. So if we seem irreverent at times, it is from Gnostic knowledge and not agnostic ignorance.

Go back far enough and you find that every one of the ancient races had its planetary Mother whose fatherless Son became the Savior of the world. To the Initiates, however, it was the saver of the Life Principle from death in matter. This is the true Messiah.

That the reader may see how universal the idea was, we offer a score or more of these divine Mothers, whose sons became race saviors. In Babylon she was Ishtar; in Libya, Neith; in Cilesia, Ate; in Armenia, Anaites, and in Assyria, Ataigates. In Crete she was Ariadne; in Phrygia, Cybele; in Phoenicia, Astarte, and in Ephesia, Artemis or Diana. In Pontus, oddly enough, she was called Ma, and in Sumeria, Mama. Then there was Ida in India; Kwanyin in China, and Kwannon in Japan. In Greece she was first Nix, then Hemera, then Gaea, and finally Aphrodite, from which with Hermes, the male aspect, we get the word hermaphrodite, originally the androgynous Life Principle. In Egypt this cosmic Mother was first Mut, then Nut, and finally Hathor, the earth-goddess. Still later she became Isis, mother of the divine Horus, the Savior of the Egyptians and prototype of Jesus. "Immaculate is our lady Isis" is an inscription on an engraving of the goddess. She it was who was immaculately conceived, not her son, and so, in keeping with this, immaculate conception to the Church is that of Mary, not Jesus. These successive mothers represent the changing, successive states of the one Creative Principle, and those who think this just a pagan idea should remember Sarah, Rebekah, Rachel, and Asenath, another Egyptian goddess.

From these virgin earth-mothers it was only a step to virgin human mothers, overshadowed by a deity whose semidivine son became a miracle-worker. The mother of Hercules was a virgin, and so was the mother of Sosiosh, the Persian. Attis was born of the virgin Nana—she who put the pomegranate in her bosom. Romulus and Remus, the founders of Rome, were sons of the god Mars, who happened to meet their virgin mother, Rhea Sylvia, on her way to a spring of water. So was it with Bacchus, Aesculapius, Zarathustra, and many others.

From this it was but another step to historical characters whose subsequent greatness was hard to explain. Pythagoras's father, we're told, was Apollo, and his mother Parthenis, from *parthenos*, which means virgin. Alexander the Great was said to be the offspring of a god who, disguised as a serpent, the genetic principle, beguiled his mother Olympias, as per Eve. Plato was the alleged son of Apollo, who, in the form of a bull, another genetic symbol, embraced his virgin mother Perictione. Later, the god, like Gabriel to Joseph, made known to Ariston, her bethrothed, the true nature of the child's parentage. The bull was Taurus, but what had it to do with Plato? Nothing, yet it illustrates how the planetary Logos became a man and walked about in Galilee.

It is useless, we know, to offer these pagan parallels, because to "the saved in Christ" they are but myths and superstitions; yet why should they be myths and superstitions here and sacred and holy truth in the case of Jesus? Can we not see that the latter is but our myth and superstition? Undoubtedly these pagan divinities were as real and sacred to their devotees as ours are to us. The slain Tamuz was so very real, the women of Haran wept for him and would not be comforted. Yet he passed and so will ours. Gods and Saviors are as successional and chronological as popes and kings; they endure longer only because they are racial and national. Already our Trinity is passing, Catholic-wise; given a few more generations and it will no longer be Father, Son and Holy Ghost, but Jesus, Mary and Joseph. Among Catholics there are some who habitually vilify the Jews, then run to church to worship three of them. In this they see no paradox because in things religious they can see nothing. And the same may be said of Christians in general; incapable of creating a religion of their own, they had to borrow one from the Jews, who, in turn, borrowed theirs.

Now from immaculate conception by a virgin, virgin birth is inevitable. That we may see how the cosmical becomes literalized, humanized and fixed in the racial mind, let us consider that first reference to a "virgin birth," namely, that in Isaiah 7:14. ". . . Behold a virgin shall conceive, and bear a son, and shall call his name Immanuel." Why not Jesus, if it were He? And just to show how the New Testament employs the Old to substantiate its arguments, we quote from Matthew, Chapter 1.

22. Now all this was done, that it might be fulfilled which was spoken of the Lord by the prophet, saying,

23. Behold, a virgin shall be with child, and shall bring forth a son and they shall call his name Emmanuel (Greek spelling), which being interpreted is, God with us.

More correctly, "all this was done," to make it appear that Jesus was the fulfillment of a previous prophecy. Yet how could it apply to Jesus since Isaiah spoke of the child as of his day? "For unto us a child *is* born, unto us a son *is* given . . ." 9:6. As for the passage itself: it was translated from the Greek text, and there the word used was *parthenos*, which does mean a virgin, but the word used in the original Hebrew, from which the Greek was taken, did not mean a virgin. The word there is *almah*, which means simply a young woman. In the later Greek translation, the error was corrected, the proper Greek equivalent *neanis* being substituted. But it suited the purpose of the Church to leave it in its "virgin" Greek, and so it has come down to us.

Those who try to explain virgin birth on the basis of parthenogenesis as found in nature are not very complimentary to the party involved, for, though it is the rule among rotifers and quite common in plants and insects, it does not appear above the plane of the amphibians. All such attempts are due to the false assumption that this virgin birth happened and therefore must be accounted for somehow. This is one of those *unprovables* we said should be thrown out. Evidently Thomas Jefferson did just that. "The day will come," said he, "when the mystical generation of Jesus by the supreme being as his father in the womb of a virgin will be classed with the fable of the generation of Minerva in the brain of Jupiter." Here is a *spiritual* declaration of independence; had the author not been capable of it, he would never have written the historical one. If the Founding Fathers were not all atheists, as some claim, they were at least spiritually emancipated. But let us return to the confounding fathers.

While parthenogenesis does not explain, it does point us in the right direction—downward and backward to the primordial and elemental. The one subject of myth and scripture is the Life Principle; this it is that was immaculately conceived and virginally born, first from the Absolute, and then from its opposite, the earth. The latter is Evolution, and this is the event the Old Testament prophesies. The Gospel writers but used it to make their tale sound authentic.

They went downward and backward for their nativity scene also. They said it was a stable, but that is either some more Jewish refinement or plain deception, for, mythologically, Christ was born where all the other saviors were born, in a cave. This cave was always in a wilderness of some kind, and according to the Protevangelion, a presynoptic source, Joseph searched for a cave and found one in a desert. From other sources we learn that this was the same cave in which Attis and Adonis were born. Still other gods and saviors born in a cave were Apollo, Bacchus, Hermes, Jupiter, Mithra, Krishna, and therefore Christ. In Latin countries the nativity is still portrayed as taking place in a cave, now *creche*, but not crib. It was the gospelists who cribbed it, the cosmic to a cradle. As for the custom: It was St. Francis of Assisi who established it, but it was not his idea; it is pure Mithraism. On December 25 the Persians celebrated the birth of their savior Zoroaster in a cave and they called him "the Ram of God who taketh away the sins of the world." Priests, candles, incense, and holy water all figured in the drama. Observing the similarity, Freiherr von Gall concluded, "There is not the slightest doubt that there exist the closest point of post-Exilic Judaism and that of Zoroastrianism."

In this cave was a manger, that is, a horse's stall. The nonliteralists interpret this part as an occult reference to the sun's position at Christmas time in the annual zodiac. It is then coming from Sagittarius, the horse, and Capricorn, the goat, hence the animals in the manger. The Gospel story, however, is not based on the annual cycle but on the cosmic or creative cycle. The meaning and the animals, therefore, lie on the other, or Involutionary, side of the zodiac. The animals are Aries, Taurus, and whatever was formerly Gemini, goats we suggest. The manger is actually the celestial manger, Praesepe, a cluster of stars in Cancer, where the Sun of God was born as a material entity.

This is the manger of the Ascelli or celestial asses, those same asses Vulcan, Bacchus, and Saul rode on, and now another god rides on them, to Bethlehem, and still later to Jerusalem.

1. Now when Jesus was born in Bethlehem of Judea in the days of Herod the king, behold, there came wise men from the east to Jerusalem,
2. Saying, Where is he that is born King of the Jews? for we have seen his star in the east and are come to worship him (Matt., Chap. 2).

Now why should Jesus be born in Bethlehem? Was this also to fulfill a previous prophecy, or due only to a tax decree? Neither; Jesus was born in Bethlehem for the same reason Joseph and David were born there. Bethlehem is the mystic "house of bread," the source of planetary substance. Thus the locale is not historical but contrived. And such is the whole story. When we look at the historical, this becomes obvious. According to the account, Herod was king at the alleged time, 1 A.D., but according to present scholarship, Herod died at least four years prior to this. According to Luke, Cyrenius was then governor of Syria, but according to Syrian records, still extant, he was not. There was, however, a Quirinus, who ruled from 13–11 B.C. This being so, either the calendar or the Gospels is wrong, some say as much as twelve years. This confusion about the date implies that uncertainty of long-subsequent authorship, which confirms our statement that the Gospels were not written until the second and third centuries. Not only is there confusion here but disagreement also. According to Matthew, Joseph and Mary "turned aside" to Nazareth against God's will, but Luke tells us they lived in Nazareth before the nativity. Matthew says they went immediately to Egypt, while Luke says they came "to Jerusalem, to present him (Jesus) to the Lord." Then there is the date. It was not until the fourth century that the time of the nativity was set at December 25. If this is the correct date, then Jesus was born in the dead of winter. Would then the shepherds be "keeping watch over their flocks by night"? And if it is the wrong date, then John was not born June 24.

O what a tangled web we weave,
When first we practice to deceive.

WALTER SCOTT

8. And there were in the same country shepherds abiding in the field, keeping watch over their flock by night.

9. And lo, the angel of the Lord came upon them, and the glory of the Lord shone round about them: and they were sore afraid (Luke, Chap. 2).

They must have been very cold also in late December. And why should sheep be out in the fields at that time? It snows in Palestine.

13. And suddenly there was with the angel a multitude of the heavenly host praising God, and saying,

14. Glory to God in the highest, and on earth peace, good will toward men (Chap. 2).

To the Christian masses this celestial demonstration occurred only at the birth of Christ, yet when Confucius was born "his mother heard celestial music and a voice of benediction from the sky. The child was saluted as a throneless king." Atkins.[1] And of Buddha, historical or not, it was said, "His mother (Maia) foresaw his conception in a dream, and at the moment of its occurrence the universe blossomed like a garden, the dumb spoke and heavenly music filled the air. His mother's side became as crystal through which the divine babe could be always seen while all the hosts of heaven guarded her city and her palace. Celestial spirits attended her delivery, the trees of an enchanted garden bent down their branches to shelter her . . ." Again, Atkins.[2] Such stories were also told of Noah and Moses, and even today they are repeated for each Dalai Lama of Tibet. "Whenever he is born trees and plants put forth green leaves; at his bidding flowers bloom and springs of water rise and his presence diffuses heavenly blessings." Frazer. This is the language of mythology, in other words, Creation allegorized.

So is the story of the Magi, their "gold, frankincense and

[1,2] *Procession of the Gods*, G. G. Atkins, 1930.

myrrh." This too is assumed to be unique, yet when Socrates was born, 469 B.C., "Magi came from the east to offer gifts at Socrates' birth, also bringing gold, frankincense and myrrh" *(The Anacalypsis).* At the birth of Krishna, 1200 B.C., "angels, shepherds and the prophets attended, gold, frankincense and myrrh were brought to him." And when Confucius was born in 598 B.C., "Five wise men from a distance came to the house, celestial music was heard in the skies and angels attended the scene" *(The Five Volumes).* Magi also attended the birth of Mithra, Zoroaster, and Osiris. Thus Magi, gold, frankincense, and myrrh are standard mythic equipment, so also angels, shepherds, and celestial music. Yet mythology contains deep and profound meanings for those who can see them. It also explains mysteries, and here it explains one no saint or savant has ever solved.

9. When they (the wise men) [3] had heard the king, they departed; and, lo, the star, which they saw in the east, went before them, till it came and stood over where the young child was (Matt., Chap. 2).

This is the mysterious "Star of Bethlehem," over which even our scientists argue and guess. Because it's in the Bible, they must find an explanation. This well illustrates the plight of those who accept absurd hypotheses then wrestle with their absurd deductions. Why not recognize it for another of those *unprovables* and throw it out?

Had such a phenomenon actually occurred two thousand years ago, it would have been recorded by someone, the great Ptolemy, for instance. It was before his time, but had it been real no doubt he would have mentioned it. The reason he did not was because there was no such phenomenon. It was a star all right but that one seen crystal clear in Maia's womb, namely a nascent sun in the womb of space. Thus as we said, "out of the womb of time and space a sun is born." Here it was a star

[3] The story of the wise men from the East was brought from the East by the Gymnosophists. It was a legend about the birth of Buddha. They also brought the story of Krishna.

in the true etymological sense, an astral entity. If our world in its solar stage, the time might be some trillion years B.C.— B(efore) (the) C(onfusion). Little wonder then it's been a mystery.

"Such stories as these echo from the dim horizon of all religions, invest the birth and infancy of the spiritually elect with wonder. Legend and symbol, memory and devotion combine to weave the fabric of them, and it is beyond our power to disentangle their strangely colored strands and find the fact." Atkins.[4] The fact is not at all difficult to find when the fact is known, namely, the creative process. This is the basis of all mythology, all metaphysics, and all religion, that is the philosophy thereof. Long before religion existed, man learned from nature the facts of Reality and put them into a form of narrative known as mythology. In this the impersonal forces were personified, they were given names, they became gods, and devils, heroes and saviors. As the natural facts underlying them were forgotten, the personifications became the realities, endowed with moral instead of creative qualities. And here mythology became theology. Thus belief in theology and religion is due to ignorance of fiction as well as fact. And yet we have such statements as this: "For theology is a science—the Queen of Sciences; it is the science of objective revelation, which has come to the rescue of reason." Reverend M. O'Connor. Come to bedevil reason would be more correct. Would you call the Gospels science? Would you call the following rational?

13. And when they (the wise men) were departed, behold, the angel of the Lord appeareth to Joseph in a dream, saying, Arise, and take the young child and his mother, and flee into Egypt, and be thou there until I bring thee word: for Herod will seek the young child to destroy him (Chap. 2).

If Jesus' omnipotent Father could save all Israel at the Red Sea, could he not have saved one little infant without sending him all the way to Egypt? And if this infant was destined to

[4] G. G. Atkins, *Procession of the Gods*, p. 120.

come, could any human agent have prevented it? It sounds too much like mythic formula to be anything else. Every Creation myth has its opposive matter trying to destroy the spirit principle. In Judea it was Herod seeking to destroy Jesus, and in Egypt it was Herut seeking to destroy Horus, and the latter is the source of the former. In the Old Testament, even God tried to kill Moses, in the inn, the same inn we now find Jesus in, namely, Involution. Saul sought to kill David, and Pharaoh the infant Moses. And like Pharaoh, Herod slew the innocents when he failed to find this Moses of the New Testament. He did not slay all the "innocents," however; he missed the future Christians. In Revelation it is the great Dragon, matter, that would destroy the child of the woman "clothed with the sun." In Greece it was Python, the serpent, who threatened Apollo, and in India, Kansa, who sought to destroy Krishna. In the latter country, all savior destroyers are called "the devourer of the young in the egg"—the "mundane egg," or world seed. This is natural generation and fact, and "the Queen of Sciences" destroyed it. But the authors secretly using its process had to get Jesus down to Egypt, earth, and so we read:

14. When he arose, he took the young child and his mother by night, and departed into Egypt (Chap. 2).

No doubt you've seen pictures of these three on their way— and it's a long way from Bethlehem to Egypt. Would Mary be capable of such a journey so soon? Joseph walked hundreds of miles but she rode on an ass. And no doubt she came to Bethlehem the same way. Would any sane man subject his wife, so near delivery, to the jolting back of an ass? No, this is just part of the asinine story.

Curious is it not, how much Jewish history (?) is bound up with Egypt? The Old Testament tells us that Jacob begat a Joseph who went down into Egypt, and the New tells us of another Jacob who begat another Joseph who also went down to Egypt. And how analogous are Joseph and Jesus: Joseph was born in Bethlehem, and so was Jesus; Joseph sets out to find his brothers and arrives in Egypt; Jesus sets out to find safety and arrives there likewise; Joseph was sold for twenty pieces of silver, and Jesus for thirty; Joseph saved his people from starvation, and Jesus from damnation. Thus the one is but a revolutio of the other.

Throughout the entire Bible, Egypt is the dark land of matter; Mary fleeing there with her infant is but the Hebrew version of Isis fleeing with the divine Horus, and Dione, wife of the Pelagian Zeus, fleeing from Python to the Euphrates.

The New Testament is as vague about the early years of Jesus as the Old is about those of Abraham, Noah, and Samson, and for the same reason—its authors knew nothing about the early part of what he personifies, namely, the world. Apparently they did know, however, that it too was an infant once, and so we have the infant Jesus. Only Luke tells us anything about his childhood, and that rather absurdly—the story of his being lost for three days, part of which was unnoticed by his parents.[5] With this absurdity, Luke passes over his formative years with the statement that the child "increased in wisdom and stature, and in favor with God and man." And of Samuel it was said, "And the child Samuel grew on, and was in favor both with the Lord and also with men." Elsewhere we learn that Jesus was a carpenter, which means a builder, in this case a world. He was the Logos, without which "nothing was made that was made." The other authors go straight from infancy to maturity with a prelude about John. Here we have another barren woman promised a son in her old age. This was John the Baptist. Nothing is given about his youth either, and for the same reason.

In the third chapter of Matthew, we have his baptism of Jesus in the river Jordan. Upon the literal interpretation of this the Baptist Church and the rite of baptism are founded. Little did those responsible realize the perverted and inverted nature of the foundation on which they built; if they had, neither church nor rite would ever have existed.

The river Jordan is the river of life—the free-flowing elements between spirit and matter; in other words, the "deep" of

[5] This too comes from Egypt. There Isis searches for her lost son Horus, later found in the Temple of the Sun teaching the priests.

Jonah and the "deluge" of Noah. Now Noah and Jonah were both Creators, and as Jesus was just another, he too was plunged into these primordial waters. And what does the word *baptize* mean? Originally it meant "to plunge under the waters of the world." And so John said he baptized only with water (primordial) but Jesus would baptize with fire. What fire? Well, what follows the primordial waters but a fiery sun, Leo, "the lion of the tribe of Judah?" Were we to interpret occultly the words here attributed to God, they would read thus: "This is my beloved sun in whom I am well pleased." John is the energy aspect of this sun, the baptizer at its zenith, and John of the Gospels makes Jesus speak of him thus: "He was a burning and a shining light: and ye (the elements) were willing for a season (the sun period) to rejoice in his light," 5:35. As the sun eventually becomes a "dead matter" planet, John, the energy, is imprisoned, that is, robbed of its power, as was Samson. From here on (Evolution) that power decreases while consciousness increases. And this is the meaning of John's statement that he will decrease but Christ will increase. His death is the release of this power, hence one with the killing of "the firstborn." And Herodias is one with Delilah.

Jesus represents creative consciousness, while John, the wild man, is that energy that dragged consciousness down from the third to the seventh plane. Elsewhere it is called Lucifer, and as the Latins said, *Lucifer antevolat,* leads on ahead, and Jesus called John a *herald.* Jesus' baptism is but the baptism of spirit in matter, not matter, the mortal man, in spirit. It is therefore none other than the "original sin." But who has ever connected the two? No one, and so we have such statements as this (Council of Trent): "From the fall of man until the hour of baptism the Devil has full power over him and possesses him." The truth is John and the Devil are one, and it is only after his baptism that the Devil, materiality, has power over consciousness. But such is Christian wisdom! It has turned everything upside down and called it truth. And upon this perverted truth the Baptist Church and the rite are founded. Out of the confusion, however, one clear point emerges—the manner of baptism. Jesus was not just dipped or sprinkled but, like Jonah, completely and wholly immersed. Today, we too are so materially immersed we cannot see the spiritual truth in anything.

Like everything else in religion, baptism comes from mythology. The gods of India, Greece and Egypt were all baptized, in fact, the Egyptian god Anup was called "the baptizer." In each case supernatural phenomena attended the baptism. Even at the call of Mohammed, "Celestial regions were shaken by the tumult in the prophet's soul." Stars fell from heaven and the frightened jinns fled from the scene. "Finally the sense of a Divine Commission objectified itself in a vision of the angel Gabriel who brought him a direct command." Atkins. And was it not Gabriel who brought Joseph Smith his command? Such is the immortal nature of mythology.

Baptism is not the only thing the Church has inverted and perverted. There are many others, a good example of which is the Lenten season. Its forty days, we are told, is the time for spiritual observance, abstinence, penance, meditation, etc. To understand its perversion we must go back to Christmas.

The forty days of the Christmas season (twenty before and twenty after) is the time when physical nature is asleep. It is at this time that the psychic forces (we will not say spiritual) are most active. As "The night time is the daytime of the soul," so winter is the daytime of the spirit. In this, Christmas is to the year what the Sabbath is to the week, a time for spiritual attainment. This is nature's time for this and the Initiates so use it. But three months after it has passed our spiritual Know-Nothings have dedicated forty days in spring to this purpose; a time when nature is "bustin' out all over"; a time when the sap runs wild and "a young man's fancy lightly turns to thoughts of" —sex. A fine time this for spiritual observance! But such again is Christian wisdom. The Catholics, particularly, demand rigid observance of the rules and threaten punishment to the indifferent. From one of their many pamphlets we quote the following: "Thus does our Savior go before us on the holy path of Lent. He has borne all its fatigues and hardships, so that we, when called upon to tread the narrow way of our Lenten Penance, might have his example wherewith to silence the excuses, and sophisms, and repugnances of self-love and pride. The lesson is here too plainly given not to be understood; the law of doing penance for sin is here too clearly shown, and we cannot plead ignorance; let us honestly accept the teaching and practice it . . . Let us not harden our hearts to this invitation, lest there be fulfilled in us the terrible threat contained in those words of our Redeemer: 'Unless ye shall do penance, ye shall perish' (Luke 13:3)." And the final shot: "Hence it is that the Church—*the infallible interpreter of her Divine Master's will*—tells us that the repentance of our heart will not be accepted by God, unless it be accompanied by fasting and abstinence." "Infallible interpreter!" when it has misinterpreted this entire book.

Thus with threats of spiritual death these babblers force the physically starved poor to deny themselves food and the emotionally starved, the simplest pleasures—as if nature and society didn't deny them enough already. This is ignorance torturing itself at the wrong time and to no purpose. Esoterically, it isn't even following the alleged example for the Creator here is gathering strength to create a world.

The time for all this is Christmas, but we have made it a time for glutting our physical appetites and grudgingly giving material trash. Instead of one of nature's most sacred and solemn moments, it is the business man's harvest and the souse's saturnalia, a drunken spree in honor of Bacchus and Mammon instead of Christ. Here in this country it's one of our mass-murder days, in which the highways are strewn with corpses. Our minds have been so robbed of the wisdom-content we can't even drive a car wisely. And who is to blame for such a humanity? A clergy incapable of enlightening the laity or even restraining it. Only when it becomes an anachronism does it move at all, hence the occasional Ecumenical Council.

The Church has had considerable difficulty enforcing its absurdities upon its people, and this it attributes to the innate cussedness of human nature. It speaks of the "impregnable ignorance" of the willful rejectors, but their rejection is not due to innate perversity but rather innate sanity, the common sense of rational humanity. Instinctively the people know there is something phony about these teachings, but due mainly to them, they do not know just what. Our purpose in dealing with them is to set that *something* forth so plainly that even the "infallible interpreter" can see it.

The next event is but more perversion, this time by the authors. This is the temptation in the wilderness, a revolutio of Eden, and a steal from the *Vendidad*. In this it is Zarathustra who is tempted. And in the Hindu literature we find the source of both stories. Buddha, as he set forth on his ministry, was tempted by the demon Wasawrthi Mora, who said to him, "Be entreated to stay that you may possess the honors that are within your reach; go not, go not." Rejected, this demon gnashed his teeth and threatened vengeance on the Hindu Savior. That Jesus did not succumb to his counterpart is a cosmological error and contrary to the Eden story, for if he had not *fallen* this world and we would not exist. This aspect could not be brought out in the New Testament equivalent; its Adam had to be a perfect being morally, and a perfect basis for a redemptive religion. And such is the diabolical cunning of the Bible. If we are wise we will learn to separate its sheep of truth from its goats of falsehood.

In this temptation story is hidden a fact we should be aware of. It tells us Satan offered Jesus the world and everything in it. How could he unless he owned it? Well, he does; Satan is matter and its energies, and the story is but a mythologist's way of telling us something we have asserted from the beginning, namely, that in the inanimate world matter and energy dominate, genetic consciousness again "inactive and asleep." The only consciousness here is the epigenetic and this, as yet, is wholly incapable of controlling these violent forces. This alone explains why our imaginary God of love and mercy allows these forces to destroy us.

There is but one other subject we would like to deal with here—the disciples. Who were they, and what were they? As presented, they were the few among millions spiritual enough to discern the divine nature of Christ, and this in spite of the recorded fact that they were "unlearned and ignorant men" (Acts 4:13). There's a lesson for us in that, but not the chief one.

If these constant companions of Jesus were historical characters, how is it St. Paul knew nothing about them? Concerning

this, Robertson in his *Christianity and Mythology* has this to say:
"On the face of all the gospels alike, the choosing of the Twelve
Apostles is an unhistorical narrative; and in the documents from
which all scientific study of Christian origins must proceed—
the Epistles of Paul—there is no evidence of the existence of
such a body. In only one instance is it mentioned, and that is
demonstrably part of a late interpolation, whatever view we
may take of the original authenticity of the Epistles." Paul then
knew nothing of a "twelve." His Jesus was the mythic, pre-
Christian symbol.

The authors of the Gospels knew quite well who these twelve
were but they had a professional reason for disguising them.
They were thus like our professional detective story writers, in
knowing something the reader doesn't know, namely, "who-
dunit." And so, like their modern counterparts they blind and
deceive the reader by every trick of their trade. It is for us to
see through this trick and thereby learn for ourselves "who-
dunit." Had Western man done this in the beginning he would
have saved himself two thousand years of spiritual madness. It's
rather late now, but suppose we apply it to this scriptural "who-
dunit."

Among occultists these twelve have ever been identified with
the twelve signs of the zodiac, but only in its annual and solar
sense. This is modern understanding and not enough. We must
learn to see them in terms of the greater, cosmogonical zodiac.
As such they are the New Testament's Elohim, the twelve creative forces; they are Jacob's twelve sons, and the twelve tribes
of Israel. Among the Chinese they were the Tien Hoang, or
"world creators"; among the Hindus, the twelve Aditya, the
twelve Nidanas, or "causes of being." In Greece they were the
twelve Titans, and in Scandinavia the twelve Aesirs of Asgard.
The gods Osiris and Marduk also had their twelve helpers. The
twelve disciples are but the New Testament equivalent of these
pagan deities, in other words, the *dramatis personae* in the drama
of Creation.

Now "in order of appearance" the first of these were fishermen or watermen, and the waters here are the same as in Genesis and Aquarius, the primordial sea. Chief of these was Peter,

whom Jesus said was the son of Jonah the fishman. Calling Peter a son of Jonah, though figurative, is an occult hint of Peter's original nature, the primordial waters. As these waters, also figurative for energies, "congealed" they became solid earth, Peter, from petra, stone. We have the root in petrified. Jesus using the assumed Aramaic equivalent called him Cephas, "which being interpreted is a stone." Maybe so in Aramæn but it sounds suspiciously like Cetus the whale that swallowed Jonah. So or not it served a useful purpose—a solid foundation for a future Church. This we'll return to later.

In like manner James and John were called Boanerges, which means "the sons of thunder." Now were they so called because as men they thundered the gospel message? No, this is also plagiarized cosmology. You will recall that about this time in the Greek myth of Creation, the Cyclopes, or fire gods, appeared. These forged the lightning and thunderbolts of Zeus, and two of them were Brontes and Arges, thunder and lightning. Now Boanerges is but these two names scrambled and rearranged. The letters are all there, the arrangement but a blind. James and John are the cosmic fire elements, and Luke presents them as such: "And when his disciples James and John saw this, they said, Lord, wilt thou that we command fire to come down from heaven, and consume them . . . ?" 9:54. The only thing that ever brought fire down from heaven is the Creative Principle and all such miracle-workers including James and John, Elijah and Prometheus are but personification of it. As fire, lightning, and other signs, John also represents light, and this is why he is called the disciple whom Jesus loved most. Apparently he was most loved because most needed. "Let there be light," was the first words of the Creator. Here then we have another John identical with Lucifer, the cosmic light-bringer. To paint the one as a saint and the other as a devil is, itself, diabolical.

They could not escape the cosmic fact, however, and so contrived another substitute. This time, Judas, who as matter betrayed the spirit. You have heard of "the bowels of the earth," no doubt. Now Peter in Acts, says of Judas, "Now this man purchased a field with the reward of iniquity; and falling headlong, he burst asunder in the midst, and all his bowels gushed out" 1:18. The bowels of Judas, bursting and gushing out, are the "bowels of the earth" bursting and gushing out the life force, as explained in other chapters. But who would ever connect Judas's "bowel movement" with the expulsion from Eden, the Exodus from Egypt, and even the "glad tidings" of the apostles, namely, evolutionary life? John tells us it was the priests who purchased the field, and elsewhere we are told that Judas hanged himself. Do these contradictions sound like veridical history? No, but they are excellent keys to the Bible's true nature, useless, of course, to those ignorant of cosmology. These simple souls look upon Judas as the enemy of Christ, yet without Judas there would have been no Christ, but only Jesus; without him, Jesus could not have consummated his destined sacrifice. This mutual dependence is but that of consciousness and energy.

In the genealogy given in Matthew we are told that Jacob begat Judas and his brethren. Nowhere else does the Bible use the name Judas for Judah, Jacob's son, but now the truth is out—the Judas of the New Testament is but the Judas of the Old. His father, Jacob, represents the Creator on the third plane, and his sons, Judas and his brethren, are the differentiated aspects of this Creator. Jesus is this same Creator and Judas and his brother disciples are the same as Judas and his brethren. Thus the Jacob and Judas of the New Testament are by no means separated from the Jacob and Judas of the Old Testament by some forty generations; the one is but a revolutio of the other.

Jesus and his twelve are the "whodunits" of the Gospels, and their "crime" was the crime of Creation. That we may see their undefined and impersonal nature, we have the doubtful Thomas Didymus, superficially, the Christ-doubting disciple. This too is but a blind for the blind. The name Didymus comes from the Greek word Didymos, the Greek equivalent of the Roman Gemini, the zodiacal twins. It means double or dual nature, here the bisexual genetic. Thus Thomas was of doubtful sex, not mind. And such were they all, including Jesus, the feminine aspect of the Trinity. Not for nothing does Christian art portray him as an effeminate man; he is the androgynous Man, the undifferentiated Life Principle. As the Zohar says: "Man, as emanation, was both man and woman as well on the side of the Father (ideation) as on the side of the Mother (substance). And this is the two fold Man." And so said Plato.

This is the miracle-worker, and so to the miracles.

21

The Miracles

Those who wish to seek out the cause of miracles, and to understand the things of nature as philosophers, and not to stare at them in astonishment like fools, are soon considered heretical and impious, and proclaimed as such by those whom the mob adores as the interpreters of nature and the gods. For these men know that once ignorance is put aside that wonderment would be taken away which is the only means by which their authority is preserved.

SPINOZA

The miracles of the New Testament should be divided into two categories: the major and the minor. The first are entirely supernatural—immaculate conception, virgin birth, and the like; the second are more natural and even humanly possible, such as healing the sick and making the blind to see. The authors have so cunningly confused the two that the subtle difference is lost. The key, however, lies in the first or major miracles, therefore we will touch upon the second only incidentally. Taken literally, the immaculate conception and virgin birth are not Christ's miracles but God's, yet in the occult sense they are, for He too is God. Yes those who say that Christ is God speak the truth in spite of their ignorance; their error lies in the fact that they do not know what God is. Neither do they know what Christ or Jesus is.

Jesus is the New Testament's God, as Jehovah is of the Old Testament. He is the word, the Logos, the Creator, as St. John makes him. The God over and above Him is, therefore, as superfluous as the God of Adam, earth. Jesus is the Creative Principle in Involution, Christ, this Principle in Evolution. See diagram page 321. When reduced by personification to the human, His

Christhood consists of human consciousness someday divinified by divine human qualities. But this is not the scriptural miracle worker, nor is it Christ; it is Jesus, and the first miracle He wrought as such is that of turning water into wine. This is number 3. The first two are the immaculate conception and virgin birth, paralleling the immaculate conception of the world, and its birth from virgin space. With these we have already dealt, and so we will begin here with the third miracle and its correlative plane. This is the starting point of all scriptural Creators, Noah, Jacob, David, and therefore Jesus. It represents the beginning of planetary substance.

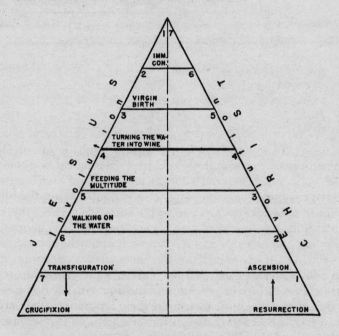

3. Turning the Water into Wine

1. And the *third day* there was a marriage in Cana of Galilee; and the mother of Jesus was there (John, Chap. 2).

Now what third day is this, and from whence reckoned? No theologian can tell us, because no theologian knows what this story means. As we do, we can answer our own question. It is the third day of Creation, and here begins the Creative Principle's miraculous manipulation of planetary substance—the mother aspect that "was there." The marriage is the union of this and ideation, from which comes all that is to be. It is here the Son fecundates the Mother, as per our last chapter. This is In-volution. The locale, Cana, is but the Old Testament Cana-an where another personification of the Creator, namely, Abraham, married and begat a world.

2. And both Jesus was called, and his disciples, to the marriage.

This is the Creator and the twelve creative forces, Elohim, Titans, Aesirs, etc.

3. And when they wanted wine, the mother of Jesus saith unto him, They have no wine.
4. Jesus saith unto her, Woman, what have I to do with thee? mine hour is not yet come.
6. And there were set there *six* waterpots of stone, after the manner of the purifying of the Jews, containing two or three firkins apiece.
7. Jesus saith unto them, Fill the waterpots with water. And they filled them up to the brim.

About sixty gallons; that's a lot of wine for a little wedding.

8. And he saith unto them, Draw out now, and bear unto the governor of the feast. And they bare it (Chap. 2).

Again, why six waterpots? Because there are six involutionary planes which Jesus, like Aquarius, fills with what is everywhere called *waters*, those same waters the Genesic Creator by his spirit moving on them turned into matter. The wine is that same wine this Creator, alias Noah, made, drank, and was drunken on, namely the wine of Life.

9. When the ruler of the feast had tasted the water that was made wine, and knew not whence it was (but the servants which drew the water knew); the governor of the feast called the bridegroom,

10. And saith unto him, Every man at the beginning doth set forth good wine; and when men have well drunk, then that which is worse: but thou hast kept the good wine until now (Chap. 2).

There is a momentous fact here quite unknown to present humanity, namely, that the best part of Creation is the last part, Evolution, and even the last part of this. This is the difference between the substantial Jesus and the spiritual Christ. Therefore those who think of the first part, God and his hosts, as the best, should ponder this statement deeply. We have challenged their concept from the beginning, and now the scriptures substantiate us. Nor is this the first place—consider the riddle Samson propounded. Out of the dead carcass of the lion, Leo the sun, comes earth and the sweetness of life.

There is still another lesson here for us. "Woman, what have I to do with thee?" "Who is my mother and who are my brethren?" "If any man come to me, and hate not his father, and mother, and wife and children, and brothers and sisters, yea, and his own life also, he cannot be my disciple." Such statements and Christ's treatment of his mother have ever been a difficulty to the Church, and so it would change them. In the latest Catholic revision it has softened them so as not to cause embarrassing questions. With a few more revisions the Bible will be "foolproof" and conformable to the faith. And thus does ignorance prevent its own enlightenment. We have here a good example of the consequence of blindly accepting a false hypothesis; in this case, a human mother and son. With this in mind the revisionists try to make the Bible conform to human standards, whereas the author offers these inconsistencies as an occult hint of Christ's true nature. He is telling us first, that no human mother is here implied, and second, that mythological Saviors have no human relationships. Such passages are the precious keys to the Bible's cosmological theme, and they are being obliterated one by one. Until our "great Bible students" know what they are dealing with, they should let such passages alone. Their scholarly revisions are but semantic tragedies, and a sickening waste of time. For years they labor over chapter and verse, then, like the mountain, bring forth a mouse, a changed word here, a comma there, but never a suspicion of the actual meaning. This is *ignorantio elenchi* at its worst. But there are other forms of it: our understanding of this miracle, for instance. We do not see in it what we are here for—to turn the savagery of life into civilized existence.

To millions of Christians, Christ came to show them "the way" in which they should live, yet to what extent do they follow His advice? It seems they prefer to worship Him rather than follow Him. It's easier on human nature, besides it takes only a few hours one day a week. Thus they are free to spend the rest of the time in the marketplace, doing the very opposite of what He taught. The result is we have sunk to the very depths of materiality; money is now our Savior, and only knowledge that helps us make it is of any value. Thus today, Christ would have to do more than turn water into wine to prove His divinity; he would have to turn the wine into cash as well. That done, He would be "very God of very God." Yea, though I speak with the tongue of men and of angels and have not money, I am as sounding brass and a tinkling cymbal. Faith, hope and money, but the greatest of these is money. If so, why don't we use it to rid the world of ignorance instead of wasting it protecting ourselves from it? Today we pour out billions for defense when half the amount in the hands of the enlightened would change the entire setup.

4. Feeding the Multitude

The next outstanding miracle is that of feeding the multitude. This occurred in a desert place, that involutionary "wilderness." Here thousands had followed Jesus and as night came on they were "ahungered," and so,

38. He saith unto them, How many loaves have ye? go and see. And when they knew, they say, Five, and two fishes.

39. And he commanded them to make all sit down by companies upon the green grass.

40. And they sat down in ranks, by hundreds, and by fifties.

41. And when he had taken the five loaves and the two fishes, he

looked up to heaven, and blessed, and brake the loaves, and gave them to his disciples to set before them; and the two fishes divided he among them all.

42. And they did all eat, and were filled.

43. And they took up twelve baskets full of the fragments, and of the fishes.

44. And they that did eat of the loaves were about five thousand men (not a woman among them; Mark, Chap. 6).

And Christians believe that! It seems the author here was trying to shock credulity into doubting, but he did not reckon with the spiritual obtuseness of Piscean man. This fellow can see nothing but the literal word, not because he lacks intelligence but because he is so materialistic the spiritual and cosmic are quite beyond him. Were he made aware of this fact he would not be so sure of his convictions or hard on those who differ with him. As suggested elsewhere, he should read other races' literature. The Judean place where this miracle took place was called Bethany, and in an Egyptian similitude it is Bethanu. And they called it "the place of multiplying bread." If this miracle by Jesus was a one-and-only-time event, how did it get into the Egyptian scriptures thousands of years earlier? The raising of Lazarus also occurred here, and that too is copied from Egyptian mythology, see page 338. So near-contemporary a writer as Origen (second century) said he could find no trace of "Bethany beyond Jordan." What then of the miracle that happened there?

The feeding of five thousand with enough for five was never done by God or man. This is but the law of increase in nature, and applies to Involution as well as Evolution. In our outline we said that on this fourth plane primordial substance greatly increased and became partite, that is, infinitely divided into the monadic host. The nature of this miracle then is the division of planetary substance. This is the bread of that "house of bread," Bethlehem, the source; it is also the "bread that cometh down from heaven; not as your fathers did eat manna and are dead: he that eateth of this bread shall live for ever" (John 6:58). Apparently John did not fully understand his subject either, for this bread and this manna are the same; the only difference is that the one is involutionary, the other evolutionary. It was of this John spoke thus: "Whosoever eateth my flesh and drinketh my blood hath eternal life and I will raise him up at the last day"—of Creation. And on such impersonal promises is our hope of immortality based. You see, the Bible is not speaking of us at all, but of the Life Principle. This, we repeat again, is "the worm that never dies," not the human soul or spirit.

The five loaves and two fishes, 5 plus 2, or 7, are the septenary elements; the twelve disciples are the twelve Elohim, or forces, that *serve*, rather control, them. Here the reader should recall the twelve caterers that Solomon set over his multitude of workers, each responsible for his cosmic month. The twelve baskets of fragments is an occult allotment in keeping with this. Even the word "fragments" has an occult meaning. This small, dense globe is by no means the sum of energy the Creator set out with. For billions of years this earth, when in the sun stage, poured out its energy into space, the solid earth being but the "fragment" remaining.

Christ has ever been associated with fish—a universal Savior symbol. As stated, the Hindus represented the first Avatar of Vishnu as half fish, half man—Pisces-Aquarius; and our Christ is called by them the Piscean Avatar. In the Talmud the Messiah is called Dag, the fish. The Phoenician and Philistian Dagon, the Chaldean Oannes, and the Greek Phoibos were all fish men. The Greek word for fish *Ichthus* is made up of the initials of the five Greek words *Iesous (Ch)ristos, (Th)eou Uios Soter*—Jesus Christ the Son of God, Savior. The Greeks had seals and talismans with this word engraved upon them, and the early Christians' signet, the Ichthus, had the same significance, so likewise the Fisherman's Ring, still worn by the pope. Thus Jesus, like Jonah, is a fish man, symbol of the Life Principle within the primordial ocean. In fact he so declared himself (Matthew 12:40).

The eating of fish on Friday is now a rule among Catholics, and these credulous souls believe it is strictly a Christian custom. It is, however, as pagan as all the rest. In the remotest times the Norsemen ate fish on Friday the year round, not because of Christ but because of Frigga, their goddess to whom fish was sacred. Of course Frigga didn't know that; fish was honored by the Norsemen because it was their mainstay in winter. From this Frigga comes our word Friday and also the custom. Until the recent change, eating meat on Friday was a sin. But against whom or what? The God of Creation? A lot he cares whether one eats at all or not. If he does, he should begin with those things that rob millions of their food—flood and drought, blight and frost, hurricane and tornado, not fish. But such is the pettiness of the religious mind, also the absurdity of its customs: You shouldn't eat meat on Friday but you can cause the slaughter of millions of animals the other six days; you mustn't eat pork, but you can be a pig every other way.

The Old Testament precedent for this fourth miracle is Elisha's feeding a company of a hundred from a few loaves with like fragments left over (2 Kings 4:43–44), and Elijah's increasing the widow's barrel of meal and cruse of oil. Thus Christ was not the first to perform this miracle. Today we look back upon these wonders and say, "That was the age of miracles." We also wonder why we, with all our science and technology, have no such power. This too is woeful ignorance. There never was an age of miracles; miracles, like Saviors, belong to mythology. Because of that their power was simply nonexistent. Once this is understood their power over us will also be nonexistent. It's obvious St. Augustine had no such understanding. He tells us he accepted Christianity only because of the overwhelming evidence of the miracles. And now we find they were not miracles at all. They are, however, morals. There are multitudes "ahungered" in our world too but we do not feed them. We do not multiply our crops to fill empty mouths, but bulging pockets. We cannot reach these empty mouths because under our system every mouthful must first be paid for. We are followers of Christ in name only.

Any system that compels the individual to think only of himself and his family is inimical to human welfare. It breeds selfishness, the very opposite of altruism and brotherly love. We think of the home as the center of love, of kindness and self-sacrifice, but how all embracing are these noble qualities; how much do they counteract the products of selfishness? Marriage, home and children are the basis of our world but with human consciousness limited to them, they become the baseness of our world as well, covert motives for overt mischief. If we would get rid of the baseness we must elevate the basis—not *the* home but *man's* home. Domesticity is not enough; we must think of Demos as well. Important as the home is, it is not the Omega but the Alpha of human society, the racial nursery in which we learn the rudiments of social civility. This accomplished, we leave the home and enter the world. This is individual maturation, and it applies to the race as well.

This was Christ's idea: "Who is my mother and who are my brethren?" But, you say, that was all right for the Son of God but not for us. No, it is not for us to carry to extremes examples set by world Saviors, but the very purpose of such Saviors, mythical though they be, is to show us how and when to do in moderation what they did in the extreme.

5. *Walking on the Water*

The fifth major miracle is that in which Jesus walks on the water, calms the sea, and so on. This one, we have in duplicate, therefore, it must have happened. The first is in Matthew, chapter 8.

23. And when he was entered into a ship, his disciples followed him.
24. And, behold, there arose a great tempest in the sea, insomuch that the ship was covered with the waves: but he was asleep.
25. And his disciples came to him, and awoke him, saying, Lord, save us: we perish.
26. And he said unto them, Why are ye fearful, O ye of little faith? Then he arose, and rebuked the winds and the sea; and there was a great calm.

The rest is found in chapter 14, probably the same story by a different author, which proves the book is not all Matthew's.

25. And in the fourth watch of the night Jesus went unto them, walking on the sea.
26. And when the disciples saw him walking on the sea, they were troubled, saying, It is a spirit; and they cried out for fear.

27. But straightway Jesus spake unto them, saying, Be of good cheer; it is I; be not afraid.

28. And Peter answered him and said, Lord, if it be thou, bid me come unto thee on the water.

29. And he said, Come. And when Peter was come down out of the ship, he walked on the water, to go to Jesus.

It takes a lot of ignorance to believe this literally, yet, literally, millions do. And then we wonder what's wrong with our world. What better world would you expect of such ignorance? We will not say that man cannot and never will walk on water; he has powers and possibilities as yet undreamed of, but if this feat is ever accomplished it will be by powers he himself develops in Evolution, and not by powers given him by gods and saviors. The latter is but personification—a factor that has done more harm to truth than all the sinners in history. It is but Noah and the ark, Jonah and the whale all over again. "But as the days of Noe were, so shall also the coming of the Son of man be" (Matt. 24:37). "For as Jonas was a sign unto the Ninevites, so shall also the Son of man be to this generation" (Luke 11:30). "For as Jonas was three days and three nights in the whale's belly," etc. The tempest is the Deluge, and the ship, the ark; the water-walking Jesus and Peter, creative consciousness and energy. What an outrage then to hold up to us the idea that with faith enough we too can walk on water, remove mountains, and so on. The faith implied here is not human faith at all; it is the Cosmocreator's. Yet because of these scriptural deceptions, we repeat, fools refuse medical aid and even let serpents bite them. Here out of ignorance we misapply the moral.

Jesus walking on the water is but "the spirit of God" moving "upon the face of the waters," the Old Testament precedent. You will recall our reference to another Creator who tried to make a world out of the *turbulentos,* turbulent elements. Here in this "fourth watch" of the involutionary "night" they are indeed turbulent, and only the Creator can control them. If you would know how turbulent they eventually become, you have only to look at the sun, their most violent stage. Our religion-perverted mystics tell us the sun is the abode of "divine beings" and therefore a "holy place." Literally and actually the sun is hell in heaven, spatially speaking, a cosmic inferno whose violence is beyond our comprehension. And do not call this blasphemy; you cannot blaspheme El Shaddai, powerwise; "the half has never been told." Telescopic observations of his violence are but reality seen "through a glass darkly." This is the original hell or Hades of the Greeks, and the hell of religion is but this perverted by priests for "benefit *of* clergy." And yet what hell it has caused us racially; millions have lived and died in the fear of it, and all for want of knowledge of Reality.

While on the subject of violence we can interpret that statement, "The kingdom of heaven must be taken by violence." This too is a grievance to our "students of divinity," so contrary is it to the teachings of Christ, and of common sense. Not so, however, when seen in this cosmic context. "The kingdom of heaven" is the postsolid, evolutionary planes, and from the presolid planes can be reached only by and through the violent sun period. This is also the meaning of that statement, "The kingdom of heaven is at hand," not an imminent moral millennium, but the time for involutionary life to become evolutionary. You will notice it does not say "the kingdom of God"—this *is* violence. Whenever this phrase is used it is of this violent period the mythologist is speaking, as for instance, "Verily I say unto you, that there be some of them that stand here, which shall not taste of death, till they have seen the kingdom of God come with power" (Mark 9:1). "The kingdom of God come with power" is the sun stage and those who would not taste of death until they saw it were the planetary elements. The death implied here is the death of the Life Principle in dense matter, and the bright sun stage comes first. This the elements would see, and this, strange to say, constitutes the sixth miracle.

This likewise is the meaning of the dire predictions concerning the last days. "For nation shall rise against nation, and kingdom against kingdom, and there shall be earthquakes in divers places, and there shall be famine and troubles: these are the beginnings of sorrow." Yes for the planetary entity—"The Sorrows of Satan" and the troubles of Pharaoh, namely, materiality. It is also Adam's Paradise Lost. These dire predictions relate to conditions trillions of years ago, yet whenever this old earth trembles, or wars arise, our literalists turn to them and cry "The end is near" and "The second coming of Christ is at hand." To have a "second coming" you must have a first, and the Christ of religion has not come yet, nor has the end of the world. Yet for two thousand years this Bible-garble has produced periodic waves of hysteria. So here again we see the tragedy of ignorance. It's still with us. Our fundamentalists are looking for the "second coming of Christ" when what they're going to get is just more violence—worldwide disaster.

In this solar violence we have the solution to another scriptural absurdity, and deception. Immediately following the fifth miracle, we read about Jesus' encounter with the wild man, whose name is Legion, and out of whom Jesus cast a host of devils. These devils are the terrible forces of the sun period, legions surely, which must be cast out ere a violent sun becomes a peaceful planet. At this same point in the Old Testament parallel, Saul was also wild and David pretended to be. He "scrabbled on the door of the gate and let his spittle fall down upon his beard" (1 Sam. 21:13). The gate on which David "scrabbled" is that "gateway of the gods," the sun, and when the Creator, Jesus, said of His word that "the gates of hell shall not prevail against it," He was speaking of this cosmic Hades. His "word" is the genetic ideation, and neither the fiery sun nor the frozen earth can prevail against it, for it will come forth in Evolution.

It is strange these devils all knew Jesus' nature while His companions did not. At His approach they cried out, "What have we to do with thee, Jesus, thou Son of God? art thou come hither to torment us before the time?" What time? The time for these violent forces to be cast out of the sun. And what were the swine that received them and "ran violently down a steep place"? Well, what receives the sun's cast-off forces? The planets of course. These are the "swine" of Jewish mythology, and this is not the only place it speaks of them as such; later we will point it out again. These swine are matter, dirt to the mythologist. The Jewish mythologists had no respect for matter; their popular name for it was *nechoshet*. Necho means dragon, the rest is obvious. And so our world is but cosmic dragon dirt, yet why did the Creator labor so long to create it if it be so despicable? Medieval Christians dominated by Jewish ideology considered matter so vile they were ashamed of their own material bodies; to them only the original spirit was holy, and so these foolish ones lived and died in the hell this ideology brought them.

Vile or not, God made the world and for a mighty purpose; why then should His Son speak of the end of it in His day? As this did not happen, agnostics point to it as proof that Jesus was not infallible. But it was not of our world He was speaking; it was of the prephysical world. Here again the translators interpreted in keeping with their own delusions. The original Greek, *teleuten aion*, did not mean the end of the world, but rather the end of an eon, in this case the presolar period. This was spirit's Gotterdammerung, the end of the Edenic world, not ours. To the Creator standing here, there was only violence and a tomb before him—the sun and earth. At the end of the sixth plane the invisible ether becomes a visible, luminous sun, and this is the sixth miracle.

6. The Transfiguration

2. And after *six* days (eons) Jesus taketh with him (the elements) Peter, and James, and John, and leadeth them up into an high mountain (fiery Sinai) apart by themselves: and he was transfigured before them.

3. And his raiment (the solar aura) became shining, exceeding white as snow; so as no fuller on earth can white them (Mark, Chap. 9).

If the authors of the New Testament were not secretly following the creative process why do these time periods accord so accurately with it? And if this be the basis, why this cunning deception? It is but added proof of our contention—the Bible is not "the word of God" but the work of priests laying the foundation for a supernaturalistic religion. Were it not so there would be no motive for this perversion of Creation's story. It was for this reason the priests substituted their own account in Genesis for the Jhwhist's intentionally mythological account.

The Gospels are perverted cosmology, and so after the sixth
plane and period comes the first part of the seventh, and here,
we repeat, the invisible elements are transfigured into a visible,
shining sun, whose "garments" are white as snow—white light.
This is the Transfiguration, an event in the life of the Creative
Principle, and therefore of Jesus only as this personified. It's
nothing new in occult cosmology: Buddha was transfigured on
a mountain in Ceylon; Noah and Moses were also transfigured,
at birth, and their light filled the whole house—not man's but
God's, the solar temple. Describing Noah, the Apochryphal
Book of Enoch says, "A body white as snow, hair white as wool
and eyes that are like the rays of the sun." Naturally, since he
was the sun. And from this our "great Bible students" conclude
that Noah was an albino—innocents abroad in an occult world.

4. And there appeared unto them Elias with Moses: . . .
7. and a voice came out of the cloud, saying, This is my beloved Son
(Sun): hear him (Chap. 9).

Here we have a new character—Elias. And who was he? The
Gospels refer to this mysterious personage many times, yet
there is no book or clear-cut account of him anywhere; that is,
exoterically, but esoterically there is, for Elias is none other than
an evolutionary Elijah, as was Elisha. In the Apocrypha, Elijah
is called Elias (Ecclesiasticus 48). And even Luke says likewise,
though indirectly. When speaking of James and John bringing
fire down from heaven, he concludes with "even as Elias did"
(9:54). It was Elijah who did this. The change in the suffix, Eli-as,
represents that isomeric change that we said takes place in matter. This is symbolized by the next major event. The long-
expected Elias, then, is one with Moses, the evolutionary aspect
of the involutionary Elijah, and also Jesus. Since the New Testament was written subsequent to the Old, we naturally assume
that Jesus lived long after Elijah, alias Elias. This is true only
in the same way that Solomon lived after David, and Abraham
after Noah—which Joshua refutes. These are not chronological
characters but mythological Creators, hence parallels. The
meaning of this meeting then is this: the mountain is Mount

Sinai, the sun-earth entity, and here Involution meets Evolution. The story is thus but a revolutio of the Old Testament account of Moses meeting God on this same Mount, so naturally he appears at this point also.

And now we find this planetary Creator preparing for the "Passover"—not a mere observance of that Passover we read about in Exodus, but the same Passover, thus another revolutio. In both, it is the passing over of the Life Principle from Involution to Evolution.

12. And the first day of unleavened bread, when they killed the passover, his disciples said unto him, Where wilt thou that we go and prepare that thou mayest eat the passover? (Mark 14).

Here again the time sequence accords with the creative process, for the "first day of unleavened bread" is the first day, or beginning, of dense matter. This is the "unleavened" bread of the scriptures. The next verse points to its zodiacal position— Libra, as of our correction. The statement would mean little if the earth sign was Virgo. We also said it was the opposite or nether hand that indicated conditions.

13. And he sendeth forth two of his disciples, and saith unto them, Go ye into the city, and there shall meet you a man bearing a pitcher of water: follow him (Chap. 14).

This is a reference to the zodiacal water carrier, Aquarius, whose thirtieth degree stands directly opposite to the first of Libra—as we made it. The nether hand is thus pointing to the earth. This applies to all the cycles, creative, precessional, and annual. When in these the nether hand enters Libra, the earth is weighed in the Balance. In the creative cycle, Belshazzar was "weighed in the balance" at this point, and now Jesus is likewise —in the Roman court.

This Passover was observed in an "upper room," the still prephysical part of the new world; and here this Sun of God and his twelve aspects ate their "last supper" in Involution, a supper of bread and wine—the nectar and ambrosia of the gods.

Here Jesus declares that one of these aspects will betray Him, as later another denied Him—Judas, matter, and Peter, rock. Thus Judas and Peter are the Delilah and Medusa of this myth. Now compare this cosmic picture with Christian art and custom—Da Vinci's "Last Supper," and the sacrament.

As they partook of this meal Jesus instituted the latter. As he ate and drank the bread and wine, he said, "Do this in remembrance of me," and ever since deluded people have been doing it, not because they understand it, but because they don't. Here perhaps they can find out. The wine and bread are symbols of the two aspects, consciousness and energy, changed or transubstantiated in the creative process. This is the transubstantiation symbolized by the "holy eucharist." The involutionary elements are different on the evolutionary side; they become isomeric, that is, same in substance but different in quality. Indeed they undergo two changes: first, in the sun-earth organism, second, in the plant-animal organism. Thus transubstantiation is a significant factor in Creation, hence also in mythology. The ancients, as we said, knew much more about these things than we do; they evidently studied nature, not divinity, and left their knowledge in esoteric allegory. This we have interpreted literally, and so become the victims of one of the most baseless and superstitious forms of religion in all the annals of theomania. The Aztecs may have been crueler, but not more credulous.

Anyone who thinks that ordinary bread and wine are actually "transubstantiated" into the flesh and blood of Christ by the mumbled words of an ignorant priest should put a little arsenic in them first. He will find then that the flesh and blood of Christ are deadly poison.

This ignorant Christian custom of eating and drinking commonplace bread and wine in the hope of gaining some Christlike virtue is but a relic of the savage rite of omophagia—the eating and drinking of another person's or animal's flesh and blood to acquire his or its qualities, strength, courage, and so on. But the civilized, so-called, have gone the savage one better; they eat a god instead of a man, and so the savage's anthropophagy is now theanthropophagy.

It is on this and the crucifixion that the Catholics base their

Mass, a pious mumbo-jumbo to which nature answers, "Me no understand." Every word and gesture is supposed to have profound significance, yet what significance can they have when the whole ritual is based on something that never happened? How educated and supposedly intelligent men can believe such antics important can be explained only by the spiritual ignorance of Western man. When *"Ite missa est"* (the Mass is over) is said for the last time, not in, but for, the Mass, there'll be some hope of enlightenment. Even in the darkness of the Middle Ages there were a few who knew the fraudulent nature of this rite. The officiating priests of Rome would, *sub rosa*, change the words *"Hoc est meum corpus"*(This is my body) to *"Panis es, et panis manebis"* (Bread it is, and bread it shall remain). And the poor, benighted people would bow their heads before the elevated Host and profess their unworthiness just as today. Such abject abasement, rite and ceremony are but a priestly mess of pottage paid for with the birthright of human dignity.

If we must play hocus-pocus, let us know what we are doing. The wine and bread are symbols of the pure, virgin elements that on the lower planes became that Demon that is Deus inversus. It is Deus then that should remember His source—and the Revelator says so. Yet we too are these elements, and when we eat and drink their earthly symbols we too should remember our own cosmic source and nature. To elevate and sublimate our worldly and materialistic consciousness is the ritual's only efficacy. This is the purpose of all religious rites, and every race of antiquity had its Judeo-Christian equivalents. In the Bacchic Mysteries a consecrated cup called the Agathodaemon was passed among the communicants, and bread and wine were served as symbols of our source. The Manichaeans partook of the "consecrated host," while the Mithraists had their "sacramental meal." In Egypt the communicants partook of a cake composed of flour, milk and honey on which the cross, the symbol of matter, was impressed. This is the origin of our "hot cross buns." Then there was the ancient Agapé, or Love Feast, in which rich and poor alike joined in communion. For the first fifty years of the Christian era this and "holy communion" were jointly observed; thereafter, according to Pliny the Younger, the communion was celebrated in the morning, the Agapé in the evening. The Jews also had and still have their sacramental bread and wine, but their communion is not "in remembrance" of Jesus Christ.

This scriptural "transubstantiation" is the key to much of the New Testament. By it the involutionary Jesus becomes the evolutionary Christ—Prometheus and Hercules, Elijah and Elias; by it "the kingdom of God" becomes "the kingdom of heaven"; by it "the Son of God" becomes "the Son of man"; by it Jesus takes His place "on the right hand of God," Evolution. Because of it the involutionary disciples become the evolutionary apostles, with their "glad tidings" of a new "gospel," biologic life. Here this gospel is transferred from the Old Testament Jews, symbols of the involutionary, to the New Testament Gentiles, symbols of the evolutionary. In this planetary isomerism lies also the meaning of the two ways Jesus, thereafter the Christ, delivered His message: the proverbs explained secretly to the disciples, and the promise of open demonstration. The one is planetary ideation impressed upon the involutionary forces, the other, their evolutionary expression. John puts it thus (16:25): "These things have I spoken unto you in proverbs: but the time cometh, when I shall no more speak unto you in proverbs, but I shall shew you plainly of the Father." Potency and epiphany, and the latter, Epiphany or Twelfth Night, is this literalized and thus obscured.

We would like to follow this inexorable process to its inevitable conclusion, but there are other incidents here that reveal quite clearly the fraudulent nature of this whole story. This, we think, the reader should know. One of these is the raising of Lazarus. This too is a miracle, but it is only a preview of Jesus' own miraculous resurrection; therefore the two are one.

1. Now a certain man was sick, named Lazarus, of Bethany . . .

4. When Jesus heard that, he said, This sickness is not unto death, but for the glory of God . . . (only the genetic's sleep in matter).

6. When he had heard therefore that he was sick, he abode two days still in the same place where he was.

11. These things said he: and after that he saith unto them, Our

friend Lazarus sleepeth; but I go, that I may wake him out of sleep (Evolution).

14. Then said Jesus unto them plainly, Lazarus is dead ("dead matter," the energy aspect).

17. Then when Jesus came, he found that he had lain in the grave four days already (middle point in Devolution).

37. And some of them said, Could not this man, which opened the eyes of the blind, have caused that even this man should not have died?

38. Jesus therefore again groaning in himself cometh to the grave. *It was a cave*, and a stone lay upon it.

39. Jesus said, Take ye away the stone. . . .

41. Then they took away the stone from the place where the dead was laid. And Jesus lifted up his eyes, and said, Father, I thank thee that thou hast heard me.

43. And when he thus had spoken, he cried with a loud voice, Lazarus, come forth.

44. And he that was dead came forth, bound hand and foot with graveclothes: and his face was bound about with a napkin. Jesus saith unto them, Loose him, and let him go (John 11).

Here we have one of the greatest frauds and deceptions in the Bible. Besides being historically untrue, it is a copy brazenly offered as unique and original. Its source, however, is Egypt. Just as Jesus, the Judean Savior, went to Bethany to raise His friend, so Horus, the Egyptian Savior, went to Bethanu to raise his father. What is more, the names Mary, Martha and Lazarus all came from Egypt. There the two sisters are Meri and Merti, and their brother, by derivation El-Azar-us, became Lazarus. The word Bethanu means "the house of God," in this case that of the Egyptian god Anu. From this we can see where the Jews got their word Beth and also the story.

Since these tales were known throughout the ancient world they must have some symbolic meaning, and that is the important part.

Lazarus was the brother of Mary and Martha, "whom Jesus loved." Why then did He not go to them at once, not wait until He knew Lazarus was dead? Because Lazarus, like Jesus himself, represents the Life Principle in Involution and this must die that Evolution might be. Later, this is raised up as biologic life, which is "the glory of God." The four days represents the middle point in Devolution, also 7, when the Life Principle is ready and waiting to be resurrected. In the case of Christ it was three days. John the Revelator is more precise; he makes it exactly three and a half days.

8. And their dead bodies shall lie in the street of the great city (earth), which spiritually is called Sodom and Egypt, where also our Lord was crucified.

11. And after three days and an half the spirit of life from God entered into them, and they stood upon their feet . . . (Rev. 11).

And this in turn was taken from Ezekiel, in whose story of "the valley of dry bones" the same thing happens. And you will recall that Elijah raised "the widow woman's" son, and Elisha, the Shummanite's. Raising "dead matter" to life then is an old story in mythology.

Now just as the story of Lazarus came from Egypt, so the story of Jairus's daughter came from India.

In the *Hari-Purana*, translated by Jacolliot, we find a story about Krishna (Chrishna) raising a young girl from the dead as Christ raised Jairus's daughter. According to the Hindu myth, Kalavatti, daughter of Angashuna, died, and as the people were mourning over her,

. . . suddenly, a great rumor spread throughout the palace and the following cries were heard, a thousand times repeated: '*Pacya pitaram; Pacya gurum!*' 'The Father, the Master!'

Then Chrishna approached, smiling, leaning on the arm of Arjuna.

'Master!' cried Angashuna, casting himself at his feet, and sprinkling them with his tears. 'See my poor daughter!' and he showed him the body of Kalavatti stretched upon a mat . . .

'Why do you weep?' replied Chrishna, in a gentle voice. 'Do you not see that she is sleeping? See she moves. Kalavatti! Rise and walk!'

Hardly had Chrishna spoken when the breathing, warmth, movement and life returned, little by little, into the corpse, and the young girl obeying the injunction of the demigod, rose from her couch and rejoined her companions.

But the crowd marveled and cried out, 'This is a god, since death is no more for him than sleep.'

The raising of the dead then is just some more Christology.

It was at this point that Jesus, looking out from the hills of Bethany, wept over Jerusalem—not for the immoral nature of men but for the nonmoral nature of Causation. We too dealt with this and concluded that nothing conscious of what it is doing could create a thing so horrible as a primeval world—billions of years of violence, warfare, and death. Little wonder this personified Creator wept! Not tears of grief but the *lacrimae rerum*—the tears of things: the struggle to live, the loneliness of souls, and over all, inevitable death. The poet Vergil sensed this, and so did the Greek dramatists, hence the sense of impending doom in their tragedies. The Jews could not face this grim Reality and so they put a *persona* on it. Now instead of the stoic fortitude that comes of knowledge, we have a loving God, a gentle Jesus and a billion Pollyannas.

Yet in spite of this, the truth comes out at times—the story of the fig tree. Jesus, finding no fruit upon it, blasts it and it dies. The figs of Palestine ripen late in May, and this event took place in March or April, Easter week, which is to say that Jesus cursed a fig tree because it did not supply him food out of season. If there is a moral here it is this: what does not serve the Creator shall be destroyed. And now the time has come to destroy the false persona the priests put on His face.

We have now reached the zodiacal point Leo, chronologically near the time when the Sun of God himself is to die and become a dense-matter earth. And so Jesus tells his disciples to procure for him an ass (with colt) to carry him to Jerusalem, which is the earth. This, we are told, is to fulfill the Old Testament prophecy in Zechariah 9:9: "Behold thy King cometh unto thee: he is just, and having salvation; lowly, and riding upon an ass, and upon a colt the foal of an ass." This is not the fulfillment of Old Testament prophecy but the New Testament using Old Testament mythology to authenticate its own. These asses are cosmic asses, the Ascelli, in the constellation Leo, on which numerous solar heroes rode to their death against the warlike material elements. Bacchus, or Dionysius, the savior of his people, came riding on an ass; so did Vulcan, Saul and even Moses. "And Moses took his wife and his sons, and set them upon an ass, and he returned to the land of Egypt (earth) . . ." (Exodus 4:20).

In this contest with matter, the Life Principle is defeated, bound, and buried that it may rise again in Evolution. With this in mind, the authors have Jesus tell his disciples, "Except a corn of wheat fall into the ground and die, it abideth alone: but if it die, it bringeth forth much fruit." The fruit implied here is biologic life. In this lies also the meaning of that statement, "And I, if I be lifted up from the earth, will draw all men unto me." Those who interpret this as meaning the lifting up of the man Jesus upon a wooden cross, that all men may be drawn up also, are those to whom He referred when he said, "To them it is not given to know the mysteries of the kingdom." And this includes the entire clergy. This lifting-up of Jesus is identical with the lifting-up of the serpent in the wilderness.

The Bible furnishes no better proof of the purely genetic nature of Jesus than these statements. The genetic principle must die, in matter, that is, become inactive; and when it rises up in Evolution it draws everything with it, including the epigenetic. Personifying this, the Bible calls them "men," and ever since men have taken it literally. But they are not consistent in their literalism; if they were they would insist that this excludes women. But sane men no longer want war and so for once they become symbolists.

This genetic must have a garden to grow in, and now we find Jesus in the Garden of Gethsemane—the word means "the wine press," symbolically, the earth. This is the scene of life's aforesaid agony, and here the Life Principle is strained through that cosmic ethmos, matter, that from it may come forth that "good wine" kept till the last—conscious, qualitative life. And here the Creator prays to his Father, whoever that might be, that the cup may pass from Him—but there was no answer. He is doomed as in the Greek tragedy. And here we see the error of New Testament theology. That a God of love should demand such a sacrifice from his "only begotten son," is incredible, but that the inexorable law of Creation should demand it is quite believable. And let us remember here that the source of this "only begotten" is the Greek word *monogene*—one gene.

Here in this New Testament Garden of Eden, the Creator becomes "heavy" and His disciples fall asleep. This is the same sleep that overtook Adam, Noah, Abraham, and others; and the "rest" they took is that "rest" God took at this same point.

Now come the priestly hirelings, symbols of materiality, to make of Jesus the New Testament's "Prometheus Bound." It seems, however, they met with some opposition.

47. And one of them that stood by drew a sword, and smote a servant of the high priest, and cut off his ear (Mark 14).

And to this day no priest or servant thereof can hear the truth. Judas, their servant, seals its doom with the kiss of death and they do the rest.

3. Then assembled together the chief priests, and the scribes, and the elders of the people (all Jews), unto the palace of the high priest, who was called Caiaphas (Matt. 26).

The word *Caiaphas* means rock or stone, and also the oppressor; and in mythology the oppressor is matter. Thus, as with Peter, what he stands for is not the rock of salvation, but the rock of oppression. If Jesus, the Christ, represents all that is right and beneficial to man, we have here a subtle confirmation of our own indictment of the priests, for now we are told they got together

4. And consulted that they might take Jesus by subtilty, and kill him.
14. Then one of the twelve, called Judas Iscariot, went unto the chief priests,
15. And said unto them, What will ye give me, and I will deliver him unto you? And they covenanted with him for thirty pieces of silver (Chap. 26).

Here again we have a New Testament effort to make its story seem the fulfillment of Old Testament prophecy. "Then was fulfilled that which was spoken by Jeremy the prophet, saying,

And they took the thirty pieces of silver, the price of him that was valued . . . (Matt. 27:9). Had Jeremy said fifty pieces, then the authors would have made it fifty also. Jesus said, "O fools, and slow of heart to believe all that the prophets have spoken" (Luke 24:25). And that's for us.

59. Now the chief priests, and elders, and all the council, sought false witness against Jesus, to put him to death (Matt. 26).

57. And there arose certain, and bare false witness against him, . . .

60. And the high priest stood up in the midst, and asked Jesus, saying, Answerest thou nothing? what is it which these witness against thee?

61. But he held his peace, and answered nothing. Again the high priest asked him, and said unto him, Art thou the Christ, the Son of the Blessed?

62. And Jesus said, I am: and ye shall see the Son of man sitting on the right hand of power, and coming in the clouds of heaven.

63. Then the high priest rent his clothes, and saith, What need we any further witnesses? (Mark 14).

Not only the chief priests but the elders and the council must have known of the miracles Jesus wrought: walking on the water, raising the dead, and so on, and they must have known no mortal man could do such things. Why then did they doubt? For professional reasons only? All this is overlooked that the inexorable process might go on.

1. And straightway in the morning the chief priests held a consultation with the elders and scribes and the whole council, and bound Jesus, and carried him away, and delivered him to Pilate.

3. And the chief priests accused him of many things: but he answered nothing.

9. But Pilate answered them, saying, Will ye that I release unto you the King of the Jews? [1]

10. For he knew that the chief priests had delivered him for envy.

11. But the chief priests moved the people, that he should rather release Barabbas unto them.

---

[1] In the nineteenth century an eminent scholar, Rabbi Wise, searched the records of Pilate's court, still extant, for evidence of this trial. He found nothing.

14. Then Pilate said unto them, Why, what evil hath he done? And they cried out the more exceedingly, Crucify him (Mark 15).

24. When Pilate saw that he could prevail nothing, but that rather a tumult was made, he took water, and washed his hands before the multitude, saying, I am innocent of the blood of this just person: see ye to it (and if we were as wise as Pilate we, too, would wash our hands of it; Matt. 27).

So much argument over the question, Who killed Jesus? yet do not the scriptures make it clear? Not the Romans, whose Governor sought to save him; not the whole Jewish people, for "many heard him gladly"; but the priests, the crucifiers then as now of truth and progress. And what hate and bigotry, persecution and war they have caused! Brother against brother and nation against nation, and all for what? A Creation myth mistaken for history. Roman and Jew, priest and apostle are but characters in the drama thereof. Jesus, the lead, is the Life Principle, His silence, its unconsciousness; His courage, its determined purpose.

Throughout the Old Testament, the Jews represent the Life Principle, and the Gentiles its opponents; in the Gospels this is reversed, then John of Revelation reverts to the Old Testament symbolism—proof that he is not the John of the Gospels. Pilate, a historical figure, is here made to represent, as in Genesis, that which would stay the descent of spirit into matter. Because of Pilate's effort, taken literally, the Coptic Church made him a saint and celebrates his day in May. In both the Coptic and the Greek Orthodox Church, his wife Claudia Procla is also a saint, October 27 being St. Procla's Day. Saint in one country, devil in another, and all for want of knowledge.

In the Barabbas incident there's an occult touch that is indeed revealing. In his effort to save Jesus, Pilate offered the crowd a murderer, but they rejected him. What an indictment of the Jews, we say, demanding that the Son of God be crucified instead of a criminal. The real indictment, however, is of ourselves, for it proves we are spiritually benighted. The Son of God and the murderous Barabbas are one. The full name of the latter was Jesus Barabbas, the first name being dropped only after the name Jesus became sacred. *Bar-abbas* means "son of the fathers"; therefore Jesus Barabbas, son of the Father(s), and Jesus Christ, Son of God, are one and the same. The only possible difference is that between creative consciousness and its violent energy, the Cain of this story. In other myths it's the murderous Set of Egypt, and the ruthless Romulus of Rome. And all are but an occult way of saying that energy dominates consciousness on the lower planes, hence nature's violence. Those still influenced by religion say such a view can be nothing but an illusion of the mortal mind, that behind it all lies the divine, the holy and the spiritual. So here again we ask such people: What's divine about an earthquake? what's holy about a hurricane? and what is spiritual about the law of the jungle? This is the real delusion of the mortal mind. It's time it learned the truth. God is not a divine prefix to savage nature; He *is* savage nature, and this alone explains the next miracle.

7. The Crucifixion
(More correctly, the Crucifiction)

A literal crucifixion is not a miracle, but in the planetary sense it is as much a miracle as any of the others; therefore we will consider it as such.

1. Now before the feast of the passover, when Jesus knew that his hour was come . . . (John 13).
14. And it was the preparation of the passover, and about the sixth hour (cycle) . . . (Chap. 19).

Now is it not strange that the crucifixion should take place during the Passover? Among the Jews this was a most sacred occasion. For them to crucify anyone at this time, they would have to break at least seven of their religious laws. Why then did they profane it with murder? The answer is, they did not. No matter what the priests and masses considered the Passover to mean, the Gnostic authors knew its occult meaning—the passing over of the Life force from Involution to Evolution as in Exodus—and so they made the crucifixion and resurrection of Jesus to coincide with it. Nor is it strange that this should coincide with the spring equinox, for this was the event celebrated after the deeper meaning was lost. At this time the sun hangs for three days upon the celestial cross formed by the ecliptic and the equator.

It was "the sixth hour." Here again the time corresponds with the creative process, the sixth hour being the sixth planetary cycle, after which comes the seventh, dense matter. Here the Creative Spirit must drink the cup of materiality.

In Genesis God warned Adam about this, and now Pilate serves the same purpose:

15. But they (the materializing forces) cried out, Away with him, away with him, crucify him. Pilate saith unto them, Shall I crucify your King? The chief priests answered, We have no king but Caesar (materiality).

And why should Jews, who hated the Roman yoke and hoped for a Messiah to free them, say that?

16. Then delivered he him therefore unto them to be crucified. And they took Jesus, and led him away.

And who is to blame, if his death was foreordained? Like Pharaoh and Judas, they were but instruments in God's horrendous scheme.

17. And he bearing his cross went forth into a place called the place of a skull, which is called in the Hebrew Golgotha (Chap. 19).

You will recall the epithet thrown at Elisha by the jeering children—"old bald head," skull. Elisha was the bare "bald" earth itself, as were "naked" Adam and Noah, and such is Golgotha. The other name, Calvary, is the Latin equivalent from *calvaria*, a skull, and *calvus*, bald. The Aramaic Gulgalta, source of the Hebrew Golgotha, means "like a skull." As these countries are not remotely separated, it might be argued that these similarities all derive from an event, but this can hardly be the case with Mexico, some five thousand miles away. Yet the place where its great god Quetzalcoatl was crucified means "place of the skull." These similarities come not from an event but from a common mythoplasm. Certain legends also spring from this. One pertinent to our subject is an Islamic tale about a "treasure cave" under Golgotha in which lie buried the bones of Adam and the treasures of Paradise. The Catholic Church must have heard about it for it has turned Golgotha into Golconda. And the skull's become skullduggery, see p. 472.

The "cave" is the earth itself,

18. Where they crucified him, and two others with him, on either side one, and Jesus in the midst (Chap. 19).

Now what is on either side of this cave but Involution and Evolution? These are the two thieves: the one steals from the Absolute, the cosmic source, the other from the earth, the biologic source. The one is Rachel stealing her father-in-law's images; the other, her descendants stealing the jewels of Egypt. While hanging on the cross Jesus said to one, and only one, "This day shalt thou be with me in Paradise." This thief is the evolutionary energy that rises with consciousness; the other ceases to be, which accords with our theory. Herein lies the reason why we put Paradise on the evolutionary side as well as the involutionary, see page 44. To the Life Principle, Paradise is anywhere outside dense matter. In Evolution, this Paradise is the heaven of religion. And here religion acquires another saint; the "good thief" is now St. Dismas—the earth divided as in Peleg's day.

23. Then the soldiers (symbols of material power), when they had crucified Jesus, took his garments, and made four parts, to every soldier a part; and also his coat: now the coat was without seam, woven from the top throughout (Chap. 19).

And so was the world. Creation began at the top (spirit) and was woven downward to dense matter. And the Egyptians declared that its symbol, the Great Pyramid, was built in like manner. Jesus' coat is Joseph's coat "of many colors," namely the involutionary aura. The garments are this in Evolution, making the four kingdoms. The stripping of Jesus is the same as that of Ishtar and Innana; and let's not forget naked Adam and Noah. Today, we grant Jesus a loin cloth, a concession to our sensitized but nonintelligized souls.

25. Now there stood by the cross of Jesus his mother (Mary), and his mother's sister, Mary the wife of Cleophas, and Mary Magdalene (Chap. 19).

But why so many Marys? Because Mary, as we said, is the name of the Earth Mother, from *Mare*, the cosmic sea or source. In mythology woman represents matter, and it is this that brings about the spirit's death. Thus, shocking as it may be, it was his saintly mother who caused Jesus' crucifixion. This is clearly stated in this story's Babylonian source. In this, Ishtar has her divine son, Tammuz, crucified, buried and then resurrected. And at the crucifixion Ishtar "stood the cross beside." In Egypt it was Meri and Merti, mourning the death of Osiris. It may have been knowledge of the mythic meaning of Mary that made the authors present Jesus as resentful towards his mother. At the first miracle she was there helping to turn the cosmic waters into the bitter wine of life. This the Creator must now drink, and so Jesus is given a sponge full of vinegar, a symbol thereof.

30. When Jesus therefore had received the vinegar, he said, It is finished . . . (Chap. 19).

"And on the seventh day God ended his work which he had made" (Gen. 2:2).

And this is the seventh day in this story, hence the same day, and what was finished was the same work, namely, Creation. Thus Jesus died on the seventh day, Christianity to the contrary. This being so, Jesus was not crucified in the spring—Easter, Aries—but in what is now Virgo but should be Libra, the symbol of matter.

Here the "evil spirit from God" that came upon Saul came upon Jesus also, and so,

50. Jesus, when he had cried again with a loud voice, yielded up the ghost (Matt. 27).

And what ghost is this? That Holy Ghost that fathered him? Yes, in subsequent form, the earth's metaphysical robes in Involution, which the earth-entity gave up when it became solid matter, the stripping of Ishtar and Innana again. In Evolution this "ghost" reappears, the planetary aura which remains with the earth till disintegration. At this point in the story it could have a more concrete meaning—the final release of the solar gases, we suggested might be the cause of novas.

44. And it was about the sixth hour (eon), and there was a darkness over all the earth until the ninth hour (Luke 23).
51. And, behold, the veil of the temple was rent in twain from the top to the bottom; and the earth did quake, and the rocks rent . . . (Matt. 27).

We have here a good example of the credulity of Western man. For two thousand years he has been reading about this convulsion and "darkness over all the earth" without ever questioning it or demanding proof of it. Yet had it happened, would not some of those able historians have recorded it? Why did they not? Because this is just some more "star of Bethlehem" history, a thing of the incalculable past. The sixth to the ninth hour is that vast period between Leo and Scorpio inclusive, the "darkness over all the earth," that night for creative consciousness when blind energy alone rules all. Beyond this there is light again and the unconscious genetic has the conscious epigenetic to aid it, a sort of planetaty paraclete. The temple here as elsewhere is the earth itself, rent in two parts, Involution and Evolution, which till now was but one, the former. In the days of Peleg "was the earth divided" (Gen. 10:25).

52. And the graves were opened; and many bodies of the saints which slept arose,
53. And came out of the graves *after his resurrection*, and went into the holy city, and appeared unto many (Matt. 27).

This is indeed more applicable to the resurrection, if it means that of Christ, but our playwright had a keen sense of the dramatic. He also tells us who "the saints" of the Gospels are—the emergent creative forces. Were they men, long dead before this time, we should see that Christ is not necessary to saintliness. The "holy city" these saints entered "after the resurrection" is the biologic organism. This is the "holy" of the scriptures, and in the eyes of nature, holy only as creative means and purpose. Christians, taking literally these fantastic events, call Jerusalem the "Holy City" and Palestine the "Holy Land," yet aside from their purely symbolic meaning, there is nothing holy about them; they are, on the contrary, a pestilential spot from which have come false theologies, racial prejudice, and religious bigotry—and now political war and conflict. Such it always was and will remain as long as Jewry, Christianity, and Israel exist.

After this came Joseph of Arimathea, "secretly for fear of the Jews," and took the body of Jesus away and buried it. This Joseph is but the first Joseph burying the body of the first Jesus, namely, Jacob.

39. And there came also Nicodemus, which at the first came to Jesus by night, and brought a mixture of myrrh and aloes, about an hundred pound weight (John 19).

This is very clever, for Nico-demus is but Neco-demon—matter and the devil. This it was that came to the Creator in the planetary night, and now assists in his entombment.

41. Now in the place where he was crucified there was a garden (Eden); and in the garden a new sepulchre, wherein was never man yet laid (Chap. 19).

This is Adam's garden, "wherein was never man yet laid," because never man was yet born, nor even an amoeba. The sepulchre is the earth, not a tomb in Judea. Yet what havoc it has wrought! Consider, for instance, the Crusades, those hellish wars for a "holy sepulchre" that never existed; three million people needlessly butchered, among them sixty thousand children. And again there are those who say, It doesn't matter what men believe; it's what they do that matters. Yet what they **do** is but the outer expression of their beliefs. Were these right and just this world would be Utopia, but since it is Pandemonium, it's time we examined them.

According to the Gospels, the Jews did not mind committing murder during the Passover, but they were greatly worried about profaning their Sabbath, and so they requested Pilate to have the legs of the three broken that they might die the sooner. But when the soldiers came to Jesus they found him already dead, so they broke not his legs but only pierced his side. And this too was stuck in to make it sound like prophecy fulfilled, "These things were done, that the Scriptures should be fulfilled, A bone of him shall not be broken. And again another Scripture saith, They shall look on him whom they pierced." This is not Old Testament foreknowledge of the death of the New Testament Christ, but personified aspects of the creative process. It represents the stricken earth releasing the life force; the piercing of Jesus' side has the same meaning as Judas's bowels gushing out, and the Jews fleeing from tortured Egypt. This wounding of the Creator is as old as mythology itself. Among the Telingonese, their god is pictured with nail holes in his feet; in the Elder Edda, Odin is "wounded with a spear." While hanging in self-sacrifice on Yggdrasil, the World Tree, he addresses himself thus:

> I knew that I hung
> In the windswept tree
> Nine whole nights,
> Wounded with a spear,
> And to Odin offered
> Myself to myself,
> On that tree
> Of which no man knows
> From what root it springs.

That tree is "the tree of life" and the root from which it springs is the Absolute. In both John and Acts *tree* is used instead of *cross*. And Jesus is just another Odin, not a son of the God of the Old Testament, but the Old Testament God now in the New.

In this little verse there is another mighty fact obscured by priestly cunning, namely, that crucifixion is a voluntary act of the Creator. He, or rather, it, lets itself be "crucified" upon that cross called matter. As this took place trillions of years ago, man is in no sense responsible for it: it is but Creation's way. Our literal-minded preachers paint a tragic picture of their Savior hanging upon this cross, for our sins, then in the next breath tell us he was "the Word," "the Logos," the Creator of the world. Very well, if he created a world like this, he deserved to be crucified, for the suffering he caused us. In the literal sense he suffered but a few hours; we, his creation, for millions of years. Let's keep our pity then for those who still suffer, not waste it on fictional pain. Such pain is easy to bear, as proved by stage and screen.

Uninformed Christians, and that means most of them, believe that only their Savior suffered death on a cross, whereas some sixteen of them died in just this way. A list may help the credulous to escape their crucifixion upon the cross of superstition.

Jesus—Nazareth
Krishna—India
Sakia—India
Iva—Nepal
Indra—Tibet
Mithra—Persia
Tammuz—Babylonia
Criti—Chaldea
Attis—Phrygia
Baili—Orissa
Thules—Egypt
Orontes—Egypt
Witoba of the—Telingonese
Odin—Scandinavia
Hesus—the Druids
Quetzalcoatl—Mexico

Please note the similarity in name of the Druidic and Christian Saviors. Occultly, they are all similar, for all are the Creative Principle crucified upon the cross of matter.

The cross is not, therefore, Christian in its origin; it is

a universal symbol found on temples, tablets, and artifacts throughout the entire ancient world. Centuries B(efore) the C(onfusion), the city of Nicaea was laid out in the form of a cross; and centuries after, the cross was used by the Aztecs, who never heard of Christ until his followers came to rob and kill them. In man himself, standing erect with arms outstretched, we see the living symbol of this cross and the model on which the mythical cross was made. The latter is cosmic, not human. The significance of the cross is not, therefore, due to the fact that a Savior was crucified upon it, but, on the contrary, all Saviors were said to have been crucified upon it because of its significance. John, more occult than the rest, has Christ carry his own cross, and thus does he imply that each of us should do likewise. Why then expect even a Son of God to carry it for us? Whether we know it or not we are carrying it, and all we need to carry it triumphantly is superreligious enlightenment.

The cross, like all Christian paraphernalia, is but an appropriation of pagan mythology. What is more, this appropriation did not occur until about three hundred years after the alleged crucifixion. Until then the Christian symbol was the swastika, originally a symbol of creative motion. The word is Sanskrit, and derived thus: *su* (good), *asti* (being), and with the suffix *ka*, becomes "It is well." As such it was worn as a talisman and token of good cheer. Later a lamb was used, Aries, "slain from the foundation," etc. When all knowledge of the natural and creative significance of the crucifixion was lost, and the tortured Savior from sin began to dominate the Christian mind, the crucifix was substituted. Now every Catholic home has one or more, and pictures of the tortured Christ hang in every room. Yet such things do not bring peace to such homes; only enlightenment can do that.

"The fourteen stations of the cross," as used by the Catholic Church, are but an ignorant adaptation of the steps the Creator takes in the creative process. If we think of these steps as seven down and seven up, as in our diagram, then there are fourteen. The Church calls them "stations of the cross" but makes them only *to* the cross; thus it has kept the mystic seven, doubled, but lost its occult meaning. That meaning is planetary and zodiacal;

the zodiac of Signs has twelve "stations," in Greece it's the "twelve labors of Hercules," and in Egypt "the twelve tortures" the neophyte had to suffer before he was given the sacred Tau, the cross of the hierophant.

The seven major miracles are identical with the seven days in Genesis, and the seven involutionary signs of the zodiac. Commenting on this, Massey makes this statement: "The Gnostics asserted truly that celestial persons and scenes had been transferred to earth in the gospels and that it is only within the pleorama or zodiac that we can identify the originals of both." Even the medieval Albertus Magnus knew this fact. To quote him verbatim: "The Mysteries of the Incarnation, from the Conception on to the Ascension into heaven, are shown us on the face of the sky and are signified by the stars." And almost contemporary with the priestly perversion of this, Irenaeus said: "The Gnostics truly declared that all the supernatural transactions asserted in the gospels 'were counterparts of what took place above.'" And "what took place above" was what took place in Involution. The locale of these miracles then is not geographical but uranographical.

Indeed there is not an incident in the whole Christ story that is not written in the stars (heavens, not Heaven), and by pagan Initiates. As we said, The zodiac is the story of creation written in the stars and as this story was written there thousands of years before the Christ of religion, it cannot refer to him. On the contrary, the gospels follow minutely the pagan sequence. Within each sign lie the details; to mention only those pertinent to this point in the story, the first decanate of Leo is the Crater, or Cup, the solar crucible; the second is Centaurus, the soldier on horseback. It was of this Cup the Sun of God drank, and it was this soldier that bound him and led him away to be crucified on Golgotha, Egypt, Earth. The color symbol of the Centaurus decanate is purple, a sign of royalty—"king of the Jews." The third decanate is the raven (cock), at whose crowing Peter, the stony earth, denied the spirit principle. The first decanate of Virgo is Boötes, the bear-driver, who scourges the Creator, and the second is Hercules, the Hellenic Christ, who died at this point from wearing the purple robe of the centaur Nessus. The last decanate of Virgo is a crown of thorns, Corona Borealis. "Then came Jesus forth, wearing the crown of thorns, and the purple robe" (John 19:5). The cross is the entire sign of Libra, as we have made it, the dense, material earth, otherwise known as Egypt, "where our Lord was crucified." And everything else with him, hence "the martyrdom of man."

That man should suffer as he does and the Cause remain blameless is a priestly lie that must be refuted. The cross itself is that refutation but because of the lie we cannot see it. We still believe that God, in his infinite love, sacrificed his Son to save us from perdition. This we call "vicarious atonement," but for what? It was not man that committed the "original sin"; it was the Creator, yet man is atoning for it. This he cannot see, nor dare he accuse.

I think it was St. Anselm who sensed these subtle truths; a metaphysician as well as a bishop, his words imply a suspicion that Christ came not to save man from the condemnation of God, but to save God from the condemnation of man. Having made a world of pain and suffering, God felt he needed exoneration, and so sent a representative to plead his case before mankind. This is the love and mercy teaching of his dutiful Son, who died to save his Father from the growing suspicion of pagan enlightenment. And he did it so well he deceived all Christendumb. Taken either way, it's still mythology, and the fact that western man can believe it literally is the key to the mess he has made of his world. He just doesn't know he's going about in a state of appalling ignorance.

Had our Gospel writers been metaphysicians, like Anselm, we would now know the true nature of Causation and our place in its creation; but no, they were religion-makers and their purpose was to procure a soft spot for themselves on the real cross, life itself. And so, with diabolical cunning, they took the facts of natural creation and wrote them up in such a way as to deceive the entire world; they diverted the race from the natural to the supernatural and thus confused the human mind. Of man, the only moral part of God, they made an immoral ingrate grieving the heart of his loving Father . . . He must be saved from this "sin" instead of his God-ordained ignorance, and this by way of a priesthood that holds up the cross as a symbol of God's love instead of his monstrous cruelty. Our priests see no theistic lesson in Managua destroyed at Christmas, or part of Alaska at Easter. Not even a church struck by lightning while its people worship can teach them anything. Some of them are looking for the Second Coming of Christ but, as we said, what they are going to get is worldwide disaster. This too is in the stars, or more specifically, the Precession of the Equinoxes, but as they have no knowledge of these things they cannot warn us. Our seers and sages have done so but not our priests. It seems that Nature gives man only six thousand years in which to make a mess of his world, then she wipes out the mess and starts him off all over again. The last clean sweep was six thousand years ago, and now the six thousand years are up. These things are "acts of God," and what are man's puny sins compared to them?

If to the reader this is just irreverence, we are sorry; it should be scorn and ridicule. Such a story as the Gospels tell is unworthy of man's respect; it is, we repeat, the greatest fraud and hoax ever perpetrated upon mankind. But do not conclude its crucifixion is bad theology; it is the one true part of it. Whatever God creates, he crucifies. Like Odin, he even crucified himself, and this is the crucifixion of Christ.

There is no love or mercy in the creation of a world; it is but a natural process in which the Creative Principle becomes involved in matter; this produces cosmic forms. In due time it rises from matter to produce biologic forms, and this is the next miracle.

The Resurrection

The Resurrection is the supreme miracle but it is Evolution, not Involution, therefore Number 8, or 1 in the evolutionary sense. This represents the dawn or first day in the new dispensation, and such the author makes it.

1. The first day of the week cometh Mary Magdalene early, when it was yet dark, unto the sepulchre, and seeth the stone taken away from the sepulchre (John 20).

Just as the crucifixion and resurrection are identical with the plagues and exodus from Egypt, so is this first day of the week with their first month. "And the Lord spoke unto Moses and Aaron in the land of Egypt, saying, This month shall be unto you the beginning of months; it shall be the first month of the year to you." And so we're not reading anything new here, just a revolutio of Exodus.

Mary Magdalene is the repentant earth after its solar debauch, and still in the darkness of the primeval dawn. The stone she found rolled away from Jesus' tomb is the same stone he rolled away from Lazarus's, namely, dense matter that had held the life force entombed. Here, as in Egypt, this obstruction was rolled away by radiation, the means of escape. Is it any wonder then that no one saw Jesus rise from the grave, or that the means of his escape is still a mystery?

2. Then she runneth, and cometh to Simon Peter, and to the other disciple, whom Jesus loved (namely, light), and saith unto them, They have taken away the Lord (life) out of the sepulchre (earth), and we know not where they have laid him.

4. So they ran both together: and the other disciple did outrun Peter, and came first to the sepulchre (Chap. 20).

Yes, light would outrun stiff old Petra, but he got there eventually. And there they saw the linen clothes but no body, another great mystery, two thousand years old. No preacher can solve it because no preacher knows that this body, Corpus Christi, is but Corpus Mundi, and the "risen" part of the Life Principle has now lost it. Now, and only now, does the involutionary Jesus become the evolutionary Christ, henceforth to sit "at the right hand of God"—Evolution. The disciples did not know this, "for as yet they knew not the Scriptures, that he must rise again from the dead" (John 20:9). Why did they not know the Scriptures? They were pious Jews. Since Jesus declared this repeatedly, human disciples would know, but light and stone would not.

11. But Mary stood without at the sepulchre weeping: and as she wept, she stooped down and looked into the sepulchre,

12. And seeth two angels in white sitting, the one at the head, and the other at the feet, where the body of Jesus had lain.

The two angels are identical with the two thieves, the invo-evolutionary powers, one on either side of the earth, and both are of the nature of light.

13. And they say unto her, Woman, why weepest thou? She saith unto them, Because they have taken away my Lord, and I know not where they have laid him.
14. And when she had thus said, she turned herself back, and saw Jesus standing, and knew not that it was Jesus (Chap. 20).

No, Mary, knowing only the involutionary Jesus, would not know the evolutionary Christ—we said they were different, iso-meric. However, when he spoke to her she did recognize "the creative word."

And now the risen Christ appears unto the elements in Evolu-tion, and "breathed on them and said unto them, Receive ye the Holy Ghost." This is but the Life Principle now clothed in its evolutionary robes. In John 21 it appears to the elements again, this time by the seashore, where Peter, like Adam and Noah and David, was naked. Here Christ asked him if he had caught any fish, and when Peter assured him he hadn't, this Christ said to him:

6. Cast the net on the right side of the ship, and ye shall find. They cast therefore, and now they were not able to draw it for the multitude of fishes.

The ship is the earth, and its right side is the evolutionary side, the right hand of God and of power. But the earth elements were not yet aware of its riches, and so still toiled away on the left or involutionary side—as our preachers are still doing. This was contrary to the onward process, and so the creative law corrected them, after which they reaped an abundance—more scriptural proof that this is the best side. And now Christ dines with them and they greatly wonder that a spiritual being lately risen from the dead should eat as physical men. And so do we, yet occultly this is the first time Christ did eat as other men, organically.

On still another occasion Christ came to the disciples straight through the walls, as he did through the walls of the sepulchre —and these two walls are one, the cosmic ethmos, earth, through which the Life Principle passes. And here our "doubting Thomas" questioned his reality. In the Dark and Middle Ages the doubting Thomases were all tortured to death, but times do change. Today there be some, even among the clergy, who are doubting, but they lack the knowledge to support their doubt. We hope this book will supply it.

And now Christ appears a third time.

14. This is now the third time that Jesus shewed himself to his disciples, after that he was risen from the dead (Chap. 21).

From this verse it is evident the Gospel writers did not realize the distinction between Jesus and Christ, for it was not Jesus who showed himself here but the evolutionary Christ.

These three showings are the three organic kingdoms. And here Christ tells Peter three times to feed his sheep—the life of these three, for without Peter, earth and water, they die.

Christ's exit from the tomb is identical with the Exodus from Egypt, and the forty days he remained on earth is the same as the forty years in the wilderness. Both represent the four material planes thus far developed; beyond these life will eventually rise, that is, make its ascension to the fifth, sixth and seventh, and so to complete the picture, Christ goes up out of sight, as did Elijah, Mithra, Hercules and Romulus. He went up to heaven from Jerusalem; had he gone up twelve hours later he would have gone in the opposite direction. Where then is Heaven?

The ascension of Christ is a very important part of Christian doctrine; it implies immortality, triumph over death, a heaven world beyond, and a possible Second Coming. Why then did Matthew and John ignore it? Luke mentions it only in one little verse of nineteen words, a sort of postscript not found in some manuscripts. And someone added to Mark a mere reference to it with the telltale little sign ¶. Is this vital event then a later interpolation, or just part of the hoax the others forgot to include?

Absurd as it is, it is not enough. We are asked to believe his mother also ascended. This is the Assumption, Mary ascending and assuming her place as "Queen of Heaven." Mary is matter and it too ascends, aurically.

This Assumption is also cosmological. In the Zodiac of Constellations it begins with Virgo, the life force's ascension from matter. In the lesser Zodiac it is annually enacted. As the sun, passing through the various signs, enters Virgo, its brilliant rays obscure the sign and Virgo disappears. In the Christian myth this is considered Mary's reunion with her son, actually sun, August 15. In about three weeks the sun passes on and Virgo reappears, about September 8, said to be Mary's birthday. As with everything else this Assumption is in no sense peculiar to Christian mythology. All the pagan earth-mothers were taken up to heaven by their divine sons, there to reign as "the Mother of God," "the Queen of Heaven," and so on. Alcmene, the mother of Hercules, ascended and became the Queen of Heaven. Semele was taken up by her son Bacchus, called "the Son of God," to reign as Queen of the Universe, and at her name "trembled all the demons." Pallas Athena was called "the one Mother of God." and also Queen of Heaven. Some six hundred years before the time of Mary, Jews in Egypt were worshiping a Queen of Heaven. In Jeremiah this term is used four times in reference to her. Jeremiah does not tell us her name; it was, however, Malaket, and like all the rest she heard prayers and interceded for those who sought her help. In Babylon it was Ishtar, also called "the Queen of Heaven." A prayer to her reads as follows:

To the Lady of Heaven and Earth, who receives prayers, who harkens
   to the petitions, who accepts beseechings;
To the merciful goddess who loves righteousness;
Look upon me O Lady, so that through thy turning toward me the
   heart of thy servant may become strong.

And how does this differ from the prayers of the Catholics to their "Lady of Heaven"? In their "Hail Marys" they little realize they are but repeating ancient customs they now condemn as superstitions.

Prior to the ascension Christ commanded his disciples to "tarry in the city of Jerusalem (earth) until ye be endued with power from on high." This they did, and on the fiftieth day (Pentecost) the power came upon them and they spoke with divers tongues, as at Babel. And why not since this is the same Babel, namely earth. The disciples are the elements within it. Thus entombed they must tarry until they receive power from on high, namely, the sun, after which they will differentiate into many forms and speak many tongues. This help from on high is the Comforter, and the Paraclete—*para*, besides or additional, and *kaleo*, call. In dealing with this same matter we said that when a sun became a planet, it wandered alone in frigid space until *called* by another sun to enter a solar system; here it is comforted with light and heat from an external source.

In reading the New Testament we must cease to think of the man Jesus, and even of "the Son of God," and think rather of the sun of God, for this is a solar myth, and its dying hero, a dying sun. In this the Life Principle is crucified on the cross of matter and later ascends from it. This is the ascension of Christ.

This whole story on which our religion is based is but a drama of Creation, Jesus the star thereof, more ways than one, and the disciples, the supporting cast. Thus those who make a drama of it, "The Passion Play," "The Nativity," etc., are but dramatizing a drama. As practically all of it is involutionary and its action that of gods, not men, the dogmas based upon it are humanly ridiculous.

And so we must face Paul's conclusion: "If Christ be not risen, then is our preaching vain, and our faith is vain also." Well, literally, it is, but instead of realizing it our teachers but repeat Paul two thousand years later: "Deny or doubt the Divinity of Christ and the whole structure of the Christian plan comes tumbling down as a shattered jigsaw puzzle." [2] Actually it was

[2] Rev. M. O'Connor, in *Modern Indifference and Theological Science*.

never anything else. That it has endured so long is no proof of its validity, but only of Western man's metaphysical inadequacy. He lacks the metaphysical knowledge and perception to see its cosmological basis. This is why those who have only denial and ridicule to fight it have failed; it takes knowledge to shatter this jigsaw puzzle. We have not denied or ridiculed but merely explained it away. And that is the end of all religions; as F. N. Morley said: "All religions die of one disease, that of being found out." Yes, but "when in the course of human events," one is found out, a crafty priesthood resurrects this ancient myth and builds another upon it. Sixteen times this Savior myth has risen thus to deceive the race; let us now, henceforth and forever, recognize it for what it is, a myth and nothing more. Its miracles are the miracles of Creation and nothing more. Do you see then the hoax that has been played on you?

Recently I heard a religious group discussing this and one of them said if ever space travel became a possibility they would carry the Gospel message to the other planets—some of which may be billions of years in advance of us. What would the beings there think of it? Would they not be surprised to learn the mother of their Creator was a Jewish girl by the name of Mary, and that their world was created by her Son saying Let it be? No, if ever we go visiting cosmically we had better leave our provincialisms at home.

Since this was written cosmic visiting is underway. Men can now go to the moon, and yet believe in Genesic Creation; they can transplant hearts but only "with the help of God," as one stated. Can we not see that this is but our way of thinking, and that the beings on other worlds never heard of this God, His mother, or His word-of-mouth creation?

22

Revelation, Part I

Even if I do not understand, I yet conceive some
deeper sense to lie in the words. Not measuring and
judging these things by private reasoning but giving
the chief right to faith, I have supposed it to be too
high to be comprehended by me.

ST. DIONYSIUS, ON REVELATION.

This is Western man trying to understand
occult cosmology without the key to Causation.

This so-called Revelation of St. John has ever been a mystery,
"too high to be comprehended" even by the other saints. It need
not be henceforth because our theory explains it completely.
But before explaining it, we would like to make two assertions
about it: it is not a revelation, and it should not be taken too
seriously.

The book is but Creation and Evolution apocalyptically, that
is, occultly, written. As these were known to all the ancients,
John required no revelation to acquaint him with them. He had
learned about them from others and but embellished them, like
Ezekiel, to give his writing power and authority. Its symbology
is common to all Creation myths; its repeated use of the number
7 can have no other significance: 7 angels, 7 horns, 7 stars and
7 seals, 7 vials, 7 plagues and 7 candlesticks, 7 churches and 7
letters addressed to them, 7 spirits before the throne, and a beast
with 7 heads. In Ezekiel 4 we find the same, identical symbols;
John, in fact, is but the Ezekiel of the New Testament. Like his
prototype, he sees the gates of heaven open, a throne therein,

and 7 lamps that are "the spirits of God"—the 7 planes and elements. Like Ezekiel, he sees four beasts, this time with wings instead of rings. Like Ezekiel he sees dead bodies lying in the street (earth), which after three and a half days rise and walk again—the life-force dead in matter, which after the first half of Devolution is alive again in Evolution. Like Ezekiel, he eats a little book, the book of life, which in its cosmic sense is Involution written on the inside, and Evolution on the backside; the one paradisical, the other purgatorial. In its human sense, it is existence, sweet in contemplation but sour in experience. All this realized, we know of nothing in all literature that needs *debunking* more than this so-called revelation.

It is not to be taken seriously, that is religiously, because it is not what it is alleged to be—a vision of the awful majesty of God, his retribution upon wicked humanity, his promise of a new heaven and a new earth, the posthumous existence of Christ, and his preeminence in heaven. This is no part of Reality; it is but priestly "stage props." So again, we know of nothing so deserving of the phrase, "Much ado about nothing," spiritually. Stripped of its nonsense, it is but the creative process, the many visions, but different aspects of this, thrown together without logic or sequence, either by the author because he did not know the sequence, or by subsequent redactors who desired to hide its true meaning.

The book opens with the 7 letters to the 7 churches, but as this is more apropos of subsequent "mysteries," we will leave it with a promise of a surprise when later we return to it. Here we will begin with Chapter 4. As the book is much too long to deal with verse by verse, we will comment only on what is most relevant.

1. After this I looked, and, behold, a door was opened in heaven: and the first voice which I heard was as it were of a trumpet talking with me; which said, Come up hither, and I will shew thee things which must be hereafter.

2. And immediately I was in the spirit: and, behold, a throne was set in heaven, and one sat on the throne.

3. And he that sat was to look upon like a jasper and a sardine stone:

and there was a rainbow round about the throne, in sight like unto an emerald.

After learning about revelators from Ezekiel, we should know what this is—ecclesiastical deception. There are no revelators, no prophets, and no prophecies in the scriptures; there are only cunning priests religionizing cosmology. There was no door opened in heaven, and there was no voice as of a trumpet; there was only pagan imagery and symbolism. The throne is the earth itself, set up in that heaven called space; the rainbow round about it is its cosmogonical trajectory as represented by the zodiac. The precious stones are but lapidarian symbols thereof, as of the Jews. The jasper, emerald and sardine (sardonyx) stones are the gem symbols of Pisces, Gemini, and Cancer. See p. 375.

5. And out of the throne proceeded lightlings and thunderings and voices: and there were seven lamps of fire burning before the throne, which are the seven Spirits of God.

The "seven Spirits of God" are the seven plane forces in Involution, and their thunder and lightning represent their violence.

6. And before the throne was a sea of glass like unto crystal: and in the midst of the throne, and round about the throne, were four beasts full of eyes before and behind.
7. And the first beast was like a lion, and the second beast like a calf, and the third beast had a face as a man, and the fourth beast was like a flying eagle.

The same old four—Leo, Taurus, Aquarius and Scorpio, the complete invo-evolutionary cycle as in the zodiac.

8. And the four beasts had each of them six wings about him (north, south, east, west and up and down); and they were full of eyes within (symbols of intelligence): and they rest not day and night, saying, Holy, holy, holy, Lord God Almighty, which was, and is, and is to come (Chap. 4).

Why is it we mortals assume the unknown part of Reality is "holy"? There's nothing holy about its creations—a flaming sun, insensate earth and savage nature. Causation is to be respected only because it is cause; without it there would be nothing. This is the scriptural meaning of both holy and sacred. What "was, and is, and is to come" is this Cause in its three stages, Involution, Earth and Evolution, thus one with the Sphinx. It is not "almighty" but only adequate for its purpose. And how could its unconscious forces say anything? This is allegory and nothing more.

1. And I saw in the right hand of him that sat on the throne a book written within and on the backside, sealed with seven seals (Chap. 5).

The throne is the planetary entity, and the book, "the book of life." What was written on the inside is Involution, and on the backside, Evolution; the one, sweet to the gods who cannot feel, and bitter to man who can. This part of the revelation is not from God but from Ezekiel, who got it from the Babylonians, the Assyrians and the Sumerians. The seven seals are identical with the seven decrees of Ishtar and Innana.

2. And I saw a strong angel proclaiming with a loud voice, Who is worthy to open the book and to loose the seals thereof?
3. And no man in heaven, nor in earth, neither under the earth, was able to open the book, neither to look thereon.
4. And I wept much, because no man was found worthy to open and to read the book, neither to look thereon.
5. And one of the elders saith unto me, Weep not: behold, the Lion of the tribe of Juda, the Root of David, hath prevailed to open the book, and to loose the seven seals thereof.

Here begins the propaganda for the faith. The implication is that the opener of this book is the Christ of the Christian religion. Well, it is if you know what Christ is, but those who think it is the man of Galilee have much to learn. The opener of this book is the Creative Principle. This alone closed it at the end

of Involution, and this alone can open it in Evolution. The Lion
of the tribe of Judah is the zodiacal Lion, Leo the sun. It is this
that wakens Life asleep in matter, and thus opens Evolution,
here called the "backside" of the book of life. The seven seals
are the laws of the seven planes, and the seven angels, the powers thereof. As each plane is opened its power prevails for a time,
then passes to the next. This is knowledgeable henotheism as
opposed to monotheism, the perfect concept for commercialists
so absorbed in their material things they do not care to learn
the *modus operandi*. The "seven spirits before the throne" are but
symbols of the septenate Creator, alias God, a generic term for
Reality, without knowledge of it. Knowledge here of the purely
cosmogonical nature of this Christ, Lion, Judah and David will
help the reader understand these things when later we deal with
them.

7. And he came and took the book out of the hand of him that sat
upon the throne.

This is Evolution taking the book of life out of the hands of
Involution, power having passed from the one to the other. This
is the subject of half the Pentateuch.

8. And when he had taken the book, the four beasts (cardinal powers) and four and twenty elders (consciousness and energy of the
twelve zodiacal cycles) fell down before the Lamb (Aries, the genetic
principle), having every one of them harps, and golden vials full of
odours, which are the prayers of the saints.

Here we see the purely symbolic nature of this book. The
odors are not odors but prayers of the saints, and the saints are
not saints but creative forces.

9. And they sung a new song, saying, Thou art worthy to take the
book, and to open the seals thereof: for thou wast slain, and hast
redeemed us to God by thy blood out of every kindred, and tongue,
and people, and nation.

The slain here is the Creative Principle symbolized as Aries,
the Ram. This is "the lamb, slain from the foundation of the

world," that is, its beginning. On the 7th plane it became "dead matter," until redeemed, raised up again in Evolution.

10. And has made us unto our God kings and priests: and we shall reign on the earth.

The Life Principle freed from matter now reigns on the earth. The "we" and "us" are not human beings but this principle personified and euhemerized. It is only with this the myths and scriptures deal. Therefore to understand them we must learn a new language, a sort of *cosmolingua*, or language of the cosmos. This was the Esperanto of antiquity. To hear a sermon in any other language is a painful experience; it reveals so clearly the cause of our present conditions. The cause of all man's troubles can be reduced to just one word—ignorance. It is this that's running our world, not wisdom.

And what better example of this could we have than our present understanding of the next chapter "The Four Horsemen of the Apocalypse"? No doubt you have heard sermons based on these dread horsemen, all in terms of man, his sin, and a *loving* God's wrath and vengeance. Myth and scripture, however, deal not with such things.

1. And I saw when the Lamb opened one of the seals, and I heard, as it were the noise of thunder, one of the four beasts saying, Come and see.

2. And I saw, and behold a white horse: and he that sat on him had a bow; and a crown was given unto him: and he went forth conquering, and to conquer.

3. And when he had opened the second seal, I heard the second beast say, Come and see.

4. And there went out another horse that was red: and power was given to him that sat thereon to take peace from the earth, and that they should kill one another: and there was given unto him a great sword.

5. And when he had opened the third seal, I heard the third beast say, Come and see. And I beheld, and lo a black horse; and he that sat on him had a pair of balances in his hand.

6. And I heard a voice in the midst of the four beasts say, A measure of wheat for a penny, and three measures of barley for a penny; and see thou hurt not the oil and the wine.

7. And when he had opened the fourth seal, I heard the voice of the fourth beast say, Come and see.

8. And I looked, and behold a pale horse: and his name that sat on him was Death, and Hell followed with him. And power was given unto them over the fourth part of the earth, to kill with sword, and with hunger, and with death, and with the beasts of the earth (Chap. 6).

The four talking beasts are again the four presiding powers of the zodiac, but the horsemen are something new. They represent the four lower planes in Evolution. As in Sagittarius, the horse symbolizes the dynamic but uncontrolled genetic force. This realized, what should we expect of it but war and conflict? This we asserted throughout and we said the Gospels affirmed it. There is no peace for us on these four planes; to attain it, we must acquire the wisdom of the White Horse of the Kalki Avatar, namely, fifth-plane consciousness. As all this was priestly knowledge two thousand years ago, it was carefully kept from the masses. To this end the horsemen and their symbols were intentionally transposed and confused. This we assert without apology, for we have found it again and again in other parts of the Bible.

The first horse is not number 1; it is number 3, black and with a balance. This is the black earth, symbolic of the darkness of matter; in plain words, the mineral kingdom. Its zodiacal symbol is the balance, as we made it, and according to St. John, rightly so. The second horse is number 4, a pale horse, "and his name that sat on him was Death, and Hell followed with him." This is Virgo, as we made it, the pale, etheric energy of the plant kingdom. As this is the beginning of biologic life, it is also the beginning of death. The reference to the wheat and oil belongs here rather than to verse 6; Virgo still carries a sheaf of wheat. The third horse is number 2, a red horse, "and power was given him who sat thereon to take peace from the earth, and that they should kill one another, and there was given unto him a great

sword." This is Scorpio, the killer, the astral element whose
awakening in the animal kingdom initiated "the struggle for
existence," warfare and carnage. Number 4 is number 1, a white
horse whose rider, bearing a bow and crown, "went forth conquering and to conquer." This is Sagittarius, the archer whose
task is to conquer the energies of the planes below. The white
horse is that White Horse of the Avatar whose wisdom will
bring peace to both man and savage nature. On the lower half
of his kingdom he too is a killer, conquering by violence as
today, but his future conquering will not be of energy over
energy, but of consciousness over energy. This fourth plane is
the *human* Armageddon on which is fought the battle of *human*
spirit over matter. Until this is won, the powers of these four
planes will make hell of a fourth part of the planetary whole,
the lower right-hand quadrant, as stated in verse 8.

And now that these four are past, in Evolution, we come to
the fifth, wherein the battle has been won.

9. And when he had opened the fifth seal (plane), I saw under the
altar the souls of them that were slain for the word of God, and for
the testimony which they held:

11. And white robes were given unto every one of them; and it was
said unto them, that they should rest yet for a little season (cycle), until
their fellowservants also and their brethren (not people but forces),
that should be killed as they were, should be fulfilled.

In Chapter 7 the thought is carried further:

13. And one of the elders answered, saying unto me, What are these
which are arrayed in white robes? and whence came they?

14. And I said unto him, Sir, thou knowest. And he said to me, They
are they which came out of great tribulation (the lower planes), and
have washed their robes, and made them white in the blood of the
Lamb.

15. Therefore are they before the throne of God, and serve him day
and night in his temple (the earth): and he that sitteth on the throne
shall dwell among them.

16. They shall hunger no more, neither thirst any more; neither shall the sun light on them, nor any heat.

17. For the Lamb which is in the midst of the throne shall feed them, and shall lead them unto living fountains of waters: and God shall wipe away all tears from their eyes.

These are not human souls martyred for the faith, as we are led to believe, but the World Soul on this nonmaterial plane. They were not slain for "the word of God," religiously, but for "the will of God," planetarily. On these high planes life's struggle with matter is over; therefore there will be no tears as of now. The white robes signify the purified planetary aura; had it any literal and personal meaning it would be but a human correlate—the human aura freed from the dark colors of the physical. In speculating on Venus we said the forms there might not be physical but astral, and in time and placement Venusian life may be on even the seventh plane. And we, the killers, would go there!

The Lamb and the God part in this cosmic process is but priestcraft using cosmology to establish Christianity.

12. And I beheld when he had opened the sixth seal, and, lo, there was a great earthquake; and the sun became black as sackcloth of hair, and the moon became as blood;

14. And the heavens departed as a scroll when it is rolled together; and every mountain and island were moved out of their places (Chap. 6).

As the sixth plane is beyond the material world, that world no longer matters for the life upon it. Counting from Leo, the maker of matter, this sixth plane corresponds to Capricorn, and as Blavatsky said, "Capricorn is connected with the birth of the spiritual microcosm and with the death of the physical universe," [1] for us, the world. This is also "the gateway into life of those who know not death." If the body here is no longer physi-

[1] *The Secret Doctrine*, vol. 2, p. 612.

cal, then it knows not physical death. Here also the heavens (planes) are beginning to roll up as they rolled down, a purely natural process, and a matter of trillions of years hence. Why then terrify present humanity with it? At that far distant day the present suns will have become planets, and this is the meaning of verse 13, "the stars of heaven fell unto the earth," more correctly, became earths.

15. And the kings of the earth, and the great men, and the rich men, and the chief captains, and the mighty men, and every bondman, and every free man, hid themselves in the dens and in the rocks of the mountains;

16. And said to the mountains and rocks, Fall on us, and hide us from the face of him that sitteth on the throne, and from the wrath of the Lamb:

17. For the great day of his wrath is come; and who shall be able to stand? (Chap. 6).

And this is called wisdom, "divine revelation," and the like. I say it is priestcraft using cosmology to frighten the ignorant into submission to it; its wild imagery, but intellectual terrorism used to gain power. Today no one should give it a moment's serious thought, that is religiously.

But to complete the story: The first two verses that follow are from chapter 8, the last three, from chapter 10. The reader may say this is tampering with text to prove our theory but no, these bits and pieces were deliberately scattered about to conceal and deceive. We are but putting them back *in their proper place*. And this is not the only case where this must be done.

1. And when he had opened the seventh seal, there was silence in heaven about the space of half an hour.

2. And I saw the seven angels which stood before God; and to them were given seven trumpets.

5. And the angel which I saw stand upon the sea and upon the earth lifted up his hand to heaven,

6. And sware by him that liveth for ever . . . that there should be time no longer:

7. But in the days of the voice of the seventh angel, when he shall

begin to sound (future), the mystery of God should be finished, as he hath declared to his servants the prophets.

The seventh seal represents the seventh and final plane in Evolution, and as time is concomitant with matter, there shall "be time no longer." Here Evolution is at an end, the work is finished, and all is well. And so said Job: "in seven no evil shall touch thee" 5:19. And such is the mystery of God—Creation and its sequel. Such also is the mystery of Revelation, not a vision of heaven but a review of time, not a revelation from God but a plagiarized account of Evolution. And how does it differ from ours save in language? We too said there were seven planes and seven cycles; we too said their manifestation was sequential and henotheistic. We also said our theory was "gospel truth," but unlike Ezekiel and John we did not take it from older sources and say we got it in a vision. We thought it out—and long before we perceived it in the ancient archives. That is why we can interpret them. As Emerson said of traveling, so with occult literature: we see in things only what we take with us, already know. This is also why the race cannot see cosmology in the scriptures; it does not know cosmology, nor has it the means of seeing it. The criterion of truth is the amount of truth we have in ourselves, so the amount and kind of truth we see in the scriptures depends on the amount and kind we have ourselves.

The other septenary visions—the seven plagues, the seven vials of wrath, etc., are like the first, so again we will leave them to the reader. In chapter 11, however, there is a reference that we should understand; it pertains to the Gentiles, non-Jewish scum.

1. And there was given me a reed like unto a rod: and the angel stood, saying, Rise, and measure the temple of God, and the altar, and them that worship therein.

2. But the court which is without the temple leave out, and measure it not; for it is given unto the Gentiles: and the holy city shall they tread under foot forty and two months.

3. And I will give power unto my two witnesses (genetic consciousness and energy) and they shall prophesy (bring about) a thousand two hundred and threescore days . . .

The "temple of God" is the planetary entity. This is that "temple not made with hands, eternal in the heavens," space. The outer court given over to the Gentiles is the lower material part. In Revelation and the Old Testament the Gentiles represent the material and subversive forces that oppose the spiritual, God and the Jews—a good example of national pride and racial conceit. In the synoptic gospels, however, the order is reversed; there it is the Jews who are the opposers; mythically they are even made the crucifiers of the spirit, Christ. This distinction should be kept in mind when reading the Bible as a whole.

The outer court is not to be measured because it is no part of the spiritual kingdom (consciousness); indeed, its destiny is but a cosmic corpse, a lifeless moon. The "thousand two hundred and threescore days," or 1,260, are the same as the "forty and two months," both but numerical symbols of the planes and periods the material dominates, namely, the four lower kingdoms and cycles.

And this "temple of God" had "a wall great and high (its "ring-pass-not") and twelve gates (zodiacal divisions), and at the gates, twelve angels (powers), and names written thereon (Pisces, Aries, Taurus, and others) which are the names of the twelve tribes of Israel," esoterically. "On the east three gates, on the north three gates, on the south three gates, and on the west three gates" (Rev. 21:13). These are the four divisions of three signs each we found in the zodiac, also in Ezekiel 48:35. And in the midst thereof, the very center in fact, there was a city, the earth, "and the name of the city from that day shall be, the Lord is there." We too said the Lord is there, the creative principle in matter, earth. It may have sounded shocking then, but you see it is "God's word."

16. And the city lieth foursquare, and the length is as large as the breadth: . . . The length and the breadth and the height of it are equal (because it is a globe).

17. And he measured the wall thereof, a hundred and forty and four cubits, according to the measure of a man, that is, of the angel.

The angel is the creative power and this and Man, capital *m*, are one. The number of cubits in the wall is the same as those who are saved, namely, 144. This and the number of the beast, 666, the number of the "woman clothed with the sun," 1,260, and even Adam, spelt in Hebrew *Adm*, are numerically the same. And all are the earth entity. And it is this drab entity that St. John describes so glowingly:

18. And the building of the wall of it was of jasper: and the city was pure gold, like unto clear glass.

19. And the foundations of the wall of the city were garnished with all manner of precious stones. The first foundation was jasper; the second, sapphire; the third, a chalcedony; the fourth, an emerald;

20. The fifth, sardonyx; the six, sardius; the seventh, chrysolite; the eighth, beryl; the ninth, a topaz; the tenth, a chrysoprasus; the eleventh, a jacinth; the twelfth, an amethyst.

The twelve zodiacal divisions with their birthstone symbology are shown in the list below.

Jewish gem symbology based on the lesser zodiac is as follows:

Jasper	March	Chrysolite	September
Sapphire	April	Beryl	October
Chalcedony	May	Topaz	November
Emerald	June	Ruby	December
Onyx	July	Garnet	January
Carnelian	August	Amethyst	February

This is "the Holy City" on which we base our faith in a heaven hereafter. If it isn't a hoax what is it? As an ideal, it is but a dream of the Zodiacal Night; now that that is passing we must wake and buckle down to the task of building this city on earth.

21. And the twelve gates were twelve pearls; every several gate was of one pearl: and the street of the city was pure gold, as it were transparent glass.

And this is our "pearly gates" and "streets of gold"! This is the city this saintly humbug saw "coming down from God out of heaven, prepared as a bride adorned for her husband"—grandiloquent symbology of this old world in its radiant sun period. Yet on such bases religions are founded. Such is the power of words, particularly on fear and ignorance. Indeed, so powerful are they, anyone with sufficient command of them can rule the world. This was the priests' original objective.

Instead of visions of God and his holy city, Revelation is but the ancient Gnosis of the pagan mystics whom the Christian Fathers with inhuman cruelty exterminated. But this so-called saint, actually gnostic, was too smart for them; he wrote their "hated doctrine" up in such a way as to make them accept it as a cornerstone in their temple of lies. And there for two thousand years they have bowed in reverent awe before the thing they hated most.

And now that we know what we are reading let us look at some of the other "visions." These again are but aspects of the planetary process, some pertaining to Involution, some to Evolution. Such is chapter 12.

1. And there appeared a great wonder in heaven (space); a woman clothed with the sun and the moon under her feet, and upon her head a crown of twelve stars.

2. And she being with child cried, travailing in birth, and pained to be delivered.

3. And there appeared another wonder in heaven; and behold a great red dragon having seven heads and ten horns, and seven crowns upon his heads.

4. And his tail drew the third part of the stars of heaven, and did cast them to the earth: and the dragon stood before the woman which was ready to be delivered, for to devour her child as soon as it was born.

5. And she brought forth a man child, who was to rule all nations with a rod of iron; and her child was caught up unto God, and to his throne.

6. And the woman fled into the wilderness, where she had a place prepared of God, that they should feed her there a thousand two hundred and threescore days (1,260 or forty and two months).

The woman, symbol of matter, is not only "clothed with the sun," she is the sun, the great Earth Mother of all mythologies; she is Isis, Innana and Ishtar. Here in this sun period is conceived and carried the nascent earth itself, with the moon under its feet as we made it. This is the child the great dragon Typhon, symbol of violence, would destroy. Had it anything to do with the Christ of religion, how equate his fantastic origin here with that of the Gospels? Typhon is the violent, turbulent forces that eventually destroyed the free energies of the sun but not the earth within it. This is saved and carried up by way of Evolution to "the throne of God," the metaphysical planes as in the first vision. In the Greek myth, Typhon is called Python, offspring of the Earth Mother Gaea. This was the slimy monster Apollo, the sun, beheld as the Deluge subsided. Thus it and the son are one, namely earth.

The time the woman remained in the wilderness is identical with the measurement of "the holy city," also earth. This wilderness of both the Old and New Testament is the four lower material planes. The stars that fell from heaven certainly were not the visible stars but the invisible ones finally dragged down to earth, matter. In our theory we assumed there are many in the invisible stage; John seems to have had the same idea.

There is nothing new in this story, rather myth. Cronus sought to destroy Jupiter, but the "holy" child was saved by being wrapped up in rags, matter, and cared for by Amalthea in the hills, wilderness. According to another myth, Dioné, the mother of Apollo, when pursued by Python, fled into the wilderness. In still another, Eurydice was chased into the woods by Aristaeus, god of herdsmen, and there killed by the sting of the serpent, matter. In Egypt it was Isis, fleeing with her "divine son" Horus, when pursued by Typhon. And let us not forget Mary fleeing with *her* "divine son" into Egypt when threatened by Herod. That this too is a myth is also revealed in Revelation. In 11:8 John says: ". . . the great city, which spiritually is called Sodom and Egypt, where also our Lord was crucified." Now, we repeat, our Lord was not crucified in Egypt unless it is synonymous with the earth. And if it is, then that's where Mary went.

7. And there was war in heaven: Michael and his angels fought against the dragon; and the dragon fought and his angels,

8. And prevailed not; neither was their place found any more in heaven (Chap. 12).

Here we see where war began—in heaven. This one is the war of Creation, very different from the peaceful process of the Priestly Account. Michael is but one of the "beasts" of Ezekiel, the primary creative power, and his angels are the *kirubs* (cherubs), creative aspects. The dragon and his angels are the violent energy principle. Here John is telling us the truth—there is nothing but war in God's creation. And now this heavenly war is earthly war and human war. The preventive force is not God but man. He alone can stop the dragon and his warfare. Fortunately he is now dimly aware of it.

9. And the great dragon was cast out, and that old serpent, called the Devil, and Satan, which deceiveth the whole world; he was cast out into the earth (became earth), and his angels were cast out with him.

Here we see the natural and impersonal nature of these so-called beings, now religious superstitions. They are not *beings* nor are they opposers of the Creator; they are but the energy, ultimately material part of the Creator, and coworker with him.

10. And I heard a loud voice saying in heaven, Now is come salvation, and strength, and the kingdom of our God, and the power of his Christ: for the accuser of our brethren is cast down, which accused them before our God day and night (Chap. 12).

If this be literally true, it is strange business to be going on in the heaven of religion. If the Devil is so evil, what was he doing there in the first place? And if God is so "holy, holy," why did he allow this evil one to accuse the brethren "day and night"? And who are the brethren, since this is Creation not Evolution? This is personified cosmogony, and its "war in heaven" is as old as the first mythologist. Among the Romans, Lucifer rebelled and was cast down to the bottomless pit called Orcus, earth. The Titans of Greece made war upon Zeus and for their impiety were hurled down to Tartarus, a place lower than Hades the sun, hence also the earth. In India, Maha-sura (great spirit), envying Brahma his glory, led a legion of rebellious spirits against him, but Siva cast them down into Honderah, the place of darkness. In Persia, Tiamat, the adversary, fought with Sosiosh, the Creator, who, overcoming her, formed the earth from her body. Here in "the bottomless pit" called matter these warring elements were bound for a "thousand years," merely an indefinite period, until loosed again through radiation. This we dealt with in another section. We also dealt with something else that now appears in Revelation 9:

1. And the fifth angel sounded, and I saw a star fall from heaven unto the earth: and to him was given the key of the bottomless pit.

2. And he opened the bottomless pit; and there arose a smoke out of the pit, as the smoke of a great furnace; and the sun and the air were darkened by reason of the smoke of the pit.

11. And they had a king over them, which is the angel of the bottomless pit, whose name in the Hebrew tongue is Abaddon, but in the Greek tongue hath his name Apollyon. (And Apollyon is Apollo, the sun, now dead.)

Here, as we said, it wanders about in space, hence a planet—wanderer—a cosmic bomb, asmoke and deadly. This is the "bottomless pit"—matter here going through its congealing and cooling process, and so we read chapter 20:

1. And I saw an angel come down from heaven, having the key of the bottomless pit and a great chain in his hand (Medusa, the congealing force).

2. And he laid hold on the dragon, that old serpent, which is the Devil, and Satan, and bound him a thousand years (Prometheus Bound).

7. And when the thousand years are expired, Satan shall be loosed out of his prison (Prometheus freed).

To start another war—this time biologic. This and the pale horseman are one—"and Hell followed with him."

8. And shall go out to deceive the nations (planes) which are in the four quarters of the earth, Gog and Magog, to gather them (the creative forces) together to battle: the number of which is as the sand of the sea.

This is Evolution but the last word has not been said about Involution, and so in chapter 16 we come to another great mystery, Armageddon. Here we will see how meaningless it is for us.

16. And he gathered them together into a place called in the Hebrew tongue Armageddon.
17. And the seventh angel poured out his vial into the air; and there came a great voice out of the temple of heaven, from the throne, saying, It is done.
18. And the great city was divided into three parts, and the cities of the nations fell: and great Babylon came in remembrance before God, to give unto her the cup of the wine of the fierceness of his wrath.

The "seventh angel" is the power of the seventh involutionary plane—the sun-earth stage, symbolized by the city Babylon. The warfare is that between the spiritual and material forces. In this the material wins. Here the creative process ends and so the voice from heaven says, "It is done." And elsewhere, "It is finished." After this the earth is divided into three parts, Involution, Devolution and Evolution.

1. And I saw a new heaven and a new earth (Evolution): for the first heaven and the first earth (Involution) were passed away; and there was no more sea (the prephysical elements; Chap. 21).

And we said these no longer existed when the physical was formed. We also said that this newborn world was no Garden of Eden, and John agrees. He calls it a seven-headed beast on which sits a whore, clothed in jewels and fine raiment; none other than the "woman clothed with the sun," now material and evil.

4. And the woman (the Earth Mother) was arrayed in purple and scarlet colour, and decked with gold and precious stones and pearls, having a golden cup in her hand full of abominations and filthiness of her fornication (symbols of materiality; Chap. 17).

This scriptural harlot is decked out just like the "holy city," and in verse 18 we find she is that city. "And the woman which thou sawest is that great city which reigneth over the kings of the earth." Not kings, but kingdoms.

5. And upon her forehead was a name written, MYSTERY, BABY-LON THE GREAT, THE MOTHER OF HARLOTS AND ABOMINATIONS OF THE EARTH. (Babylon, like Egypt, is a mythic symbol of the earth.)

6. And I saw the woman drunken with the blood of the saints, and with the blood of the martyrs of Jesus: and when I saw her, I wondered with great admiration (Chap. 17).

The earth is drenched with blood, not just of martyred saints, but of martyred life. This is "the will of God," but because of a false theology no man dares say so.

7. And the angel said unto me, wherefore didst thou marvel? I will tell thee the mystery of the woman, and of the beast that carrieth her, which hath the seven heads and ten horns.

8. The beast that thou sawest was, and is not; and shall ascend out of the bottomless pit, and go into perdition: and they that dwell on the earth shall wonder, whose names were not written in the book of life from the foundation of the world, when they behold the beast that was, and is not, and yet is (Chap. 17).

Such an explanation does not explain; it only compounds the mystery. But this is as it was meant to be. It is the language of one who knew but wished to conceal the true meaning, namely, creation. It is, we repeat, priestcraft using this to found a religion. And so its foundation is dragged in—Jesus. And what had he to do with Creation unless he too is a symbol?

The beast that was is the sun-stage of this earth; this is Involution and therefore "is not" today; and yet it is, because it is now the earth itself. Theoretically, the seven planes are now evolutionary.

9. And here is the mind which hath wisdom. The seven heads are seven mountains on which the woman sitteth.

11. And the beast that was, and is not, even he is the eighth, and is of the seven, and goeth into perdition (Chap. 17).

The eighth stage of this cosmic beast, the earth, is a moon and we too said it would go into perdition—dissolution. All material elements will someday be destroyed, radiated away, and this is the destruction of the Great Babylon, earth, scripturally called a whore. This is what "the word of God" calls the work of God.

Here follows an account of her wealth in silver and gold, precious stones and fine raiment, the merchants' fornication with her, and their consternation at her fall. All symbolic language but it has its human correlate—the commercialist, his absorption in matter and obsession with material things. He has read this many times but he has never seen in it a warning; in fact, as far as he is concerned, the wise of all the ages may as well have never lived. And so he goes on his way plundering and despoiling. His one objective is financial profit and in the interest thereof he has poisoned the air, the water and turned the soil into a dust bowl. Were he allowed to continue he would render the planet uninhabitable. He hasn't intelligence enough to correct his own false mental trends and so nature must. For this purpose she instituted the law of cycles. Under this we change whether we like it or not. This is what is happening now—Pisces to Aquarius, but never having been taught the wisdom-knowledge we don't even know what's taking place. Thus we are but blind actors in a play we do not understand.

In this commercialistic age man, generic, is but economic man, and from every moral and spiritual standpoint economic man is a fool—in the sense of unwise. He does not know what he is doing, to himself or his world. Apparently he has never heard of what in occult circles is called "the dweller on the threshold"—the malevolent product of primeval savagery, now his subconscious. This can be aroused and is being aroused in his daily practice. With a few more decades of this practice he will breed a generation of monsters. There is no such thing, in our age, as physical lycanthropy, but there is such a thing as psychic lycanthropy—moral man into amoral beast, and we are producing him. He is walking our streets and invading our homes, a creature that would kill for the price of a meal. So to all the ologies economic man must study to be a good business-man, he should add teratology, the study of monstrosities, also

theronistics—the creation and maintenance of monsters. Fortunately his age and dominance are passing, from commercial
theronistics to social therapeutics.

It is of these things and their cause the Revelator is now
speaking.

1. And I stood upon the sand of the sea, and saw a beast rise up out
of the sea (cosmic), having seven heads (planes) . . . and upon his heads
the name of blasphemy.

2. And the beast which I saw was like unto a leopard, and his feet
were as the feet of a bear, and his mouth as the mouth of a lion: and
the dragon (energy) gave him his power, and his seat, and great authority (Chap. 13).

In an early chapter we said that the celestial bodies are cosmic
beasts, and asserted that "holy writ" was our authority. Well,
here it is. This particular one is Leo, the sun, king of the cosmic
beasts. This is the beast of all mythologies—Cosmosaurus, the
planetary entity, particularly in its solar stage. As it is the sun
that creates the planet's matter, it is the Cosmocrator, and so
this Cosmosaurus and this Cosmocrator are one, and his Judeo-
Christian name is God, hence our theronistic world. Elsewhere
we said that secretly, the Bible is the greatest indictment of God
ever written. In dealing with his work the saints and prophets
consistently use such terms as *beast, whore, blasphemy, Satan, sin*
and *evil*. And for two thousand years Western man has been
worshiping their creator. What now, little man, what now?
Well, now perhaps, he can see his own metaphysical incompetency in not seeing this; also the solution to the paradox—divine
source and savage nature. The rest of this chapter reveals even
his own source and nature.

3. And I saw one of his heads as it were wounded to death: and his
deadly wound was healed: and all the world wondered after the beast.

The wounded head is number 7—mortal matter forming in
the sun. This is Achilles' heel, that part of Being subject to
mortality.

4. And they (the creative forces) worshipped the dragon (energy) which gave power unto the beast (matter): and they worshipped the beast, saying, Who is like unto the beast? Who is able to make war with him?

5. And there was given unto him a mouth speaking great things and blasphemies; and power was given unto him to continue forty and two months (Chap. 13).

As this is the same number as that of the "great city" and "the woman clothed with the sun," these three are one.

11. And I beheld another beast coming up out of the earth (entity); and he had two horns like a lamb (consciousness and energy) and he spake as a dragon (energy dominant).

This second beast is the physical earth, born of its own sun parent.

12. And he exerciseth all the power of the first beast before him, and causeth the earth and them which dwell therein to worship the first beast, whose deadly wound was healed (not religious, but biologic sun-worship).

13. And he doeth great wonders so that he maketh fire to come down from heaven on earth in the sight of men (Chap. 13).

The solar fire is brought down or reduced to dense matter in the sight of the creative elements, personified as men. This is identical with the myth of Prometheus.

14. And deceiveth them that dwell on the earth by means of those miracles which he had power to do in the sight of the beast; saying to them that dwell on the earth, that they should make an image to the beast, which had the wound by a sword, and did live.

15. And he had power to give life unto the image of the beast (man), that the image of the beast should both speak, and cause that as many as would not worship the image of the beast should be killed (elimination of the unfit; Chap. 13).

The "they" of this vision, so called, are the creative forces and the image they made of the first beast, the sun, is the earth; and this accomplished, "they" made another image, generically, man. And so if man is made in the image of God, he is made in the image of a beast—Cosmosaurus. This is the esoteric wisdom of the Bible. And how different from chapter 1.

18. Here is wisdom. Let him that hath understanding count the number of the beast: for it is the number of a man; and his number is six hundred threescore and six (666).

This is God's number; then let us get it and stop worshiping him. The text says it is the number of a man, but its source belies that. It is written ' ' ' which is the Hebrew letter *yod* (God) repeated three times, a good example of the concealed indictment. It is branding the Creator in a way the ignorant cannot discover.

This fraudulent saint did not see the God of religion or its Christ but he did see something and saw it clearly—the true nature of Causation. This he continues in various chapters:

13. And I beheld, and heard an angel flying through the midst of heaven, saying with a loud voice, Woe, woe, woe, to the inhabiters of the earth . . . (Chap. 8).
10. The same shall drink of the wine of the wrath of God, which is poured out without mixture into the cup of his indignation; and he shall be tormented with fire and brimstone in the presence of the holy angels, and in the presence of the Lamb (Chap. 14).
1. And I heard a great voice out of the temple saying to the seven angels, Go your ways, and pour out the vials of the wrath of God upon the earth.
2. And the first went and poured out his vial upon the earth; and there fell a noisome and grievous sore upon the men which had the mark of the beast, and upon them which worshipped his image (economic man).
3. And the second angel poured out his vial upon the sea; and it became as the blood of a dead man: and every living soul died in the sea.
4. And the third angel poured out his vial upon the rivers and fountains of waters; and they became blood.
8. And the fourth angel poured out his vial upon the sun; and power was given unto him to scorch men with fire (Chap. 16).

11. And the smoke of their torment ascended up for ever and ever: and they had no rest day nor night . . . (Chap. 14).

9. And men were scorched with great heat, and blasphemed the name of God, which hath power over these plagues . . . (the plagues of Exodus; Chap. 16).

And why shouldn't they, if this be God?—an *inhuman* "beast" compared with which the

> . . . Dragons of the prime,
> That tear each other in their slime
> Were mellow music matched with him.
> Tennyson, *In Memoriam* LVI

Where then is the God of love and mercy? There's not a trace of him in Revelation (the New Testament), nor yet in Ezekiel (the Old Testament). Neither is there in the Pentateuch. The God of Joshua is but this same mad "beast" reveling in blood and battle. No, save for the Gospels, which are truth perverted for benefit of clergy, there are only savagery, cruelty, pain and death in the Bible. And this is what constitutes its truth; the rest is lies. Savagery, cruelty, pain and death are the way of life and therefore "the will of God." When in outlining the creative process we spoke in similar terms, we were, no doubt, accused of blasphemy, but our indictment was purely negative; we only denied God divinity, whereas St. John writes a whole book to prove His diabolical savagery. Compared to his charges, we think ours are defensive and exonerative; we even said the Great First Cause is not responsible for its cruelty.

The mystery of Revelation is no mystery at all, but only occult knowledge of Causation, Creation and Evolution—exactly as we wrote of them. As these are all that was, and is, and ever shall be, we see the significance, and also insignificance, of the author's warning not to add or take anything from it, which the rest of the scriptures do with their moral unreality.

We see also the fraudulent nature of this alleged authority. Every race of antiquity knew the content of Revelation, yet John, like Ezekiel, had the audacity to say that he himself saw and heard these things. "And I John saw these things and heard them. And when I had heard and seen, I fell down to worship before the feet of the angel which showed me these things." And we have been worshiping ever since instead of civilizing ourselves. Worship, we repeat, is the wasteful act of an ignorant soul.

Once our souls are enlightened what wrath exists will not be "the wrath of God" but the wrath of man. Aside from the punitive laws of nature, this scriptural "wrath of God" is but the priesthood's terror weapon.

What then is the "salvation" this book offers us? It is planetary, not human. Of the countless billions who have lived on this earth, our literalists believe that only 144,000 will be saved. Such people should read their Bible with more understanding or not at all, for St. John tells them that all will be saved. "And the seventh angel sounded; and there were great voices in heaven, saying, The kingdoms of this world (that is all life) are become the kingdoms of our Lord" 11:15. But think not this is exclusively Hebrew knowledge. Older far than this is the Hindu story of Vishnu pacifying humanity and pardoning the devils Siva threw into the bottomless pit, after which all will dwell with the gods again on Mount Meru. What then becomes of the doctrine of eternal punishment? Even Origen pronounced this doctrine false and well he might for it is but mythological double talk and nothing more. What is mythically "lost" is the Life Principle itself; its "sin" was that of falling into matter (Involution); from this it rose again and was "saved" (Evolution). This is the Bible's theme, not "lost" human souls, or salvation. Had this been understood from the beginning, we would not have wasted two thousand years saving our souls that were never lost. Do you not see then the necessity of knowing something more than the literal word? This is neither fact nor history; it is priestly perversion thereof. The rest of Revelation is but more of the same.

23

Revelation, Part II

Behold, I show you a mystery; we shall not all sleep,
but we shall all be changed.

St. Paul

You have all heard of "God's plan of salva-
tion," and you've been told it is of Christ's sacrifice on the cross.
The Gnostics knew better and in words that are occult, cryptic
and terse one gives us the *real* "plan of salvation," but where,
you might never guess.

4. John to the seven churches which are in Asia: Grace be unto you
and peace, from him which is, and which was, and which is to come;
and from the seven Spirits which are before his throne (Rev. 1).

Here begins Exodus and Evolution according to the New
Testament, but let us present the whole preamble.

10. I was in the Spirit on the Lord's day (the planetary sabbath), and
heard behind me (as did Moses) a great voice, as of a trumpet,
11. Saying, I am Alpha and Omega, the first and the last: and what
thou seest, write in a book, and send it unto the seven churches which
are in Asia; unto Ephesus, and unto Smyrna, and unto Pergamos, and
unto Thyatira, and unto Sardis, and unto Philadelphia, and unto
Laodicea.

12. And I turned to see the voice that spake with me. And being turned, I saw seven golden candlesticks;

13. And in the midst of the seven candlesticks one like unto the Son of man, clothed with a garment down to the foot, and girt about the paps with a golden girdle.

14. His head and his hair were white like wool, as white as snow; and his eyes were as a flame of fire;

15. And his feet like unto fine brass, as if they burned in a furnace; and his voice as the sound of many waters.

16. And he had in his right hand seven stars: and out of his mouth went a sharp two-edged sword: and his countenance was as the sun shineth in his strength.

17. And when I saw him, I fell at his feet as dead. And he laid his right hand upon me, saying unto me, Fear not; I am the first and the last:

18. I am he that liveth, and was dead; and, behold, I am alive for evermore, Amen; and have the keys of hell and of death.

19. Write the things which thou hast seen, and the things which are, and the things which shall be hereafter;

20. The mystery of the seven stars which thou sawest in my right hand, and the seven golden candlesticks. The seven stars are the angels of the seven churches: and the seven candlesticks which thou sawest are the seven churches (Chap. 1).

No doubt the reader has seen pictures of this monstrosity, an awesome figure with eyes of fire and a flaming sword proceeding from his mouth—fear engendering priestcraft, this and nothing more. It has no literal meaning whatever but is, as in the Eden story, symbolic only of the punitive laws of nature. And since the stars are but symbols of angels and the candlesticks symbols of churches, and the angels and churches themselves but symbols, it is all symbolic imagery.

Who then is this Alpha and Omega, "girt about the paps with a golden girdle"? Certainly not the man Jesus Christ. Men do not wear girdles, nor are their breasts referred to as paps. Paps are the female nipples and a symbol of fecundity, sustenance, and the like. This too is but a symbol of the androgynous Life Principle, as much female as male. It is also the evolutionary antiscion (shadowy opposite) of Nebuchadnezzar's image of Involution. Put them together and you have our diagram of the

Creative process, the Alpha and Omega of Being. In the midst of this is the Creative Principle, and this it is that was alive in Involution, dead in dense matter, and now alive again in Evolution. In Revelation 11:17 the same words are used in reference to God: "Saying, We give thee thanks, O Lord God Almighty, which art and wast, and art to come." Now this, you say, is quite all right since Christ is God, but chapter 17 makes use of practically the same words and here the subject is "the great beast," Satan, earth. "And the beast that was, and is not, even he is the eighth"—yet to come. Thus again we see that esoterically the scriptures make God, Christ, Satan, and the beast all one— the earth and its Creative Principle. This is the beginning and the end of all things in this world, and from the seventh plane *"was, is, and is to come."* The idea is by no means peculiar to Hebrew scripture. In the Bhagavad-Gita, Vishnu says of himself, "I am the beginning and the middle and also the end of existing things." And Horus of Egypt said: "I am yesterday, today, and tomorrow." I think we've had enough of this symbolic nonsense; it's time now we learned the facts of Reality instead.

Our metaphysicians respectfully consider Christ as the highest aspect of evolutionary consciousness, and with this we would agree, but the Revelator pays him no such tribute, but makes him a symbol of the entire evolutionary side of Being, as shown in our diagram. His feet were like brass, symbol of the lowest, densest plane; his body was clothed in a garment, the planetary aura, while his hair was as white as wool, this part alone signifying the higher, diviner planes. Thus he represents the creative power throughout Evolution. And this it is that said, "For lo, I am with you all days, even unto the end of the world." Upon this, and similar statements, the Church bases its claim to "indefectibility," or security from destruction by its foes, but here we see this claim is as spurious as all the rest. We are not dealing with a personal Christ or a man-made church, but with an impersonal principle and the planetary entity.

And as with the Christ, so with the churches; they are not man-made edifices but planetary planes, thus naturally, seven. When this alleged revelation was written, supposedly near the close of the first century, there may or may not have been seven churches in Asia Minor, but the number is not important; seven

was chosen regardless of fact, because of its symbolic significance. Indeed we have some evidence on this point. The Alogi,
who opposed the Montanists, contended there was no church
in Thyatira at that time, and since then the only proof of this
church's existence is this revelation itself. Now that we understand its true nature, we see the Alogi may have been right.

The seven letters to these churches, or planes, are but descrip-
tions of and admonitions to the life thereof. As anything else
they aren't even good sense. So many practical things to be said
and this mentor deals only in symbols so fantastic Western man
has not been able to comprehend them in two thousand years.
What he needs is cosmology, not theology. The seven spirits are
the seven divisions of planetary life, and as such, stand figuratively before the throne of the planetary Logos. This latter,
actually the genetic intelligence, warns, threatens and ad-
monishes the lazy, lagging epigenetic, exactly as in Exodus,
Joshua, Judges, and so on. The seven churches are identical with
the seven zodiacal stages from Leo to Aquarius. And this is the
mystery of Revelation 1–3.

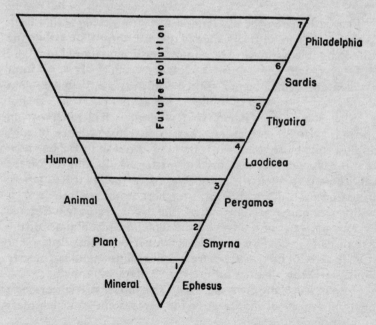

Ephesus

1. Unto the angel of the church of Ephesus write; These things saith
he that holdeth the seven stars in his right hand, who walketh in the
midst of the seven golden candlesticks;

2. I know thy works, and thy labour, and thy patience, and how
thou canst not bear them which are evil: and thou hast tried them
which say they are apostles, and are not, and hast found them liars:

3. And hast borne, and hast patience, and for my name's sake hast
laboured, and hast not fainted.

4. Nevertheless I have somewhat against thee, because thou hast left
thy first love.

5. Remember therefore from whence thou art fallen, and repent,
and do the first works; or else I will come unto thee quickly, and will
remove thy candlestick out of his place, except thou repent.

6. But this thou hast, that thou hatest the deeds of the Nicolaitans,
which I also hate.

7. He that hath an ear, let him hear what the Spirit saith unto the
churches; To him that overcometh will I give to eat of the tree of life,
which is in the midst of the paradise of God (Chap. 2).

This is the language of Genesis and its meaning is identical.
What has borne with patience is the earth itself, or rather the
Life Principle within it. Here in matter it has labored long and
suffered much, bondage in Egypt, so to speak. If it will not
awaken and remember its source and purpose, it will remain
there. And as there is no biologic life at this point, it is it, not
us, that should remember from whence it had fallen—from
spirit to matter. Therefore "do this in remembrance of me"
applies to it more than to us. Its first love was spirit, but now
that it has *fallen* it is enamored of matter, a sufficient reason for
punishment in ancient philosophy. Nevertheless this is where
it was meant to be at this time, for here it has a job to do. If it
will hasten and overcome matter, the first work, it will become
organic and "eat of the tree of life which is in the midst of the
paradise of God." This should read "the tree of knowledge" for
it *is* "the tree of life." Elsewhere we said the Jews did not clearly
understand this distinction.

Here in Revelation we see what the apostles really were, not
men but aspects of the Creative Principle, some of which meet

evolutionary requirements and some of which do not—not all matter will become auric and free in Evolution. Those that the spirit hates are the latter, the slag pile, and so it sends them to perdition. Collectively they are called Nicolaitans. Is this but Nicodemon again? Historically, there was a sect at that time called Nicolaitans, much given to material pleasure; thus they symbolize laziness, gluttony, and complacency, and these creativity cannot tolerate.

"Do the first works." More than once we suggested the same thing; no doubt it fell on deaf ears then, but those ears should heed it here if this be "the word of God." But what are these "first works"? According to the Church, they are worshiping God and saving our souls, but as these are not based on Reality they should be the last works. God is not something to be worshiped, but to be made intelligent use of, and in this, the "first works" for us are those elemental things of life and human society that must be done before a peaceful, civilized world is possible. Utopia here and Heaven hereafter are but states in which these elemental problems have been solved. Yet we have not solved the most elemental of them all—human sustenance; half the race is still half fed. We talk of honesty, justice, brotherly love, yet our economics are but jungle tactics on the human plane; to survive, every animal instinct is daily aroused and augmented. We talk of peace, yet we haven't learned how to stop one man bent on war and world domination. We have developed a kind of emotional sensitivity that objects to cruelty to children and animals, yet our consciousness is still so limited we are solicitous only of what we see. Beyond this, is measureless cruelty throughout the world, and we do nothing about it—"out of sight, out of mind." We have a social culture so delicate we must not say "damn" over the air, yet literally we damn millions to a life of poverty, toil and misery. We cannot write the plain, blunt truth about these things lest we offend the sensitive public, yet underneath its delicate skin lies such cruelty, savagery, stupidity and ignorance as keep the whole world in blood and tears. How then can we have the last things, Utopia, peace, brotherly love? Do "the first works" first and the rest will follow: rid God's world of savagery, cruelty and war, and our own of poverty, disease and ignorance.

Smyrna

8. And unto the angel of the church in Smyrna write; These things sayest the first and the last, which was dead, and is alive;

9. I know thy works, and tribulations, and poverty, (but thou art rich) and I know the blasphemy of them which say they are Jews, and are not, but are the synagogue of Satan (Chap. 2).

Is it blasphemy (defamation of God) for a Gentile to say he is a Jew? Certainly not, literally, but this is not meant literally; this is precisely what it is said to be, apocalyptic, which means hidden or more correctly, the hidden revealed. But what is apocalyptic about it if this literal nonsense is the one and only meaning? And where is the wisdom in these admonitions if this Alpha and Omega is speaking only of a primitive church and a few dozen Jews? This John is using the Jews, as did the Old Testament authors, to symbolize the life force, and this and God are one. He is also using the Gentiles to symbolize the opposer. Therefore it is blasphemy against the Creator for the opposer to claim to be a helper. And as Evolution is the Creator's will, such are our antievolutionists.

This second church is the second plane and kingdom, and life there is poor indeed compared to that above, but rich compared to that below, "dead matter." "Consider the lilies how they grow." Their plane is the first part of the evolutionary "paradise."

10. Fear none of these things which thou shalt suffer: behold, the devil shall cast some of you into prison, that ye may be tried; and ye shall have tribulation ten days: be thou faithful unto death, and I will give thee a crown of life.

11. He that hath an ear, let him hear what the Spirit saith unto the churches; He that overcometh shall not be hurt of the second death (Chap. 2).

The Life Principle is indestructible and having overcome the first death, that in matter, it will not be hurt by the second, that of the organism. Misapplied, this sounds like proof of immortality, but it isn't. The subject is not man but the real immortal, the Life Principle; if for ten days (a certain period), it is faithful to the cosmic plan, it shall possess the crown of still higher life.

Pergamos

12. And to the angel of the church in Pergamos write; these things saith he which hath the sharp sword with two edges (life and death);
13. I know thy works, and where thou dwellest, even where Satan's seat is: and thou holdest fast my name, and hast not denied my faith, even in those days wherein Antipas was my faithful martyr, who was slain among you, where Satan dwelleth (Chap. 2).

Now why, from all the other churches, should John pick this third one as the seat and dwelling place of Satan? And if it was the seat and dwelling place of Satan, what kind of a church would it be? Just typical? We could say this is just an apocalyptic truism, but we're not trying to be sarcastic. This church represents the third, or astral plane, the zodiacal Scorpio, and the astral element is Satan's seat and kingdom. This is the source of desire, passion, and greed, and it was in this third plane, or animal kingdom, they were aroused and developed. But if life will just hold fast it will overcome even this. Antipas is a contraction of Antipater, which has no religious or historical meaning here. It would have some evolutionary meaning were it Antepas, meaning the innocent life of the preceding kingdom, the plant, figuratively martyred by the animal.

15. So hast thou also them that hold the doctrine of the Nicolaitans, which things I hate.
16. Repent; or else I will come unto thee quickly, and will fight against them with the sword of my mouth.

Sloth and gluttony developed here to be a stumbling block to man. But who developed it? Is the animal kingdom supposed to repent of it? And, if this be Christ, why should he threaten with a sword?

17. He that hath an ear, let him hear what the Spirit saith unto the churches. To him that overcometh will I give to eat of the hidden

manna, and will give him a white stone, and in the stone a new name written, which no man knoweth saving he that receiveth it (Chap. 2).

As life transcends the purely animal condition it partakes of the food of the spiritual human qualities. This is the hidden manna that life shall eat after the days of unleavened bread, i.e., purely material existence. It also receives a new name—Humanity, which only a human being knows. The symbolism of the white stone may have been suggested by the Roman *tessera*, a white stone given to the victors of the arena. These *tesserae* had written on them the letters *SP, spectatus,* and were a badge of honor and passport to social functions. The white stone and the new name therefore symbolize the reward and status of life when it reaches the human plane, as yet but a promise.

And now we must do violence to the text, for the proper sequence is broken here, perhaps intentionally, to conceal the true meaning. The fourth church is number seven, set away off by itself in the text. For these liberties we take with the Bible, we repeat, we offer no apologies whatever, for the compilers themselves have done likewise. The whole book is a hodgepodge of mythic excerpts, whose correlation is the work either of men less enlightened than the authors, trying hard but failing to achieve the proper sequence, or that of deliberate mischief-makers, confusing the sequence to hide its natural meaning. You may choose for yourself which you believe.

Laodicea

14. And unto the angel of the church of the Laodiceans write; These things saith the Amen, the faithful and true witness, the beginning of the creation of God (Chap. 3).

Here the truth comes out—"the creation of God." This is precisely what John is writing about, this time the evolutionary side of it.

15. I know thy works, that thou art neither cold nor hot: I would thou wert cold or hot.

16. So then because thou art lukewarm, and neither cold nor hot, I will spew thee out of my mouth.

17. Because thou sayest, I am rich, and increased with goods, and have need of nothing; and knowest not that thou art wretched, and miserable, and poor, and blind, and naked (Chap. 3).

Is not this clearly our present worldly humanity? Neither wholly material nor wholly spiritual, believing itself rich because of its money and material gadgets, when all the while it is mentally, morally, and spiritually poor and wretched, blind and naked—economic man. And the same may be said of nations. All of them wrapped up in their pride and self-sufficiency when not one of them has done even the "first work." Not one of them can properly feed, clothe and educate its people; not one of them can settle its foreign problems without recourse to war and conflict. We still glorify war and its warriors are our heroes; we spend so much of our wealth upon it there's nothing left for worthier purposes. It's time we forgot our stupid wars and did something to rid our nature of its cause. And here we are shown the way.

18. I counsel thee to buy of me gold tried in the fire, that thou mayest be (truly) rich; and white raiment (spirituality), that thou mayest be clothed, and that the shame of thy (material) nakedness do not appear; and anoint thine eyes with eyesalve, that thou mayest see (Chap. 3).

Now what is this eyesalve but enlightenment, a "new dimension of consciousness" by which we may see the error of our ways and the falseness of our faiths? With this we will know that truth that will set us free. Had the Christian Church, at any time, known and used this eyesalve, we would not now be poor, and blind, and naked. John prescribes this eye-opener but because he did not use the language of the kindergarten our spiritually benighted teachers cannot see it. The only use they make of his esoteric words is to terrify the ignorant into belief in their own false doctrines. And what time they have wasted!

What vast futility their effort! In our present subject we have a good example. There is in the library a ponderous volume about these seven churches and letters. The author is a man of vast erudition, and many degrees adorn his name, but alas, he had no eyesalve, and so to write his book he read the history of these churches and cities, then went to Asia Minor to study the land and its people. There he made photographs, maps and sketches to illustrate his thesis; all told, the work of a dozen years perhaps, yet what is the result? One of the most pitiful examples of Christian literalism and spiritual blindness in all literature. What a waste of human effort, and all for want of a little eyesalve. Had he possessed one grain of this he need not have left his own comfortable study. But this is only one man's waste, what of the Church as a whole? A billion wasted years is not too high an estimate—millions of individuals multiplied by two thousand years.

One of the highest hopes of the Christian Church derives its name from this apocalypse—apocatastasis, the final restoration of the lapsed race to holiness and the favor of God. How is it going to achieve this apocatastasis with its present understanding of the apocalyptic plan? Another word dear to its heart is acatalepsy, the unknowableness of things. All is mystery known only to God, and it is but presumption for man to pry and to inquire. What it needs is a little eucatalepsy, actual understanding of things. But this would liquidate the Church, and, so, is anathema.

All is not mystery; in fact, the truth about life is astonishingly obvious, but for thousands of years something has been blinding us so that we cannot see it. That something is religion, the spiritual "opiate of the people." The remedy would be euphrasia—"that which opens our eyes and clears our spiritual vision." This would be a cosmo-metaphysic—"the cosmic facts of life"—uncontaminated by religious thought. This is the "eyesalve" John counsels us to use. It is good advice for our greatest need today is a clarification of the mystery of life, and a proper orientation of the mind with Reality. And this, a supernaturalistic religion is keeping from us.

Thyatira

18. And unto the angel of the church in Thyatira write; These things saith the Son of God, who hath his eyes like unto a flame of fire, and his feet are like fine brass (Chap. 2).

We said John of the Gospels knew not the Christ of religion, and neither did the Revelator. To him the Son of God is a power, not a person.

19. I know thy works, and charity, and service, and faith, and thy patience, and thy works; and the last to be more than the first.

The church of Thyatira, number five, represents life and consciousness on the fifth major plane. Here the "eyesalve" has been found and used, and so the greed and selfishness, blindness and ignorance of the fourth plane consciousness become charity, service, faith, and patience, and altruistic work more than all. These are some of those *last things*, now attained. They are also things the Church would have us practice but does not know how to condition us so that we want to do them. This is a matter of consciousness, a factor the Church cannot develop. Yet we are what our consciousness is; therefore if we are "wretched, and miserable, and poor, and blind, and naked," it is because our consciousness is likewise, and morally and spiritually the Church is to blame. In this vast enterprise it has nothing to offer but that worn-out tale of Christ and him crucified, and what is there in this to enlighten and thus develop consciousness? It is new knowledge that does that. And what is there in business? Verse 20 answers that.

20. Notwithstanding I have a few things against thee, because thou sufferest that woman Jezebel, which calleth herself a prophetess, to teach and seduce my servants to commit fornication, and to eat things sacrificed unto idols (the Borborites; Chap. 20).

This implies unwise adherence of spiritual consciousness to material things, and we not only adhere to them, we are bogged down and mired in them. Not even fifth-plane consciousness is perfect and so it lets in these fourth-plane desires to make a brothel, *fornix,* out of it—and this is the fornication of Thyatira.

In the modern book just referred to, this Jezebel is referred to as a woman contemporary with this church and the suggestion is made that she may have been the bishop's wife. And such is priestly understanding. Not even the Old Testament Jezebel is referred to, yet she too stands for all that undeveloped nature consists of. She is therefore used here to symbolize the desires and passions of the lower planes.

21. And I gave her space to repent of her fornication; and she repented not.

22. Behold, I will cast her into a bed, and them that commit adultery with her into great tribulation, except they repent of their deeds.

23. And I will kill her children with death; and all the churches shall know that I am he which searcheth the reins and hearts: and I will give unto every one of you according to your works (Chap. 2).

The space of time to repent, that is, change, is the period allotted life on the higher part of the fourth plane, our position. We are in it yet, still clinging to faiths, systems and institutions of the lower part, hence our "tribulations." Are not our children killed in war, as in the text? Our religion-stunted consciousness is just not equal to our present place in Evolution and so we suffer. You will recall our former statement about this matter. If the human will lags behind the planetary will, disaster follows. This planetary will has a goal and we must realize that we are the medium through which it is reached. To our ignorance of and indifference to this force is due our present Aquarian-forced "tribulation." We just don't realize we are scheduled to go on and leave the dead Piscean past to bury itself. Until we learn, Nature must bury it for us, and one of her ways is war. War is Nature's ruthless way of blasting us out of our stupid status quo. The symbolic name of this status is Jezebel, and we are still fornicating with her. We have just criticized the crass materialism and commercialism of our age but we advocated no economic and political reformation, and this because the change lies not in these but in human consciousness. And this is what lies before us in the Aquarian Age, but who is enlightened enough to tell us of it or prepare us for it? Well, Revelation as here interpreted should throw some light on it.

24. But unto you I say, and unto the rest in Thyatira, as many as have not this doctrine, and which have not known the depths of Satan, as they speak: I will put upon you none other burden.
25. But that which ye have already hold fast till I come (Chap. 2).

No other burden save to keep up with the planetary will. Thus we do not have to waste our time worshiping God and saving our souls from a hell hereafter. The hell we have to save them from is here and now.

The worshipers see in this last verse a promise of Christ's second coming; there is, however, no such thing. The Christ comes but once and it is not a man nor yet a divine being; it is Evolution. There is, however, a planetary similitude of this personal Second Coming—the coming-down into manifestation in us of the higher group-soul qualities. But before these can come down as something divine they must be made divine and placed there by us. Here they become a collective beneficence, the "World Soul" divinified.

The Christian Church should not preach or pray for the second coming of the gospel Christ, for should such a being come even once, his first act would be to destroy the Christian Church. Even as literally portrayed, he labored to destroy its priest-ridden prototype, the Jewish synagogue.

26. And he that overcometh, and keepeth my works unto the end, to him will I give power over the nations:
27. And he shall rule them with a rod of iron; as the vessels of a potter shall they be broken to shivers: even as I received of my Father.
28. And I will give him the morning star.
29. He that hath an ear, let him hear what the Spirit saith unto the churches (Chap. 2).

The "nations" here are the planes, but the lesser significance is no less pertinent. Only the power and wisdom of the fifth-plane consciousness can break to shivers the rule of the fourth-plane tyrants. These, our dictators, military and industrial, are but media through which nature's savage forces operate. Feeling their impelling power, yet lacking fifth-plane wisdom, they fancy themselves instruments of destiny. Thus they gain malevolent "power over the nations." He who shall have beneficent power over them is he who becomes the medium of fifth-plane forces. But where is he? And where is the "morning star"? The objective "morning star" is Venus, and Venus represents love. Well, perhaps that is the angel of Venus: we said it was further advanced than earth.

Sardis

1. And unto the angel of the church in Sardis write; These things saith he that hath the seven Spirits of God, and the seven stars; I know thy works, that thou hast a name that thou livest, and art dead (Chap. 3).

This is sixth-plane consciousness, alive yet dead to all material desires. But even this is not the end.

2. Be watchful, and strengthen the things which remain, that are ready to die: for I have not found thy works perfect before God.

Not even sixth-plane life is perfect, yet, as we said, it becomes a beneficent influence, strengthening and illuminating the planes below. The latter are spoken of as "ready to die." This is not personal death; it is plane death. Just as the involutionary forces become violent after the fourth plane, then die in dense matter, so the evolutionary forces become violent up to the fourth plane and die thereafter. These on the higher planes are noncreative energy—earth's potential almost spent. Perhaps on the lowest planes these forces no longer sustain life, and so their forms may no longer exist.

3. Remember therefore how thou hast received and heard, and hold fast, and repent. If therefore thou shalt not watch, I will come on thee

as a thief, and thou shalt not know what hour I will come upon thee (Chap. 3).

The life that reaches this exalted plane and violates its law, its condition, "shall be seven times worse than before." As the scriptures were written by religionists, great emphasis is put upon repentance and punishment, but here in Revelation we can see how little they apply to us religiously; they are not even personal but planetary. Without some consciousness of the whole vast, cosmic process, it is difficult for us to understand our present status, social and personal. We think of ourselves as the ultimate of life and that life will never be any different. We just can't realize that we are not at all what nature intends life to be someday, and that we are but preparation for it. The fact is we are but tentative humanity, the real thing lies ahead. The next verses suggest its nature.

4. Thou hast a few names even in Sardis which have not defiled their garments; and they shall walk with me in white: for they are worthy.
5. He that overcometh, the same shall be clothed in white raiment; and I will not blot out his name out of the book of life, but I will confess his name before my Father, and before his angels.
6. He that hath an ear, let him hear what the Spirit saith unto the churches (Chap. 3).

The white raiment is merely symbolic of perfection. In our previous treatment of Revelation we said this raiment was the auric elements, and on these high planes the one and only Holy Ghost, morally. Here the garments are no longer material but finer even than mental matter, therefore *scripturally* pure. So is consciousness; it is becoming divine, and so life then will be different.

Confessing its name before the Father is all very well figuratively and Hebraically, but not otherwise. The implication that the Creative principle was morally perfect, a priori, is the great delusion of the Hebrew people. Here the reader should recall our distinction—quantitative and qualitative. Only evolutionary life is morally qualified and man makes it so. This is the great truth the Hebrew priesthood robbed us of, and considering the results of their false God-concept *in toto*, it is time we ourselves did a little blotting out. Instead of *their* God blotting *us* out of his book of life, we should blot *him* out of ours.

Philadelphia

7. And to the angel of the church in Philadelphia write; These things saith he that is holy, he that is true, he that hath the key of David, he that openeth, and no man shutteth; and shutteth, and no man openeth (Chap. 3).

Philadelphia, the city of brotherly love. Not without reason did John choose this name for the last church, or plane, for only on this last and highest one is that divine quality, love, complete. In this lies the meaning of that statement, "Love is the fulfilling of the law." This law is the law of life, of Evolution, and love, spiritual, is its end, not its beginning. Here we see the magnitude of the aforesaid Hebrew error—attributing to the involutionary Creator this strictly evolutionary and human quality. In this difference lies the whole span of invo-evolutionary being and the purpose of Creation itself. Can anything then be further from the truth than Hebrew theology?

And what has David, the man, to do with all this? Nothing; but as we presented him, he is the involutionary king of the earth whose throne is symbolized by Jerusalem. As such his keys are the same as Peter's; he who holds them opens and shuts the seven doors of evolutionary life. In Revelation, this is Christ, but it seems that Isaiah thought of it first. In chapter 22, verse 22, similar words are spoken of Eliakim: "And the key of the house of David will I lay upon his shoulder; so he shall open and none shall shut; and he shall shut and none shall open." The house of David is the earth, and Eliakim means a plurality of gods, like Elohim. In Egypt the same thing was said of another god, namely Ra, and Ra was the sun.

> He that openeth and he that closeth the door;
> He who said "I am but one,"
> Ra who was produced by himself.

In this last line lies a greater truth than anything in Hebrew theology—a sun is its own creator. This we asserted from the beginning; the Hebrews said an extrasolar Deity created it by word of mouth. The Egyptians knew better.

8. I know thy works: behold, I have set before thee an open door, and no man can shut it; for thou hast a little strength, and hast kept my word, and hast not denied my name (Chap. 3).

As spiritual advice to a church this is meaningless trivia, but as cosmological knowledge it is deep and profound. The "open door" is the exit of planetary consciousness when Evolution is over. And who can shut that? Not even the Creator himself. The "little strength" at this point is the little earth-energy left at this last moment.

9. Behold, I will make them of the synagogue of Satan, which say they are Jews, and are not, but do lie; behold, I will make them to come and worship before thy feet, and to know that I have loved thee (Chap. 3).

Every race writes its mythology in terms of its own people, and so in Jewish mythology the Jews are "the people"; all who are not are of Satan's kingdom, including the Christians. But even these pariahs must eventually join the Jews and all in the end will be saved, an idea by no means Jewish in origin. The Persians stated it thus: "Then comes the general resurrection when the good will immediately enter into this happy abode (the regenerated earth); and Ahriman and his angels and the wicked, be purified by immersion in a lake of molten metal. . . . Henceforward all will enjoy unchangeable happiness, and headed by Sosiosh, ever sing the praises of the Eternal One" (Nork). And older even than this is the aforesaid Hindu story of Vishnu purifying humanity and pardoning the devils thrown into the bottomless pit by Siva, after which all will dwell with the gods again on Mount Meru. Actually these stories refer to the resurrection of the Life Principle from that "bottomless pit" called earth, yet they all imply the forgiveness and salvation of all beings, including Satan. The Jews have never given "the devil his due"; to them he was, is, and ever shall be the enemy of God. Yet His Satanic Majesty is the energy aspect of God and therefore the creative power. As long as that power is on a low material plane, as in us, it is, of course, Satanic and evil, but that power when raised up is also the power of the spiritual planes. A long time ago we said that *Demon est Deus inversus*, and now we say that in respect to energy, *Christus est Demon inversus*. And so "none shall be lost, no, not one." What then of the doctrine of eternal punishment? It is, like everything in literal scripture, false. Even the great Origen so pronounced it.

10. Because thou hast kept the word of my patience, I also will keep thee from the hour of temptation, which shall come upon all the world, to try them that dwell upon the earth.
11. Behold, I come quickly: hold that fast which thou hast, that no man take thy crown (Chap. 3).

Having struggled long and risen high above the evil material forces life now receives that crown that is given "to him that overcometh." But what is that crown? Something a divine, prehuman deity bestows upon it? No, that crown is its own creation—perfected life—the only divinity there is. Upon a fully evolved planet this sits like a crown of glory, and this it is the world is warned to hold fast, lest cosmic forces take it away. This is the temptation that "shall come upon all the world," and every world someday. Today Venus is holding fast that crown, but it's only a matter of time, not sin. Mercury has lost it. This part of Revelation is not only an outline of Evolution but also a cryptic account of the stages the life of this earth will pass through on its inward journey to Venus, thus scriptural confirmation of our previous assertion. How many have seen in this mysterious part of the scriptures an outline of Evolution? None, in fact it has not been seen in two thousand years.

Here we would remind the reader of still another assertion, namely, that the planetary law will force man eventually to create in actuality his now imagined ideality—a God of moral and spiritual perfection—his present concept being but nature's "primitive substitute for future reality."

12. Him that overcometh will I make a pillar in the temple of my God, and he shall go no more out: and I will write upon him the name of my God, and the name of the city of my God, which is new Jerusalem, which cometh down out of heaven from my God; and I will write upon him my new name.
13. He that hath an ear, let him hear what the Spirit saith unto the churches (Chap. 3).

The "World Soul," now perfected, becomes a pillar in the temple of God, the universe, and goes no more out into objective manifestation. All has been learned that can be learned and so there is no more need of experience. But what of the Creative Principle? Eventually it comes forth again to build a new world. And this is the New Jerusalem.

2. And I John saw the holy city, new Jerusalem, coming down from God out of heaven, prepared as a bride adorned for her husband (Chap. 21).

True, only John saw nothing of the kind, but only the Gnostic lore of Creation. Our poor, deluded priesthood believes this "bride adorned for her husband" is the Church, but no such inconsequential thing is meant here—this is Cosmology. The God referred to is creative consciousness and its bride is creative energy. This the former wed in the creative process, and at the end of Evolution stands in the white robes of perfection.

We see then that this "Revelation" is no revelation at all, but only ancient, esoteric Cosmology. As such, its ominous threats and glorious promises have no meaning for the individual either here or hereafter. What then of the soul-saving Church that is based upon it? It is a house built on less than sand—mythologized cosmology. How tragic that Piscean man should be so ignorant of these things that a little knowledge of them mystically written should seem to him a "divine revelation," nay, "the word of God" himself. How tragic that he should have wasted two thousand years saving his soul instead of perfecting it as outlined here. The goal of Evolution is the ultimate perfection of mankind. Had this divine goal been seen instead of monkey origin, there would have been no opposition to it. Those responsible cannot plead lack of time as an excuse: some twenty-four hundred years ago Democritus and Leucippus taught both the evolutionary and atomic theories. Now that we know that Christ and Evolution are one, there should be no opposition.

This should settle the question, Does the Bible teach Evolution? We now see that several of its books are Evolution occultly written, their endless variations but mythic fugue and counterpoint. But their Evolution is not science's Evolution, and they are right and science is wrong. Evolution applies only to the planet, a coming out (Exodus) of what went in, namely energy and ideation. These come forth in Evolution in inverse order, hence the three kingdoms.

Actually, there is no such thing as human evolution; there is development and progress but it is involution, the involving of qualities in astral and mental matter as in Involution. Experience must have something to register in else it is lost. In the living it becomes memory, character, soul, and these at death become race-memory and the group-soul, and there withdrawn by other forms.

The religionists have some reason for opposing the scientific theory, ape to man, for it is not true. Man was never in the animal kingdom. Turn back the evolutionary clock and man would disappear on the threshold of the animal kingdom. Is man then a special creation? No, he is a special ideation.

Paul

O wretched man that I am! who shall deliver me from
the body of this death?

ST. PAUL

But there was that man Paul; surely he was
real; surely his words are those of a convert fired with faith in
a living Christ. There is no proof that Paul believed in a personal
Christ; to him Christ was a principle, "dwelling in the light
unapproachable, whom no man hath seen or can see" (Epistle
to Timothy). Chronologically he could not have seen or read the
canonical Gospels but only their Gnostic source. Even his
period and that of his writings are a matter of doubt. Justin
Martyr, who wrote so voluminously about the early Christians,
never mentioned Paul or his Epistles. All things considered, we
might even wonder if such a man ever existed, Acts being all
a part of the priestly myth. And if this be so of Acts, it is so also
of the Epistles. Those attributed to Paul are not letters written
by a certain man to certain groups but merely preachments of
the doctrine. If this be not so, what is the meaning of the foot-
notes to these letters, as in the King James Version? This for
instance: "The first epistle to the Corinthians was written from
Philippi by Stephanus, and Fortunatus, and Achaicus, and
Timotheus." And under the second: "The second epistle to the
Corinthians was written from Philippi a city of Macedonia by

Titus and Lucas." Who then wrote these Epistles? It seems the compilers had their doubts. So did Tertullian; according to him "The Epistle to the Hebrews" was written by one Barnabas. Of this one, Origen, the greatest Bible student, said: "Who wrote this Epistle God only knows." Even the names were sometimes changed. Marcion, a second-century writer, said The Epistle to the Ephesians was formerly called The Epistle to the Laodiceans. There were others writing Epistles in those days and some of them were used in the churches for several centuries, Clement's for instance. In a letter Bishop Dionysius wrote thus: "We have been reading in church today Clement's Epistle."

Paul is but the Moses of the New Testament, carrying on where its Joseph left off. Just as Moses was reared an Egyptian but became the leader of the Jews, so Paul was reared a Jew but became the leader of the Gentiles. Just as Moses became the lawgiver of the Jews, so Paul became the lawgiver of the Christians. As God spoke to Moses from a burning bush, so Christ spoke to Paul from a blinding light. As Moses was told to go to Sinai to receive power and do great works, so Paul was told to go to Damascus for like reasons. Moses built a tabernacle, Paul a church. Moses preached biologic rightness, Paul, moral righteousness. Moses fought against Pharaoh for the release of the Life Principle, and Paul fought against Peter, the rock, for the same purpose. As the Israelites were imprisoned, so were the apostles, and both were released by miraculous powers. The cue to this parallel is given in Acts, which gives Paul's history. Chapter 7 recounts the whole story of Moses that we may see the connection.

The account of Moses is very convincing, and so is that of Paul, but the conviction lies not in historical fact but in the art of literature. The Jewish literati instead of divinifying man, so divinified falsehood that it looks like truth. As the founding of a new priesthood was their purpose, they falsified even the Pauline doctrine. The crux of this lies in a fact wholly unknown to the Christian masses, namely, the distinction between the words *Christ* and *Chrest*. By the time the Christians got done with it, second and third century, the title given to Jesus was everywhere spelled Christ, but prior to this it was Chrest, possibly from the Greek word *chre*, which meant kind, gracious, etc., or the Egyptian *karast*, meaning fleshed—the word made flesh. In his *Apology*, Justin Martyr calls his coreligionists Chrestians. And so it was for three centuries. To quote from Massey: "In Bockh's [1] *Christian Inscriptions*, numbering 1,287, there is not a single instance of an earlier date than the third century wherein the name is not written Chrest or Chreist." This was changed by those "who added or removed what seemed good to them in the work of correction," as Origen said. It was this pre-Christian Gnostic symbol of spiritual being that Paul preached, and so came into conflict with the priests and their prerequisite.

This conflict, presented as between Paul and Peter, is not understood today, even by the most learned theologians. They assume it was some internal dispute about the teachings of the gospel Christ. It was, on the contrary, the conflict between the supporters of this gospel Christ and the pregospel Greek Chrestos, the universal Logos, as of John. The adherents of this more esoteric doctrine called themselves Chrestianoi. Their headquarters was in Antioch, in Asia Minor, and it was there, not Jerusalem, that the sect first became known as Chrestians, as set forth in Acts but now written Christians. The Judean sect was not even known as Christians, though later this was applied to them derisively; they called themselves Nazarenes, Galileans, and Brethren. These were priestly minded and bent on founding a religion on a personal Christ; naturally then they were shocked and annoyed to learn of an antecedent and rival sect appropriating the name Chrestians without reference to their Christ. This they called "the heresy of Antioch," see Acts, and after the Gentiles took over and the Jews withdrew it became a heresy to Rome—no hierarchy, no empire could be built upon it. That is why the Petrine doctrine prevailed and the Pauline was made to conform to it. Thus the *Chrestos Logia*, "which certain impostors in the Church of Rome propagated concerning Christ," became the Christine doctrine.[2]

This Gnostic and pagan doctrine was the source of Pauline

[1] Philipp August Bockh, 1785–1867.
[2] The quote is from Higgins.

Christianity. In it lies the true esoteric basis, a universal principle available to all, and such also is that of the two Johns. This
the Jewish priests rejected for the narrow, literalized and per-
sonalized Christ of the synoptic gospels. This was strictly for
them, and their attitude towards others is well expressed where
Cornelius, a Gentile, sought to join them. Peter speaking, Acts
10:28: "Ye know how that it is an unlawful thing for a man that
is a Jew to keep company, or come in unto one of another
nation." And Peter having done this, they accused him "saying,
Thou wentest in to men uncircumcised, and didst eat with
them." How horrible! It took a miraculous dream to convince
them they were wrong. Without this they might have killed
Paul had he not fled. This is not likely history but it illustrates
the conflict between the two systems.

At any rate Christianity began not in Rome nor yet in Jerusalem, but in Antioch in Syria—and it was operative before the
time of Christ. It took three hundred years to blend its two
components, and now we live by a synthetic faith whose name
and purpose derive from the Greeks and whose theology and
psychology derive from the Hebrews. Its morality derives from
neither exclusively but from humanity in general, and this is
the one good apple in the whole rotten barrel.

Paul preached neither Jesus nor Christ but Christhood, that
deified consciousness developed within the individual rather
than from a Christ without. This was the method of the schools
of the Mysteries, their long, arduous and dedicated work of
initiation resulted in a spirituality that can never be achieved
vicariously. Rightly understood, this is the heart of all religions
but the literalists destroyed it. Elsewhere we said that the
Church during two thousand years had failed to spiritualize the
race. Here we see the reason. We said also that the purpose of
Creation was the development of qualities, and Christianity
sidetracked it.

It has been said that Paul was the real founder of Christianity,
but not the Christianity that came down to us. His was Gnostic
Christianity, the other but a priestly perversion of this. Paul,
however, was a combination of both: priestly zeal, and knowledge he could not absorb because of his racial heritage. He too

was a victim of Jewry, and therefore burdened with its false theology and conviction of sin. Thus he was a man torn between two philosophies. While he spoke as a Gnostic, there is much that is deep and profound in his words, but alas, he could not escape his heritage. His preachments, like those of his forebears, are all of the goodness of God and the unworthiness of man, the sins of the flesh and salvation by faith. Indeed faith was his watchword and by faith he endures. Faith has its place, but what does it get us if what we have faith in doesn't exist—a loving God and a saving Christ? Were two such wondrous beings running the world, how could it be as it is? And why should we worry about it? The fact is, we don't and because of our faith in these false doctrines. Such faith is well expressed in this little offering of pious ignorance.

> A year untried before me lies;
> What it shall bring of strange surprise,
> Of joy or grief, I cannot tell,
> But God, my father, knoweth well;
> I make it no concern of mine,
> But leave it all with love divine.
>
> Anon. (and it is well)

For two thousand years we too have left it all with "love divine," and what a mess it has made of it—incessant warfare, poverty and ignorance. In peace and plenty we live by "faith in Christ" and the "grace of God," and when war comes they fail us miserably. Fair-weather allies, these! If we must have faith in something, let us first determine whether that something exists, or at least has a substantive in Reality. But this, we are told, is not faith at all; faith is belief in the unknown. But since the unknown is likely the unreal also, what good is faith in it? Faith in the unknown is foolishness; it should have no place in human thought whatever, and especially in religion. When you come to the unknown, let suspended judgment take over. Beyond this lies only belief in other believers' ignorant assumptions. Intelligent faith is faith in the known and its as yet, unrevealed powers and possibilities. As for instance: the world is known and it has limitless powers and potencies still unmanifested; man is known and he too has limitless possibilities, still to manifest. Here then are objects of intelligent faith, yet these are the very things those who advocate faith refuse to have faith in.

As an example of intelligent faith we might quote the following from Condorcet. "No bounds have been fixed to the improvement of the human faculties; the perfectability of man is absolutely indefinite; the progress of this perfection, henceforth above the control of every power that would impede it, has no other limit than the duration of the globe upon which nature has placed us." And this magnificent faith was written while Condorcet was in prison and facing the guillotine.

This is intelligent faith—belief in the, as yet, unseen possibilities of the known. There is plenty in this, still unknown, to satisfy any intelligent worshiper thereof; yet its substantive is known and that is what makes faith in it intelligent. Once this is realized, what time and argument it will save. We do not argue about the known, but only about the unknown—and what a waste of time it is! All talking about something they know nothing about and all convinced that they are right. When nations take it up they go to war to prove that "my God is better than your God." Let's stick to the known and the real, make that the object of our faith, and knowledge of it the object of our search. This is that planetary parallel—Reality and Truth. To put it in terms of our own theory: causatively and substantially the genetic and its planetary and biologic creations are all that is; the task of the epigenetic is to learn its nature, the result of which is Truth. In this Project Evolution, we have no time to waste on the unknown and the unknowable.

Apparently Paul, like Christ, never heard of this Project. Had he known the nature of Causation and its constructs he would have known the cause and source of the evils he saw in man; he would have known likewise that his God of righteousness was but man-made rightness, and that the real enemy this rightness has to fight is God himself, or itself—the nonmoral genetic force and its unmoral construct.

This is the vital truth religion hid from us; it taught us to believe the divine in us is the God part, the evil, of the devil. One purpose of this work is to put misplaced things back in their proper place, and we should not overlook this opportunity. The distinctly God part within us is in our generative organs, the creative genetic; the so-called divine, our own moral nature, epigenetic and man-made. What we call the spiritual mind is the higher mental part of this, and what we call the carnal mind is the lower part, the body mind, a wholly prehuman and wholly unaided construct of God. This body-mind with its desire element is the source of our so-called evil, but no saint has ever yet seen that the way of the body is the will of God. To St. Paul its vice is vice versa:

7. . . . the carnal mind is enmity against God; for it is not subject to the law of God, neither indeed can it be.
8. So then they that are in the flesh cannot please God (Rom. 8).

This is a sample of the confusion wrought by the false God concept of religion. The carnal mind is not in enmity against God for it is God, and wholly subject to his purpose, procreation. Therefore it is only those who are in the flesh that do please God. The Old Testament itself confirms this fact. As long as the Israelites remained in the flesh and followed the law of the body and the jungle, they pleased God immensely; as soon as they turned to pacific ways his wrath was kindled against them. Attributing punishment for their acts to God, however, is but more ignorance of Evolution and its constructs. It is only man's own moral sense that condemns the evil doers, and only when this legally or psychologically catches up with them are they punished. This it is that sees in secret and rewards openly, but Paul, like his forebears, attributed it to God.

19. For the wisdom of this world is foolishness with God: For it is written, He taketh the wise in their own craftiness (1 Cor. 3).

The wise here are not wise or they would not set in motion the punitive laws in nature. Its subtle law (cause and effect), operating on the psychic and mental planes, was just too deep

for Paul. As the ignorant saints have always done, he interpreted
it as detection and punishment by divine Omniscience.

Paul understood Hebrew and Greek but apparently he did
not understand Latin—*Demon est deus inversus.* If he had he
would have known that a fallen God becomes a devil, and that
it was this that was bedeviling him.

18. For I know that in me (that is, in my flesh), dwelleth no good
thing: for to will is present in me; but how to perform that which is
good I find not.

19. For the good that I would I do not: but the evil which I would
not, that I do (Rom. 7).

And so said Ovid before him: "I see and approve the better
things of life, the worse things I follow."

23. But I see another law in my members, warring against the law
of my mind, and bringing me into captivity to the law of sin which
is in my members.

The perplexed saint did not realize that this law in his members was the very God that he thought so good—the Creative
Principle with its constructs—desire, lust, passion, greed—at
war with his own human morality, the genetic versus the epigenetic.

The trouble with Paul was that he had too much of the genetic
in him and not enough of the epigenetic. He was not one of
those "lukewarm" fellows of Laodicea; he belonged to Pergamos
—or is it Pergonos?—the *per* standing for perversion, the
"thorn" in his flesh.

20. Now if I do that I would not, it is no more I that do it, but sin
that dwelleth in me (Rom. 7).

Very well, if it was not he, why not learn who it really was
and stop agonizing about it? Since it was not the epigenetic Paul,
it was the genetic God. As Whitman said:

> It was not I that sinned the sin;
> The wretched body dragged me in.

And so said the Hindu seers: "Desire does it. I do not do it. Desire is the doer. I am not the doer. Desire is the agent. I am not the agent." [3] And who made desire, and its astral source? And who put it in our "members"? These things neither Paul nor his forebears knew, and so he rambles on:

21. I find then a law, that, when I would do good, evil is present with me.
24. O wretched man that I am! who shall deliver me from the body of this death? (Rom. 7).

Like all his kind, Paul's wretchedness was due to his own ignorance. He understood neither the law nor the Lawgiver. So let us see if we can make this still clearer. In the course of world creation the Creative Principle, the genetic, developed mental, astral, etheric energies and physical matter. These, in Evolution, are the body and its energies. They are the source of body hunger and astral lust, and doing what they want is what we call sin. It is these that are warring in our flesh, and it is these we call the devil in us, whose sectarian name is God. In the course of Evolution man developed reason and morality, the epigenetic. These and the devil both indwell us and the warfare is between them. It is this devil that drives us to war both military and commercial. The moral and rational want peace and security, but cannot, as yet, secure them. Thus moral man has an incubus on his back and it antedates him by billions of years. This is the vital truth a cunning priesthood concealed from us. Only when we recognize the deception and learn who our enemy really is will we know what our problem is.

If Paul had known these things there would have been no wretched Christendom, for he is mainly responsible for it. "For if ye live after the flesh, ye shall die: but if ye through the spirit do mortify the deeds of the body, ye shall live." And so taking his advice about the body and sex, the benighted saints castrated themselves, the illustrious Origen among them. And it wasn't enough that he should suffer; during the Dark and Middle Ages

[3] From the *Taittirya Aranyaka.*

he caused millions to suffer like him. You should read their lives; you should know about their self-inflicted tortures, their lice, their scabs, their starvation and flagellation to realize the havoc this man, or his creators, wrought. Nor is it now a thing of the past; our monasteries and nunneries are filled with people denying themselves the life that nature intended for them; missionaries go forth to die inspired by false doctrines and ideals; millions waste their lives saving souls from sin instead of God-ordained evils: savagery, cruelty and war. Neither God nor man demands such sacrifice. The only virtue required of anyone is social decency, beyond that lies only error born of ignorance.

There is none of this self-inflicted martyrdom in the truth; it springs only from error, and the extent of it in Christianity is the measure of its error. It is from these things that the truth sets us free, then let us get it and be free.

Because of Christianity's false teachings the Church has opposed every forward step in the past two thousand years. Even today it is opposing sane laws concerning divorce, abortion and birth control. The latter, it believes, are tampering with souls. It doesn't even know there is no soul involved in conception and early fetus; there isn't even life but only the Life Principle, a promiscuous and unconscionable force. Were this allowed free rein in our disease-controlled society, it would produce six billion bodies by the end of this century. This leads straight to war, for when man overproduces, nature plows under.

To the religionist this mass production is quite all right if done in wedlock, otherwise it is a sin. So the mumbled words of a priest make sin a virtue. If sex is for procreation only, why a billion times that required? If meant only for the marriage bed, why does it develop at twelve instead of twenty? It is this too early urge, for our society, that constitutes the tragedy and agony of adolescent youth. In some this impelling urge is so strong it results in rape and murder. This we call evil but not its source.

Sex is but a cosmic lust manifesting in man, that astral source of desire now biologized. This in biologic life is the Creator and its one and only purpose is form-creating and it cares not whether it's in wedlock or without. How then can its use for

pleasure only be against its will? In the myriad forms in this
world it is getting a perpetual sex thrill. We've been told the
Creator made this world for his own good pleasure; well, this
is part of it. Thus it is from our own false God-concept our false
ideas spring. This being so, those who adhere to them should
not be allowed to decide such vital things as divorce, abortion
and birth control, for they have no knowledge of the fundamentals of Being.

The philosophy of Christianity consists of false knowledge
due mainly to misunderstood scripture. For this we have another name; it is ignorance, and it is this that's defeating the
moral effort. Right understanding comes from knowing, not just
believing. Now if those who preach and teach Christianity
knew the nature of Causation they would not waste their time
worshiping it. If they knew what the "original sin" was, they
would not see man as under the condemnation of God. If they
knew what the soul is they would not think it lost but only
undeveloped. If they knew it is quality, not entity, they would
not try to save it but rather to develop it. If they knew the nature
and purpose of Evolution they would not think these qualities
came from God; they would know they were created by man
himself. Lacking such knowledge, they cannot enlighten those
they teach, and without enlightenment the people can do nothing to improve the human estate.

You purely biologic parents, you do not know you have to
create soul (quality) do you? In fact you have been told you
don't. You have only to provide bodies, six, ten, a dozen, and
God will furnish the souls, ready-made and perfect. Your only
task is to protect them from sex and bad company. Some of you
have done just that and they walked out and killed someone
"just for the hell of it." Then you wring your hands and cry,
"What have we done to deserve this?" It isn't what you've done
but what you haven't done. You didn't enlighten them, you
didn't develop within them a civilized consciousness. You let
them grow up with only the savage, prehuman soul your God
did create, and now it has overthrown the human part. You did
not teach them right values because you do not have them yourselves. You did not hold up character as a worthy objective; your

every word and deed convinced them that money is more important. You did not tell them what constitutes true manhood; you let commercial morons teach them that the two-fisted, jaw-bustin' brute is the ideal man. You did not remove all reasons for and examples of cruelty from your children; you let them see, read and listen daily to gangsters, warfare and murder, all produced for money and by adults who should be jailed instead of enriched. You did not rise up in righteous wrath and demand these things be stopped; you let the marketplace rob your children's souls of all spiritual food and drink. So now you must take the consequence. When once you learn it is you, not God, who creates souls you will be more careful of what you create.

If our saints would save us they must learn what human nature is and what produced it: not Edenic sin but "the struggle for existence" and "the survival of the fittest." These developed such qualities as cunning, cruelty, competition and greed. These are not removed by belief in God and Jesus Christ. They are removed only by supplanting them with their opposites, love, mercy, compassion, justice. And this we are not doing; in business only the jungle qualities succeed; in war they are the only qualities.

We all want a peaceful, warless world but we haven't the faintest idea of how to achieve it. War is a conflict between two powers waged with ferocious cruelty. Yet every game we play in peace is also a conflict waged with cruelty and cunning. Thus, whether we know it or not, we are following Washington's advice: "In time of peace prepare for war," not just militarily but psychologically also. We don't approve of killing, yet we train millions to kill, and if one kills sufficiently he becomes a national hero, and we are proud of him. We are proud of our armies and navies never realizing that if we were civilized there would be no such things. We are proud of the size and efficiency of our police force when this is due only to the number of criminals in our society. We are proud only because we haven't sense enough to be ashamed.

We would rid the world of religious bigotry and prejudice, then passionately defend their source, religion. This, we've been told, is the one great binding force, when it is the most divisive force in all the world—Catholic against Protestant, Arab against Israeli, Mohammedan against Hindu. Thus instead of binding us together it makes killers of us. Throughout its history it has caused the death of untold millions. See page 463.

For two thousand years rationalists have tried to destroy the source of all this—Christ and his false God-concept. They failed because they lacked the knowledge necessary to see the errors in his knowledge. So let us see how knowledgeable this Christ was.

25

Christianity:
Its False Doctrines

Salvation is not begged or bought;
Too long this selfish hope sufficed;
Too long man reeked with lawless thought,
And leaned upon a tortured Christ.

ELLA WHEELER WILCOX

Before we attribute authority to anyone we should ask this question: What does he know of his subject? Thus far, no one has asked this question of Christ; no one has pronounced Him ignorant, and this because no one has had sufficient knowledge to see the errors in His teachings. Yet this will be the basis of our proof that this God and Savior is but a creation of an ignorant priesthood. Those priestly scribes were ignorant of Causation and Creation, Evolution and the origin of qualities and so they made their creature likewise. They were ignorant even of the meaning of Genesis and so made their Son of God believe in its literal word; in fact, His whole salvation purpose is based on that literalism.

According to these literalists Christ was the Creator of the world, yet he accepted the absurd account of creation as given in Genesis. He believed in a historical Noe, a Moses, a David, a Solomon and even a Jonah for it was he who told us the fish was a whale. He believed in a historical Adam, his sin and his fall. But Adam was not a man; therefore it wasn't man that sinned. And if man didn't sin he is not lost. And if he is not lost he does not need a Savior. Thus Christ's whole salvation mission was based on a misunderstanding of Genesis. In fact, the entire New Testament is based on a misinterpretation of the Old Testament.

One would think that the Creator of the world would know the origin and genesis of qualities and therefore of love, and yet we have such proof of Christ's ignorance of these fundamentals as this: "God is love." "For God so loved the world that he gave his only begotten son that whosoever believeth in him should not perish but have everlasting life." [1]

No greater number of didactic fallacies were ever strung together in one short sentence. God does not love the world; God does not *give* the world anything; he has no "only begotten son," belief will not save anyone, and there is no such thing as everlasting life.

God is not even the source of love, but only of life; love is not a gift but a slow and painful product of evolutionary life—very recent at that. Nowhere in all creation is there any evidence of it save in man. True, we find it dawning in the animal mother but that only proves its biologic and evolutionary origin. A Christ would know these things but as his creators did not, they made him as ignorant as themselves. Thus no further proof of Christ's human and syncritic origin is needed than this statement for it is not that of a divinely wise being but only a later expression of an ancient Hebrew fallacy—moral perfection on the wrong end of Being. The gospelists, accepting this, put it into the mouth of their creation, and for two thousand years Western man has not had sufficient knowledge of Reality to know that it is false. He still accepts it; his moral guides still cite it as Christ's unique discovery. "Upon his lips Abba meant more than any name for God ever meant before. So purely and ardently did it issue from the depths of his own experience as to communicate itself to his disciples and through them to others in such a vivid reality as to make a new and transforming epoch in the life of the human spirit. This is originality. By this token Divine Fatherhood may be rightly regarded as a discovery, and

---

[1] These words are, of course, from the gospel writers but since these created this Christ their words are cognate and of equal authority.

Jesus as the discoverer."—Dr. F. N. Buckham. In other words, Jesus was the discoverer of the greatest error in all human thought; by implanting it firmly in the racial mind he was guilty of the greatest deception in all human history. If this be originality, it resulted in the complete destruction of the ancient wisdom-knowledge of Reality. Such teaching has robbed man of all knowledge of Causation, the reason for disasters, the source of truth, the origin of qualities and the purpose of his own being. Had this Christ lived a few years longer, how would He have accounted for the destruction of Pompeii and Herculaneum? Was this too a "token" of "Divine Fatherhood"? For millions of years these violent forces have destroyed both life and property, but instead of drawing the logical conclusion our teachers but repeat the words of this ignorant Christ after him. Elsewhere we said that poets know more than priests and now it seems they know more than Christs also—a logical deduction since Christs are priest-creations. Poets make no claim to omniscience, yet having looked on nature they know their "Father's" nature:

Cry against your day as men have forever done, believing it the worst —believing themselves to inherit the age of darkness after the age of the sun.
I say all days are evil, since first the spirit moved on the waters. The bomb, the gun were fashioned in chaos; so indeed were the breasts of desire, and the beauty of beasts that, born to terror run like music round creation's wheel of fire.

                                                    Dilys Bennet Laing

Why did Christ not know this also? Because either his creators were ignorant of it or they did not want the truth revealed— truth and priests are not concomitant. And so they put still more false words into his mouth: "He that loveth me shall be loved of my Father," "Father forgive them for they know not what they do," and so on. The only father of Christ or man is a natural principle, and this is not conscious of what it creates. How then can it forgive man for his sins? Having made man savage and ignorant, how can it hold him guilty? Had this metaphysically ignorant Christ possessed any knowledge of Causation, his prayer would read in reverse—Man, forgive God, for he knows not what he does. All life attests this tragic fact, and so the question is not, Will God forgive man for his sins? but can man forgive God for his cruelty? That man caused his own suffering through an "original sin" is a perversion of the truth. That "sin" was God's—the creation of matter, the source of evil. But God does not suffer for his sins; he lets man do it. Yet where does Christ show his awareness of this fact? Where a word of pity for man's martyrdom? There is none, yet this is the basis of his wish, the brotherhood of man. Only when the individual sees blind, suffering humanity as the victim of a cause that knows not love and mercy will sympathy awaken. Only when all see this cosmic plight of man will they do unto others as they would be done by. This is the source of *divine* compassion and it is human, not theistic. This "the Son of God" did not know, and so he taught the opposite.

No other teacher was guilty of such misguidance. Buddha, or his creators, saw quite clearly the true nature of God and stood aghast at its cruelty. "If God," said he, "permits such misery to exist he cannot be good, and if he is powerless to prevent it, he cannot be God." Nowhere in Christ's words do we find such recognition of fact or accusation of Cause. Like Michael in Jude, he "durst not bring against him a railing accusation."

There is a story told of a heavenly messenger sent by God to bring report of man. Filled with zeal and prejudice against this mortal rebel, he came to earth, but there he learned a shocking truth—that man is God's moral superior, and filled with zeal for man and prejudice against God, he too became a rebel—and "I do well to be angry," said another of his kind. Now if the Gospels are literally true, Christ was also a messenger from God to man, but instead of recognizing the suffering of man and the cruel indifference of God, he widened the gulf between them: "None is good save one, that is God," while we are sinners, all; the things of man are as nothing compared to the things of God, and so we must "render unto Caesar the things that are Caesar's, and unto God the things that are God's." The implication is, of course, that the things of Caesar (man) are vile and evil, whereas the things of God are divine and holy. Had this "Son of God" known His Father's nature he would have realized that, morally at least, the things of Caesar are incalculably superior to the things of God. But having learned of God from Hebrew theology, man was to him a helpless creature wholly dependent upon a God of love for everything—with prayer as the logistic key. He has but to ask this loving God for peace, justice, health and prosperity and they will be given him. If these things come from God, and prayer be the modest price thereof, why is the world so devoid of them? Because we do not pray enough? No, but because in that vast preponderance of time not spent in prayer, we let their vicious opposite grow up in our hearts, and there they become the disposing factors in our lives, and neither prayers below nor God above can overrule them. It is for us to create these things, not beg them from alleged divinity. For thousands of years we have been begging this divinity for peace, and only now are we realizing that we ourselves must establish it, hence the United Nations.

Had Christ known the nature of Reality he would not have taught the love of God for man or its reverse. Yet the Gospels have him say: "And thou shalt love the Lord thy God with all thy heart, and with all thy soul, and with all thy mind, and with all thy strength: this is the first commandment" (Mark 12:30). It is not the first of an enlightened Christ but only of a priesthood that needed it professionally. God being but the ruthless creative power, man has no right to love it, since from it spring all his pain and suffering, his savagery and war. If he would escape from these he must not only cease pretending to love it but oppose and conquer it. Mythologically man rebelled against this one—to become human; he must now rebel against it mentally and morally to become divine. And this he is doing, all unknowingly because of religion. His search for truth, his hope for peace, his efforts towards law and order, what are they but human efforts to overcome this primal savagery within himself? This being the case, why should he love it? The truth is he doesn't but only pretends to. This results in hypocrisy, and then our teachers wonder why we are hypocrites one toward the other.

Were honest opinion allowed for just one day, they would

learn a most shocking truth—there's not a man among us that would not, if he dared, denounce this ruthless power for the suffering it has caused him. Whether the Church knows this or not, it is the truth; I do but make articulate the latent thought of millions. No man loves God, and any man who says he does is "a liar and the truth is not in him." You cannot love what you do not know, and no man knows the God of religion. Why then poison your soul, and the group-soul too, with words you know are lies? The least you might do for the human cause is to be honest with yourself; that done, "thou canst not then be false to any man."

Love is not the solvent for man's sins nor yet his savagery, therefore not even on the human plane are Christ's precepts those of wisdom—"Love thy neighbor as thyself." You cannot love your neighbor as thyself nor should you try. The error here lies in the word—not love but good will, and unemotional good will comes not from love but from enlightenment. This is the solvent of our social ills and Christ ignored it. He gave us the goal, peace and brotherhood, but He did not tell us how to solve the moral, social and economic problems that prevent its attainment; He did not tell us we are still far down the ladder of Evolution and therefore ignorant; He made no mention of the savage God-forces here man has to contend with; on the contrary He offered only the faith of childlike innocence and trust in the supernatural. He was guilty therefore of misdirection of human energies.

A humanity, ignorant of the cause, turned these savage God-forces upon itself, the result, fraternal war and conquest. A genuine Savior would have taught primitive man that his enemy was not his equally needy brother, but his ruthless, warlike Father—nature, if you prefer it. This Savior, on the contrary, taught him this Father alone was good and therefore should be loved and worshiped. And now, considering the time we've wasted on war and worship, it's little wonder we're still savage. It's time man learned he has no time to waste on God, or energies to waste on war. He needs them both in the all-important project Civilization. This implies love and justice, peace and brotherhood, and man alone can create them.

And now what has this world Savior to say about these

things? The very opposite. Instead of revealing to us our purpose in Creation and responsibility for our world conditions, He tells us to "take no thought" for anything, "for your heavenly father knoweth your need before ye ask him"—a perfect example of that "false security" under which we have lived. The statement has no literal significance whatsoever. Refuse to take thought for your own welfare and this "heavenly father" will let you starve. Take no thought for health and hygiene and you die of this "heavenly father's" murderous parasites. Take no thought for economic justice and you become an industrial slave. Take no thought for political justice and you have a world at war. Caring for these things is precisely our business, and in the present state of the world we see the result of leaving them to God—prayers for peace and incessant wars; wrong on the throne and right on the cross; the virtuous impoverished, the vicious enriched; our benefactors toiling alone, while the wealthy parasites loaf and play—this is "divine providence." What we need is a little human providence: knowledge and intelligence to right these God-ordained wrongs, and a sense of values that will help our benefactors help us. In these things God is helpless, and God's extremity is man's opportunity.

Whatever God does for any individual is done between conception and physical maturity—body-building; thereafter he *rests*, just as He did after He built His own body, the earth. Anything subsequent that seems from this source lies in the category of psychic phenomena. In evolution we build our own protective powers; they are not, therefore, cosmic and prehuman. What then does the quoted statement mean?

It does not take great wisdom to understand this statement; therefore our misunderstanding of it reveals our lack of wisdom. Here, as elsewhere, it is the Creator speaking, and this Creator brought with it all things whatsoever this world would need. In this story Jesus is this Creator and he is assuring the world that its needs are known; therefore about the world and its needs we do not have to worry—*"Qui plantavit curabit,"* He who planted it will take care of it—but think not this applies to man. He has made his own world, human society, with new and specific needs the Creator knows not of; therefore man and man alone can supply them. This is the vital truth this Christ obscured, i.e., his creators obscured. Their need was a weak, subservient humanity dependent on them for "all this and heaven too."

In spite of our science their teaching is still with us. To illustrate this we quote from a religious notice in one of our metropolitan papers. Speaking of Christ and his salvation, it says: "It means simply that God comes down and does everything that needs to be done. He has to, because we are helpless—because the very effort to save ourselves by our own 'good works' is blasphemy, idolatry, arrogance, presumption, the very essence of sin." If Christ taught such things, He was a saboteur of His Father's actual plan—Evolution. And there is no "if" about it; He did teach it. We, the creators of reason, morality and someday divinity, can do nothing, nor do we need to since God knows our needs before we ask Him. Thus He led the race from nature's order to human chaos, diverted the mind from Reality, and wasted two thousand years on a false salvation. If such a teacher actually lived and led the race so far astray, then Mani was right—"he was a demon"; he was in fact the Antichrist. To spare him this, we say instead, he was the instrument of ecclesiasticism. It was this and this alone that needed the false theology and philosophy.

This we find epitomized in that perversive parable of "the prodigal son." In this, Christ likens man to a rebel, a sinner and a fool who separates himself from his righteous father, only to repent, return and be forgiven—proof positive of his ignorant priestly origin, for no real Christ would draw such a parallel, for none exists. You cannot compare things unlike in nature. The human father and son are comparable, both being moral, self-conscious beings; the cosmic Father and Son are comparable, both being nonmoral, unconscious principles, but the human and cosmic pairs are wholly dissimilar. A Christ would know this also; he would know too that the cosmic Father and Son ran away together and that both fell into materiality. He would know that this was the "original sin" and that all others are but the results thereof. Had Christ known and taught these things, Christianity would never have got started, for the most ignorant would have seen that the sins of man are but the sins of God in man, and that man, instead of a thing apart and despised of God, is the best part of God, the only part that knows what love or mercy is. As it is through man this fallen God regains his kingdom, then instead of God being man's redeemer, man is actually God's redeemer. This is the "atonement," and man is the atoner; in other words, Evolution alone can atone for the "sin" of Involution—the creation of matter, the source of evil. Where then is the worth of this perverted parable? The occult key to it lies in the word *sun*, not son. When Apollo, the sun, was banished, he fed the flocks of King Admetus. This is the real prodigal, wasting its substance and reducing itself to the swine of scripture—the planets. This eventually returns to its father, the Absolute. But where is the preacher who knows such things?

In their literal interpretation, our preachers tell us we are the prodigal while they are the virtuous son at home. The fact is, they are the prodigal, the renegade from Reality, living on the husks of truth—literal mythology. It is for them to return to this source of Truth and be forgiven, not by God but by humanity.

This Christ admonished us to do the will of God, but apparently he did not know what the will of God is or where it manifests. To him it is in some far off-place called Heaven. "Our Father who art in heaven," and "thy will be done on earth as it is in heaven."

The will of God is the way of nature, "red in tooth and claw with ravine." [2] If Christ did not know this he was less wise than philosophers also, John Stuart Mill for one. ". . . if imitation of the Creator's will as revealed in nature were applied as a rule of action in this case, the most atrocious enormities of the worst men would be more than justified by the apparent intention of Providence that throughout all animate nature the strong should prey upon the weak." And again, "Not even on the most distorted and contrasted theory of good which ever was framed by religious or philosophic fanaticism can the government of Nature be made to resemble the work of a being at once good

[2] *In Memoriam* LVI

and omnipotent." And yet again: "If we are not obliged to believe the animal creation to be the work of a demon, it is because we need not suppose it to have been made by a Being in infinite power." [3] And so thought Buddha: "If God permits such misery to exist He cannot be good, and if He is powerless to prevent it, He cannot be God." "Are God and Nature then at strife, that Nature lends such evil dreams?" Tennyson.[4] No, it is only Nature and man's false God-concept that are at strife. To kill or be killed is Nature's law and therefore the will of God. As long as man is ignorant of this violent will he will remain a victim of it. Thus far he has consistently misinterpreted it. Feeling its impelling urge within him he thinks it a call from heaven and so sets out to make hell on earth. "God wills it! God wills it!" was the cry of every mass murderer on record. And he was right: God wills anything man is foolish enough to do. In our burning cities and starving nations we see what we can do under his will, and we will keep on doing them until we see that it is our will, not God's, that must put a stop to them. In things moral and social the genetic God of nature has no will for us; what we mistake for such is our own desire for the moral epigenetic's domination. Here the will of God for man is but the will of man for man acting upon God principles:

> A will that wills above the will of each,
> Yet but the will of all conjunctively.

If we would see it realized we must build our own moral world and live in it. We see then that man's task is the very opposite of that taught by Christ and Christianity—not "to do the will of God" but to get as far away from it as possible. This is "Free will"—the moral epigenetic's complete freedom from the domination of genetic energy and instincts.

But if no such being exists as the God of these false Gospels, to whom did Jesus pray—in the garden of Gethsemane, for instance? No one; the prayer is a pure invention, the work of

[3] *Essays on Nature*
[4] *In Memoriam* LV.

priestly-minded mythologists who wrote the rough, hard facts of Esau with the smooth, sly hand of Jacob. The garden of Gethsemane is one with the garden of Eden, and Jesus another Adam. As both are the Creative Principle, what need is there of another? And what greater prayer-answering power is there than the "Word," the Creator of the world? If greater power exists why did it not answer then? Why does it not answer now? The whole world is praying that wars may cease, but now as then there is no answer. A Christ would know the reason why, and so not waste his words on mindless space. If this Christ did not, he was again less wise than poets.

> And that inverted bowl we call the sky,
> Whereunder crawling cooped we live and die,
> Lift not thy hand to it for help—for it
> Rolls impotently on as thou or I.
>
> Omar Khayyam

What the Gospels present us with is a Son of God who believed in all the human fallacies of the preceding five thousand years. And this is the key to His origin and genesis—a priesthood which also believed in them. This is why he did not and could not give us any knowledge other than that of his day and generation. And yet what an opportunity was here! The Logos, the Word, the Creator. Could not such a being have cleared up the mysteries that have plagued us ever since? Could he not have solved even "the riddle of the universe"? Were his contemporaries so dumb and incurious they did not ask? Not entirely; one did ask but got no answer. "What is truth?" said Pilate, but the Christ-makers, themselves not knowing, hustled Pilate off before Omniscience could answer. Very clever but not knowledgeable. He might at least have told the Roman where to look for truth—in the book of life, not a book of lies.

So what is truth? To answer that we must know its source, Reality, and this the scriptures falsified. Reality, for us, is the world and all that it contains. As this includes its physical content, its genetic consciousness, the forms this created, and their consciousness, it is all in all. Reality in any broader sense is but this in multiple—the cosmos. Thus Reality is both quantitative and qualitative, objective and subjective. The human qualitative and subjective are our creations; the quantitative and objective were created for us. Our senses were made to contact and learn from the external Reality; they are the intelligizers of our consciousness, personal and racial. Our consciousness is thus the subjective part of objective Reality and right only to the extent of our experience with it. A given truth is a conceptual correlate of some aspect of Reality, objective or subjective. This aspect constitutes a fact, and knowledge consists of our awareness of it. Hence the criterion of truth is the amount of truth one has in himself, and because of that one man can be right though three billion declare he is wrong. It depends on how much his consciousness has learned from and conformed to Reality, which includes the wisdom content of the planetary group-soul. We see then that God is not Truth; God is Reality, Truth, man's knowledge of it. This being so, calling the scriptures "the word of God" is no guarantee of their truth.

Since Truth comes from Reality these two should fit together like the edges of a torn sheet of paper. Today they do not because religion inverted one of them, hence the inharmony. Herein lies our reason for stressing the need of a "reorientation of the mind with Reality." As of now it is oriented to nonreality, hence the warfare 'twixt creed and fact. Set this straight that the mind may not be confused by the variance in the facts of Reality it sees and the concepts of Reality it is taught. Concepts and percepts should also fit together; when they do not one of them is wrong. And this is the wrong of the scriptures.

Of the *cosmic* "facts of life" their creators knew nothing and so they could not make their creation know more. Aware of this they blinded us with miracles instead of facts. And what good were they to subsequent millions save to deceive them? Miraculous powers are not transmissible, nor are they possible to natural man, but knowledge of germs and therapeutic drugs is. So instead of miraculously healing a few to prove his divinity this Christ might have shown his humanity by teaching the ignorant the cause and cure of disease. Had he done so, a hundred million of his deluded followers would not have died of plague and pestilence. And if God is love, why should these even exist?

However, there is more to religion than knowledge. Religion is a duality—philosophy to enlighten the mind, and morality to civilize the soul. Christ gave us the latter but it is no more his than his philosophy. It came not from him nor from his God; it is from man and from man came Christ's. It antedates him by untold millenia, and even in his day Hillel taught the same fine precepts: "Judge not thy neighbor until thou hast been in his place." "Do not do unto others what thou wouldst not they should do unto thee; this is the whole of the law—the rest is only commentary." And so taught Socrates and Plato, Buddha and Confucius. "The doctrine of our master (Confucius) consists in having an invariable correctness of heart, and in doing towards others as we would that they should do to us." "Socrates and Plato are far superior to the Jewish moralists." And "let us add that no modern theology has taught higher and purer moral notions than those of Aeschylus and his school." Professor Mahaffy, D.D. "In reading Epictetus, Marcus Aurelius or Seneca, I often believe myself hearing the sage of Nazareth. The dignity of man, the all surpassing value of virtue, the independence and fortitude of the righteous man, the superior value of spiritual qualities as compared to all worldly goods, the sacrifice of selfish enjoyments and of life for the sake of virtue and truth—all these ideals, so worthy of reverence, we find in the one as well as in the other. The striking resemblance between the Christian and the Stoic doctrine . . . cannot escape being noticed by all." Staeudlin, in his *History of Moral Philosophy.*

Believers in the Christian origin of morals might also read Josephus's account of the Essenes, whom he calls "the most virtuous men on earth," and whose cult, according to Pliny, existed for ages before the time of Christ. To quote Josephus in part: "They are eminent for fidelity, and are ministers of peace; whatsoever they say is firmer than an oath, but swearing is avoided by them, and they esteem it worse than perjury." Speaking of the vows that each must take, he says: "And before he is allowed to touch their common food he is obliged to take tremendous oaths; that in the first place, he will exercise piety towards God; and then that he will observe justice towards men;

and that he will do no harm to anyone, either of his own accord or by the command of others . . . that he will keep his hands clear from theft and his soul from unlawful gain . . ." And what more did Jesus teach? Nothing, save false doctrines about God and man. The result is hypocrites and corruptionists instead of Essenes.

No, morality and wisdom came not from Christ; on the contrary, this Christ's teaching came from the morality and wisdom of his day. Thus we may say that man himself is the moral Christ.[5] Love and mercy, justice, truth are his creations; why then divide them into warring faiths in racial Saviors; why call them Christian, Jewish, Buddhist, Mohammedan? Call them human virtues and let it go at that. The sectarian divisions are the great dividers in our world; the cause of hatred, bigotry and prejudice. Ethnic divisions can live together until the sectarian enters in; the "melting pot" can fuse all *isms* except religious fanaticism. This endures and perpetuates the divisions. Today great effort is being made to combat "religious prejudice," but we simply do not know how to go about it; we cannot see that the only way to rid the world of "religious prejudice" is to rid it of religion, its cause and source. The substitute? That truth that would set us free—from religion's errors. This was the goal of all world teachers; it was only the priests who came after them that founded religions on them. These were not based on fact but fiction, the miraculous and the supernatural. So false a basis brought us little save stupefaction, chaos and war. If it ends in total extinction it will not be because we have found a power that would destroy us, but because we have not found the truth that would save us.

The ineffectuality of Christianity is due to nothing else than its God and Christ. It is the injection of these into everything that negates its moral teaching for those who need it most, the amoral and irresponsible. These want no part of them, and so, reject their associate. If then we would make morality a force in the world, we must rid it of its mythical Gods and Saviors.

[5] Scripturally, Christ is divine consciousness, but this consciousness called itself the Son of man, implying source.

That done, we could spend the time we waste on them on the betterment of man. Fortunately others are aware of this. "Man makes himself, and he only makes himself completely in proportion as he desacrilizes himself and the world. The sacred is the prime obstacle to his freedom. He will become himself only when he is totally demysticized. He will not be truly free until he has killed the last god." Mircea Eliade. "For man is the maker of all deities, inventor of all abstractions, builder of all laws, and from first to last, the measure of all things, the very meaning of the earth." Harry A. Murray. True; for us, there is only the earth and the life upon it; why waste time then on unrealities?

During the Piscean Age we had our political, social and industrial revolutions, but they did not change us inwardly. Something is needed to change the internal content. This will not be a religious revolution but a metaphysical one—the return of the wisdom-knowledge of the cosmos. Already man is besieging this physically; he must also besiege it mentally. This will bring him that "new dimension of consciousness and right orientation with Reality" so long denied him by religion. The latter, we know, is sacred to millions, but it's the sacred that's blinding us. Criticism, we know, is shocking to millions, but "A shock upon our minds is long overdue." Max Frankel.

26

The Church:
Its False Foundation

False shores and false securities ye were taught by the good. In the lies of the good ye were born and hidden; through the good everything has become crooked and deceitful from the bottom.

ZARATHUSTRA

The Catholic Church asserts it was founded by Christ and on the apostle Peter. Let us see just what this claim amounts to.

In one of its many pamphlets we find this claim set forth. Under the heading "St. Peter's Supremacy—Can it be proven from the Bible?" it begins thus: "There are three texts in the Bible for which Anglicans seem unable to assign satisfactory place in their system, viz., Matthew 16:13–20, Luke 22:31–32, and John 21:15–17." After a lengthy exposition of these texts, in true Catholic fashion, the writer concludes by saying there is no escape from the Catholic position.

There is no escape for those who cannot see beyond the literal word, and such is the pamphlet's author. Reversing his selections that we may deal with the most important last, they read as follows:

15. So when they had dined, Jesus saith to Simon Peter, Simon, son of Jonas, lovest thou me more than these? He saith unto him, Yea, Lord; thou knowest that I love thee. He said unto him, Feed my lambs (John 21).

As already explained, Peter is the earth, and this it is that must feed its lambs, the life upon it. As the statement is repeated three times it implies the three biologic kingdoms. The text then has nothing to do with the Catholic Church—save to refute it. As Jonah is purely mythological, calling Peter his son makes Peter also mythological. Today intelligent people do not swallow Jonah, yet they do swallow this similitude.

31. And the Lord said, Simon, Simon, behold, Satan hath desired to have you, that he may sift you as wheat:
32. But I have prayed for thee, that thy faith fail not: and when thou art converted, strengthen thy brethren (Luke 22).

Now this text has something to do with the Catholic Church; its close identification of Peter with Satan is very revealing to those who understand occult literature, but of this more in a moment. Of the last text, verses 18 and 19 will suffice.

18. And I say also unto thee, That thou are Peter, and upon this rock I will build my church; and the gates of hell shall not prevail against it.
19. And I will give unto thee the keys of the kingdom of heaven: and whatsoever thou shalt bind on earth shall be bound in heaven: and whatsoever thou shalt loose on earth shall be loosed in heaven (Matt. 16).

Thus the Catholic Church is founded on Peter whom, four verses later, Jesus openly calls Satan.

23. But he turned, and said unto Peter, Get thee behind me, Satan: thou art an offence unto me . . .

Thus if the Catholic Church is founded on Peter, it is founded on Satan—a fact we have long suspected. Satan means matter, and so does Peter the rock; therefore the two are one. Peter is but the New Testament Esau who founded, or rather was, the city called Petra, rock, and also Edom, atom, earth. This it is that binds and looses according to its laws—St. Peter's keys— and what it binds and looses is the Life Principle. The seven churches of Revelation are an outline of this. This binding and loosing Peter is also the New Testament Pharaoh; he too bound and loosed the life force. Moses' warfare with him represents this, and Paul's quarrel with Peter has the same meaning, cosmologically. As this binding and loosing is of nature, that of the Church is utterly false and pretentious. And this includes its blessings and its cursings; its excommunication, so dreaded by its people, has no moral or spiritual effect whatever; its results are political and social only and so but another means to power. And such also is Peter.

Aside from its cosmological meaning, Peter's story is the veriest nonsense—one mortal man endowed with the power over all humanity for all eternity; we thought that only God had this authority. In things religious, Catholics are indeed credulous but can they be so credulous as to believe that pre-Christian sages like Pythagoras, Plato, Socrates, and even Buddha require this ignorant Jewish fisherman to bind and loose their souls? And what of those pre-Christian Initiates from whom these ignorant religionists got their knowledge? Are they too bound and loosed by Peter? No, and neither are we.

Such a man as Peter never existed; what then of the Catholic claim that he founded the Papacy of Rome? It is one with Romulus founding Rome itself; thus Peter is but an eponym. Yet the *Catholic Encyclopedia* says his founding of the Roman bishopric is "among the best ascertained facts of history," and "no scholar now dares contradict it." This is just a sample of Catholic scholarship. With its capacity for intellectual dishonesty, anything can be proved. And if no scholar dares contradict it, it is only because no scholar has sufficient knowledge to do so, thanks to two thousand years of Catholic scholarship.

Concerning Peter, Catholic apologists pretend to examine his position fairly and honestly, then present us with statements now known to be forgeries; they offer us documents dating back to the Dark Ages and ask us to accept the words of its benighted people. Then, to cap it all, quote from the source that deceived them. Of course the Bible proves "Peter's Supremacy"—but the Bible is a book of mythology. That it does not provide a successor to Peter is a difficult point for the priestly sophists, yet they argue, and ably, that a successor is implied. When once they realize that Peter is the earth, they will see why no successor was provided. We trust they will also see the dishonesty of their arguments. They are not sincere examinations of the evidence, but only efforts of frightened little souls to defend a commitment, a refuge and a job.

Now what applies to Peter applies to the whole mythic *personae*. The twelve disciples were but the twelve planetary forces in Involution, later appearing as the twelve apostles with their "glad tidings" of life's evolutionary resurrection. As such, they are the twelve sons of Jacob and the twelve tribes of Israel, of the New Testament. What part then did they play in the founding of the Church? None whatever; this was the work of priests three centries later. What the mythic twelve founded was the earth, and not by love but by violence. What then of their martyrdom? Why this was it; the violent death of the spirit principle. James and John were its *thunderers*. Peter was hung head downward, but so was the Tree of Life, and the pyramid "built from the top downward." James was thrown from the top of the temple, but what temple? The planetary temple, and his fall made what the tree and the pyramid symbolize. Thomas, like Jesus, was a *tekton*, and like Jesus, a builder of this temple. Stephen was stoned to death, but according to apocryphal accounts, so was Jesus. As one version states it, he was "lapidated at the junction of two streams." A deeper meaning than *stoned* would be *turned to stone*, at the junction of Involution and Evolution. This was Peter's fate; not only was he hung head downward but from water he became *petra*, stone. This is the New Testament version of *Demon est Deus inversus.* And such is the painless record of apostolic martyrdom; such also is some of that attributed to the first Christians. They were thrown to the lions, but so was Daniel; they were imprisoned but so was Joseph. Actual martyrdom there was, and secular persecutions too, but they began not with the symbolic characters of this Creation myth, but with the actual characters who later, believing blindly in this myth, sought to impose it upon others. This they finally did, and because of it no one in two thousand years has had the intelligence to see the deception. What is needed here is "eyesalve."

We need this also to understand the Church. Jesus was not speaking of that institution we call the Church, Catholic or otherwise; in fact, there was no such word or institution in his time. The original was the Greek *ecclesie*, and it meant only a gathering, an assembly—no pope, no priest, no hierarchy. Now to understand this gathering or assembly we must again remember the position of the Creator when these alleged words were spoken. It was immediately before the Transfiguration—the invisible elements made visible. The *ecclesie* was therefore the gathering, or assembling, from space of the planetary elements in the sun, Hades. The choosing of its personnel is therefore but the New Testament parallel of the Old Testament's "chosen people." So likewise is the rock on which it is founded. The precedent for this is the rock or stone that grew in Nebuchadnezzar's dream until it filled the whole entity. This is the earth itself. Here we see why "the gates of hell shall not prevail against it." Why should they, since this hell or Hades created it? After its creation, the elements were again gathered and assembled in Evolution, and the *ecclesie* here is the organic forms —and the Life force will be with them "even unto the end of the world." Thus the Church founded on Peter, the rock, is but the earth and its biologic life. This is the only *catholic* or universal church there is. If the human institution was meant, why did it become divided, instead of assembled, into some seventy odd sects? If Christ chose Peter to head this institution, why did the apostles ignore his wish and elect "James the Just" instead? He, not Peter, was the first Pope. Later he was deposed and stoned to death. And Ananus who deposed him was also deposed. Does this sound like divine selection?

All this forgotten now, we're taught that Christianity was a new revelation of truth and its founders enlightened men and saints. Nothing could be farther from the truth. Ignorance is the soil in which religions grow and Christianity is no exception. The New Testament itself calls the disciples "unlearned and ignorant men," and the Jewish judges before whom their converts were brought pronounced them *idioti*, from which we get the word idiots. Still later they were called "fools in Christ." The Samaritan doctors called them Thartacs, and their period, "the Reign of Thartac." Thartac was the Egyptian god of "credulity and the vulgar faith." He was portrayed as a man with a book, a cloak, and the head of an ass. He appears in the Old Testament as Tartak, one of the foreign gods that Solomon worshiped.

If then the leaders were ignorant and credulous, what of the masses that followed them? According to Lecky, they were "in all intellectual virtues, lower than any other period in the history of mankind." "They were made up mostly of the poor and obscure, who were drawn to embrace the Gospels by an inner need, and whose low position in the social scale was a standing ground of reproach against the new religion from the side of its adversaries." G. P. Fisher. "It is only the simpletons, the ignoble, the senseless—slaves and women folk and children—whom they wish to persuade to join their congregation or can persuade." Celsus. And again, Celsus: "The rude and menial masses, who had hitherto been almost beneath the notice of Greek and Roman culture flocked in." And Hodges, on Celsus: "He disliked them for their poverty and ignorance. They seemed to be presumptuous and impertinent people who undertook to be teachers, having never learned." "I will not sit in the seat of synods while geese and cranes confusedly wrangle." St. Gregory Nazianzus. "The 'many' had begun to play with psychic and spiritual forces let loose from the Mysteries; and the 'many' went mad for a time and have not yet regained their sanity." G. R. S. Mead. "They had their full share of tumult, anarchy, injustice and war." Lecky. "The primitive Christians were men whose ardor was fierce in proportion to their ignorance." Massey. And speaking of the fierceness of their ardor, one of their own number, Jerome, said this of some who came to join but fled in fear: "Lo, they desire to depart—nay they do depart, saying that it is better to live among wild beasts than with such Christians." And Julian, who tried to enlighten them, left them with this: ". . . the deadliest wild beasts are hardly so savage against human beings as most Christians are against each other." And again, ". . . There is no wild beast like an angry theologian."

Julian tried to restore some sanity and sense to his day by

replacing Christian absurdity with pagan philosophy, but as with Ikhnaton of Egypt, the fanatical priests were too much for him. To this day he is known as Julian the Apostate, yet which was right, the apostate or the apostle? "The glory that was Greece and the grandeur that was Rome" compared to the Christian Greece and Rome answers that question.

All this the apologists smothered in lies and now our deluded preachers, teachers, playwrights and scenarists paint these early Christians as the inspired few, fighting and dying for the one true faith, and brand the really inspired as ignorant pagans. In Chapter 19 we dealt with the intelligentsia of the day; it might be of interest to know what these thought of the new religion. "It is a pernicious superstition." Tacitus. "The new faith is a perverse and extravagant superstition." Pliny. "A superstition vain and frantic." Suetonius. Today a still-deluded race looks upon these statements as pagan opposition to "the light of the world" when they were but prelude to our spiritual *dämmerung*. Little wonder the Jews did not accept this "superstition vain and frantic"; they knew too well what it really was—their old mythmakers at it again.

Thus whatever the early Christians suffered, it was not as the Church asserts, because of the new gospel they preached, but because of the old absurdity they resurrected—belief in literal mythology. Another "Son of God," No. 16, had appeared, miraculously conceived and virginly born, a third part of the Trinity walking about in Galilee. This was that "blasphemy barbarously bold," Porphyry had denounced, yet a band of fanatics called Christians was actually demanding its restoration, which meant in plain words, a return to the dark night of pre-historic Greece and Rome. Well, this just must not happen—but by heaven it did. The darkness fell, and for two thousand years it covered the Western world. All the wisdom-knowledge of the ages was burned in the market place; the "light of the world" had triumphed and the light of reason died. As Canon Farrar said: "The triumph of Latin theology was the death of rational exegesis." This is hindsight; those with foresight might well have anticipated Earl Grey: "The lights are going out all over Europe."

In the light of these facts, the "tyrants" Nero, Tiberius, Domitian, seem less monstrous; indeed they stand out as the defenders of truth. They tried to save the world from two thousand years of ignorance, but that ignorance was too much for them. They found themselves accused of the very things they tried to prevent, riot, arson, rebellion. The Christian priesthood, inheriting the libelous cunning of its Semitic prototype, caused the burning and the fighting and blamed them on its enemies. Whether it burned Rome or not, it burned the truth and that is worse.

The destruction of all evidence of Christianity's gnostic and pagan source was "the first work." It was the evangelists themselves who started it, in Antioch, as stated in Acts. Speaking of just such things the Emperor Julian said he would deal with them more at length, "when we begin to explore the monsterous deeds and fraudulent machinations of the evangelists." And of their followers, Edward Carpenter wrote thus: ". . . they took special pains to destroy the pagan records and so obliterate the evidence of their own dishonesty." By order of the Church all the books of the Gnostic Basilides were burned, likewise Porphyry's thirty-six volumes. Pope Gregory VII burned the Apollo library filled with ancient lore. Emperor Theodosius had 27,000 schools of the Mysteries paprus rolls burned because they contained the doctrinal basis of the Gospels. By offering rich rewards Ptolemy Philadelphus gathered 270,000 ancient documents; these too were burned for the same reason. As someone has said, the early Christians heated their baths with the Ancient Wisdom. And what knowledge they may have contained!

Nor did the destruction end with the Founders; the fanatics they made carried on the work: the Crusaders burned all the books they could find, including original Hebrew scrolls. In 1233 the works of Maimonides were burned along with twelve thousand volumes of the Talmud. In 1244 eighteen thousand books of various kind were destroyed. According to Draper, Cardinal Ximenes "delivered to the flames in the square of Granada eighty thousand Arabic manuscripts." On finding similar lore in the New World, the Spanish Christians destroyed it and the temples that contained it.

All evidence of source destroyed, the Christian Fathers could now substitute their own absurdities. And to substantiate them they altered words and inserted verses that did not exist in the original texts. Celsus, a witness to this falsification, said of the revisionists, "Some of them, as it were in a drunken state producing self-induced visions, remodel their Gospel from its first written form, and reform it so that they may be able to refute the objections brought against it." On this same subject Massey wrote thus: "They made dumb all pagan testimony against the unparalleled imposture then being perfected in Rome. They had almost reduced the first four centuries to silence on all matters of the most vital importance for any proper understanding of the true origins of the Christian superstition. The mythos having been at last published as a human history, everything else was suppressed or forced to support the fraud." It is well known the Christian Fathers were notorious forgers: even the Catholics admit that. According to the *Catholic Encyclopedia*, "In all these departments forgery and interpolation as well as ignorance had wrought mischief on a grand scale." Indeed Pope Stephen II went so far as to write a letter and sign St. Peter's name to it. When we know that Peter never existed these deceptions take on new meaning; they give the key to the Church's entire history, motive and purpose—domination, wealth, and power. To this end all else was done, including the fakeries, forgeries, and the burning of books.

In spite of all this we are told the founders of our faith were good men, filled with the Holy Spirit and therefore above the crime and cruelty of common clay. Such is the teaching, yet their own words belie these lies. Consider this from Jerome, for instance: "If thy father lies down across thy threshold, if thy mother uncovers to thine eyes the busom which suckeled thee, trample on thy father's lifeless body, trample on thy mother's busom and with eyes unmoistened and dry, fly to the Lord who calleth thee." This is Christian zeal and the very opposite of religion. And Tertullian, gloating on the prospects of seeing the philosophers in hell, exclaimed: "How shall I laugh! How shall I rejoice! How shall I triumph when I see so many illustrious kings who were said to have mounted into heaven groaning with Jupiter their God in the lowest depths of hell." And St. Augustine on his religion: "The enemies thereof, I hate vehemently; O that thou wouldst slay them with thy two-edged sword."

And who were these "enemies"? Atheists, infidels, destroyers of the truth? No indeed, the keepers of the truth, those abhorrent Gnostics. Here we should recall the words of Frances Swiney: "It may truly be said that the blackest and bloodiest records that history can show us are the attacks of the Orthodox Church upon the Gnostic mystics." Oh yes, it takes more than ignorance to found a religion; it takes dishonesty, cruelty and war as well.

That Christianity had such a beginning may seem to the faithful quite incredible, but if so, it is only because the little that they know about it came from priestly apologists lying for the same reason as their predecessors. The unbelieving should read contemporary historians, Eusebius, for instance, in 250 A.D., that's, A(fter) the D(elusion). He left a record of the Church at that time and it reads like this: "But since from our great freedom we have fallen into neglect and sloth when each had begun to envy and slander the other, when we waged intestine war against each other, wounding each other with words as with swords and spears, when leaders assailed leaders, and people assailed people, hurling epithets at each other, when fraud and hypocrisy had reached the highest heights of malice . . . when devoid of all sense, we gave no thought to the worship of God, but believing like certain impious men, that human affairs are controlled by no providence, we heaped crime upon crime. When our pastors despising the rule of religion, fought with each other intent on nothing but abuse, threats, jealousy, hatred and mutual enmity, each claiming for himself, a principality as a sort of tyranny." And we are asked to believe these men were saints guided by the Holy Ghost.

We see then that the early Christians were by no means a united band against a pagan world; they were, on the contrary, a number of fanatical cults all contending for place and power.[1] As the Church acquired both, internecine war broke out for the

---

[1] To cite only the principal ones, there were Arians, Nestorians, Martionites, Marionites, Jacobites, Basilidians, Carpocratians, Collyridians, Eutychians, Sabellians, Valentinians, Gnostics, Ebionites, etc. Each of these had its own interpretation of the scriptures and the form that came down to us was but the one that triumphed over the others.

spoils—and now the noble martyrs began to martyr one another. Hundreds fell at the hands of their greedy rivals; thousands died in battles fought for churches, papal elections, and the right to conduct services. With such a beginning, the Crusades, St. Bartholomew, and the Inquisition become more understandable.

Another fallacy perpetuated by the Church concerns its creeds and dogmas, rites and rituals. The gullible laity is led to believe these all drive from God, or Christ, the apostles and the scriptures. They should read their own Bishop Hilary. He told them where they came from. "It is a thing equally deplorable and dangerous that there are as many doctrines as inclinations, and as many sources of blasphemy as there are faults among us, because we make creeds arbitrarily and explain them as arbitrarily. Every year, nay every moon, we make new creeds to describe invisible mysteries; we repent of what we have done; we defend those who repent; we anathematize those whom we defend; we condemn either the doctrines of others in ourselves, or our own in that of others; and reciprocally tearing each other to pieces, we have been the cause of each other's ruin." Here we have the source of our sacred doctrines. Where they are not the work of ignorance trying to explain what it does not understand, they are the result of priestly endeavor to control the human mind.

According to their teaching "the blood of Christ washed away the sins of the world," still with us. What it actually washed away was the sanity of the world. In due time its doctrines so bedeviled the Western mind that Agobard of Lyons wrote thus: "The wretched world lies now under the tyranny of foolishness; things are believed by Christians of such absurdity as no one ever could aforetime induce the heathen to believe." Should the skeptical reader wish a sample, we offer another tale of Christian martyrdom, this time about the precursor of the curse, John of the Gospels. According to the saints, John, when very old, incurred the anger of the Emperor Domitian. To punish him, the latter had this holy man thrown into a caldron of oil and resin. A fire was lit, and when the liquid began to boil the jeering crowd heard a voice singing in the flames—the Christian Shadrach, etc. When the caldron boiled dry, there was John still alive and quite unharmed. Jerome, Eusebius, Tertullian all relate this miracle and practically all hagiographies contain it. And now, if these eminent Christians could believe this absurdity, they could believe anything, even the Gospels. And do you realize that what they believed was that "faith once delivered to the saints"? It was, and for fifteen hundred years their word was law, and men were burned at the stake for doubting it. It would seem that these saints were the most ignorant men who ever left their mark on human thought. Of Causation and Creation they knew nothing; of Evolution and its qualities they knew no more, yet their substitute "superstition" still dominates the religious mind.

Anyone dominated by religious thought is under the influence of a reason-perverting power. Such were Christianity's Confounding Fathers. Today we honor these misbegotten for their courage without realizing the crime they committed—the complete destruction of ancient science and philosophy. This resulted in fifteen hundred years of darkness, in which the Christian people did not even know the earth is round. And yet as early as the sixth century *Before the Confusion*, Pythagoras taught that the earth was not only round but going 'round the sun. In the third century B.C. Aristarchus outlined the true heliocentric theory developed as a great discovery nineteen centuries later by Copernicus. In the third century B.C. Eratosthenes measured the circumference of the earth, and in the second Hipparchus invented longitude and latitude, determined the obliquity of the ecliptic and discovered the precession of the equinoxes. In the fifth century, Democritus and Leucippus taught the atomic theory of matter and the evolutionary theory of life. These men were doing what man is supposed to do—turn Reality into Truth—but "the game was called on account of darkness," the night of Christianity. In the Dark Ages the "blackout" was complete—a curious effect for "the light of the world."

Obliquity, precession, longitude and latitude are complex subjects requiring much scientific knowledge about the earth, its shape, its size and motions. Now let us compare Greek scientists with Christian saints. Against some scientist still surviving one had this to say: "This fool wishes to reverse the entire system of astronomy; but sacred scripture tells us that Joshua commanded the sun to stand still and not the earth"—and some thirteen hundred years later a pope issued a bull to the same effect. Another famous argument was that "in the day of Judgment men on the other side of a globe could not see the Lord descending through the air." Concerning the earth's motion, St. Augustine had this to say: "It is impossible there should be inhabitants on the opposite side of the earth, since no such race is recorded by Scripture among the descendants of Adam." And Father Inchofer: "The opinion of the earth's motion is of all heresies the most abominable, the most pernicious, the most scandalous; the immobility of the earth is thrice sacred." And Lactantius concluded, "It is impossible that men can be so absurd as to believe that the crops and trees on the other side of the earth hang downward and that men have their feet higher than their heads. . . . Now I am really at a loss what to say of those who, when they have once gone wrong, steadily persevere in their folly and defend one absurd opinion with another." How peculiarly applicable are these words to those who uttered them. We know now these men were wrong scientifically, but we still do not know they were wrong theologically.

Among those most active in this perversion of truth was the great Augustine—not an ignorant man scholastically but certainly ignorant metaphysically. The proof of this lies in his own words, his *Confessions.* Though he did not know the earth is round, he presumed in these, to explain its creation, as of Genesis. This is how it reads:

This then is what I conceive O my God when I hear thy Scriptures saying, In the beginning God made heaven and earth: and the earth was invisible and without form, and darkness was upon the deep, and not mentioning what day thou createst them; this is what I conceive, that because of the heavens—that intellectual heaven, whose intelligences know all at once, not in part, not darkly, not through a glass, but as a whole, in manifestation face to face; not this thing now, that thing anon; but (as I said) know all at once, without any succession

of times; and because of the earth invisible and without form, without
any succession of time, which succession presents 'this thing now, that
thing anon'; because where there is no form, there is no distinction
of things; it is then, on account of these two, a primitive formed and
a primitive formless; this one, heaven, but the heaven of heavens; the
other earth but the earth movable and without form; because of these
two do I conceive did the Scriptures say without mention of days, In
the beginning God created heaven and earth. For, forthwith it sub-
joined what earth it spoke of; and also in that the firmament is recorded
to be created the second day, and called heaven, it conveys to us of
which heaven he before spoke, without mention of days.

And this goes on for pages, ending in rhapsodical raving. And
for this the Christian world renounced Greek science and
philosophy; for this all ancient learning was burned in the marketplace. If ever Disraeli's words were applicable it is here: "It
is worse than a crime; it is a mistake." A crime may affect only
a few, and for a brief period, whereas a mistake of this proportion affects the destiny of the race; it can even subvert Evolution
—and did. Thus are the sins of the Christian Fathers visited
upon their sons, and not just to the fourth generation, but to
the present time. But for this crime the light of Greece might
have burned on, from Aristarchus to Copernicus, from Aristotle
to Bacon, and from Democritus to Darwin. Hero's steam engine
might have been perfected, America discovered in *492*. Why, we
might now be civilized. But no, that guiding light went out and
darkness was again upon the deep.

Until this triumph of fanaticism, the ancient world was on
its way to true enlightenment. Besides those already mentioned,
it had produced such men as Pythagoras, Plato, Socrates, Aristotle, and many others. Collectively, they laid the philosophic
and even scientific bases for true civilization; the Christian
Church destroyed them. "The Emperor Justinian closed the
doors of the Academy at Athens, and the seven philosophers,
who alone represented the Neoplatonic faith, took their books
and sought the hospitality of the East." Hodges. And not until
their philosophy reappeared did the darkness disappear. The
Church's separation of religion from philosophy and cosmology

was its greatest crime and error. By so doing it robbed the racial mind of cosmic perspective without which it could not distinguish truth from error, the personal from the universal.

No one ignorant of the Mystery schools and the kind of consciousness they developed can realize the blight that Christiantity became. With its tortured Christ and sense of sin, it robbed us of the joy of life the earlier people knew. With its fake salvation and false God-concept, it denied us knowledge of Evolution and our place and purpose in it. This alone explains our plight yet the pagan philosophers taught it. Thereafter, our philosophers fell asleep at the switch, and while they slept a train load of devils passed right through and founded the kingdom of error on earth—Christianity, the greatest mistake man ever made.

A good example of their work is the Athanasian Creed. This consists of thirty-seven items, much too long to quote in full, yet here is the wisdom of the Christian Fathers, here is Western man proclaiming his metaphysical competency; we think they should be heard.

1. Whosoever will be saved, before all things it is necessary that he hold the Catholic Faith.

2. Which Faith, except everyone do keep whole and undefiled, without doubt he shall perish everlastingly.

3. And the Catholic Faith is this: That we worship one God in Trinity and Trinity in Unity.

4. Neither confounding the persons nor dividing the substance.

5. For there is one Person of the Father, another of the Son, and another of the Holy Ghost.

6. But the Godhead of the Father, of the Son, and of the Holy Ghost, is all one; the glory equal, the majesty coeternal. (They aren't even coexistent in one body.)

7. Such as the Father is, such is the Son, and such is the Holy Ghost.

8. The Father uncreate, the Son uncreate, and the Holy Ghost uncreate.

9. The Father incomprehensible, the Son incomprehensible, and the Holy Ghost incomprehensible.

And under such a creed everything else becomes incomprehensible.

As everyone knows today, the word *person* as used in this creed comes from the Latin *persona*. This did not mean a person, an individual as we use it; it meant a mask. In the Roman theater the actors wore *personae* to hide their real identity. The Greek equivalent was the word from which we get *hypocrite*. Thus instead of identifying, the word implies something false and deceptive. Esoterically it might be thought of as matter, the mask behind which the ever unknowable Creativity conceals itself. Today, however, it is but a mask behind which a cunning priesthood hides from us the true nature of our source. Tear off that mask and the mystery disappears, likewise the incomprehensible. And this we will do.

The Trinity has nothing whatever to do with things religious or with religion's God. That we may see this let us consider the Hindu Trinity: Brahma, Vishnu, and Siva—Creator, Preserver and Destroyer. But of what? Why, of the world, of course, hence cosmology, not religion. Brahma creates the substance of the world, Vishnu preserves it for billions of years, but finally Siva destroys it through radiation. If you would see all three at once you have only to look at the sun, the earth and the moon, the three stages in the cosmic process. Now compare this with the Christian Trinity.

In his metaphysical incompetency Western man turns to his semi-Oriental Bible for his spiritual knowledge, but if this be the source of it, there should be no doctrine of the Trinity or belief in it, for this does not come from the Bible; indeed the word *Trinity* does not appear in the Bible, at least in the original. The nearest approach to it is the reference in John's gospel to "three witnesses in heaven," and all authorities today pronounce this an interpolation as late as the ninth century. How then did it get into the creeds?

The doctrine of the Trinity is a wholly pagan concept, taken over by triumphant Christianity without its authors' understanding of it. One of the chief contenders with early Christianity was Mithraism, the religion of the Persians. This had a Trinity, and in their efforts to win the Mithraists over to Christianity the Founding Fathers incorporated this pagan Trinity in their faith. Thus the Athanasian Creed is but an ecclesiastical attempt to harmonize Jewish monotheism with pagan polytheism. Originally the Trinity was part of ancient cosmology; it was only in the Zodiacal Night that it became religionized. The Christian Fathers took the pagans' concept literally and on it founded the most spiritually illiterate Faith in all the annals of religious fanaticism. All others have some relic of the wisdom-knowledge in them; Christianity not only lacks it, it destroyed it.

By the time this creed was written, all knowledge of Causation and Creation was lost, and so these creed makers knew no more about cosmogenesis than little children know about biogenesis. Over the one little word *filioque*, son, the Pope of Rome, Leo IX, and the patriarch of Constantinople, Michael Cerularius, excommunicated each other. And neither knew what he was talking about. This mutual excommunication occurred in 1054 and it took the Church 911 years to revoke it, in 1965. That is its pace and tardy reform.

Only when the more enlightened laity makes of it an anachronism does it hasten to reform, hence the recent Ecumenical Council. Another "gathering" of the "ecclesia," but how different from the first—some twenty-five hundred lords and princes of the Church in which "Solomon in all his glory was not arrayed like one of these." And what was the purpose thereof? To discuss the great fundamentals, Causation, Creation, Truth, Reality? No, for of these they know nothing. And in what were "the sweeping changes" wrought? Poverty, ignorance, commercialism, communism, birth control? No, only in liturgical minutia: a bit of the mass can now be said in the native tongue instead of in Latin; the celebrant can now turn his face instead of his behind to the congregation; the communicant can now fast one day instead of three before communion; save Ash Wednesday and Good Friday, he can even eat meat during Lent; a nun can now appear in something other than a symbol of the Black Death.

If the former decrees are wrong now, why have they been right for two thousand years? If they can be changed by man, they were made by man. And that a man in far off Rome can tell millions the world over what they can eat and when they can rise is sheer mental tyranny. That this tyranny endure, no change was made in creed and dogma; heaven and hell remain and love and mercy preside over them. No change should be expected here. These "innocents abroad" haven't even discovered the demoniac nature of Causation yet. The theological significance of the dictum *Demon est Deus inversus* is quite beyond the ken of ecclesiastics. What then of the "infallibility of the Pope"? It is indeed pitiable. Of the more than two hundred and sixty, not one of them had the slightest knowledge of the true meaning of the scriptures.

For these recent changes credit is now given to John XXIII but in the long perspective of time it may be seen he but set in motion the beginning of the end.

For nearly two thousand years Christianity has been trying to save us instead of civilizing us and it has ended in a century of savagery, an era in which two hundred and fifty million Christians died in Christian wars. See p. 463. It has failed because it has not enlightened us; it has not developed our consciousness, the evolving factor. Our present problems are the product of our present consciousness but consciousness that creates problems cannot solve them. Only a higher degree of consciousness can do that, and until it is attained we will remain victims of that "will" that manifests in Nature.

Such is Christianity, a religion based on a fraud, founded by "fools" and confirmed by an assassin—Constantine the Great. If we can believe history, he killed with his own hands two of his brothers-in-law, had his wife, his son Crispus and two nephews murdered, bled to death his political rivals, threw the unbelieving into a well, and caused uncounted thousands to die on the field of battle. Constantine was another "man of God," and so was favored with a vision, the cross, and under its banner *"In hoc signo vinces,"* he conquered all Europe for Christianity. And we're told it was the teachings of the gentle Christ did that. Gibbon, the historian, knew better. "The Church of Rome defended by violence the empire which she had acquired by fraud." [2]

---

[2] In *The Decline and Fall of the Roman Empire*.

The Dark and Middle Ages

And now that Christianity is firmly established, what do we find? "The kingdom of heaven upon earth"? On the contrary, a moral and intellectual degradation unparalleled in human history. According to Lecky, "The two centuries after Constantine are uniformly represented by the Fathers as periods of general and scandalous vice." And the following two were no better. Bishop Gregory of Tours wrote an account of them and it is one of the darkest pictures in all history. On reading it, Gibbon remarked: "It would be difficult to find anywhere more vice or less virtue." As for the fifth century, Salvianus, a priestly historian, had this to say: "Besides a very few who avoid evil, what is almost the whole body of Christians but a sink of iniquity? How many in the church will you find that are not drunkards, or adulterers, or fornicators, or gamblers, or robbers, or murderers—or all together?" And we are told Christianity uplifted the race, rid the world of pagan sin and paved the way for true civilization. This too is Catholic scholarship.

According to this, the saved and sanctified Christians were not responsible for these wretched conditions; they were the result of the invasion of the barbarians and their destruction of the Roman Empire. Only after this, they say, did morality and learning sink to abysmal depths. They do not tell us these "awful barbarians" were also Christians. A hundred years before the invasion Bishop Ulfilas had given them a Gothic Bible, and they had embraced the faith.[3] It was not then a case of barbarous pagans against civilized Christians, but barbarous Christians against semicivilized Christians. And of the two, the former were the more morally decent. Immorality is a civilized vice, and the higher the civilization, the more depraved its viciousness. Tacitus, in his book *The Morals of the Germans*, shamed the Romans by holding up to them the superior morals of their invaders. Hodglein, in his history, *Italy and Her Invaders*, called these Vandals "an army of Puritans"; and so did Salvianus. The

---

[3] They were "in the main, converts to Christianity before they crossed the boundaries of the empire." *Myers Ancient History*, p. 576.

latter also said that the invaders were scandalized by the moral indecencies of Christian Carthage. And here for once Catholic scholarship concurs, "Crimes of all kinds made Africa one of the most wretched provinces in the world." *Catholic Encyclopedia.* Dean Milman, a Protestant historian, admits that "Christianity has given to barbarism hardly more than its superstition, and its hatred of heretics and unbelievers. Throughout assassinations, parricides and fratricides intermingle with adultery and rape." After examining the morals of Italy under the Ostrogoths, he implies that those of pagan Rome were better than those of Christian Rome. To quote him directly: "Under the Ostrogothic kingdom the manners in Italy might seem to revert to the dignified austerity of the old Roman Republic." The Vandals were ignorant and hence destructive but the Church has put upon them far too much blame for the havoc she herself had wrought. As Draper said: "It was not the Goths, nor the Vandals, nor the Normans, nor the Saracen, but the popes and their nephews who produced the dilapidation of Rome." This was Christian Rome. As for Christian Greece:

> Eternal summer gilds thee yet,
> But all, except thy sun, has set.
> Byron, *Don Juan*, Canto III

Nor was it pagan sin that destroyed the Roman Empire; since it was thoroughly Christianized by the fifth century, the claim that its fall was due to the enervating influence of Christianity would be more logical; in fact, it was the natural result of Augustine's *City of God*—take no thought for this world, prepare for the next. Such was the Christian teaching. When Celsus reproved the Christians for not helping the pagans defend the Empire, Origen replied, "We defend it with our prayers." And so it fell, and with it, a thousand years of darkness.

The nadir of this Christian night was around the seventh, eighth and ninth centuries, practically a blank page in European history. Nothing was done of any consequence, yet this period was most prolific in the production of saints. From this we can see where the saints come from—out of the night of ignorance, fear and superstition, the three grey hags with the single eye, the eye of faith. With this all Christendom saw Reality inverted: truth was error, right was wrong, and science of the devil.

During this "Reign of Thartac," education was frowned upon. As Compayre said, "Once the pagan schools were closed Christianity did not open others, and after the fourth century a profound night enveloped humanity. The labor of the Greeks and Romans was as though it had never been." The only effort to restore education was made by those barbarians the Church claims to have civilized. Theodoric the Goth brought to his court all the artists and scholars of his day, and his daughter Amalasuntha carried on the work after his death. Charlemagne tried to reestablish general education because, as he said, "the study of letters is well-nigh extinguished through the neglect of our ancestors." But "the monks and bishops resisted the pressure of Charlemagne and closed nearly the whole of the schools as soon as he was dead." Bishop Brown in *The Bankruptcy of Christian Super-naturalism*, p. 102. It is the proud boast of the Catholic Church that its "monks and bishops" kept alive the light of learning throughout this night. It did, but it also kept it to itself and for the very good reason that this light was also a means to power. For the same reason it kept it from the masses; these could neither read nor write. This was indeed Christendumb!

Yet there were knowledge and learning everywhere except in Catholic Europe. At a time when even kings could not read or write, a Moorish king had a private library of six hundred thousand books. At a time when 99 per cent of the Christian people were wholly illiterate, the Moorish city of Cordova had eight hundred public schools, and "there was not a village within the limits of the empire where the blessings of education could not be enjoyed by the children of the most indigent peasant," and "it was difficult to encounter even a Moorish peasant who could not read and write." S. P. Scott in *The History of the Moorish Empire in Europe*. In Christian Europe scholars were burned at the stake; in Moorish Europe they were the highest paid men in the realm. One Moorish king gave his leading scholar forty thousand pieces of gold each year, while in Christendom, Roger Bacon, credited with inventing the camera, clock, telescope and lens, gunpowder and steam power, was imprisoned fourteen years as a sorcerer and heretic. Pope Sylvester II was an educated man, but he had to go to these Moorish universities to get his education. On his return and elevation, he manifested some interest in medicine, and so fell under the suspicion of sorcery. He escaped the witch-burners only because of his high office.

The Church's opposition to science, and particularly medicine, is too well known to recount here. We might, however, offer a keynote by way of illustration. This too comes from the saints.

For a thousand years benighted Christians took their cue from St. Augustine, who informed them that "All diseases of Christians are to be ascribed to demons; chiefly do they torment first-baptized Christians, yea, even the guileless newborn infant." The remedy was also of the saints, their bones, the most efficacious of which were those of St. Rosalie of Palermo, which Professor Buckland found later to be those of a goat. The real "goat," however, was the Christian people—some fifty million of them died of the plague in the Middle Ages. The saints were responsible for this also, for they had taught that filthiness was akin to holiness, and cleanliness unbecoming pride in that body reviled by Saint Paul. So ignorant were they of the cause of disease a law was passed that every peasant bringing food to the city must carry back in the same cart a load of the city's waste, thrown out on the street during the night. Little wonder plague followed plague and the life-span was twenty-one years. Under such conditions Europe did not double its population in a thousand years. What these people needed was knowledge, scientific knowledge and the power over nature that it gives. Yet this was precisely what the Catholic Church opposed, for it well knew that "Ignorance is the mother of devotion"—and the supporter of the Church.

Most writers on this subject attribute the decline of science and learning wholly to ecclesiastical opposition. We think the cause lies deeper than this, deeper even than the Church. The ultimate cause is religion itself. The Christian religion diverted the human mind from the natural to the supernatural, from the inductive method of science to the deductive way of religion. This resulted in a loss of interest in the natural and the scientific; this molded the Christian mind for a thousand years. It was this that created the opposition; it was this that made what brilliant minds there were, ineffectual. Unlike our scientists, they had no accumulated knowledge to work from. Thus we lay the blame for both the decline of science and the opposition to it on religion, not just men. During the Renaissance conditions improved considerably, but what was the Renaissance but the return of pre-Christian enlightenment? It was this that raised the standards of Christendom, not Christianity. "Far from being a Christian concept, the value and dignity of the individual is a Renaissance notion which infiltrated Christianity in opposition to the Christian doctrine of providence and sin." Reinhold Niebuhr.

Yet in spite of this the claim is made that Christianity put an end to pagan slavery and thereby dignified the common man. It did not; it only changed the name to serfdom. And what was a medieval serf, if not a slave? The Greek and Roman slave had definite rights,[4] the medieval serf had none—not even the right to his bride the first night: this was *"le droit de seigneur."* The Church not only condoned medieval slavery but also practiced it. During the feudal period some of the Catholic hierarchy had as many as forty thousand serfs, and their condition was unspeakable. They were unlettered, lived in filth and died of preventable disease. As a reason for being, the Church has always done charitable work for the poor, but never in all its history has it done anything to rid the world of poverty. At that time it was too busy burning heretics to bother with that. Its sins were not all of omission either; it opposed the efforts of others to improve the serfs' condition. Montesquieu, a humanitarian and agnostic, was assailed because he opposed slavery and the use of torture. His book *The Spirit of Laws* was condemned and

[4] Can Christian slavery show anything comparable to this: Antonius Felix (spoken of in Acts) was a slave, yet became Procurator of Judea under Claudius, married the daughter of Marc Antony, and also Drusilla, daughter of Herod Agrippa I.

put on the Index. And what about the trade in African slaves? It was not only unopposed by the Church but carried on in the name of all that was high and holy. The Spanish Government signed its slave charters "in the name of the Most Holy Trinity." The notorious slave trader, Captain Hawkins, named his slave ship *Jesus*, and from it threw the sick slaves to the sharks. In those days slavery, like smallpox, was "the will of God," and the Bible sanctioned it. Did not Noah say, "Cursed be Ham and all his eggs (seed); a servant of servants shall he be unto his brethren"? "So we see that God not only instituted slavery but he also made it to forever be a part of the moral probation of the human race, and to be a great lesson to the end of time of his abhorrence of sin." (From *Slavery, Its Institution and Origin*, written by a minister, 1860.) His Reverence split not only the infinitive but the Infinite as well; he put the blame for slavery right where it belongs. We said religion was a reason-perverting influence; this well illustrates it. Slavery is not a sin; it's God's punishment for sin. This God cannot see sin in his unjust punishment but only in the punished. All right for the benighted past, you say, but we don't take the Bible so literally today. "I would accept every statement in the Bible literally, no matter how it contravened my reason." [5] W. J. Bryan. And this man aspired to be President, and others like him succeeded, hence Palestine for the Jews, the Bible says God promised it. So where again we see the mind-perverting influence of this unholy book; whatever it says or sanctions is "the will of God," including slavery, cruelty, war and conquest.

It took Christianity nearly seventeen hundred years to perceive the evil in slavery, and it wasn't the priestly mind that did perceive it, as per our quotation. There is a clue in this indifference we should follow. In Christ's day slavery was everywhere, yet he made no effort to abolish it; his only words concerning it were parables about unworthy servants, a euphemism for slaves. Does this not imply this priestly indifferent mind created him? Perhaps this is why he did not concern himself with slavery.

---

[5] "I'd believe the Bible even if it said that Jonah swallowed the whale." A Jehovah's Witness at a convention in 1973.

No evil or injustice is seen as such in its own blind cycle; it is only as its cycle passes that it is seen as such. Who, for instance, saw the evil of colonialism in the eighteenth century? Who saw the injustice of segregation in the nineteenth? Why, even inquisition and crucifixion were accepted in their day. It is only as our consciousness and sentiency develop that we see these things for what they are. So is it with our own ways and institutions: nationalism, patriotism, capitalism, commercialism, and even theism. These are all barbarism, and seeds of war. Not one of them will exist in a civilized world. And strange it is that only "the kids" can see them for what they are. All unknowingly they are responding to the impulse of the coming Aquarian Age; their Piscean parents cannot, and so are shocked. Now just as with the above institutions, so with Christianity and Churchianity. They are of, for and by the benighted Piscean Age and will disappear with it. What is needed now is a super-Christian philosophy for post-Christian man.

Here we come to another false claim for Christianity—it softened the pagan heart, made us less brutal, cruel and warlike, yet where do you find more cruelty and brutality than that of the Christian Crusaders in the Near East and the Christian conquistadors in the far West? For their God and gold they plundered cities and destroyed nations. To such heights of bigotry did religion inspire ignorance that wholesale massacres were resorted to—St. Bartholomew's Day, for instance, which "for perfidity and atrocity . . . has no equal in the annals of the world," wrote Draper. Here ten thousand Protestants were slaughtered, after which Gregory XIII had a medal struck to commemorate some more "Christian martyrs." Nor was this all; in a letter to Charles IX of France, 1572, he expressed his Christian kindness thus: "We rejoice with you that with the help of God you have relieved the world of these wretched heretics." Such also was the fate of the Albigenses and the Knights Templars. Add to these the ten million the Inquisition destroyed, of which "nearly thirty-two thousand had been burnt." Again Draper. In the city of Verona alone sixty men were burned alive in thirty days, and let's not forget the five hundred witches in two years. In those days murder was so common carts were sent out each morning to gather up the corpses. So frightful became conditions that

Pagliarici exclaimed, "It is hardly possible for a man to be a Christian and die in his bed." Christ's "kingdom of heaven" was now Dante's *Inferno* on earth. Oh yes, there's a way out of the Catholic position but not its condition.

It is difficult for modern man to realize the cruelty of medieval man; it seems he did not have our capacity to feel. One of the emperors, becoming interested in the mystery of metabolism, had two live men dissected in his presence; the great artist da Vinci could and did watch the contortions of tortured heretics that he might put agony on canvas. Add to this natural cruelty the fervor of religious fanaticism and you have those saintly sadists of the "Holy Inquisition." Yet these were the days of courtly manners and fine speech. Culture it seems is of two kinds, soul and social, the latter often but feline niceties to hide porcine natures. The history of the Middle Ages bears this out— fine manners and foul murders, chivalry and slavery, powdered wigs and plundered nations.

Such were the Bible-inspired Crusades, those "holy wars" for a wholly mythical tomb. Under the cross and the cry "God wills it," millions of those "fools in Christ" went forth to die, including sixty thousand children. And in the name of a kindly Christ they committed crimes unspeakable. "If you would know how we treated our enemies at Jerusalem know that in the portico of Solomon and in the Temple our men rode through the unclean blood of the Saracens which came up to the knees of our horses." [6] "See thou then to what damned deeds religion urges men." [7] If religion no longer urges us to kill, it is not because of religion but because of what religion opposed—science and enlightenment.

After five bloody attempts, these "fools in Christ" wrested the Unholy Land from its rightful owners—and to what end? Eight hundred years of Arab-Christian enmity. Here we'll let the *Encyclopaedia Britannica* complete the tale. "So was founded the Latin kingdom of Jerusalem whose history is one of the most

---

[6] Letter from the leader of the Crusade to Pope Urban II, on receipt of which all Christendom held a jubilee.
[7] Lucretius.

painful ever penned. It is a record of almost unredeemed envy, hatred and malice, and of vice with its consequent disease, all rendered the more repulsive in that its transactions were carried on in the name of religion. For eighty-eight turbulent years this feudal kingdom was imposed on the country, and then it disappeared as suddenly as it came, leaving no trace but the ruins of castles and churches, a few place names, and an undying hereditary hatred of Christianity among the native population." A hatred so undying that seven hundred years later we are confronted with it—the Middle East problem. And here again Christian ignorance sets the stage—Palestine for the Jews; and here again the Bible is the inspiration. What have we learned in those seven hundred years? "Three million lost their lives in a futile attempt to rescue a tomb from the Mussulmans. Ten million were slain during the Inquisition. Fourteen million were slain in Christian wars of the Nineteenth Century. Thirty million lost their lives in wars between Christian nations during the first two decades of the Twentieth Century. Wars, tyranny and oppression of Christian nations since the days of Constantine have caused the death of more than 200,000,000 people." [8] And now we must add to this "Some 23,000,000 men in uniform from 53 nations, countries and dominions were killed or died; at least 28,000,000 civilians died from bombs or guns, hunger or disease or in the concentration camps." Hanson Baldwin on World War Two. Such is the legacy left us by "the Prince of Peace." "Put not your faith in princes," particularly of the Church.

No account of this period would be complete without a word about them, also their claim to divine authorization, selection, and protection. What we offer here is admittedly and intentionally a one-sided picture, the dark and shameful side. Our reason for so presenting it is that millions of misguided souls are painting the other side and holding it up to a credulous world as the only side. We think both sides should be known, not only in the interest of truth but also of those who are living in spiritual bondage to a fraudulent authority. For these, a thousand years

[8] Colonel Emery Scott West.

of crime and corruption are glossed over with the statement, "There were a few bad popes." Were their informers honest they would admit there were a few good ones.

We have spoken of the dishonesty of Catholic scholarship. Nowhere is it more evident than in its whitewash of wicked popes. Their crimes were all done by others and "unavoidable," their burning of heretics, a "necessity of the times," their debaucheries, but "love of good cheer." All save three it cannot whitewash were good, great and courageous men. Contemporary records completely refute these claims, and these records were not written by the Church's enemies, but mainly by its own historians, popes and cardinals: Victor II, Pius II, Cardinal Baronius, Bishop Liutprand, Father Salvianus, and historians, Milman, Gerbert, Buchard, Guicciardini, Vacandard, Draper, and others. These are the authority for the *dark and shameful side.* What we offer here is but a hop, skip and jump over some 1500 years, but sufficient, we think, to disprove any claim to divine selection and guidance.

To begin with, the first fifty popes were all saints, save one, and some, as we said, couldn't write their own names. This brings us to about 500 A.D. After that, the popes were such that not even Catholic scholarship can apply such a term to them. The Papacy had then become a means to power, and only the power-seekers achieved it—and not by right but by might. It was war to the finish. As the *New Standard Encyclopedia* states it, "In the furious strife of local parties, the papacy came to be hardly more than the spoils of party victory. Candidates of every variety of incapacity and unsuitableness were set up by rivals." And among these were twenty-nine antipopes, all told. The authority for this is Hergenröther, Cardinal Prefect of the Vatican Archives.

During the Dark Ages these divinely guided popes murdered one another at such a rate there were ten in twelve years (891–903) and forty in little more than one hundred. Sergius III was a wholesaler; according to Cardinal Baronius and also Vulgarius, he murdered his two predecessors. In 708 Toto, a noble at the head of a rabble following, had his brother appointed pope. This was Constantine II whose eyes were put out by

Christopher, his chief official. Then Christopher and his son plotted against Pope Gregory for which they too had their eyes put out. The two nephews of Leo III, Pascal and Campulus, themselves clerics, conspired to replace Leo and set a band of paid assassins upon him as he rode through the streets. When the hirelings failed, the two nephews dragged the pope into a monastery and completed the work. Pure fiction, downright slander, you say. But no, it is from the record of the papal biographer.

This was the order of the day. Pope Leo the V was deposed by another Christopher, who was in turn deposed and succeeded by the aforesaid criminal Sergius III, who murdered his predecessors. At this time it was not the Holy Ghost that selected the popes but what Cardinal Baronius called *scortas*, whores. This was the "rule of the courtesans," sometimes called the Pornocracy, or reign of the whores. Among them was one Baronius called the "shameless whore," Theodora, and her equally shameless daughter Marozia. Both had sons by Sergius III, and both put their illegitimates on the papal throne—John XI and John XII. The first was imprisoned, the second "turned the Lateran Palace into a brothel." There was no crime he didn't commit—murder, perjury, adultery, incest with his two sisters, bleeding and castrating his enemies, etc. He died, we are told, at the hands of an outraged husband.

According to the record, Cardinal Francone had Benedict VI strangled, after which he became Boniface VII, "a horrid monster surpassing all other mortals in wickedness," according to Gerbert. He was no worse however than Boniface VIII—"a strong and courageous Pope." Yes indeed! To gain his tiara he had the halfwit Celestine V disposed of. He did not long enjoy his victory for soon he was driven out by the Romans. Under a successor, Clement V, he was tried posthumously and found guilty of every crime including pederasty and murder. And when Clement died, his successor, John XXII, revealed that Clement had been so very clement he had given his nephew the equivalent of five million dollars of papal money. It was at this time the papal court was moved to Avignon, and now St. Peter had two successors, one at Avignon and one at Rome. But even this was not enough; there were at one time three—Gregory XII, Alexander V, and John XXIII.[9]

So corrupt was the latter, Sigmund of Hungary called a council to investigate him. The result was fifty-four articles describing him as "wicked, irreverent, unchaste, a liar, disobedient and infected with many vices." As a cardinal he had been "inhuman, unjust and cruel." As Pope he was "an oppressor of the poor, persecutor of justice, pillar of the wicked, statue of the simoniacs, addicted to magic, the dregs of vice . . . wholly given to sleep and carnal desires, a mirror of infamy, a profound inventor of wickedness." He secured the Papacy by "violence and fraud and sold indulgences, benefices, sacraments and bulls." He practiced "sacrilege, adultery, murder, rape and theft." And now we can understand Petrarch's remark—"a sink of iniquity." Some of these popes so outraged decency they were exiled. At least two of them had their eyes and tongues cut out, then were dragged through the streets tied to the tail of an ass. Still others were so despised their corpses were exhumed and thrown into the Tiber. After fourteen hundred years of Christianity morals had sunk so low that Pius II tells us "scarcely a prince in Italy had been born in wedlock." A statement as applicable to the princes of the church as of the state.

Bad as all this was, the worst was yet to come—the Borgias, particularly Rodrigo. Of all the wicked popes perhaps he deserves the crown. By bribing fifteen cardinals with the equivalent of three million dollars he secured the election of one of the worst men in history—himself, Alexander VI. Guicciardini, the historian, describes him thus: ". . . private habits of the utmost obscenity, no shame or sense of truth, no fidelity to his engagements, no religious sentiments, insatiable avarice, unbridled ambition, cruelty beyond the cruelty of barbarous races, burning desire to elevate his sons by any means: of whom there were many, and among them one—not any less detestable than his father." This was the notorious Cesare Borgia who to gain a cardinalate murdered his brother John, his sister's husband,

[9] Later repudiated, the title was annulled and recently assumed by the successor of Pius XII.

and two cardinals, only to renounce it for more profitable enterprises. As Guicciardini tells us, his father had a "burning desire to elevate his sons by any means," and so Cesare became the Duke of Valentinos, his brother became Duke of Gandia, and his sister, the Duchess of Ferrara, and a princess after her marriage to a son of the King of Naples. Religion had become what it was designed to be, a means to power, honor and wealth. This Prince of the Church was, by the way, the inspiration for Machiavelli's book *The Prince*, an honest account of dishonest Christians.

While still a cardinal this rake and murderer turned his quarters in the Vatican into a brothel. According to Burchard, the papal historian at the time, he indulged in nightly revels in his rooms above the Pope's, and courtesans "danced naked before the servants of the Lord and the Vicar of Christ." And his sister, Lucrezia, distributed prizes to those who "had had carnal intercourse with courtesans the largest number of times." This is that gaiety explained as "love of good cheer."

Such were the Princes of the Church in those days. During the Middle Ages the College of Cardinals was as corrupt a body as could be found in all history. Securing a cardinalate was but a matter of money and influence. Neither character, learning nor aptitude played any part in it. Indeed boys of fourteen and fifteen were sometimes invested with the office. Paul III appointed two of his teen-age grandchildren to this high office, and when criticized for such absurdity declared he would follow the custom until "examples might be cited of infants in the cradle becoming cardinals." Von Ranke. Paul IV made his nephew a cardinal, though, as he said, "his arm is dyed in blood to the elbow."

Yet these were the men who, with the help of the Holy Ghost, selected the popes. On this matter King Ferdinand had his doubts. At the Council of Trent he wondered out loud: "How is it possible that the cardinals should choose a good pope, seeing that they are not good themselves?" Some of the elections were so violent that the Holy Ghost had no more chance than it has in an American nomination of a President. So with some of the investitures, that of Alexander III, for instance. As the cope was placed upon him, Cardinal Octavian tore it from him and putting it on himself, backwards we are told, proclaimed himself pope. The cope was then torn from him by one of Alexander's supporters, but here by prearrangement, a group of soldiers burst in and declared Octavian the winner. And that is how Victor IV was chosen. But not for long; Alexander fled to France where he raised an army and returned. In the battle that followed several churches were wrecked and the floor of St. Peter's was, as the historians tell us, "strewn with corpses." The outraged Romans drove the invader out but on a second attempt he won and for three years thereafter wreaked vengeance on his rivals.

Now why isn't this disgraceful record known as well as that of the good popes? Why aren't Catholics told it was such men as these that caused the Reformation and not "that devil Luther"? Protestantism sprang not from Luther exclusively but from centuries of protestation against the crime and corruption of the Catholic Church. Satan Peter had outraged all Europe; as Draper tells us, "Erasmus and Luther heard with amazement the blasphemies and witnessed with a shudder the atheism of the city. Things steadily went on from bad to worse, until at the epoch of the Reformation no pious stranger could visit it without being shocked." In time the shock produced reformers but instead of heeding them, the divinely guided burned them at the stake: Huss, de Molay, Savonarola, Arnold of Brescia, and others. And let us not forget the lesser known millions the "Holy Inquisition" destroyed. A thing of the past, you say. Yes, but not the authority; it still exists and was reaffirmed in our own century, under Leo XIII. "The death sentence is a necessary and efficacious means for the Church to attain its end when rebels act against it and disturbers of the ecclesiastical unity, especially obstinate heretics and heresiarchs, cannot be restrained by any other penalty from continuing to derange the ecclesiastical order and impelling others to all sorts of crime . . . When the perversity of one or several is calculated to bring about the ruin of many of its children it is bound effectively to remove it, in such wise that if there be no other remedy for saving its people it can and must put these wicked men to death." *Institutiones Juris Ecclesiastici Publici*, by Father Marianus de Luca, Papal University, Rome. "Wicked men" like the aforesaid reformers, and we have just seen the nature of the "ecclesiastical unity" that must be maintained.

Under this unity every effort to improve the conditions of the poor was met with fire and sword. Innocent III even urged the King of France to invade England because something had happened there that threatened the "divine right" of popes and kings. This was the signing of the Magna Charta which he declared was "devil inspired," whereas the Inquisition was divinely inspired. Well, which was inspired, the Magna Charta or the Magna Charlatans?

Neither mental, moral nor social welfare played any part in the Catholic Church of the Dark and Middle Ages. As it was written, "The Hebrews seek after a sign and the Greeks seek wisdom," but the Catholics seek only wealth and power. As this was our contention from the beginning, we should not fail to offer some proof of it now.

Ever and always a Catholic empire was the objective of the Catholic Church, an empire with all Europe and northern Africa for its domain. It began under Constantine, but the church then lacked the ecclesiastical power to dominate the political power. It therefore began to build by piecemeal accretion. By the time of Gregory the Great in the sixth century, it was doing fine. Though eminently qualified for the acquisitive "Great," this man was not mentally great enough to allay the prevailing fear of his time—"the end of the world"; nor was he morally great enough to refrain from using this Bible-inspired fear for the benefit of the Church. On the contrary, he used it to great advantage, hence "the Great." By convincing the wealthy landowners that their heirs would never live to enjoy their property, he secured it for the Church. That he believed the Church would survive to enjoy it, suggests that his belief was based more on financial policy than scriptural eschatology.

It was in the interest of this temporal power that the famous forgeries were committed. Desiring more and still more land, Stephen II (752–757) forged the letter bearing St. Peter's name. This was done to force the superstitious Pippin, father of Charlemagne, to drive the Lombards out of Italy and turn over their holdings to the Church. As this was not sufficient, the forged "Acts of St. Silvester" were produced through which additional claims on Italy were made. Another of the "great" popes, Hadrian I, was also guilty of forgery, or the use of it. Under him appeared the infamous document known as "The Donation of Constantine" in which the first Christian emperor was alleged to have given most of Italy to the Papacy. Even Avignon was secured by dishonesty, moral and spiritual as well as economic. The Church acquired it by absolving the Italian Queen Joanna of the murder of her husband. Such were the means employed to gain material wealth and power, and so successful were they that at one time one-third of all arable land in Europe belonged to the Church, while its power lay over all. Indeed, it could give away whole kingdoms. Having taken France from Philippe le Bel, Boniface VIII wrote this to Albert of Austria: "We donate to you, in the plentitude of our power, the kingdom of France, which belongs of right to the Emperors of the West." So was it with Aragon, Sicily, Hungary, Denmark, Portugal, and Ireland. Here the Church achieved its original objective—wealth, power and authority.

And now a word to the Irish Catholics: For centuries they have reviled England for her domination of them. We wonder how many of them know that one of their revered popes gave England this right? To Henry II of England, Adrian IV wrote this: "It is not doubted, and you know it, that Ireland and all those islands which have received the faith, belong to the Church of Rome; if you wish to enter that Island, to drive vice out of it, to cause law to be obeyed and St. Peter's Pence to be paid by every house, it will please us to assign it to you." And so for the sake of Peter's Pence the Irish lost their freedom.

Money, then as now, being the all-essential, the best financial minds were employed to devise ways and means of raising it—the sale of offices, pardons, indulgences, relics, etc. Among these was John XXII, who out of the people's money built the magnificent court of Avignon and palaces for his cardinals. Being a lawyer also, he had ways and means of making money, among which was robbing the rich Knights Templar. With the aid of

his cat's-paw King Philip, he despoiled and dispersed them.
Another means was the confiscation of the revenues of ecclesiastical offices. In the jubilee year of 1300 pardons and indulgences
were sold, not given, to pilgrims to Rome. So many came bringing their wealth to Saint Peter's that the officials used rakes and
shovels to gather up the money. Here we should recall the
remark of one of the popes: "What profits have we not derived
from this fable of Christ." Many, however, were too poor to
make the long and expensive trip, which was a grief to the holy
financers, so they decided the fee when paid at home carried the
same blessing and absolution.

As today, this robbing of the people was called "giving unto
the Lord," and so needy was he, not even prostitution was
overlooked. During "the brilliant thirteenth century," the
clergy operated brothels, and so numerous and prosperous were
they the financiers decided to tax them too.

The treasury was also enhanced by the sale of spurious relics.
These were manufactured by the thousands, and included everything the mythical Christ, his family, and his followers were
imagined to have had. There was Christ's milk teeth, navel, and
even foreskin, two or three of them in fact; there was Mary's
hair, and vials of her milk. Enough nails and wood from the
cross were discovered to build a score of them, though Constantine's mother in her day could not find the original. Washington
Irving went further: concerning the wood of the cross, he said
"There is enough extant to build a ship of the line." Every
church in Europe had these "holy relics"; indeed three of them
had the one spear with which Longinus pierced Jesus' side.
This, by the way, caused a serious internal strife. A Sultan
presented the supposedly real one to the city of Rome. The
French cardinals were horrified; the original was in Paris, they
said. The German cardinals ridiculed both for, as they said,
everyone knows the original is in Nuremberg. Such antics
seemed bad enough while we believed in the historicity of the
Christ story, but when we know its purely mythical nature they
take on a double meaning—dishonesty as well as credulity.

And speaking of credulity, another "money-making scheme"
was, and still is, the "holy places" of Palestine. Concerning these

and the gullibility of pilgrims thereto, the *Encyclopaedia Britannica* has this to say: "It is a pathetic record. No site, no legend is too impossible for the unquestioning faith of these simple-minded men and women. And by comparing one record with another, we can follow the multiplication of 'holy places' and sometimes can even see them being shifted from one spot to another as the centuries pass. Not one of these devout souls has any shadow of suspicion that, except natural features (such as the Mount of Olives, the Jordan, Ebal, and Gerazim) and possibly a very few individual sites (such as Jacob's well at Shechem) there was not a single spot in the whole elaborate system that could show even the flimsiest evidence of authenticity." Thus does modern scholarship bear out our contention. Not one of these places or relics is genuine, not even Jacob's well. They are all mythic material, now commercial material of a money-hungry Church. This is the meaning of our statement—the Church turned Golgotha into Golconda.

It was for plunder this Golconda was turned into a battle-ground—that of the Crusades. Ostensibly the purpose was to wrest the tomb of Christ from the "unclean" hands of the infidels, but the real motivation was hungry Europe's envy of the comparative wealth and splendor of Araby. This has long been overlaid with Christian sanctity but the contemporary Pope, Urban II, made no bones about it; in fact, it was his inducement to volunteers. In an address at Clermont he said: "The wealth of our enemies will be yours, and you will despoil them of their treasures." This was also the motive for the plunder and exile of the wealthy Jews and Mohammedans in Spain. Several hundred thousand were killed or banished and their property confiscated by the Church. And "the Pope granted indulgences to all who carried on this pious work," wrote Vacandard, a Catholic historian. "Pious work!" This is some more of their intellectual dishonesty. It's quite amazing the pious persona they can put on priestly deviltry.

In this same framework lies another "pious work" of the Middle Ages—the great cathedrals and the "religious art" that adorned them. These noble edifices were not built for the glory of God but for the glory of the Church, and no matter how beautiful they may be, they are but monuments to human ignorance. So with their art, pure literalism proving, as we said, Western man's inability to think in the abstract. As art, it is a worthy expression of man's esthetic sense, but like its saints and lilies, it sprang from a soil as foul and putrid as any in human history; it sprang, in fact, from the moral nadir—the period of Alexander VI and his two successors, Julius II and Leo X. Its purpose then was not moral uplift but papal upkeep. Great art makes error attractive; it brought millions of pilgrims and hence millions of *lira*. The artists themselves painted not from religious inspiration but from papal command, and on pain of severe punishment.

It took great courage to defy the all-powerful "Mother Church" in those days. Many tried but they paid for it with their lives. The reformers of those days did not have the knowledge to effectively defy it. After fifteen centuries of Christianity, the racial mind was naive and credulous. Thus the Reformation was but adolescent rebellion against maternal prostitution. It was left for futurity (us) to turn this semirebellion into triumphant revolution. And this is not so far distant as some of us suppose; the list of future popes is not a long one. As the present cycle closes, another historian will write another book and he will call it THE DECLINE AND FALL OF THE ROMAN CHURCH.

Index